Economic Warfare
or Détente

International Perspectives on Security Series
Richard Ned Lebow, Series Editor

The purpose of the International Perspectives on Security series is to make available to audiences in the United States important works written by non-Americans. Most of the books in the series will be original studies, although some will be translations of previously published works. The series will treat theoretical and substantive aspects of security. Special emphasis will be given to European security problems, but other regional and comparative studies will also be published.

Also of Interest

About the Book and Editors

This book analyzes East-West economic and political relations in the context of the policies of the major Eastern and Western countries. The authors, a group of international scholars, examine the potential use of East-West trade as an instrument to influence Eastern policies, and they assess the effects of U.S. unilateral imposition of embargoes and sanctions against the Soviet Union and Eastern European countries. They conclude that although East-West economic relations suffer during times of increased international tension, trade between them is an important stabilizing element.

Reinhard Rode is a senior research fellow at the Peace Research Institute in Frankfurt. **Hanns-D. Jacobsen** is a visiting fellow at the American Institute for Contemporary German studies at Johns Hopkins University.

Economic Warfare or Détente

An Assessment of East-West Relations in the 1980s

edited by Reinhard Rode
and Hanns-D. Jacobsen

Westview Press / Boulder and London

International Perspectives on Security Series, No. 1

This is a Westview softcover edition, manufactured on our own premises using equipment and methods that allow us to keep even specialized books in stock. It is printed on acid-free paper and bound in softcovers that carry the highest rating of the National Association of State Textbook Administrators (NASTA) in consultation with the Association of American Publishers (AAP) and the Book Manufacturers' Institute (BMI).

Published in 1985 in the United States of America by Westview Press, Inc.; Frederick A. Praeger, Publisher; 5500 Central Avenue, Boulder, Colorado 80301

Library of Congress Cataloging in Publication Data
Economic warfare or détente.
    (International perspectives on security)
    Bibliography: p.
    Includes index.
    1. East-West trade (1945–   )—Addresses, essays,
lectures. 2. Economic sanctions—Addresses, essays,
lectures. I. Rode, Reinhard, 1947–   . II. Jacobsen,
Hanns-Dieter. III. Series.
HF1411.E265   1985   382'.091713'01717   85-3245
ISBN 0-8133-0118-1

Composition for this book was provided by the editors
Printed and bound in the United States of America

10   9   8   7   6   5   4   3   2   1

CONTENTS

TABLES AND FIGURES

TABLES

FIGURES

PREFACE

There is a clear need for a reassessment of East-West economic relations following the Afghanistan sanctions imposed by President Carter in 1980 and the Euro-American gas deal controversy of 1982. The first question in any such reassessment must be whether, in contrast to the 1970s when East-West trade and détente were blooming, the 1980s will be a decade of tension and decay in East-West business. While there is also a clear need to sort out the political and economic processes at work in East-West economic relations, it must be recognized that given their inherent complexity a single, generally applicable delineation between economics and politics is simply not possible. The task of making a political reassessment in the mid-1980s would therefore, necessarily overtax a single author. For this reason the editors elected to invite contributions from a number of colleagues.

In order to analyse all the relevent issues, including the policies of the major countries involved, and to do so in good time, it was necessary to draw on the work of colleagues outside of the Federal Republic of Germany. It was in addition the intention of the editors to make use of the wide range of expertise that exists in the field of East-West economic and political relations, which meant going beyond the confines of a single discipline. Indeed the issues considered are such that expertise in economics and political science is required. The subject matter, lying as it does at the center of the East-West conflict, also represents a challenge to the peace and conflict research field.

Interdisciplinary and comparative research of experts from various institutes is still more of an exception than a rule despite the need for precisely such an approach in a number of fields. The editors were therefore gratified by the enthusiasm with which the researchers involved agreed to cooperate. The various contributions were intensively discussed and prepared for publication at two conferences, one in May 1983 in Frankfurt and one in October of the same year in Berlin. With regard to the respective contributions, the editors considered it advantageous to have a division of labor on the country studies, with the chapter on the Federal Republic being written by an American colleague and the chapters on the United States written by European authors. The results show that this not only helped to illustrate the Euro-American controversy over East-West trade policy but also to guarantee the necessary mixture of distance and engagement.

Despite the participation of 18 authors it was still necessary to deliniate the field of study. As the project concentrated on East-West economic relations within the broader East-West conflict, it was possible to leave aside Japan and the People's Republic of China. In the economic field the East-West conflict is

xii

still largely a Euro-American affair, in which the Soviet Union can be considered in its role as a European power.

The editors are grateful to the German Society for Peace and Conflict Research for granting sufficient funds to cover the two conferences as well as publication in both German and English. The Peace Research Institute Frankfurt had overall responsibility for the project and provided the necessary administrative and organizational support. The editors would like to thank Stephen Woolcock for his assistance in completing the English edition, as well as the publishers, Westview Press and Verlag Neue Gesellschaft, for generously agreeing to fit the book into their publishing programs at an early stage.

March 1985   *Reinhard Rode*
Hanns-D. Jacobsen

PART I

INTRODUCTION

1
East-West Trade and Détente

Reinhard Rode

The significance of economic relations in the East-West conflict remains unclear, and the assumptions of academics and politicians are numerous and contradictory. There is disagreement on the importance of economic relations as such, as well as disagreement on whether they have favorable or damaging consequences for Eastern and Western countries. The different components of East-West economic relations such as trade, credit, technology transfer, industrial cooperation and energy also vary in their importance and their consequences. A concrete analysis must therefore seek to address more detailed questions. In order to arrive at a lower level of generalization one can first of all consider a limited time frame. Alternatively it is also possible to compare the various components of relations with respect to their similarities and differences. The latter poses no great problem, but a too much limited time frame makes an analysis of the links between economic relations and détente impossible.

One further fundamental question concerns the general relationship between economics and politics in the East-West conflict. Because this question cannot be resolved, it is necessary to have a more limited but operational question on which to base research on East-West relations. As East-West trade and détente were both booming during the 1970s, it seems logical to ask specific questions about the relationship between political and economic relations in that period. However, the crisis suffered by both trade and détente at the end of the 1970s and the beginning of the 1980s may have created conditions more amenable to an analysis of the relationship between East-West trade and détente than during the period of euphoria in the 1970s when the well-known assumptions were developed. An analysis covering both the rise and fall of trade and détente may also provide more far-reaching insights than one of the boom period alone.

In addition to this analytical argument there is also a normative case for a new research effort on the relationship between East-West trade and détente. The increase in tensions between the two superpowers, and consequently between the antagonistic alliances, at the end of the 1970s and the beginning of the 1980s, puts the question of a new era of détente on the agenda in dramatic fashion. The difference between the political and economic accents set by the superpowers on the one hand and their respective smaller partner countries on the other also underline the relevance of this question. Whereas the interest in détente has declined on the part of the superpowers, especially in the United States, the countries in Eastern and Western Europe still favor détente and perceive the increase in tension not as a necessary clarification of the relationship but as a danger. In this context economic relations have again become the focus of more attention.

The specific importance of trade within East-West economic relations can easily be seen from its distinctive quantitative importance. Trade is the main component of economic interaction between capitalist and communist countries. Other fields are rightly seen as supporting trade, as is for example the case with credit or even special types of trade such as technology transfer, industrial cooperation, and energy. Before we can analyse these assumptions systematically and pose meaningful questions about the effects of East-West trade on détente, we need an operational definition of détente.

There are two overinterpreted and seemingly optimistic definitions of détente as: the "structure of peace"; and the pejorative characterization of "containment" by other means.[1] The first is more based on wishful thinking than analysis, and the second overlooks the qualitative difference between the era of containment and the period of détente. We define détente, following Czempiel, as a complex process in which the military dispute is replaced by political, economic and ideological competition.[2] In this Czempiel tried to clarify the different planes of the relationship introduced by Marshal Shulman *(Foreign Affairs,* Oct. 73, p. 36 ff.), and defines détente as a process in which the pattern varies between the different planes of security, economic welfare and power competition. In a structure of conflict détente means to decrease or to abolish the tension inherent in different positions. A relaxation of conflict therefore means a reduction in readiness to use violence. The conflict itself remains stable, as does the difference in positions.

This definition avoids the misunderstanding that détente is identical with reduction of conflict, a misperception which was to be found in the discussion of détente in the United States during the first half of the 1970s. Within a specific plane multiple dimensions of conflict occur, and conflicts differ in intensity within each of the security, economics and power planes. In the plane of economic relations competition and embargoes are present as well as cooperation. There can therefore be different degrees of conflict, and the connection between the cause of conflict and détente varies. A strategy of détente can therefore only be considered as a long-term process.

Having explained what is understood by détente, it is now possible to try to bring the heterogeneous assumptions into a systematic order.

Assumptions on the Effects of East-West Trade

gains for the East	gains for the West	favors détente and peace	works in favor of a convergence of the systems
access to modern Western technology	penetration of socialism via capitalist methods of production, technology and patterns of consumption	interdependence promotion of détente peaceful co-existence cooperation spill-over mutual advantage ambivalence	contributes to a change of systems interdependence cooperation spill-over convergence optimal system mix of capitalism and socialism
frees resources for arms build-up			
provokes Western dependence on Eastern raw materials	dependency of planned economies from continuation of cooperation		
opens the West to blackmailing	chance for leverage (linkage)		
endangers the market economies	asymmetry		

These assumptions on the effects of East-West trade are to be found in the academic as well as the political debates. Despite all the overlapping, which makes rigid classification appear problematic, two main themes emerge. These are cooperation and détente on the one hand, and conflict and power on the other.

Cooperation and Détente: Liberalism and Functionalism

Academics and politicians differ, in their specific assumptions about the relationship between East-West trade and détente, not so much in content but in the intensity of their search for convincing arguments. For politicians a persuasive statement may be sufficient, but academics have to consider the pros and cons more systematically and carefully.

Western politicians have made many statements establishing a relationship between cooperation, détente and peace. The 1969 Brussels' Declaration of NATO is one.[3] There was also President Nixon's strategy for relations with the Soviet Union which explicitly relied on functionalist philosophy. His Secretary of Commerce, Peter G. Peterson, declared that the aim of economic cooperation was "to build in both countries a vested economic interest in the maintenance of an harmonious and enduring relationship".[4] West German statesmen also made a number of similar statements, but there existed a clear difference of emphasis between the various approaches. The lowest common denominator was the assumption that trade brings about mutual advantage. This implies that East-West trade is purely beneficial for both partners and has positive economic wel-

4

fare effects. The relationship as such, however, could be discontinued at any time, because the costs of interruption remain low.

Cooperation resulting in mutual dependence (interdependence) is of a higher order because the costs of discontinuation are higher. Such cooperation can result in a spill-over effect in which the reinforcement of interdependence has a positive influence on developments in other fields. This is the core of the functionalist argument developed by David Mitrany.[5] His hypothesis was that cooperation between nations in non-political areas forms a network of closer relations which leads to a spill-over into the political area. Although functionalism implies elements of theoretical eclecticism,[6] the liberal origins are evident. The main interest of functionalists is in political integration, as is, for example, illustrated by the work of Ernst B. Haas[7] on the Common Market of the West European states. Neo-functionalists like Joseph Nye[8] have drawn attention to the possibility that increasing transactions in the form of trade, capital transfer and communication may have ambivalent effects on relations. Besides the spill-over there is also a chance of spill-back.

In East-West relations it is not integration, but the functionalist assumptions about the political consequences of economic cooperation which are of interest. In this respect the functionalist argument follows the classical liberal tradition of the peace promoting effects of trade. Without a fixation on free trade, positive effects are expected according to the motto "Trade is Better than no Trade". But the relationship between capitalism and socialism was not a major area of functionalist research, so attempts to apply functionalist assumptions to East-West relations are very rare.[9]

For convergence theory, however, East-West relations were of central importance. Whereas both politicians and academics have assumed that East-West trade can further détente, convergence theory was mainly a product of academics, and the basic lines of argumentation go further than functionalist ideas. The theory of convergence not only took up the idea of the promotion of peace but also that of integration. Haas' expectation of the integration of homogeneous social systems is explicitly assumed by the theory of convergence for capitalism and socialism. These assumptions have different origins, however, and cannot generally be attributed to the liberal tradition.

During the 1950s, assumptions about an overall or partial convergence of the capitalist and socialist economic systems were developed.[10] These included the idea of an "optimal" system based on a mixture of the positive elements of both, and produced by the convergent development advocated by Walter S. Buckingham, Pitirim Sorokin, and Jan Tinbergen.[11] Raymond Aron and John Galbraith supposed that this would come about through the pressures generated by modern industrial society[12] and Walt Rostow and Erik Boettcher identified the different phases of growth through which industrialization must pass before convergence can occur.[13] The theory of economic convergence has already suffered so much criticism,[14] that assumptions about an overall convergence of societies are made less frequently. Overall convergence can follow three possible developments; positive convergence towards a perfect society (Sorokin), negative convergence leading to increased alienation in East and West (Marcuse) and the decay of totalitarian systems through the liberalizing effects of industrialization (Duverger).[15] None of these can seriously claim to be based on an elaborate theory. Positive convergence is mainly based on hope. It is built on the image of an exciting utopia that surpasses the unpleasant realities in both systems and the dangers inherent in a possible confrontation. But there is a tremendous gap between the desirability and the plausibility of such a convergence. The cultural pessimism of Marcuse sharpens the critical view of the deficiencies of both systems, but negative convergence is not inevitable, even under conditions of alienation. Finally the assumption that industrialization leads to liberalization and convergence underestimates the possibility that there are equivalent functional pressures in the antagonistic systems which may produce a different outcome. Functions and structures like rational-bureaucratic organization, political participation, enlargement of welfare, etc.[16] can exist without convergence, just as systems can perform as functionalism demands while setting different goals.

This means that the theory of convergence is mainly a normative theory of integration in which the functional and analytical elements are not well developed. The discussion of convergence reached a peak during the 1960s, which suggests it was based on the anticipation of better East-West relations in the 1970s, but also on speculation, given the lack of any empirical foundations. The theory of convergence involves the approximation and assimilation of systems not détente.

East-West trade did not, therefore, attract much interest in the theory of convergence. It was not the interaction or cooperation between the systems that was seen as the driving force behind convergence, but inherent characteristics of technical progress. In convergence theory the decisive characteristic of a system was no longer seen to be the ownership of the means of production, but technology. There was also thought to be a causal link between the objective requirements of technological development and the need for the development of appropriate social systems. This was to take place automatically, regardless of the social structure and ideology and thus ignoring the distinction between capitalism and socialism. In addition to a normative inclination towards the perfect society, the theory of convergence can therefore also be interpreted as a product of the 1960s' fascination with technology and belief in the power of science. Another element was a confidence in unlimited growth and incremental, positive technological progress.

What follows does not deal with questions of approximation, assimilation or change.[17] It is therefore possible to disregard the assumption of convergence, and focus more on functionalist considerations. If the emphasis is also placed on cooperation and its effects, rather than integration, one can apply functionalist ideas in the interesting case of East-West trade and détente. This implies that trade, including East-West trade, is seen as cooperative interaction. Functionalism within the liberal tradition underlines this cooperative element. Marxism and Realism, however, put the accent on power and conflict.

The functionalist view of East-West economic relations focuses on coopera-tion and interdependence. The cooperative aspect of East-West trade which proponents praise and opponents fear is generally common sense. Just what interdependence means in practice is a matter of dispute, particularly in the case of East-West trade. Waltz's classical definition of a "relationship costly to break"[18] is still the most attractive one, so that the conflict centers on the mean-ing of "costly".[19] Nye's and Keohane's criteria of sensitivity and vulnerability aim at more precision[20] but do not solve the operational problems, which are again particularly difficult in the case of East-West trade. It is, and will, probably remain, unclear at what level interaction can be designated as interdependence. Volumes of trade can be calculated, but the critical measure of how dependence and mutual dependence are perceived cannot be computed. In this context use of the term "costs" is more illustrative than quantitative because political and economic costs run together making any evaluation more or less arbitrary. The functionalist perspective is inclined to interpret even low margins of interde-pendence in East-West trade as positive in order to highlight the element of co-operation, to calculate the costs of interruption as high, and to assume positive political spill-over. This is based on the pre-theory that interaction and commu-nication between societies, even if they have different political and economic orders, is mutually advantageous and creates a common interest in maintaining links. Within the East-West relationship, which includes both conflict and co-operation, the emphasis is on cooperation, and conflict, whilst not overlooked, is qualified as secondary and manageable. Here the influence of the liberal tradi-tion becomes apparent with its inclination to harmonize political and economic relations. The liberal normative bias for peace therefore leads to the pre-theory that only détente makes sense in East-West relations.

Conflict and Power: Marxism and Realism

It is no accident that the renaissance of the power perspective in the inter-pretation of the East-West conflict coincided with the increase in East-West ten-sions at the end of the 1970s. Politicians who had doubts about détente from the beginning were quick to recognize its demise. At the same time academics found it interesting to rediscover the illusive concept of power and try to use it in analysis. Although one cannot be certain, because political discussion in the East lacks transparency, the renaissance of the power perspective probably took place to the same degree in both East and West. Eastern elites have, of course, discussed President Carter's economic sanctions and obviously discuss President Reagan's ambitions of waging economic warfare.

The central problem with the concept of power is that it serves as both a means to an end and an end in itself, which results in a lack of analytical precision. Furthermore, Max Weber's classical, offensive definition of power as "any chance in a social relation to enforce one's own will upon the opposition no matter what this chance is based upon,"[21] which was transferred to international relations by Hans J. Morgenthau, has the implicit disadvantage of being limited to the model of a world of states. Just as complexity and interdependence within the international system have not overcome the national state, which was declared dead too early, the world has not remained a pure world of national states. The concept of power is still mainly understood in its military sense, and very rarely in the sense of the defensive capacity of not yielding to the demands and pressures imposed by others, as Karl W. Deutsch saw it.[22]

The standard work of the Realist School was first published by Morgenthau in 1948, just as the Cold War began.[23] Morgenthau argued explicitly against idealistic, liberal-internationalist hopes, and confronted them with dispassionate, realist interpretations of power, power politics and national interest. By power he understood the dominance of human beings over the thinking and behavior of others. Although the terms national interest and public welfare have been shown to be questionable,[24] the realist perspective has nevertheless shown a new attraction for some American scholars.[25]

With a determined conservative president like Ronald Reagan the perspective of power politics with all its inherent simplifications has won a decisive influence on government policy in the United States. Policy towards communist countries and especially towards the competing world power, the Soviet Union, is based on the assumption that the East-West conflict is a zero-sum game. Accordingly, although compromise is not excluded, the basic structure of conflict remains unchanged, which means that tension between the superpowers is considered the normal state of affairs and détente the exception. The emphasis is on conflict and competition for power, not cooperation, and this includes the evaluation that East-West trade was a one-way street favoring the East. The export of Western technology is seen as assisting and reinforcing the system in the East, which is unable to modernize sufficiently without imports from the West. Imports of technology are also seen as helping the Soviet Union to save on the costs of development, thus freeing up resources for the arms industry and indirectly contributing to the modernization of the Soviet military apparatus. Raw material imports from the East are seen as increasing Western dependence and providing the East with the hard currency it needs to finance imports of technology. This is the "no trade with the enemy" logic which resulted in the restrictions on East-West trade and economic warfare so favored by the hardliners in the Reagan administration.[26]

As a revolutionary theory which predicts the death of capitalism and the victory of socialism, Marxism is clearly a deterministic theory of power. In its idealized form the goal of world revolution allows for nothing but conflict in relations between capitalist and communist states. What remains indeterminate is the form of the conflict which ultimately results in the world-wide victory of communism. The Marxist-Leninist variation of Marxism ran into contradictions between theory and policy shortly after the October Revolution in Russia. On the one hand, there was the thesis that the capitalists would sell the rope that would be used to hang them; on the other there was already a concept of "peaceful coexistence" with the Western states, developed by Lenin himself. Besides the economic advantages of trading with capitalist states, Lenin also expected it would be possible to skillfully use trade to systematically play off one competing capitalist country against the other to the advantage of the Soviet Union. He assumed that the use of trade policy as a continuation of war by non-military means could divide the West and thus render it less able to form a new "imperialistic front of unity" and to intervene militarily in the Soviet Union.[27]

Lenin's tactical concept was elevated to a long-term strategic concept of peaceful coexistence with capitalist states by the XXth party convention of the communist party of the Soviet Union in 1956. The objective of a world-wide transformation from capitalism to communism was not abolished, but it was no longer argued that this transformation could only be achieved through war and the use of violence in each country. As a means of avoiding war the doctrine of peaceful coexistence was an expression of the interest of both superpowers in preventing armed conflict in the nuclear age. The contradictions between the assumptions of the Marxist tradition and the concept of peaceful coexistence are obvious. Within the Eastern bloc such contradictions are taboo, but in the West they provide the basis for dispute about the ultimate goals of the Soviet Union. One cannot say just how far the Soviet Union has moved away from Marxist theory. Some theoretical elements of Marxism-Leninism have obviously been dropped in the justification of the Soviet détente policy, but the significance of this phenomenon must remain controversial.

The East also displayed elements of a functionalist way of thinking when it underlined the role of East-West trade in peace and détente in the Declarations of the Warsaw Pact in 1966 in Bucharest and 1969 in Prague.[28] One must, however, be very cautious before interpreting rhetoric about the mutual benefits of trade between countries of different social systems and its importance for détente, as an expression of Eastern functionalism. As long as the asymmetry in East-West economic relations predominantly favors the West, it seems more plausible to interpret this Eastern assessment as the consequence of a desire to gain from East-West trade. For communist countries, functional spill-over would mean a limitation on their freedom of movement and at least a partial penetration of their social systems. Such fears of penetration reflect the traditional Stalinist view of East-West economic relations which receded into the background after the rise of the doctrine of peaceful coexistence, but did not disappear altogether. Under Carter and Reagan this Eastern discussion has probably intensified, but the ritualistic nature of debate in the East precludes any open dispute. As a consequence the definite analysis of East-West economic relations from a dependency perspective has Western authorship. Johan Galtung concludes that, due to the vertical division of labor and colonial structure of East-West trade, the East will become increasingly dependent on Western technology and there will be spiralling consumer demands.[29]

From the preceding it is possible to construct the following systematic comparison of the various analytical and political approaches to East-West trade.

Analytical and political approaches to East-West trade

general pattern of East-West relations	pattern of relation between East and West in general	pattern of East-West trade	gains from East-West trade	consequences for the conflict
liberalism/ functionalism/ policy of détente	conflict↔cooperation game with variable sums	cooperation > conflict	mutual	détente
Marxism-Leninism/policy of coexistence (unresolved contradiction between theory and policy)	conflict zero-sum game	cooperation > conflict	mutual but more favorable for the East	peaceful coexistence
realism/ power politics	conflict zero-sum game	cooperation < conflict	more favorable for the East	tension

The State of Research

Empirical research offers no clear conclusions on the significance of East-West economic cooperation, and most general economic studies are, at best, equivocal. As the following six chapters of part II of the book look in detail at the significance of economic cooperation, this introduction shall be confined to a short outline.

– Compared to world trade, East-West trade experienced above average growth during the 1970s, but still remained relatively unimportant. The boom in the first half of the decade was followed by a period of consolidation in the second half and stagnation and decline from 1980 onwards (see Jochen Bethkenhagen, chapter 2).
– East-West trade remained primarily a European affair, with the U.S. and Japanese shares of trade remaining relatively low.
– Asymmetries in East-West trade favor the West, because East-West trade accounts for a larger share of overall foreign trade and a greater percentage of

GNP in the East than in the West. This asymmetry is also evident in the complementary character of trade in which the East imports mainly capital goods, and the West mainly fuels and other raw materials.

- The boom in East-West trade was made possible by Western credits. This resulted in a high but, by international standards, not dramatically high Eastern debt (see chapter 3 by Klaus Schröder).
- More intense forms of interaction, such as industrial and long-term cooperation and joint ventures, have not occurred on a large scale and their importance is more symbolic than quantitative (see chapter 5 by Klaus Bolz).
- Western energy imports from the Soviet Union assumed a leading role in East-West trade and induced the Western discussion on dependence (see chapter 6 by Friedemann Müller).

Dependence marks the line where empirical results end and problems of interpretation begin. In chapter 7 Peter Knirsch concludes that there is not a high degree of dependence in any aspect of East-West economic relations. He also finds that both sides are only partially dependent and that the resultant interdependency is of only limited significance. The East's dependence is also found to be higher than the West's. The majority of the authors in this edition generally agree with this interpretation.

Of great interest, but also very complicated, is the relationship between trade and the process of détente. There is a striking correspondence between the boom period of East-West trade in the first half of the 1970s and the policy of détente in the years from 1972 to 1975. Werner Link draws attention to the fact that this boom occurred after the governments had abolished political obstacles and created new political conditions. He concludes that economic cooperation followed political cooperation.[30] This clear interpretation is, however, qualified by Link's view that international economic trends were more important than foreign policy. He therefore comes to the more cautious general conclusion that East-West economic relations had an ambivalent effect on détente. In this volume Peter Knirsch does not venture beyond this cautious view and finds that economic relations have only the potential of promoting détente. He also underlines the primacy of politics and the special importance of political relations. Compared to the period of Cold War, conditions have also been changed by the dominance of superpower relations in the East-West conflict and the increased relevance of the smaller countries within the alliances for the broad range of East-West relations. Although economic relations did not prevent growing tensions in East-West political relations in the years 1980 to 1983, one cannot exclude the possibility that they had a moderating influence.

For the 1980s, there is obviously still no adequate empirical base nor valid indicators to enable one to arrive at a generalized interpretation of the interrelationship between trade and détente. There is evidence of the existence of a formal relationship but it does not shed much light on the causality between trade and détente. Wall and Goldmann/Lagerkranz[31] have tried to contrast the development of East-West tension and trade, and have prepared informative diagrams. Both analyses point to a correlation between increased tensions and the decrease in trade at the end of the 1940s. The Goldmann/Lagerkranz analysis includes the first half of the 1970s and therefore also shows the correlation between détente and the boom in East-West trade during the first half of the decade. Without discussing the validity of the indicators they use to measure tension and détente, the results clearly give no definite evidence of cause and effect.

Jodice and Taylor[32] present a clear hypothesis. From their work they conclude that the process of détente did not fundamentally change intra- and inter-alliance trade. However, there appear to be major problems with their indicator of "relative acceptance". Their research also seeks to answer the question of how intensive East-West trade would be in absence of all non-economic factors. As East-West trade involves interaction between antagonistic blocs it has, inevitably, a political quality. It therefore seems implausible to start by assuming, as a constant, the optimum of a political East-West trade which can clearly never exist. Given the questionable nature of this indicator it makes little sense to conclude that economic relations had no impact on détente because growth rates were low; low compared to what?

Of more interest are the results of Frei and Ruloff[33] on the psychological aspect of East-West relations during the period of détente. Given the inability, as indicated above, of arriving at a quantitative interpretation of the relationship between East-West trade and détente on the basis of empirical data, the decision-makers' perceptions of the reality become very important. Frei and Ruloff try to show potential contradictions between perceptions and reality. Again, however, there are problems with the choice of indicators. Their indicators of economic cooperation are imports plus exports as a share of overall trade of the EEC and CMEA. They also use a complicated factor analysis approach to the development of dimensions of East-West relations, and a content analysis of documents of the Conference on Security and Cooperation in Europe. They find that commercial and industrial cooperation is not seen to be very important by decision-makers, who have a 3 per cent awareness of such cooperation and rate it fourth out of ten dimensions to East-West relations. This result, however, says more of the unresolved problems with the indicator than the limited importance of economic relations in the perceptions of decision-makers. One highly interesting finding is the different importance given to economic cooperation in East and West, with its importance in the East being of a higher order of magnitude. Compared to other issue areas, economic relations always range behind disarmament, peace and security or conflict. The authors see the general cause for the decline of détente at the end of the 1970s as a cyclical trend in the political climate. As détente went through a trough at the beginning of the 1980s, this idea of political cycles leads one to conclude that there will be another peak in détente or some equivalent sometime in the future and confirms the primacy of politics over economics in the perceptions of decision-makers. With regard to our main question concerning the relationship itself, or the mutual influence of economics and politics on each other, we are none the wiser.

This underlines the need for a reappraisal of the question in the mid-1980s. The decline of East-West trade and détente at the turning-point of the two decades and the subsequent indications of a new slow rise in the mid-1980s provide us with more empirical material and may facilitate more far-reaching answers. Despite the fact that the unresolved question of the relationship between economics and politics prevents us from reaching any definitive conclusions, it does not exclude some tentative new findings. This is especially the case if the central question is supplemented with more detailed questions. This leads us to a catalog of six questions which will be addressed in the following chapters and especially in the summary of the final chapter.

1. What is the relationship between East-West trade and détente?
2. To what extent do East-West economic relations cause partial interdependencies?
3. What are the effects of East-West economic relations?
   What can be said about the economic and political distribution of benefits for both sides?
4. Has East-West trade benefitted particular constituencies on both sides who have brought political pressure to bear to decrease tension?
5. Are restrictive policies and sanctions really obsolete and ineffective?
6. Do common alliance interests and alliance policies in East and West prevail, or are they limited by differing interests and policies of the alliance leaders and their smaller partners?
7. Are intra-western divergencies really Euro-American, or are there transatlantic pro- and anti-coalitions?

Notes

1 Ernst-Otto Czempiel, 'Von der Parität zur Superiorität: Die amerikanisch-sowjetischen Beziehungen', in: *Amerikanische Außenpolitik im Wandel. Von der Entspannungspolitik Nixons zur Konfrontation unter Reagan*, Stuttgart 1981, p. 22; Connie M. Friesen, *The Political Economy of East-West Trade*, New York 1976, p. 1 ff.

2 Ernst-Otto Czempiel, Die Vereinigten Staaten von Amerika und die Entspannungspolitik, *Aus Politik und Zeitgeschichte*, B 37/1977, p. 400.

3 *Europa-Archiv*, 4, 1970, p. D 79 ff.

4 Richard Nixon, *U.S. Foreign Policy for the 1970's. Shaping a Durable Peace*. Report to the Congress, Washington, D.C., GPO, 1973, pp. 8, 10, 15, 16; Franklyn D. Holzman/Robert Legvold, 'The Economics and Politics of East-West Relations', *International Organization*, vol. 29, no. 1, winter 1975, p. 300.

5 David Mitrany, 'The Functional Approach to World Organization', *International Affairs*, vol. 24, London 1948, pp. 350-360.

6 Ernst B. Haas, *Beyond the Nation-State. Functionalism and International Organization*, Stanford University Press 1964, p. 19.

7 Ibid., *The Uniting of Europe. Political, Social, and Economic Forces 1950-1957*, Stanford University Press, 1968, p. 317.

8 Joseph S. Nye, *Peace in Parts — Integration and Conflict in Regional Organizations*, Boston 1971.

9 A. J. R. Groom, 'The Functionalist Approach and East/West Cooperation in Europe', *Journal of Common Market Studies*, vol. XIII, 1975, pp. 21-60.

10 Bernd Windhoff, *Darstellung und Kritik der Konvergenztheorie*. Gibt es eine Annäherung der sozialistischen und kapitalistischen Wirtschaftssysteme?, Bern/Frankfurt 1971.

11 Walter S. Buckingham, *Theoretical Economic Systems*, New York 1951; Pitirim Sorokin, 'Soziologische und kulturelle Annäherungen zwischen den Vereinigten Staaten und der Sowjetunion', *Zeitschrift für Politik*, NF, vol. 7, 1960, pp. 341-370; Jan Tinbergen, 'Kommt es zu einer Annäherung zwischen den kommunistischen und den freiheitlichen Wirtschaftsordnungen?', *Hamburger Jahrbuch für Wirtschafts- und Gesellschaftspolitik*, 8, 1963, pp. 11-20.

12 Raymond Aron, *Die Entwicklung der Industriegesellschaft und der sozialen Stratifikation*, Berlin 1977; John Kenneth Galbraith, *Die moderne Industriegesellschaft*, München/Zürich 1969.

13 Walt W. Rostow, *The Process of Economic Growth*, Oxford 1953; ibid., 'The Take-Off Into Self-Sustained Growth', *The Economic Journal*, vol. 66, 1956, pp. 25-47; ibid., *Stadien des wirtschaftlichen Wachstums. Eine Alternative zur marxistischen Entwicklungstheorie*, Göttingen 1967; Erik Boettcher, 'Phasentheorie der wirtschaftlichen Entwicklung', *Hamburger Jahrbuch für Wirtschafts- und Gesellschaftspolitik*, 4, 1959, pp. 23-34.

14 Gernot Gutmann, 'Die Argumente vom Wandel durch Handel', in: Alfred Schüller/Ulrich Wagner (Eds.), *Außenwirtschaftspolitik und Stabilisierung*

14

von Wirtschaftssystemen, Stuttgart 1980, p. 57; Günther Rose, *Industriegesellschaft und Konvergenztheorie. Genesis, Struktur und Funktionen*, Berlin (GDR) 1971; Herbert Meissner, *Konvergenztheorie und Realität*, Berlin (GDR) 1969.

15 Maurice Duverger, *Introduction à la Politique*, Paris 1964.

16 Gerda Zellentin, *Intersystemare Beziehungen in Europa. Bedingungen der Friedenssicherung*, Leiden 1970, p. 133 ff.

17 Zellentin (Ed.), *Annäherung, Abgrenzung und friedlicher Wandel in Europa*, Boppard 1976.

18 Kenneth N. Waltz, 'The Myth of National Interdependence', in: Ch. P. Kindlberger (Ed.), *The International Corporation. A Symposium*, Cambridge, Mass., 1970, p. 205 ff.

19 Mary A. Tetreault, 'Measuring Interdependence', *International Organization*, vol. 34, summer 1980, no. 3, pp. 429-443.

20 Robert O. Keohane/Joseph S. Nye, *Power and Interdependence. World Politics in Transition*, Boston 1977, p. 11 ff.

21 Max Weber, *Wirtschaft und Gesellschaft. Grundriß der verstehenden Soziologie*, Tübingen 1972, p. 28.

22 Karl W. Deutsch, *The Nerves of Government. Models of Political Communication and Control*, The Free Press, New York 1966.

23 Hans J. Morgenthau, *Politics Among Nations*, New York 1948.

24 James N. Rosenau, 'National Interest', in: ibid., *A Scientific Study of Foreign Policy*, New York 1971, pp. 239-250.

25 Stephen D. Krasner, *Defending the National Interest. Raw Materials Investment and U.S. Foreign Policy*, Princeton University Press 1978; Robert W. Tucker, *The Purposes of American Power. An Essay on National Security*, New York 1971; Norman Podhoretz, *The Present Danger*, New York 1980.

26 Harald Müller/Reinhard Rode, *Osthandel oder Wirtschaftskrieg? Die USA und das Gas-Röhren-Geschäft*, Frankfurt 1982.

27 Ursula Schmiederer, 'Zur sowjetischen Theorie der friedlichen Koexistenz'. *Probleme sozialistischer Politik 8*, Frankfurt 1968, p. 13 f.; Gerhard Wettig, *Konflikt und Kooperation zwischen Ost und West. Entspannung in Theorie und Praxis. Außen- und sicherheitspolitische Analyse*, Bonn 1981, p. 101 f.; Dietrich Geyer (Ed.), *Osteuropa-Handbuch. Sowjetunion. Außenpolitik 1917-1955*, Köln 1971, p. 19 ff.

28 Groom, *The Functionalist Approach and East-West Cooperation in Europe* (note 9), p. 30, *Europa-Archiv* 23, 1969, p. D 551 f.

29 Johan Galtung, *The European Community. A Superpower in the Making*, Allen and Unwin, London 1981, p. 86 ff.

30 Werner Link, *Der Ost-West-Konflikt. Die Organisation der internationalen Beziehungen im 20. Jahrhundert*, Stuttgart 1980, p. 195.

31 Kjell Goldmann/Johan Lagerkranz, *East-West Tension in Europe 1971-1975. Updating of a Data Set and Retesting of a Model*, The Swedish Institute for International Affairs, Stockholm 1977, p. 28; Roger G. Wall, *The Dynamics of Polarization*, Stockholm 1975, p. 113, a. 115.

32 David A. Jodice/Charles Lewis Taylor, 'Détente and its Effects. A Measure-

ment of East-West Trade', in: Daniel Frei (Ed.), *Definitions and Measurement of Détente. East and West Perspectives*, Cambridge, Mass., 1981, p. 166 ff.

33 Daniel Frei/Dieter Ruloff, 'Entspannung in Europa: Perzeption und Realität', *Politische Vierteljahresschrift*, vol. 23, April 1982, no. 1, pp. 27-45.

PART II

ECONOMIC RELATIONS – INTERDEPENDENCE OR MARGINAL FACTOR?

2
Trade

Jochen Bethkenhagen

Specific Determinants of East-West Trade

Different Political Systems. East-West trade is the exchange of goods between countries with different social systems. It is thus an ever-present factor in East-West political relations. Since these relations are characterized by perennial controversy, the question of what instrumental role trade policy should play in this controversy is often asked. The debate over harmonizing trade policies toward the East, which has taken on a renewed intensity since the USSR's entry into Afghanistan, does not reflect a politicization of trade with the East but rather a divergence of political concepts. Specifically, the question is whether these trade relations should be used as the motivation for an East-West policy based on cooperation in the spirit of the Final Act of the Conference on Security and Cooperation in Europe (CSCE) in Helsinki, or whether they can also be used as sanctions in cases of political conflict. A further question is whether increasing interdependence inevitably leads to more stable East-West relations, or whether it might result in undesirable political constraints. How these questions are answered will determine whether trade policy towards the East promotes partial interdependence or whether it relegates cooperation to the role of a peripheral phenomenon.

Different Economic Systems. East-West trade involves countries with differing economic systems. Foreign trade is subject to complete government control in CMEA (Council of Mutual Economic Assistance) countries (state monopoly of foreign trade and foreign currency). The state determines the volume of foreign trade, its regional structure and composition, though the details of this control are not published. In the West, government influence on trade with the East is in fact relatively large compared to regulation in other areas. But state intervention, such as in the form of lists of banned exports, import quotas, or tariff regulations is always clearly recognizable – and thus also more open to criticism. These differences become especially significant where matters of preferential reciprocity, such as for example, most favored nation status, are concerned. State monopoly of foreign trade also entails concentration of foreign trade on a

17

few suppliers. Indeed, in most cases there is a complete separation of domestic and foreign markets which also often involves efficiency losses in East-West trade relations. In addition, prices are set by criteria completely different from those in the West, thus creating a potential danger of dumping. These differences inherent in the system necessitate specific political measures in the West. The creation of mixed bilateral commissions, extensive liberalization of import quotas, but protection from ruinous price competition through anti-dumping regulations and price investigation procedures, as well as the establishment of trade promotion agencies in CMEA-country embassies, can be seen as a reflection of Western efforts in the late 1960s to ameliorate trade barriers caused by systemic differences.

Different Levels of Economic Development. East-West trade also takes place between countries with differing levels of economic development. In comparison to the highly industrialized Western countries of the EEC, Japan, and the U.S.A., most of the CMEA countries must be classified as agrarian or agroindustrial such as Rumania, Bulgaria, Poland. Others such as East Germany, Czechoslovakia and Hungary are mature industrialized societies; but classed by their economic or technological level of development, they would fall within the less-developed half of the hierarchy of industrialized countries. Finally, the Soviet Union – the West's most significant Eastern trading partner – occupies a special position. Its level of economic development would put it with the agroindustrial countries. But the magnitude of its domestic market as well as its wealth of natural resources make it a "self-sufficient naturally endowed economy", largely independent of foreign economic developments. With the partial exception of most favoured nation status, the developmental problems of the CMEA economies have scarcely figured in the import tariff policy of Western countries. Indeed preferential or free trade agreements such as those the EEC countries have concluded with Third World countries and other Western European industrialized countries have in fact resulted in indirect discrimination against CMEA countries.[1]

East-West trade is therefore influenced by both political and economic factors. It is very difficult to weigh the importance of the various factors, particularly given that besides the specific factors general economic developments such as rising raw materials prices, interest rate changes, and economic crises naturally also affect East-West economic relations. But it does appear that in the discussion on the use of East-West trade as a political instrument, its economic significance is overrated and economically conditioned developmental problems are underrated. The following analysis will therefore explore the economic determinants of East-West economic relations. This should not, however, be interpreted as an underestimation of the political factors influencing East-West trade, which are analysed in Parts 3 and 4 of this volume.

The Development and Structure of East-West Trade

East-West trade here refers to the exchange of goods between the seven European CMEA member countries and the 24 OECD countries. For purposes of analysis, a distinction will be made from time to time between the USSR and the smaller CMEA countries, also referred to as East European countries. The study is essentially based on CMEA countries' foreign trade statistics. In analyzing the composition of East-West trade, however, OECD foreign trade statistics, presently available to 1981,[2] are used.

Imbalance. The development in East-West trade since the beginning of the 1970s can be summarised as follows: expansion, efforts at consolidation, and stagnation.

The first half of the 1970s saw a steep rise in East-West trade, when the value of trade tripled in only five years from 13 to 37 billion transfer roubles,[3] an average annual expansion rate of 23 per cent. The CMEA countries' imports from the West grew much faster than their exports to the West and in the five years 1971 to 1975 they were about 25 per cent higher. The result was an accumulated deficit for the CMEA countries of nearly US-$ 25 billion.

The CMEA states accepted these deficits; indeed some actively encouraged them because, in view of the shrinking reservoir of labor, labor-saving technologies and processes were becoming increasingly important for these states' economic growth. They saw an expansion of trade with the West as a way of using foreign trade as a "growth factor". The plan was to make use of modern Western technology to develop, among other things, a strong export industry. The expectation was that the imports from the West would pay for themselves through increased exports, so that the loan repayments seemed assured.

At the beginning of the 1970s, the political conditions for an intensification of co-operation between East and West were favorable. As early as 1967 the NATO countries established, in the Harmel Report, the position that "military security and a policy of détente are not contradictory, but rather mutually complement each other."[4] This policy was actively pursued in the USA particularly during the Nixon-Kissinger administration[5] and in the Federal Republic during the Brandt-Scheel administration.[6] The FRG's treaties with the East (Ostverträge), the natural gas pipeline agreements, the conclusion of the U.S.-USSR trade agreement in October, 1972, and not least, agreement on the CSCE Final Act raised expectations in East and West that a qualitatively new, enduring phase of East-West relations would succeed the Cold War. The change signified an easing of the conflict between the capitalist and socialist systems, which was viewed as an ongoing and constant factor in East-West relations.[7] The conflict continued but was to take a less destructive form than it had during the Cold War, in which one side's advantage was always achieved at the expense of the other. With détente, a constructive confrontation of systems was envisioned which would be advantageous for both sides.[8]

Economic conditions also favored a credit-financed expansion of East-West trade. After the first dramatic oil price increase in 1973/74, the OPEC states had large balance-of-payments surpluses. These petrodollars were recycled into the Western banking system. When recession followed the first "oil price shock" in Western industrialized countries, there was a lack of demand for credit that was partially filled by the CMEA countries. Thus credit to the Soviet Union and to Poland in 1975 made up 27 per cent of all long-term foreign loans granted by banks in the Federal Republic. CMEA countries were considered good credit risks. In addition, some Western countries used subsidized state credits in order to compete with other Western exporters for the expanding markets in the East, or transferred the risk to the state via guarantee agreements. When some CMEA states – mainly the USSR – managed to get interest rate concessions, these were mostly neutralized by higher export prices.

Insufficient Consolidation. As early as 1975/76, it became clear that the expansion of East-West trade was imbalanced as a result of special factors, and that measures had to be taken to prevent a further widening of the gap between imports and exports.[9] This applied particularly to the smaller CMEA countries, whose trade deficit with the OECD countries was about US-\$ 6.5 billion in 1975 alone.

In the consolidation phase which followed, the import growth slowed dramatically while the growth in exports ceased to accelerate. By this time the imbalance had become so large that the cumulated deficit in the second half of the 1970s was two-thirds higher than in the period 1971 to 1975.

The Eastern European countries' trade with the West (excluding the USSR)

Average annual growth (nominal)	1971-75	1976-80	1981-82
		in per cent	
Exports to the West	15	14	- 1.3
Imports from the West	23	7	- 11.3
		in US-\$ billion	
Cumulated deficit	16.4	27.5	- 1.1

For various internal and external reasons it was not possible to step up exports to earn the foreign exchange needed to cover interest charges and capital repayments. Loans were used not just for investment, but also often to finance imports of raw materials and semi-finished manufactures. In addition, the "consequential costs" of plant imports from the West – such as raw materials and spares – were underestimated and no allowance was made for the fact that the productivity of Western plants in Eastern Europe is often lower than in the West. On top of this, there were internal growth problems associated with consumers' expectations of further rises in living standards, which political leaders were only able to satisfy by incurring trade deficits. On the export side, the CMEA countries did not manage to adjust the range of goods or offer to meet Western requirements.[10] Marketing and the overall organization of foreign trade, also remained unsatisfactory. Finally, external factors prevented successful consolidation. The recession in the West weakened demand for imports from Eastern European countries; their share of the OECD countries' total imports fell. The United States' high interest rate policy imposed additional unexpected burdens on the balance of payments as interest rates doubled between 1978 and 1981. The situation was exacerbated at the beginning of the 1980s when Western banks changed their credit policy after their confidence was shattered by Poland's de-facto insolvency, and to a lesser degree by a similar situation in Rumania.[11]

The following statistics show just how difficult things became for the smaller CMEA countries. In 1980, East European countries (USSR excepted) had to pay US-$ 6.3 billion (net) in interest alone. To do so required a trade surplus of roughly the same amount. Instead they incurred a deficit of about $ 3.2 bn. The pressure from Western banks was one reason why major adjustments became necessary, and East-West trade moved into the phase of stagnation or decline mentioned above. In 1981, there was a 6 per cent absolute decline in the smaller CMEA countries' imports from the West. In 1982, the brake on imports was applied even more drastically and they declined by 16 per cent. This shows that the smaller CMEA countries are in fact able to control their balance of payments, and that Poland's inability to come to grips with its economic problems is the exception rather than the rule in Eastern Europe. Brainard notes that in the period from 1979 to 1982 there was a dramatic turnabout in capital flow for the East European countries: In just three years "a net inflow of $ 5 billion had become a net outflow of $ 10 billion".[12]

Gains in the Soviet Union's Terms of Trade. The USSR's policy for trading with the West, unlike the smaller Eastern European countries', was not constrained by acute balance of payments problems. As an oil exporter in its own right, the USSR benefited from the dramatic increases in energy prices. It was able to increase its real imports from the West a good deal faster than its own exports without coming up against a critical debt limit. The net debt of the USSR was $ 10 bn at the end of 1982, of which $ 4 bn was with BIS banks (Banks reporting to the Bank of International Settlements). However, the Soviet Union also reduced the pace of its import growth in the second half of the 1970s:

USSR trade with the West and terms of trade

	real average annual increase in per cent		
	1975/70	1980/75	1981/80
Exports to the West	4.8	2.8	- 3.3
Imports from the West	17.1	6.4	4.8
Terms of trade	5.1	14.0	2.4

The terms of trade in Soviet trade with the West improved by over 152 per cent between 1970 and 1981. Thus trade with the West provided the USSR with additional resources for its domestic economy.

Differences in the Composition of Trade. The composition of the USSR's exports is different from that of the other CMEA countries'. Whereas the smaller states' export pattern is relatively differentiated, the Soviet Union's has become heavily concentrated. In 1982 exports of oil, oil products and natural gas alone accounted for 80 per cent of export earnings compared to only 33 per cent in 1970. The share of natural gas in total energy exports has increased. In 1970, exports to the West amounted to only 1 billion m^3. The decision, taken at the end of the 1960s, to export natural gas as well as oil to Western countries has, in retrospect, turned out to have been highly beneficial. Soviet reserves of natural gas are probably larger than of oil, and natural gas production costs are lower. The USSR also achieved large "windfall profits" with natural gas because gas prices are linked to those for oil products. Total Soviet earnings from energy exports between 1973 and 1982 increased from 1.3 billion to 15 billion TRbl; yet the volume only rose from 76 million tonnes to 127 million tonnes of coal equivalent. In other words price increases in the energy market were the main growth factor in Soviet trade with the West. Consequently, it has now become highly dependent on events in the world energy markets, and in 1982, Soviet trade with the West suffered its first downturn when the decline in demand due to the recession made Western European natural gas importers cut their imports from the USSR by 3 billion m^3, reducing Soviet earnings by 7 per cent.

The smaller CMEA countries have also tried to cash in on the rise in oil prices. In the second half of the 1970s they significantly expanded their oil processing business, and by 1981 about 20 per cent of their earnings from exports to the OECD countries came from oil products. In order to be able to export oil products, however, they had to import crude from OPEC countries. Because of the significant reduction in the price differences between crude and oil products this business has become less important.

In the 1970s, the smaller CMEA countries increased their exports of finished products at above-average rates with the result that their share of total exports increased from 21 per cent in 1970 to 28 per cent in 1981. But since 1978, the share of this sector has been falling again. Apart from the undoubted short-comings in sales policy, trade in these products was also hampered by higher tariffs and other protectionist measures taken in the West to safeguard its consumer goods industries. This is confirmed by the respective shares of consumer goods and other sectors in the smaller CMEA countries' exports to the OECD. The CMEA countries' shares of OECD markets fell most in the consumer goods sectors. By contrast, they largely held on to their relative positions in raw materials, semimanufactures, chemical products and engineering products, including electrical products and vehicles.

The pattern of CMEA imports is homogeneous. There has been a dramatic rise in the share of foreign exchange absorbed by imports of agricultural products, from 10 per cent in 1974 to 27 per cent in 1981. The only exceptions are Bulgaria and Hungary. The reason for the large import requirements of the other CMEA countries is the low efficiency of their agriculture. The sector is unable to produce enough feedstuffs and to organize meat production economically, so that the planned increases in meat supplies are only possible with large agricultural imports. All CMEA states still have the long term aim of a high degree of self-sufficiency in food supplies. But the conclusion, in 1983, of the "embargo-proof" long-term grain agreement between the USSR and the USA, which provides for minimum purchases of 9 million tonnes per annum, proves that import requirements of grain are expected to remain high.[13] For the United States the grain exports are the only important item in its trade with the East. In general the CMEA countries account for about 10 per cent of total US farm exports.

On the whole therefore, the composition of East-West trade does not correspond to the usual pattern for trade between industrialized countries. There is no exchange of similar goods, substitution trade, such as cars for cars, but – and this is particularly true of Soviet trade with the West – raw materials are traded for industrial goods in complementary trade. Complementary trade results on the one hand, in different dependencies, so that supply interruptions can create short-term economic disruption in the West. In the energy sector, however, the existence of back-up reserves as well as options for regional and product substitution in energy supplies means that such disruptions would not be serious. On the other hand even future growth options are negatively influenced in the USSR. The economic costs for the USSR of a trade war would most likely be less than for the West in the short run, but greater in the long run. In general, however, the impact of these effects should not be overrated given the relatively small volume of trade.

The importance of trade

Asymmetry characterizes not only the development and composition of East-West trade, but also its relative significance to East and West and within the East and the West.

East-West trade accounts for about 30 per cent of the CMEA countries' foreign trade but only about 3 per cent of OECD countries' foreign trade. East-West trade is therefore of greater relative importance to the CMEA countries than to OECD countries. In general terms trade with the East is something of a peripheral phenomenon for OECD countries. Stagnation in the smaller CMEA countries' trade with the West has meant that these countries accounted for only 1.5 per cent of the OECD countries' trade in 1981 down from 2 per cent in 1970. The intensification of trade with Eastern European countries in the mid-1970s must therefore be considered as only a temporary episode. This leads to the conclusion that it is primarily economic factors which determine the course of trade relations, because these countries — with the exception of Poland — were excluded from Western economic sanctions. In the mid-1970s, favorable political and economic conditions enabled East European countries to live above their means. The modernization concept failed with the result that trade expansion had to be readjusted to their own export options and capacities. In this context it should also be noted that it was the countries which, by a wide margin, imported more from the West that showed the greatest economic and payments difficulties in the early 1980s. In 1975, 50 per cent of Poland's and 42 per cent of Rumania's imports came from the West. Whether this is a mere coincidence or whether a causal link exists is surely a matter for more careful investigation. In the meantime, this development should not be ignored in the discussion of whether or not Western credit supports the socialist system.

In contrast to Eastern European countries, the USSR was able to gain ground in Western markets. The USSR's share of OECD trade increased from 1.2 per cent to nearly 2 per cent between 1970 and 1981. In terms of imports, however, this was not due to an increased Western trade involvement in the USSR, but in large part to higher prices of Soviet oil and natural gas supplies. For example the average value of Soviet exports to the Federal Republic increased by 161 per cent between 1977 and 1982, but the volume of exports only increased by 24 per cent. The USSR's terms-of-trade[14] improved by 65 per cent. In other words the USSR was able to import about two-thirds more goods for the same quantity of exports than six years before.[15] The USSR also became a more important trading partner for the West than the remaining CMEA countries. At the beginning of the 1970s, it only accounted for 35 per cent of the total trade with the West, less than the 65 per cent of the remaining CMEA countries. By 1981, however, its share was 55 per cent, and thus more important than the rest of the CMEA put together.

Whereas in the CMEA the leading political power is also by a large margin the West's leading trade partner. On the Western side the leading political power, the U.S.A., has only a peripheral trading position. The USA's share of total OECD imports from the East is only between 3 and 5 per cent, while its share of OECD exports range, depending on the scale of grain supplies, between 4 per cent (1970) and 14 per cent (1979). Excluding agricultural trade, the USA accounts for a mere 0.4 per cent of nonagricultural OECD exports (1981). If one also considers the share of exports to the East in total U.S. foreign industrial trade, which is only 0.6 per cent, it is clear that the United States can formulate its Eastern trade policy in industrial goods with little regard to the costs of any disruption to such trade. In agricultural trade, where the CMEA accounted for 10 per cent of U.S. exports in 1981, the United States is only prepared to incur the costs of restrictive trade policy in the short term, such as with the partial grain embargo between January 1980 and April 1981. The conclusion of a long-term grain agreement running from August 1983 to September 1988 demonstrates the U.S. interest in a secure market. The contract included explicit assurances that supplies will not be interrupted by possible future embargoes.

In comparison trade with the East is of greater economic importance to the West Europeans. In 1981 the Federal Republic conducted about 6 per cent of its foreign trade with CMEA countries and thus exhibited the highest degree of involvement with Eastern Europe of all the seven countries that participate in the Western economic summits. Also noteworthy are the different regional emphases among some Western industrialized countries. While the Federal Republic is more heavily involved with Eastern Europe than with the USSR, mainly because of the high proportion of inner-German trade, the USSR is Japan's most important trading partner by a wide margin.

On the whole, however, East-West trade accounts for only a small percentage of the West's total trade, and there has even been a decline in its relative importance in recent years. Rather than increased interdependence, there has been a progressive economic disengagement in trade between East and West Europe. This view is also supported by the figures on the structure of Western imports from the CMEA. Only in the case of energy and raw materials does the CMEA surpass 5 per cent of total Western imports. It is also only in energy, where Soviet natural gas deliveries will generally represent more than a third and in the case of the Federal Republic of Germany about 35 per cent of domestic consumption by 1990, that one can speak of a partial interdependence.

The importance of trade with the East for employment in Western countries is also often overrated. One analysis of the employment effects revealed for example, that in the FRG, in 1979, about 220,000 jobs were directly or indirectly dependent upon exports to CMEA countries and 92,000 upon exports to the USSR. This represents 0.9 per cent of total West German employment,[16] which is scarcely a dangerous degree of export dependency offering politically useful leverage to the USSR.

Sectoral analysis also shows that in no branch of the economy has employment become dangerously dependent on exports to the East. The highest levels of employment dependency are in metal production and metal processing with 5 per cent, and mechanical engineering with 4 per cent. For some companies, however, trade with the East could be important or even vital to continued existence. For example the annual reports of the Mannesmann Corporation

– one of the biggest FRG-exporters to the East – show that an average of 15 per cent of the business of its West-German branches was with CMEA countries during the 1970s; the extremes being 18 per cent in 1976 and 8 per cent in 1977.

It is difficult to evaluate the negative employment effects of imports from the East and it remains an open question as to whether these imports in fact destroy jobs. In the case of imports from the USSR, the answer must be no, because the raw materials supplied could not be produced domestically. In general the same applies to imports from other CMEA countries. The goods do not as a rule compete with domestic products, but rather with those of third countries. If, for example, Hungary were to halt the supply of leather goods or textiles, the products would not be produced domestically, but imported at lower cost from newly industrializing countries. The employment effects of trade with the East must therefore be evaluated as quite positive. But for both the economy as a whole and individual sectors, they are too slight to engender any politically dubious dependency.

Summary and Outlook

In the early 1980s, East-West trade is only a peripheral phenomenon in Western foreign trade relations. Partial interdependencies are to be found, if anywhere, in Western Europe's long-term energy procurement contracts and the U.S.A.'s grain supplies. Since the mid-1970s, trade with the smaller CMEA countries has slackened. The increased importance of imports from the USSR is almost exclusively due to energy price rises, not to improved competitiveness of Soviet exports. Thus the expectations of more intense economic relations that were harbored in both Eastern and Western political and economic circles at the beginning of the 1970s have not been fulfilled. On the one hand economic interdependence did not reach the level at which it might assume a stabilizing role. East-West relations are therefore still characterized by the primacy of politics. Economics has, however, of course had some impact on political decision making. For example the controversy over the gas-pipeline project as well as that over the United States' grain export policy, was in the main prompted by economic interests. On the other hand, it would be wrong to attribute stagnation in East-West trade to the concurrent worsening of East-West political relations. Developments in trade can be largely explained by economic factors, such as the insufficient competitiveness of CMEA exports, recession in the West and also partly in the CMEA, as well as the rising cost of raw materials and credit.

The outlook for growth in East-West trade at the beginning of the 1980s is considerably less favorable than at the beginning of the 1970s. At the beginning of the 1970s, there was a desire to intensify economic relations between the two blocs which does not exist in the early 1980s. Although the U.S. government has lifted its embargo against the gas pipeline it has in no way given up its objections to the creation of partial interdependencies in East-West trade relations. Since November 1982, committees of NATO, CoCom, the OECD, and IEA have been working to harmonize trade policy toward the East. The result, if any, cannot be expected to be a promotion of trade with the East. If there is no substantial extension of the CoCom embargo list or ban on future energy procurements from the USSR, and credit policy remains a matter for national discretion, it will mean that the Europeans have succeeded in prevailing with their approach. From the tenor of the current debate it would appear that the question is not how East-West trade could be promoted by a political initiative, but what form and degree restrictive measures should take. The U.S.A. acts on the premise that East-West trade confers unilateral benefits on the USSR. These enable the USSR to strengthen its military potential and thus oblige the West to bear new defense burdens. But there is no basis for this premise. On the contrary trade only occurs when it benefits both sides, and the West is likely to benefit most.

Critics of the restrictive U.S. approach doubt whether trade with the East can be used as an instrument in the pursuit of generally recognized political goals. They argue, among other things, that general export limitations will scarcely weaken the Eastern military potential. In CMEA countries, as in other countries, preservation of the system and external security have priority. Military expenditure is therefore largely independent of the country's economic situation, so that trade restrictions would take their toll primarily in the CMEA countries' standard of living. Experience teaches us that power elites respond to latent dissatisfaction of the population by a domestic political clamp down and possibly also a hardening of the foreign policy stance. Moreover, smaller CMEA countries would be forced into a greater trade dependence on the USSR. Restrictive trade policy is not, therefore, a suitable tool for implementing generally accepted political goals.

The debate on restrictive East-West trade policies may dissipate if there were a more general recognition of the fact that growth prospects for East-West trade are poor for purely economic reasons. In the medium term the smaller CMEA countries will be unable to increase their imports and will have to use a large portion of their export earnings to service debt. The difficult economic situation in the West inhibits trade with the USSR, because it holds back any energy price increases on which any growth would be based. Against this political and economic background, it could be considered a success if the existing relative importance of East-West trade is maintained. A further decline of its importance is, however, more likely.

Notes

1 *See* Jochen Bethkenhagen, Hans Martin Duseberg, Maria Lodahl, Heinrich Machowski: *RGW, EG und Ost-West-Handel. Möglichkeiten der Zusammenarbeit unter den Bedingungen der regionalen Teilintegration.* Teil I: Textband. Berlin 1980, p. 312. Distributed as manuscript.

2 The two sources however, differ sometimes significantly. Systematic differences result from the geographical definition (including or excluding intra-German trade), the type of trade covered (general or special trade), the coverage by country of origin and destination (country of purchase or sale or country of manufacture and final destination), the coverage of special transactions (including or excluding gold for monetary purposes), and whether trade is fob or cif. In addition, there are discrepancies in timing and different rules on confidentiality. It seems likely that there are other reasons as well, as some of the discrepancies are considerable. According to CMEA statistics, CMEA countries had an import surplus of more than $ 3 bn in trade with OECD countries in 1981. According to OECD statistics, this was an export surplus of $ 140 m (including inner-German trade). *See* Heinrich Machowski: 'East-West trade still facing difficulties'. *Economic Bulletin*, January 1983.

   Marer has shown that CMEA statistics are better suited for balance of payments analysis. *See* P. Marer, 'Toward a solution of the mirror statistics puzzle in East-West commerce'. Friedrich Levcik (Ed.) *Internationale Wirtschaft − Vergleiche und Interdependenzen*. Festschrift für Franz Nemschak. Vienna and New York, 1978, p. 430 ff.

3 The TRbl is the CMEA countries' common external currency unit. Its parity against other − Eastern and Western − currencies is set by the International Bank for Economic Co-operation, one of the two CMEA banks. The parity against the US-$ in 1981 was 1 TRbl = $ 1.39 US.

4 The Harmel Report is found in: *Europa-Archiv*, vol. 3/1968, p. D 75 ff.

5 The key to U.S. policy was a "linkage concept" designed to make relations with the USSR dependent on its action in other parts of the world. In return for trade expansion, the U.S. expected Soviet restraint in crisis areas such as the Near East, Berlin, and Southeast Asia. *See* Hans-Dieter Jacobsen, *Die Ost-West Wirtschaftsbeziehungen als deutsch-amerikanisches Problem*. Ebenhausen, 1983, p. 56.

6 See Angela Stent: *From Embargo to Ostpolitik*, Cambridge 1981.

7 *See* Jochen Bethkenhagen, Siegfried Kupper und Horst Lambrecht: 'Über den Zusammenhang von außenwirtschaftlichen Interessen der DDR und Entspannung'. In *Die DDR im Entspannungsprozeß − Lebensweise im realen Sozialismus*. Edition Deutschland Archiv. Köln, p. 17.

8 However, only if the profits for both sides are equally high can this policy persist in the long run. Otherwise the losing side will not be interested in continuing the policy. See Jochen Bethkenhagen, Siegfried Kupper and Horst Lambrecht, *op. cit.*, p. 17. On this question, Kissinger commented: "We must be mature enough to recognize that a relationship, if it is to be

stable, must offer both sides advantage; and that the most constructive international relations are those in which both parties see an element of profit. Moscow will derive benefit from others. Here one can not balance accounts daily in each case, but only for the whole area of relations and over a period of time." Henry A. Kissinger: 'Die Entspannungsdoktrin der Vereinigten Staaten.' *Europa-Archiv*, vol. 20, 1974, p. D 164.

9   *See* Jochen Bethkenhagen. 'Osthandel der Bundesrepublik Deutschland in einer Konsolidierungsphase'. *Wochenbericht des DIW*. No. 14/1976.

10 "However, it must be admitted, that the process of adaption of socialist countries' export to the needs and requirements of Western markets was also inadequate". Jozef Soldaczuk: 'East-West economic relations: Expectations a decade ago and actual outcome'. Paper presented at: Workshop on East-West European Economic Interaction. Session Eight. Moskau, September 1983. Distributed as manuscript.

11 Rumania's payments problems stem largely from the Polish repayments moratorium of March 1981. This event most likely provided the occasion for Western banks to initiate a new, more cautious credit policy toward CMEA countries. It took the form, among other things, of a reduction of the credit line, or in omitting the customary net increase. *See* Lawrence J. Brainard, 'Handels- und Zahlungsprobleme in Osteuropa'. *Europa-Archiv*, vol. 14/1983, p. 408.

12 Lawrence J. Brainard, *op. cit.*, p. 409 f.

13 *See* Heinrich Machowski, *Ost-West-Handel weiter unter schwierigen Bedingungen. op. cit.*, p. 567. The Soviet Union has also concluded long-term grain agreements with Canada (1981 through 1986; 4 - 5 million tons annual minimum purchase guarantee), Argentina (1980 through 1985; 4 million tons), Brazil (1983-1986; 0.5 million tons), and France (1982; 1.5 million tons).

14 Index of export prices divided by index of import prices.

15 *See* Jochen Bethkenhagen. 'Handelsverflechtung mit den kleineren RGW-Ländern auf neuem Tiefstand', *Wochenbericht des DIW*. No. 12/1983, p. 163.

16 For methods and further results *see* Jochen Bethkenhagen and Hans Wessels. 'Beschäftigungseffekte des Osthandels nicht überschätzen'. *Wochenbericht des DIW*, No. 13/1981.

30

Table 1: *The CMEA countries' trade with the West*[1]

CMEA countries	Exports[2]					Imports[2]				
	1970	1975	1980	1981	1982	1970	1975	1980	1981	1982
					Billion TRbl[3]					
Bulgaria	0.26	0.35	1.15	1.10	0.91	0.32	0.96	1.10	1.54	1.39
Czechoslovakia	0.70	1.17	2.21	2.18	2.14	0.82	1.57	2.53	2.40	2.24
GDR[4]	0.90	1.69	2.95	3.87	4.66	1.17	2.45	4.11	4.23	4.08
Poland	0.91	2.42	4.04	2.96	2.67	0.84	4.63	4.51	3.30	2.24
Rumania	0.54	1.39	2.82	2.68	2.47	0.70	1.68	2.78	2.37	1.49
Hungary	0.59	0.95	1.99	1.89	1.93	0.67	1.41	2.43	2.64	2.33
CMEA (6)	3.90	7.97	15.16	14.68	14.78	4.52	12.70	17.46	16.48	13.77
USSR	2.21	6.17	16.19	17.57	19.00	2.57	9.75	15.83	18.24	18.98
CMEA (7)	6.11	14.14	31.35	32.25	33.78	7.09	22.45	33.29	34.72	32.75
					Change on previous year in %					
Bulgaria	+10.1	+3.8	+23.7	−4.5	−17.3	+38.0	+40.7	+25.3	+40.6	−10.1
Czechoslovakia	+9.4	−6.0	+23.5	−1.4	−1.5	+26.0	+2.0	+10.0	−5.2	−6.6
GDR[4]	+7.8	−5.3	+26.6	+31.2	+20.4	+32.1	−0.4	+10.5	+2.9	−3.6
Poland	+19.2	+9.0	+14.5	−26.6	−9.8	+4.2	+17.2	−1.0	−26.8	−32.1
Rumania	+20.2	−8.8	+13.5	−5.1	−7.8	+5.1	−13.1	+5.3	−18.8	−37.1
Hungary	+22.5	−8.8	+15.3	−4.6	+1.6	+42.2	+3.5	+11.5	+8.8	−11.8
CMEA (6)	+20.8	−0.5	+18.5	−3.2	+0.7	+19.0	+7.5	+7.2	−5.5	−16.4
USSR	+4.7	−2.4	+26.5	+8.5	+8.2	+11.5	+57.4	+18.5	+15.2	+4.1
CMEA (7)	+14.4	−1.6	+22.5	+2.9	+4.7	+16.2	+24.7	+12.3	+4.3	−5.7
					Share of trade with the West (total exports or imports = 100)					
Bulgaria	14.2	10.1	16.8	14.5	11.1	19.1	23.8	17.2	20.2	16.6
Czechoslovakia	20.6	20.0	22.0	19.9	18.0	24.8	24.7	24.8	22.2	19.0
GDR[4]	22.1	22.6	24.1	27.4	29.0	26.9	29.2	30.5	29.5	27.3
Poland	28.5	31.5	34.6	29.6	23.7	25.9	49.5	34.4	28.2	22.4
Rumania	32.3	35.0	36.9	31.7	32.3	39.6	42.2	31.4	28.4	23.5
Hungary	27.0	22.3	25.0	21.2	20.0	26.9	28.4	29.3	29.2	24.7
CMEA (6)	24.0	24.3	26.9	24.5	22.8	27.2	34.2	29.0	26.6	22.4
USSR	19.1	25.7	32.6	30.8	30.1	24.3	36.6	35.6	34.7	33.7
CMEA (7)	22.0	24.9	29.6	27.6	26.5	26.1	35.2	31.8	30.3	27.8

Figures for 1982 are provisional.
[1] OECD countries. − [2] Fob; Hungary's imports: cif. General trade. Purchasing and selling country; USSR and Hungary (from 1975): country of origin and destination. − [3] The transfer rouble is the CMEA countries' external currency unit: its value in 1970 was US-$ 1.11; in 1975 US-$ 1.39; in 1980 US-$ 1.53; in 1981 US-$ 1.39; and in 1982 US-$ 1.38. − [4] So-called capitalist industrial countries (as a group).
Sources: CMEA countries' foreign trade statistics; DIW estimates.

Table 2: *The CMEA countries' trade balance with the OECD countries*

CMEA countries	1970	1971 to 1975[1]	1976 to 1980[1]	1980	1981	1982
Balance in billion US-$[2]						
Bulgaria	−0.1	−1.4	−1.0	+0.1	−0.6	−0.7
Czechoslovakia	−0.1	−1.4	−3.4	−0.5	−0.3	−0.1
GDR[3]	−0.3	−3.6	−7.9	−1.8	−0.5	+0.8
Poland	+0.1	−7.0	−10.2	−0.7	−0.5	+0.6
Rumania	−0.2	−1.3	−1.1	+0.3	+0.4	+1.4
Hungary	−0.1	−1.7	−3.8	−0.7	−1.0	−0.6
CMEA (6)	−0.7	−16.4	−27.5	−3.3	−2.5	+1.4
USSR	−0.4	−7.1	−10.7	+0.5	−0.9	+0.0
CMEA (7)	−1.1	−23.5	−38.2	−2.8	−3.4	+1.4
Exports as % of imports						
Bulgaria	81.3	58.3	83.1	105.0	71.4	65.5
Czechoslovakia	85.3	81.5	77.0	87.3	90.8	95.5
GDR[3]	77.4	71.0	67.3	71.8	91.5	114.2
Poland	108.4	61.5	69.0	89.4	89.7	119.2
Rumania	76.9	84.3	91.6	101.4	113.1	165.7
Hungary	88.9	72.8	74.0	81.8	71.6	82.8
CMEA (6)	86.5	70.7	74.6	86.8	89.1	107.3
USSR	85.9	79.8	87.6	102.2	96.3	100.1
CMEA (7)	86.3	74.2	80.4	94.2	92.9	103.5

Discrepancies in the totals due to rounding. Figures for 1982 are provisional.
[1]) Cumulated figures. − [2]) At current prices and exchange rates; trade surplus: +; trade deficit: —. − [3]) With so-called capitalist industrial countries (as a group).
Sources: CMEA countries' statistical yearbooks and foreign trade yearbooks.

Table 3: *The CMEA countries' debts in convertible currencies*
1971 to 1982

	1971	1975	1980	1981	1982

Net indebtedness[1] in US-$ billion[2]
at the end of each year

	1971	1975	1980	1981	1982
Bulgaria	0.72	2.26	2.73	2.23	1.77
Czechoslovakia	0.16	0.83	3.64	3.53	3.26
GDR[3]	1.21	3.55	11.75	12.50	11.09
Poland	0.76	7.38	24.50	24.73	23.76
Rumania	1.23	2.45	9.18	9.82	9.40
Hungary	0.85	2.20	7.51	7.81	7.03
CMEA (6)	4.93	18.67	59.31	60.62	56.31
USSR	0.60	7.45	9.30	12.44	10.10
CMEA (7)	5.53	26.12	68.61	73.06	66.41

Debt service ratio[4] in per cent

	1971	1975	1980	1981	1982
Bulgaria	15.6	32.0	17.1	19.6	15.2
Czechoslovakia	1.2	3.5	12.2	16.1	12.7
GDR	7.4	10.5	28.6	32.4	18.5
Poland	4.3	15.3	46.4	87.6	70.9
Rumania	11.3	8.8	24.3	33.8	31.1
Hungary	9.7	11.6	27.3	30.0	40.2
CMEA (6)	6.9	11.7	29.0	41.3	31.6
USSR	1.4	6.0	4.2	7.1	4.2
CMEA (7)	4.8	9.2	16.0	22.7	15.9

[1]) CMEA countries' total liabilities (government credits, bank credits, supplier credits, Eurobonds and World Bank and IMF credits for Rumania) minus CMEA assets with Western banks reporting to the Bank for International Settlements (BIS). – [2]) At current exchange rates. – [3]) Including intra-German capital transaction. – [4]) Interest based on average interest rates in the Euromoney market in per cent of exports to the OECD countries.
Sources: Figures on gross indebtedness: Allan J. Lenz: Controlling international debt: Implications for East-West trade. Paper submitted to the Workshop on East-West European economic interaction. Session eight: World economy and East-West trade – a reconsideration after a decade. Moscow, September 19-22, 1983.
Debt service ratio: DIW calculations.

Table 4: *Importance of East-West-Trade*
. shares in per cent

Reporting country	CMEA (6)			USSR		
	1970	1975	1981	1970	1975	1981
	Total exports of reporting countries = 100					
OECD	2,0	2,7	1,6	1,2	2,2	1,8
EEC (10)	2,7	3,4	2,1	1,2	2,0	1,5
of which:						
West-Germany	4,4	5,5	3,7	1,2	3,1	1,9
France	2,1	2,8	2,0	1,5	2,2	1,8
Italy	3,0	3,3	1,6	2,3	2,9	1,7
Great Britain	1,9	1,9	1,2	1,3	1,1	0,8
United States	0,5	0,9	0,9	0,3	1,7	1,0
Japan	0,6	1,0	0,5	1,8	2,9	2,1
	Total imports of reporting countries = 100					
OECD	1,9	1,8	1,3	1,2	1,5	1,9
EEC (10)	2,4	2,4	1,9	1,3	1,6	2,3
of which:						
West-Germany	4,3	4,3	3,8	1,1	1,8	2,5
France	1,3	1,7	1,3	1,1	1,5	2,8
Italy	3,6	2,7	1,8	1,9	2,3	3,4
Great Britain	1,6	1,2	0,8	2,4	1,7	0,8
United States	0,4	0,5	0,5	0,2	0,3	0,1
Japan	0,6	0,4	0,2	2,6	2,0	1,4
	Shares of reporting countries in total OECD exports to the East					
OECD	==================100=====================					
EEC (10)	70	68	65	53	49	40
of which:						
West-Germany	35	35	34	16	23	15
France	8	10	11	10	9	8
Italy	9	8	6	12	8	6
Great Britain	8	6	6	9	4	4
United States	5	6	10	4	15	11
Japan	2	4	4	13	13	15
	Shares of reporting countries in total OECD imports from the East					
OECD	==================100=====================					
EEC (10)	71	69	68	56	54	60
of which:						
West-Germany	32	31	34	12	15	16
France	6	9	9	7	9	14
Italy	13	10	9	10	10	13
Great Britain	8	6	4	19	10	3
United States	4	5	7	3	3	1
Japan	3	2	1	17	13	8

Source: OECD: Foreign Trade Statistics, Serie A.

Table 5:
*The CMEA countries' respective shares
of trade with the West, 1970 to 1982*

shares in per cent

	1970	1975	1980	1981	1982
CMEA (7) exports to the West = 100					
Bulgaria	4.3	2.5	3.7	3.4	2.7
Czechoslovakia	11.5	8.3	7.0	6.8	6.3
GDR	14.7	12.0	9.4	12.0	13.8
Poland	14.9	17.1	12.9	9.2	7.9
Rumania	8.8	9.8	9.0	8.3	7.3
Hungary	9.6	6.7	6.3	5.9	5.7
CMEA (6)	63.8	56.4	48.4	45.5	43.8
USSR	36.2	43.6	51.6	54.5	56.2
CMEA (7) imports from the West = 100					
Bulgaria	4.5	4.3	3.3	4.4	4.2
Czechoslovakia	11.6	7.0	7.6	6.9	6.8
GDR	16.5	10.9	12.3	12.2	12.5
Poland	11.8	20.6	13.5	9.5	6.8
Rumania	9.9	7.5	8.3	6.8	4.5
Hungary	9.4	6.3	7.3	7.6	7.1
CMEA (6)	63.8	56.6	52.4	47.5	42.0
USSR	36.2	43.4	47.6	52.5	58.0

Figures for 1982 are provisional.
Sources: CMEA countries' foreign trade statistics; DIW calculations.

Table 6: *The OECD countries' respective shares of trade with the East
1970 to 1982*

shares in per cent

	1970		1975		1980		1981		1982	
	CMEA (6)	USSR	CMEA (6)	USSR	CMEA (6)	USSR	CMEA (6)	USSR	CMEA (6)	USSR
Respective exports to the West = 100										
Western Europe[1]	93.1	81.4	93.0	86.4	92.4	93.0	91.1	93.9	92.1	95.0
of which: EEC (9)	66.9	54.8	62.4	53.8	60.8	64.5	57.8	64.5	52.1	67.3
of which: West Germany	28.7	10.4	25.8	15.1	27.5	19.1	27.0	20.7	27.2	21.4
United States	3.3	2.7	4.0	2.3	5.2	0.9	5.9	1.0	5.3	0.8
Japan	2.1	1.5	1.5	10.9	1.5	5.9	1.4	4.7	1.1	4.0
Respective imports from the West = 100										
Western Europe[1]	92.0	76.3	86.8	64.0	82.0	68.2	82.2	67.3	83.0	62.5
of which: EEC (9)	63.4	50.6	57.4	45.3	53.0	46.1	53.7	40.7	61.1	38.1
of which: West Germany	24.2	13.2	23.9	20.0	23.4	18.9	24.0	14.8	27.0	15.3
United States	4.4	3.9	7.7	15.0	11.3	8.5	10.8	9.1	9.0	10.9
Japan	2.0	12.1	4.0	12.8	3.6	11.2	4.2	12.1	3.9	15.4

Figures for 1982 are provisional.
[1]) EEC (9), Efta, Greece, Spain and Turkey.
Sources: CMEA countries' foreign trade statistics; DIW calculations.

Table 7: *Importance of imports from Eastern Europe by commodity as a percentage share of total World imports of industrialized West*

| Sitc | Rev. Category | Percentage shares | | | | | |
		1976	1977	1978	1979	1980	1981
	Total	1.5	1.4	1.4	1.3	1.3	1.2
0	Food and live animals	2.1	1.8	1.9	1.8	1.7	1.7
1	Beverages and tobacco	1.8	1.6	1.3	1.3	1.2	1.3
2	Crude matls excl fuels	1.5	1.5	1.5	1.5	1.5	1.4
3	Mineral fuels etc	1.3	1.0	1.0	1.2	1.0	0.9
4	Animal, vegetable oil, fat	1.9	2.5	1.9	1.7	1.3	1.6
5	Chemicals	1.4	1.3	1.2	1.2	1.4	1.5
6	Basic manufactures	1.7	1.8	1.7	1.7	1.6	1.6
7	Machines, transport equip	0.8	0.8	0.7	0.7	0.7	0.6
8	Misc manufactured goods	2.6	2.5	2.3	2.3	2.2	1.9
9	Goods not classd by kind	1.2	1.4	1.1	1.0	0.7	0.6

* The industrial countries include: Austria, Belgium, Canada, Denmark, France, West Germany, Italy, Japan, Luxembourg, Netherlands, Norway, Sweden, Switzerland, The United Kingdom and The United States.
Eastern Europe includes: Bulgaria, Czechoslovakia, East Germany, Hungary, Poland, and Rumania.
Source: Doc/ITA from UN series D trade tapes.

3
Credit

Klaus Schröder

Introduction

The West still regards Eastern Europe as a region with unusually high credit risks. This poor image has negative economic as well as political consequences. This chapter analyzes the causes of strain in East-West financial relations as well as why they have been overrated. It does so in order to demonstrate that a) an easing in strained East-West financial relations is not only a question of the willingness of the Western banks to provide the funds, but also depends on a complex set of factors which is essentially determined by what happens in the West; and b) that all in all Eastern Europe's debt does not represent a major challenge to the Western financial and monetary system.

Comecon's Debt with the West

Up to the early 1970s the Comecon countries hardly figured as borrowers in the Western money and capital markets. In 1971 their debt with the West totaled US $ 8.4 bn. The restraint of the East European borrowers disappeared however, when, during the period of East-West détente, the changed political as well as economic conditions came to favour stronger financial relations, and lenders signalled their willingness to promote more capital exports to Eastern Europe. From this followed an unprecedented acceleration of lending activity, which reached its climax at the end of 1981 with US $ 92 bn. Consequently, the Comecon countries' gross debt with the West increased elevenfold in the ten years between 1971 and 1981. In 1975, the annual rate of new debt reached its peak with an increase of US $ 14 bn. Although the rate of growth of the new debt clearly decreased during the second half of the 1970s, the total debt nevertheless continued to grow averaging US $ 11 bn. each year.

In an international comparison the development of this debt is also considerable. During the ten years to the end of 1981 the average annual growth rate of loans to the Comecon countries of 27 per cent was clearly above the general international credit development. Since 1980, however, new credit transactions have been drastically reduced. For instance, loans to East European borrowers on the Euromarket sank from US $ 4.9 bn. in 1979 to US $ 1.5 bn. in 1981 and US $ 0.7 bn. in 1982. As a result of these changes the total indebtedness of the Comecon countries sank for the first time in a long while in 1982. Working with OECD statistics, which showed a gross debt of US $ 92 bn. in

1981,[1] the gross debt was expected to be US $ 87 bn. at the end of 1982 with a current account surplus of US $ 5 bn.

Poland has received by far the most credit, about US $ 27 bn. at the end of 1982, which amounted to one third of the total loans to Eastern Europe. The Soviet Union rates second with around US $ 19 bn. but has, at the same time, deposits of US $ 10 bn. with Western banks. Measured by net debt (debt minus deposits) the GDR still stands above the Soviet Union with US $ 11 bn.

Changes in Western Credit Policy

The abrupt change in the credit policies of Western banks towards East European borrowers was caused by a highly complex and primarily economic set of factors. These economic factors were, however, temporarily intensified and superseded by political developments.

Developments in the Euromarkets. The starting point for the change in credit granting policies was a shift in the structure of lenders and borrowers on the particularly sensitive Eurocreditmarkets that was induced by the wave of oil price changes in 1980. On the creditor side the OPEC cartel countries were able to strengthen their dominant capital supplier role by vigorous oil price increases. On the borrower side there set in a strong process of displacement as industrialized countries increased their relative demand for credit in order to balance their current account deficits which had increased with the oil prices. They thus absorbed more than half of the newly granted Eurocredits, with the result that developing and Comecon countries could only satisfy part of their credit requirements. In 1980, the Comecon countries received only US $ 2 bn. against US $ 5 bn. in 1979 and their share of new business in the Euromarket dropped from 6 per cent to 3 per cent.

Internal bank factors and Poland's insolvency. This process of intensified selection of debtors particularly hit the Comecon countries, because, aside from the shifts due to the rise of the oil prices, there existed at the same time a bundle of "internal bank factors" which caused the creditors to be more restrictive when granting credits to East European debtors or debtors from developing countries. The diminished willingness to grant credit was caused, for instance, by the increased concern about the control of the Euromarkets, the introduction of minimum reserves for Euromarket transactions, and the inclusion of foreign lending in the national credit policies (so-called consolidation). In addition, banks were less willing to take upon themselves the growing risks of the by now essential rescheduling and to lend for long-term credits, money that was tied up in short- and medium-term projects. Added to this was the fact that the ratio between credit loans and capital funds had obviously approached a critical threshold, with the result that limits were set on readily available credits. Apart from these general factors there were also "Comecon-specific" reasons for changes in lending policy. For example, there were indications that the individual banks had, to a large extent, exhausted their internal lending limits and the expected problems of debt management – due, among other things, to rising interest rates – made it inadvisable to exceed those limits.

The growing consciousness among Western financiers of the increased economic risk assumed new proportions with the crisis in Afghanistan. In 1980, it was apparent that:
– the sensitivity of Western creditors in calculating economic as well as political risks had clearly increased;
– the political risks were still of secondary importance;
– Afghanistan prepared the ground so that subsequent political influences, directly or indirectly connected to Poland, clearly changed the willingness of Western banks to grant loans to Eastern Europe.

The general reluctance to lend to Eastern Europe became more concrete when Poland actually became insolvent in March 1981, and martial law was declared in December 1981. This happened because it confirmed the economic expectations of the creditors, in respect to the sinking debt service capability of Poland, just six months after they had signed the DM 1.2 bn. credit in October 1980. They took a more concrete form for three reasons. First, the Polish "shock" hit the central nerve of Western bank managers and forced them to change their "lending model" towards East European countries. Second, for the first time the defaulted credits of a large debtor, and moreover one from Eastern Europe, had to be rescheduled. Third, also for the first time, credit relations with Eastern Europe became influenced by political developments in the West in a massive and direct manner, after the imposition of martial law in Poland.

Although Poland's insolvency had been predicted in internal bank statements years before, it nevertheless hit the Western governments and especially the Western banks like a bombshell. After all, during the détente period, Western politicians had seen Poland as an important mediator between East and West, and the banks had also concentrated their Eastern credits primarily on Poland. When, in the spring of 1981, Poland could no longer maintain its debt service, it had a total Western debt of around US $ 24 bn. The banks alone, and above all the West European banks, had lent US $ 15 bn. to Polish borrowers. The fact that Poland, which had received 27 per cent of all credits granted to Comecon countries, became insolvent, therefore hit the Western creditors particularly hard and helps explain the extremely abrupt shift in their credit policy.

There were already signs of difficulties in 1980, when several Eastern applications for credit were declined and a trend towards rising interest rates and shorter credit term was already visible. But these difficulties became worse after the Polish "shock", when interest rates rose significantly and even the sale of bills of exchange to export financing banks (Forfait market) ceased, because it was no longer possible to assure that other Eastern countries would succeed in their debt management. This expectation soon came to dominate all Western capital markets. Consequently, the particularly risky budget or balance of payments credits were scarcely granted any more, even in smaller sums, and admittance to the Euromarkets was denied not only to Poland but to all other Comecon countries.

Bank credit policy. Poland's insolvency and the need to reschedule its debts led to such a strong reaction towards *all* Comecon countries, including those with a comparatively good credit standing, because it was realized that key Western assumptions on credit policy were at least partially unrealistic. For example, there was the so-called umbrella theory which worked on the principle that, in order to maintain stability in its satellite system, the Soviet Union would grant financial assistance to any satellite country threatened by a default of payment to Western creditors. Western credit policy was, and to some extent still is, based on the assumption that such an umbrella existed. This helps explain not only the generosity in granting credit, but also why more information on the purpose of loans and total indebtedness was not obtained from the borrowers in Eastern Europe. When the Soviet Union did not jump into the breach, as Poland and in 1982 also Rumania became insolvent, one corner-stone of Western capital export policy was destroyed. As a result Western banks have been forced to reformulate their policy. The decisive factors in the banks' future behaviour will be disappointment at their false judgement of the Soviet position and the resultant insecurity concerning financial investments in the East.

Consequently, in terms of credit policy all of Eastern Europe is cum grano salis treated the same way as Poland. The assumption that all Comecon countries came under a Soviet umbrella was also disastrous insofar as while it facilitated calculation of the overall regional risk of Eastern Europe it encouraged over-lending to individual countries. A more balanced allocation of credits might have prevented the excessive Polish indebtedness. In addition, Eastern Europe, like many other regions, has been regarded as an independent area for competition, and rivalry between the banks has encouraged thinking in terms of market shares and growth rates. Even within banks, internal competition between the different foreign departments, has meant that their attention has been focused on the volume of new credit agreements rather than the growing risks.

Finally, it is remarkable that, during the 1970s, the Western banks assumed that state-trading countries with central economic and financial planning would exercise strict financial discipline. When this assumption also proved to be unrealistic it accentuated the overreaction of the banks. Such unrealistic expectations were, or are possibly the result of either a lack of sufficiently expert bank personnel with special knowledge on Eastern Europe or that these employees were not able to assert themselves in the internal bargaining within the banks. All the above-mentioned reasons help explain why the period of relatively easy financing, which prevailed during the 1970s, suddenly turned into a phase of overreaction in the early 1980s in which the banks reduced new credit to a minimum.

Withdrawal of Capital and the Domino Theory

The period of overreaction was also characterized by the termination of short-term credit lines which had formerly been prolonged on a roll-over basis, and the banks actually equating the rest of the Comecon countries with the insolvent Poland. Since the banks were used to considering the Comecon region as an area of equal risk, it was only logical to assume that all of Eastern Europe would follow Poland and become unable to service their debts. Consequently, short-term credits were not rolled-over but terminated in *all* Comecon countries wherever this was possible.

Such a withdrawal of capital began in *Poland* during the spring of 1981 (US $ 1.2 bn.) and increased pressure for a rescheduling of the debt. During the second half of the year *Rumania* was particularly hard hit by the withdrawal of short-term funds totaling US $ 1.5 bn. The enforced repayment of these funds was possibly a major factor in the Rumanian liquidity crisis. There is enough evidence to suggest that Rumania would have remained solvent had it not been forced to refund such credits to Western financiers, because the current account deficit, reduced by rigorous cuts in imports, could probably have been financed through medium- and long-term credits and additional IMF resources. The withdrawal of short-term assets, however, made the ensuing rescheduling of debts inevitable.

During the spring of 1982, the termination of short-term credits amounting to US $ 1.1 bn. by Western banks caused even *Hungary*, the favoured son of the Comecon borrowers, to experience a major liquidity crisis. It is paradoxical that Hungary, which distinguishes itself from other Comecon countries by its economic policies and the quality of its financial management, faced a liquidity crisis because of the behaviour of Western banks. Western politicians and representatives of the central banks did, however, recognize this. Assuming that the banks' overreaction meant they would be unable to arrange any compensation for such withdrawals, the central banks therefore acted quickly and arranged bridging credits for Hungary from their own funds through the Bank for International Settlements (B.I.S.).

The *GDR*, which had made only moderate use of short-term credit on the inter-bank money market, lost only US $ 0.2 bn. in withdrawal of short-term funds. It was more affected by the fact that after receiving an average of US $ 0.5 bn. from the Euromarkets between 1979 and 1981 it could only raise US $ 69 m. in 1982. This caused a liquidity gap in 1983 which could only be closed by circumventing the still almost closed Euromarkets, and through the intervention of political authorities with the DM 1 bn. credit.

The withdrawal of capital was, as described above, a result of the old "Eastern Europe approach". But from the banks' point of view other considerations also played an important role. As growing debt problems became obvious and the risk of rescheduling increased, the banks thought they could avoid this dilemma by granting short-term credits which could be extended as appropriate but also reclaimed in case of more serious risk. This view has encouraged many diverse and extremely risky credit commitments, and favored the entry into the inter-bank markets of banks of doubtful standing.

In contrast to Poland, which is confronted with a serious debt crisis, the other Comecon countries mentioned merely have to deal with liquidity problems, although these are in certain cases very serious. These liquidity crises can be explained by the panic and unnecessary claims for repayment by the Western banks.

The so-called "domino theory" which expresses a certain expectation in regard to all of Eastern Europe, has already been described in its practical impact without actually using the term. According to this theory the fall of one domino (Comecon country) causes others to follow in a chain reaction. It is based on the view that these countries exhibit similar characteristics such as the homogeneity and inherent sluggishness of their economic systems as well as their strong economic interdependence. However, the more decisive factor appears to be the widespread subjective expectation of Western creditors concerning parallel shifts in the debt or liquidity ratings of all Comecon countries. This process of self-fulfilling expectations can be recognized in Eastern Europe; it started with Poland, was transferred to Rumania and then concentrated on Hungary. Two dominos had already fallen before Western institutions intervened to prevent Hungary and probably others following suit.

Strains caused by political factors

In a historical perspective reaching back to the 1920s, the 1970s represented a period of relatively "normal" financial relations. During this period the Comecon countries had easy and direct access to the Western capital markets, they were considered as good credit partners, and were all in all treated like any other borrower. In contrast there were virtually no significant credit relations between East and West between the end of World War II and the late 1960s. The Western banks' assessment of Eastern Europe's creditworthiness, however, changed almost over night when the détente of the early 1970s reduced political risks, leaving only negligible economic risks. The total indebtedness of the Comecon countries was, at that time, only around US $ 7 bn.

In any assessment of the overreaction of Western banks it is important to recognize that, having downgraded political risks in the early 1970s, financiers subsequently paid very little attention to them. Evidently, they were confident of détente, were even drawn further in by Ostpolitik and official economic policy towards the East, and were not discouraged by the financial reluctance of American banks.

Following the Soviet invasion of Afghanistan in 1980, the banks again recognized the political risks but did not begin to include them in their calculations until a year later when Poland became insolvent and when Western governments felt obliged to react both directly and indirectly to the declaration of martial law in Poland.

Besides the political events in and around Poland the reactions of Western governments are of special significance for the Western creditors. Although primarily caused by the declaration of martial law in Poland, the political involvement of Western governments has implications for all of Eastern Europe. The politicization of East-West trade and financial relations has caused the banks to be more circumspect in their political risk assessment. The politicization was largely due to the U.S. emphasis on the security implications of East-West trade. This view assumes that East-West trade and credit links mainly benefit the East, and that by strengthening its military potential, they contribute to a growing threat and must therefore be limited.

Just how this view is translated into practical policy depends on a range of variables and is still the subject of discussion. Measures will, however, either be primarily directed against the Soviet Union, against the Soviet Union and Poland or in an undifferentiated fashion against all Comecon countries. These measures not only affect East-West relations but also represent a special challenge to the cohesion of the Western alliance. For example, there are differences between the United States and Germany over the Hermes credit guarantee system which the U.S. claims is subsidized and must therefore be restricted. More generally there are also differences between the United States and Europe over American demands to standardize Western capital export policies towards Eastern Europe and to standardize the minimum interest rates for credit receiving official support.

Even though proposals to limit credits were rejected, nearly unanimously by Western Europe, the demands of the American administration inevitably caused uncertainty on Western credit markets. This led the banks to become even more reluctant because, on one hand, they did not know whether West European governments would be obliged to follow the U.S. lead in seeking a more security-related approach to East-West trade and credit policies. On the other hand, the American demands could be transmitted to the markets by way of the American banks, even if the European governments were able to assert themselves and refuse to follow the U.S. lead. This shows the pervasive influence of politics, and that discussion, especially when it is on the application of sanctions, can by itself influence the behavior of the banks in granting credit. Thus discussions on the intended use of financial relations as a sanction or a political lever helped increase the potential risk of lending to Eastern Europe to new almost "astronomical" levels at which even creditworthy countries like the Soviet Union could no longer negotiate credits. Consequently the period of overreaction was prolonged.

Polish Default. The idea of extending security policy considerations to include credit relations with Poland and Eastern Europe as a whole, gained ground in the United States during the spring of 1982 with the discussion of a so-called "Poland-Default" and the possible imposition of monetary sanctions. At this time repayment of several million U.S. dollars, guaranteed by the Commodity Credit Corporation (CCC), was due but could not be made by Poland. Consequently there was pressure from several U.S. constituencies, including high ranking officials of the U.S. Department of Defense, for an official declaration of default on Poland. This strategy was justified on the following grounds:
- "The weapon of capital is potentially one of the most powerful and least used in the Western world. Poland affords us a chance to use it;" and
- "The capital requirement of Soviet satellite countries might cause a change in Soviet attitudes in other fields and could lead to progress on significant reductions in armaments."[2]

After an extremely controversial debate the Reagan administration did not force a declaration of default, and the CCC rules, which require a formal declaration of default before creditors can avail themselves of CCC guarantees, were circumvented. The U.S. government took over the arrears and paid the Polish liabilities at the American banks.

Misgivings on the part of U.S. banks, as well as European banks and governments, about the economic repercussions of a default were probably the reason why the hard-line of the Pentagon's security experts did not prevail. Nevertheless the financiers remained concerned because the decision not to press for a default was explained with the remark that the United States wished to reserve use of this trump card as a second line of attack.[3]

Monetary Sanctions. The discussion of monetary sanctions was obviously influenced by the idea that the introduction of governmental controls over capital flows would enable the West to exert political pressure on the Soviet Union and its allies. Of all the politically motivated approaches to East-West trade the banks rejected a declaration of default and monetary sanctions most vehemently. They did so not only because of an old tradition of nonintervention, but also because they were concerned that monetary sanctions could plunge the Western money and capital markets into chaos. Monetary sanctions, in the form of a credit stop or a vigorous reduction of Western capital exports, represent a powerful instrument whose impact would by far surpass that of trade sanctions in the fields such as technology or grain.

A politically motivated credit stop would have fatal results for Eastern Europe. First of all these countries would be obliged to maintain a balance of trade surplus *uno actu* with the West to cover the relatively high interest payments and redemption obligations. This would result in a marked loss of growth for the duration of the sanctions, which would add to the already considerable economic problems. Second, in order to finance large projects, the Comecon countries would have to accumulate hard currencies over several years by increasing exports or reducing imports and then paying cash, unless they gave up such projects altogether. As for the Eastern European response to such sanctions, it is doubtful that all countries would concentrate all their efforts on the fulfillment of interest and redemption payments to the West at the expense of their domestic economic and socio-political objectives.

In order to demonstrate the possible effects of sanctions, the Eastern reactions can be reduced to what would be the worst case. This would consist of the Soviet hegemony reacting to the politically motivated Western monetary sanctions by declaring itself and its satellites free of all obligations to pay back anything. If one proceeds from this quite realistic scenario and examines its implications for the creditors, the following conclusions may be drawn:

- A moratorium would be inevitable for all Eastern debts, and any offers by individual banks to reschedule the debts in order to avoid the moratorium would be ignored by the East;
- The creditor banks would be forced to write off their total Eastern claims resulting in unavoidable cutbacks or passing of the dividend payments;
- The financial and trade relations between East and West would be severely disrupted for many years to come;
- The financial relations among the Western states would also be affected by a general Eastern moratorium.

Official discussion of the application of monetary sanctions in 1982 was probably silenced by a realization that the costs of such sanctions would be high for both the East *and* West, and the politicians' concern about their ability to control and limit the ensuing chaos.

Towards a New Credit Policy. Despite doubts about sanctions the American ideas were kept alive in the form of a "credit standardization policy towards Eastern Europe", which the United States injected into the Versailles summit meeting of the Western heads of state in June 1982. Although it was not clear by what means and by which coordinating mechanism a limitation of credit to Eastern Europe was to be achieved, the American approach was clearly to restrict credit flows to Comecon countries. This has had an effect on the banks even though it was emphasized in different European capitals that the formula found in the declaration of Versailles did not include tangible political commitments. For the Federal Republic of Germany no shift of the credit policy is considered necessary, either in quantity or in the kind of financing,[4] and there is no thought of any politically imposed limit of credits.

Subsidies in the Export Credit Guarantee System. One essential American demand focused on the reduction of subsidized credits. This may be relevant to some other European countries but not to the Federal Republic of Germany. No official credits are granted in the FRG and interest rates subsidies out of public funds are only available for Eastern credits insofar as a so-called credit ceiling B exists in the Export Company mbH (AKA) which the German Federal Bank holds at its disposal. Because there are neither government credits nor interest subsidies, the attention of the U.S. administration focused on the question as to whether or not the German *export credit insurance system* is a subtle form of subsidization. The American assumption that this was the case, was apparently supported by an American study[5] commissioned by the Pentagon. In reality, however, only insufficient evidence can be furnished to support this view.

Due to the principle[6] of limited coverage and long-term self-financing,[7] the German Hermes system provides no direct subsidies. Furthermore because the self-financing principle is currently endangered for the first time due to the enormously increased "political" claims and because a considerable long run financing deficit is projected, it is planned to increase premiums and remove even the indirect element of a subsidy from the system. In addition, no more guarantees may be granted in cases where claims have already occurred or can be anticipated. This drastic measure has already been applied on credit to Poland and Rumania.

In German trade with the East, government guarantees constitute one of the most important means of trade promotion. First, because it is only through Hermes AG that political risk can be covered and second, because the German exporter cannot refinance his supplier credit at the AKA without the coverage of Hermes. In the present economic conditions the increase in premiums forced by budgetary considerations, together with a politically motivated reduction of guarantee liabilities must result in a direct limitation of German exports to the East, especially when only a few Western banks are willing to grant credits to Eastern Europe.

Certainly the West must consider more seriously whether and if so on what conditions it should satisfy Eastern demand for credit. But it appears extremely doubtful that such problems can be properly addressed when each national system of financing credit is suspected of containing strong elements of subsidy, or when every new credit granted to the East is seen as strengthening the Eastern military potential.

Conclusions

The period of overreaction and of overrating the financial problems of the East continues. At the moment this is due more to problems in the Western hemisphere than the situation in Eastern Europe. For example, there are the difficulties in Brazil and nearly the entire Latin American region, the problems of coordination among the banks and the international organizations with regard to an acceptable burden-sharing, the financial bottleneck which now also confronts the IMF and finally, as shown above, the problem of political intervention by Western governments. Because East-West financial relations are overshadowed by these Western problems, the view that Eastern Europe represents a special credit risk has persisted for a long time in both public and expert circles. It is now time for this judgement to be revised. It is no longer correct to maintain that Eastern Europe is insolvent and overindebted. There are neither delays in payment for all countries nor negotiations on rescheduling, and none are expected. It is more correct to say that it is only *Poland* that cannot repay its debts and that rescheduling can be expected in the coming years. Poland will remain the exception and the number one debt problem in the near future. For Poland balance of trade surpluses achieved, at great sacrifice, will not even cover interest payments with the result that under the present conditions debt will continue to rise for some years.

Following the Polish "shock" for the Western banks in 1982 and 1983, Rumania also had to reschedule debts it could not pay. The causes, severity, and the duration of the Rumanian insolvency differ, however, from the Polish problems. Rumania seems to have resolved the worst of its problems, at least for the time being, and no further rescheduling is expected in 1984. Rumania will probably also be able to repay the relatively modest sum of about US $ 0.4 bn. which it is obliged to pay with the support of the IMF and further import reductions. Besides Poland and Rumania *Hungary* and the *GDR* are of course also facing problems, but these are of a specific nature. Thus Hungary's temporary liquidity shortage was not self-induced but due to the withdrawal of short-term bank credit. Hungary has also received at least quantitative compensation for the consequences of the abrupt capital withdrawal through new Western credits, and is trying very hard to be respected as a reliable borrower. At this time special doubts only exist about the credit risk of the *GDR*. If the Western umbrella can be opened once again for the GDR, it would probably be able to fulfill its repayment obligations, and could in addition realize important projects that have had to be deferred. One must, however, take care that the improved political relations with the GDR, which are hoped to follow this financing, are not bought at the expense of new financial burdens which would in turn jeopardize progress on the political front. *Bulgaria, Czechoslovakia* and the *Soviet Union* were able to decrease their debts during the past years and are, from an economic point of view, considered as good credit partners.

It is therefore possible to draw the following conclusions:
— The debt situation of the Comecon countries is not comparable with that of the developing countries or the newly industrialized countries in either its extent or the degree of adjustment necessary to ensure a healthy balance of payments.

- In the West the centrally planned economies of the East are always depicted as being rigid and little able to react to global economic or foreign trade problems. The worldwide repayment difficulties suggest, however, that in contrast to many developing and newly industrializing countries, the Comecon countries are quite capable of making the necessary adjustments. For example, the small countries of Eastern Europe not only succeeded in reducing their balance of payments deficit from US $ 6.7 bn. in 1980, but also achieved a current account surplus of nearly US $ 2 bn. in 1982.[8]
- The Soviet Union which ran a current account surplus with the West in each of the past three years, will continue to adjust its balance of payments through the export of energy, raw materials and gold and thus hold debts down in order to minimize dependency on Western capital markets and Western governments.
- Contrary to the widespread public impression, the conditions for rescheduling in Poland are also more favorable than in many other rescheduling candidates for the following reasons: even in the third year of rescheduling the bank's exposure remains nearly unchanged, whereas in other cases additional credit has had to be granted in the first year; the commercial credit lines allowed to Poland are comparatively low and are available only for merchandise trade not for other purposes; agreement with Poland could be achieved, in contrast to other cases, without the support of international organizations such as the IMF and BIS or Western governments.
- The energy requirements of the small Comecon countries are largely secured without hard currencies. In addition the compulsion to save energy has increased dramatically because of the Soviet quantitative limits and the price increases. This means that these countries have only occasionally to burden their foreign exchange balances with energy imports from the West. The small Comecon countries do not therefore appear on the world markets and force prices up. Equally Western investment in the Soviet energy and raw materials also helps reduce tensions on world markets.
- The realization that the East can no longer finance current consumption through Western credit also suggests that, in future new credit agreements will serve to finance Eastern investment in enhanced productive and export performance. The resultant faster amortization of loans should serve to reduce the total risk for Western financiers.
- At present all Comecon countries are focusing on a consolidation of their foreign trade; in the long run, however, this strategy is only viable if the Western capital markets are flexible enough to support it.
- If the Western capital markets do not react flexibly small Comecon countries will be in danger of becoming more indebted to the Soviet Union and thus even more tied to the superpower. Such a reorientation would make them even less competitive internationally, because they would lose their ability to usefully integrate into the worldwide economic division of labor.

This would ultimately lead to a rediscovery of the advantages of Western financial markets as financier for imports of Western technology needed to strengthen Eastern efficiency. This would create much higher Eastern demand for credit which would be unloaded, with a vengeance, onto our markets causing problems of instability as great, if not greater, than those experienced in recent years.

— There is room for more moderation of the West's overreaction to the East European debt, because of the improvements in economic and financial affairs, and the fact that problems are worse in other regions. Furthermore attitudes may be changed by the expectation that the volume of credit for Eastern Europe should be maintained in order to soften the harsh consequences of economic adjustments over the past few years. Finally, doubts caused by the security related political controversies may be mitigated if the view prevails that the behavior of Western creditors over the past three years[9] constituted a de facto finance sanction which hit the small Comecon countries particularly hard but did not affect the Soviet Union. If this were to happen the negative assessment of East-West financial relations could then be altered and strains in the discussion of East-West trade and the technology transfer also reduced. This stage has not yet been reached. The banks, which are not interested in a blockade or confrontation with Eastern Europe, continue to monitor the political controversies and their implications for the financial markets. The chances of finding a solution to the problems of East-West financial relations must be seen in the context of the restraints imposed by the Western financial system and the general tensions in East-West relations.

Notes

1 OECD, *Financial Market Trends*, No. 24, March 1983, p. 17.
2 Felix G. Rohatyn, Shift the Burden to Moscow: Declare Poland Bankrupt, *International Herald Tribune*, March 2, 1982.
3 *Neue Zuercher Zeitung*, Polens Auslandsschuld − Moskaus Achillesferse?, February 2, 1982, p. 10.
4 Thus concurring remarks by the Chancellor and the Minister of Finance of the Federal Republic of Germany. *Sueddeutsche Zeitung*, Westen will Ostkredite begrenzen, June 7, 1982.
5 Daniel F. Kohler, Kip T. Fisher, *Subsidization of East-West Trade Through Credit Insurance and Loan guarantees*, Santa Monica, January 1983.
6 The guarantee can only take certain risks and insure these only at a certain percentage. In addition, the Hermes company has to be paid for services.
7 The income of the Federal Republic from the guarantee activities had until 1982 always surpassed expenditure on claims. The surplus (totaling about 1.2 billion DM) has been fed annually in small sums into the Federal budget.
8 See Lawrence J. Brainard, Handels- und Zahlungsprobleme in Osteuropa, *Europa-Archiv*, No. 14, 1982, p. 409.
9 Klaus Schröder, 'Wirkungen monetärer Sanktionen gegenüber den RGW-Ländern', in Friedemann Mueller et al., *Zur Frage von Wirtschaftssanktionen in den Ost-West-Beziehungen: Rahmenbedingungen und Modalitäten*, Baden-Baden 1983.

4
Technology Transfer

Jürgen Nötzold

Introduction

Within the Western Alliance it has never been disputed that the transfer of technology to CMEA countries, and in particular to the Soviet Union, involves political and security risks. For this reason CoCom (Coordinating Committee for Multilateral Export Controls), to which all NATO countries (except Iceland) and Japan belong, was established in 1949. Since the 1970s, the United States has increasingly voiced its displeasure with Soviet foreign policy. Concurrently, there has also been a shift in official American assessments of Soviet foreign policy goals. This has ultimately brought about discussions within NATO on the extent to which Western technology exports bolster Soviet arms production and undermine détente. In particular, the question as to the degree to which economic-technological relations not regulated by CoCom tend to foster Soviet military capacity is judged differently by various NATO members.

Above all the Reagan administration, as the Carter administration before, is convinced that the Eastward flow of Western technology buttressed the Soviet arms industry in the 1970s. This interpretation of events has visibly shaken American confidence in trade cooperation with the Soviet Union[1] and led to American demands for limiting economic relations with the USSR. Furthermore, the United States also called for an extension of the CoCom list to include all modern technology and know-how. There is, however, also a pro-trade view in the United States.[2] Advocates of this view argue that economic relations with the Soviet Union are not only economically significant, but also politically beneficial. In fact, proponents of this direction are of the opinion that increased trade could eventually contribute to a *modus vivendi* with the USSR.

Economic relations with the East are a particularly important element of West Germany's détente policy.[3] Through trade the Federal Republic hopes to strengthen the ties between Western and Eastern Europe, thus creating the preconditions for peace in Europe. Discussions within the Atlantic Alliance on the scale of — and the objectives to be pursued in — economic relations with Eastern countries particularly affects West German foreign policy. The United States is West Germany's most important ally. As long as the military threat dominates the East-West conflict, the Federal Republic relies on the American defense guarantee for its security. At the same time however, West German defense and security policy, also attaches great significance to détente with Eastern Europe. This is, at least in part, due to the fact that the development of inter-German relations stands or falls with the quality of bilateral relations between the Federal Republic and the Soviet Union.

Compromise proposals, put forward with the aim of bringing about a coherent Western policy on East-West trade, have not been able to free West Germany from this dilemma inherent in its relations with the United States and the USSR. Such proposals include, for example, restrictions in transfer of technology to CMEA countries.[4] In their extreme form limitations of this type would end in a dissolution of existing East-West economic ties, which would in turn hamper West-Germany's political dealings with Eastern Europe and the Soviet Union. It is, therefore, important to seriously consider, whether, and to what extent, the flow of Western technology to the USSR really constitutes a risk for the defense and security of the West. The following factors must be taken into account in any pertinent assessment of this problem:

- the volume of Soviet imports of technology from the West since the marked expansion of Soviet trade with the West at the beginning of the 1970s;
- the importance of technology imports for the Soviet economy, and to what degree is the Soviet Union dependent on technology imports from the West;
- the extent to which Soviet arms production is influenced by the import of Western technology;
- the consequences for the USSR of limitations on the Eastward flow of Western technology.

Scale and Characteristics of Soviet Technology Imports

To date Soviet foreign trade relations with Western industrialized countries have focussed on the import of capital goods. Plant and equipment make up the bulk of Soviet imports from the West; by comparison, the transfer of other types of technology has remained a *quantité negligeable* in the foreign trade of the USSR. The latter pertains also to those types of technology transfer which were to be promoted according to the terms of the CSCE Final Act, i.e. research cooperation between states, academic exchanges, patents and export licenses, international business cooperation and direct foreign investments. The Soviet Union has concluded quite a few cooperation agreements with Western industrial enterprises, but on the whole these have been framework agreements that have only led to discussions between experts and in some instances to agreements on export licenses. In only a small number of cases was agreement reached on mutual research and development projects. In general, the different type of economic system in the Soviet Union inhibits increased foreign trade with Western industrialized countries.

Given the significance that is often attributed to Soviet technology imports, one could be led to believe that plants and equipment make up more than a proportional share of the Soviet Union's trade with the West. In reality, however, capital goods have never amounted to more than about one-third of total Soviet imports from the West. The reason for this is that proceeds from exports are spent on other commodities, such as raw materials, food and industrial consumer goods. This is also in large part true for the other CMEA countries. Moreover, the share of Western trade in total CMEA country trade generally declined. There has also been a reduction in the volume of technology imported from the West and, with the exception of Czechoslovakia and Hungary, a growth in the volume of food imports.

The Soviet economy's limited absorption capacity can hardly suffice as an explanation for reductions in the USSR's imports of technology from OECD (Organization for Economic Cooperation and Development) countries. In 1930 imports made up 19 per cent of Soviet domestic consumption of plant and equipment. In 1931 the share of machine tools imported from the West even reached a level of 66 per cent. At that time there were big problems caused by the great need for raw materials and basic commodities as well as a lack of qualified workers. Ever since the beginning of the Soviet Western trade offensive in the early 1970s, the share of capital goods imported from the West has always been much lower than the volume of related Soviet domestic investments.

It has also been widely assumed that Soviet imports from Western industrialized countries are concentrated in the area of high technology. This is incorrect. On average, Western exports of capital goods to the Soviet Union and other CMEA countries do not include more advanced technology than exports to other parts of the world.[5] The pattern of Eastern imports is clearly dominated by conventional products of the mechanical engineering branch, while more modern products – such as electronics – prove to be of far lesser importance. The trend towards extensive growth in the Soviet economy also appears to effect its pattern of imports from the West. Advanced technology is mainly transferred through business cooperation, direct investments and patents and licences. But as these forms of East-West cooperation have so little significance, they can be virtually neglected. Indeed, mainly due to the different types of economic systems, the volume of these transactions lies well below the normal level in Western economic relations.

Soviet capital goods imports from Western industrialized countries have mainly focussed on the following branches, some of which are definitely in the proximity of consumer-related industries: chemical industry, motor vehicle construction, ship-building, wood and cellulose industry and light industry. Particular stress has been placed on equipment for the chemical industry, in which imports were increased as far back as the end of the 1950s and the beginning of the 1960s. The role of OECD countries in supplying equipment for the chemical industry grew dramatically in the second half of the 1970s when their share of Soviet imports grew from 38 per cent in 1970 to 56 per cent in the first half of the 1970s and an average of 75 per cent in the second half of the 1970s. There is therefore clearly a continuous demand for imported products of this branch.

Technology Imports and the Soviet Economy

Since the Soviet Union manufactures most of its plant and equipment, it has little incentive or need to import these items. Even during the middle of the 1970s, when there were record imports of plant and equipment, imports from OECD countries did not amount to more than about 7 per cent of total Soviet investment in capital goods. According to Soviet sources imports of plant and equipment from OECD members reached the level of 4 per cent in 1970, followed by an upward trend to between 5 and 6 per cent in 1977.[6] Other calculations come to the conclusion that Soviet investments in plant reached an all-time-high of 11 per cent in 1975. But ultimately it is not decisive whether the peak import rate was 6 per cent or 10 per cent. Of far more importance is the structural pattern of technology imports and the degree to which imported technology benefits the Soviet economy.

The pattern of Soviet technology imports will therefore be examined at this point. In general, there is no pronounced Soviet dependency on plant and equipment imports from the West; however, the Soviet Union is dependent on Western capital goods in some branches of production it is seeking to develop rapidly. As a consequence of the desired rapid development of such industrial branches, the emphasis placed on certain import commodities is always temporary in nature. For example, the rapid increase in auto industry capacities was the reason for extensive imports in 1970 and 1975. The expansion of equipment for the food and textile industry in 1960 is another example of this phenomenon. In contrast the Soviet chemical industry needs the continuous flow of Western capital goods to overcome its under-development. Without question, the chemical industry is most dependent on imports. This is particularly evident in the case of synthetic materials. In order to increase its output of natural gas, the Soviet Union has had to import pipes, especially wide diameter pipes.[7] The rapid growth in natural gas production since 1970 has come about as a consequence, not only of the 'natural gas-pipeline' deals with Western countries, but also of the 'Orenburg-Pipeline' which was constructed in cooperation with other CMEA countries.

The question, therefore, is whether this should be interpreted to mean that the Soviet Union is dependent on imports? In this regard it must be borne in mind that, in almost all cases, Soviet requirements are so immense that they cannot feasibly be covered by Western imports indefinitely and the USSR must substitute them by its own products as soon as possible. Limited availability of hard currency also compels the Soviets to neglect imports for certain branches when other, newer lines of import have priority. Thus Soviet import dependency on specific Western products and technologies is therefore always only temporary in nature.

Possession of foreign technology is in itself no guarantee that the receiving country is able to utilize it effectively, and may even result in an increase in imports of the technology concerned. Here reference should be made to a representative opinion poll taken among West German exporters on the problems of absorbing Western technology in the Soviet Union. According to this poll, the centrally planned economy of the USSR not only impedes indigenous technological innovation, but also hampers the effective absorption of Western technology. The opinions expressed were along the following lines. "The initiation phase for installations procured from the Federal Republic of Germany generally takes longer in the Soviet Union than in Western countries ... In comparison to Western countries, the time needed in the USSR to assimilate technological knowledge on the fundamental features of imported installations is considerably longer. It can be observed that at least five years are necessary to copy single machines. The imitation of complex installations takes up to 10 years. The industrial plants are set on fulfilling production plans. Innovation is regarded above all as a disturbance, which endangers plan fulfillment and thus jeopardizes premiums." Some business firms questioned even went as far as to describe Soviet industrial plants as essentially hostile to modernization.[8]

These conclusions about the effect of specific technology transfers on the Soviet economy, can be supplemented by data on the economy of the USSR as a whole. During the 1970s the Soviet Union rapidly expanded imports of machines and transport equipment. The value of these imports rose from 0.9 billion rubles in 1971 to 4.4 billion rubles in 1981. This rapid expansion of capital goods imports was actually accompanied by a reduction in the rate of economic growth from 6 per cent in 1971 to 2.3 per cent in 1981. There has also been no increase in labor productivity, which would normally accompany technological progress. In fact, there has even been a slight downward trend in the rate of growth of labor productivity, which was 7 per cent in 1971 but only a mere 2.6 per cent in 1980.

It is necessary to qualify observations on the effect of Western technological imports on the economic growth if particular cases are also taken into account. Those sectors which have been given high priority in Soviet economic planning are also in a position to overcome the problems arising from the utilization of new (i. e. innovative) technologies. These examples of the successful application of modern Western technology by the USSR contrast sharply, however, with the inefficiency generally observed in absorbing and utilizing imported high technology. This can be partially explained by the fact that Soviet imports of technology are concentrated in those sectors which have been relatively neglected by economic planning and therefore have particular difficulties.

It has often been assumed that imports of technology would relieve the Soviet Union of the burden of economic reforms. But the problems in applying imported technology show that the contrary is true. Imports of technology are no substitutes for organizational improvements of the Soviet economy. Indeed 1970, a time when imports were growing, brought a number of changes to the economic planning and control process of the USSR. It is now apparent that these changes involving improvements in the innovation process have not been enough to raise the technological level. In fact these improvements in planning techniques have not had as favorable an effect as would the introduction of some element of competition within the context of continued centralized planning. One could expect more success if business enterprises had a more direct interest in operational results, and more competence in the field of investment decisions.

From the beginning the Soviet economy has been, and still is, guided by the principle of giving priority to various branches of industry. The Soviet economy is successful when resources, such as investment, material and research and development, are concentrated in specific areas. This explains why the USSR has obtained excellent results in certain areas of research and development, while trailing behind the level of development of Western industrialized countries in others. When the Soviet Union focuses on certain economic sectors, it can bring to bear the world's largest scientific potential. The USSR — together with the United States, Japan and the Federal Republic of Germany — spends record amounts of its gross national product on research and development, and it has at its disposal the biggest potential of scientists, engineers and technicians active in research and development.

The level of technological progress achieved, therefore, depends, to a high degree, on the administratively ordained priorities. Certain areas of fundamental research bear witness to this fact. The capability of centrally planned economies to concentrate financial and personnel resources has brought about outstanding achievements in sectors such as nuclear physics and laser research. Accordingly, an international comparison shows that Soviet research is first-rate in those areas which require large capital-intensive installations, such as plasma physics. Topnotch technological achievements are evidenced by the issuance of patent licenses on an international scale. In such cases the Soviet Union even issues licenses to the United States. These exports of concessions quite clearly pinpoint the areas the USSR has promoted most, namely iron and non-iron metallurgy and coal industry.

Technology Imports and the Soviet Arms Industry

The principle of emphasizing certain industrial sectors particularly applies to the arms industry. During the first Five-year-plan Stalin was motivated to further develop the Soviet economic planning system by the need for greater efforts in armaments in the light of external conditions. The Soviet centrally planned economy was correctly described by theorist Oscar Lange, who later had a strong influence in socialist Poland, as a "war economy *sui generis*". The arms industry is supported in two ways. First, products of special economic importance for the industry are emphasized. Second, the economy as a whole is systematically screened for products of that kind. Military representatives (voenpredy) stationed in industrial plants and research facilities also help in this effort. These officials not only have permission to identify, but also to induce production of resources required for armaments.

One can therefore also assume that all imported Western technologies are also checked to see whether they can serve military purposes. Most of these goods can be used either directly or indirectly to improve efficiency because modern weapon systems are based on the application of technological know-how which also finds application in the civilian sector. The following examples of the use of Western technology in the Soviet arms industry have become known. In 1972 the Bryant Chucking Grinder Company delivered a number of precision machines to the Soviet Union, which were to be used for the production of miniature bearings. After the machines were supplied it was noticed that the targeting of Soviet intercontinental missiles become much more accurate. It can therefore be assumed that these machines were put to use in the Soviet arms industry. Another example has to do with the military use of trucks manufactured at the Kama River truck plant, where most of the equipment was originally imported from Western industrialized countries. According to American sources trucks of the type manufactured in this factory were used by the Soviet army during their invasion of Afghanistan in 1979.[9] There will be other examples because the USSR is obviously interested in utilizing foreign technology in its armaments when it can.

The Soviet arms industry, however, also goes to great lengths to achieve the highest possible level of self-sufficiency. Given that the USSR is competing with the United States in the arms field, planning in this area cannot rely on imports for contingency supplies. In any case most weapon systems combine a large number of technologies so that any single imported technology has only a limited beneficial effect. Soviet efforts in developing larger-scale weapon systems have been successful because they could fall back on the findings of their own fundamental research. The development of nuclear weapons and delivery systems during the 1950s and 1960s are examples of Soviet advances in armaments achieved without utilization of foreign innovations. The Soviets were also the first to ignite the hydrogen bomb, and to begin the exploration of outer space, which brought about the well-known "Sputnik shock" in the United States.

The differences between Soviet military and civilian technological capacities can be seen, for example, in the area of computer manufacture and application. Time and again it has been assumed that the Soviet arms industry relies on Western computer technology — due to the underdevelopment of the Soviet and Eastern European electronics industry. But this supposition cannot be verified. At the end of the 1940s and the beginning of the 1950s, the Soviet Union — together with Great Britain and the United States — even had a leading position in computer technology. Subsequently, Soviet computer production has always been sufficient to fulfill the requirements of the high priority areas, such as armaments, astronautics and research. But the application of computer technology on a broad industrial scale was neglected until some steps were taken in the 1960s and 1970s with the help of other East European states and/or imports from Western industrialized countries.

The general picture that emerges in technology is therefore that the Soviet technology lags behind the West. This is not primarily a problem of innovation, but more often one of inadequate capacity hampering the realization of necessary structural change in industry. Moreover, the need for structural modifications, which in many cases will have already taken place in the West, is either not seen in time or when it is necessary changes are not carried out fast enough.

Imports from the West do, however, have an indirect effect on arms expenditures. As the practice of setting priorities leads to the neglect of certain industrial branches, imports are necessary to off-set undercapacity or underdevelopment in these branches. This not only helps improve overall Soviet economic efficiency but also facilitates the distribution of resources according to economic objectives. For instance, food imports – in particular from the United States – helped compensate for the backwardness in Soviet agriculture. It must be stressed, however, that the backwardness of various sectors is not a consequence of resource concentration on the arms industry, but rather the shortcomings of a centralized capital distribution system, which either fails to recognize new production opportunities in time or cannot put them to work fast enough in industrial plants.

Sanctions and the Soviet Economy

The observations made so far would suggest that the Soviet Union could be expected to overcome a partial embargo on technology by setting new economic priorities. This can be illustrated by two cases which led to heated debates within the Atlantic Alliance on the question of economic cooperation with the Soviet Union.

As is well known, the first case, that of the Urengoy Project linking the exploitation of the big Soviet natural gas reserves in the northern part of western Siberia with Western Europe, touched off a serious controversy within the Western alliance. The United States considered that the foreign exchange earnings from the 'natural gas deal' would enable the Soviets to sustain trade with the West. It also thought the deal would lead to an inadmissible dependency of Western Europe on Soviet natural gas supplies. These reservations were not shared by West European countries, a fact to which the United States reacted by extending the sanctions, imposed on the Soviet Union on June 18, 1982, to commodities produced either by subsidiaries of American companies or by foreign companies licensed to use American technology. These embargo measures affected West European suppliers of the Urengoy pipeline, and above all those using American compressor construction technology. To be sure, the

United States lifted all sanctions directed against construction of the natural gas pipeline on November 13, 1982, because of an impending compromise within the Western Alliance on a common trade policy toward the USSR. But the Soviet Union had already begun to produce the necessary technology for compressor construction of its own.

This example shows that Soviet interest in imports was not a consequence of technological deficiencies, but, rather, of a bottleneck in capacities resulting from rapid enlargement of the natural gas network. The Soviet steel industry can produce its own large-diameter pipes but has insufficient capacity. In contrast to pipe production the technical performance and reliability of Soviet compressors is certainly well below Western supplies. But as the successful development of the Soviet natural gas network since the 1960s shows it would be wrong to conclude that the Soviet natural gas pipeline system also has a lower level of efficiency. The problem is that the Soviet Union simply has trouble meeting its requirements for large pipes, compressors and construction machines needed for laying natural gas pipelines. By taking advantage of Western import opportunities, the USSR saves more time and money in the construction of natural gas pipelines than if it made everything itself.

The second example concerns the case, mentioned above, of the grinding machines used to make high-precision miniature bearings. It was assumed that the increased targeting precision of Soviet intercontinental missiles would not have been possible without the use of these machines. For this reason, an embargo was placed on the export of American machines to the USSR. The Soviet Union probably already knew how these machines were made at the time it imported them from the United States, but lacked the necessary advanced technological experience to actually produce them. Typically the Soviet economy reacted to the embargo by making the development of high-precision machines for the production of bearings a major priority in the Five-year-plan running from 1976 to 1980.

General Soviet dependency on foreign trade is limited because imports make up no more than 6 to 8 per cent of the gross national product. In some cases this rate can reach a level of 10 per cent, but never goes higher. Only about one-third of Soviet foreign trade is conducted with Western industrialized countries – so that this accounts for at most 2 to 3 per cent of its gross national product. The USSR is also endeavoring to decrease its dependency on the West and develop its own capabilities as a consequence of worsening East-West relations and threat of embargoes.

The United States and West Germany are traditional suppliers of machines to the Soviet Union. However, due to global economic developments even the most modern technologies are now offered by more suppliers. The best known example in this respect is Japan. Thus, politically neutral industrialized countries, as well as various newly industrializing countries have become efficient suppliers of technology on the world market.

When considering the extent of Soviet dependence on suppliers of Western technology it is often overlooked that countries of the Council of Mutual Economic Assistance (CMEA) are still its most important suppliers of plant and equipment. Since the Second World War the Soviet Union has imported most of its capital goods from CMEA countries. In the 1950s, Soviet purchases of plant and equipment from the CMEA's leading exporters of these items, namely the German Democratic Republic, Czechoslovakia, Hungary and Poland, made up 75 per cent of its total imports of equipment. In 1955 the CMEA's share of Soviet plant and equipment imports even reached almost 80 per cent.

During the 1970s, there was a rise in the volume of imports from Western industrialized countries. But even West Germany, which holds a prominent position among Western suppliers of machines and manufacturing equipment to the USSR, only accounted for a share of Soviet capital goods imports comparable to that of Czechoslovakia. West Germany's share is far exceeded by that of the GDR. In the mid-1970s, the emphasis in Soviet capital goods imports did, indeed, shift from CMEA countries to Western industrialized countries. The CMEA's share dropped from 71.5 per cent in 1973 to 54.9 per cent in 1976, while the share of Western industrialized countries rose from 25.9 per cent to 40.3 per cent over the same period. This level represented the peak of imports from the West and since 1978 the CMEA's share of Soviet machine imports has increased and the West's receded.

When imports of Western plant and equipment were at their peak they represented 6 per cent of investment, while the corresponding share for CMEA countries was about 11 per cent. Soviet economic performance was therefore clearly more dependent on imports from CMEA countries. Since 1978 there has once again been a tendency to import more capital goods and technology from CMEA countries than from Western industrialized countries which continued on into the beginning of the 1980s. For example, the 36th Council Meeting of the CMEA, held at Budapest in June 1982, decided on closer cooperation in the field of microelectronics with the explicit aim of gaining more independence from the West. This goal was again confirmed at the CMEA summit meeting in June 1984.

The question of the effects of Western technology exports on the Soviet Union can therefore be answered as follows. A reduction in Western exports would hit the USSR in various civilian technological areas while having little or no effect on Soviet military technology. Even CoCom could not prevent the Soviet Union from becoming a military super power. Nonetheless, security problems involved in the East-West conflict warrant the cut-off of certain technology exports, and in the case of military relevant "high technology" CoCom controls must be effective. The advantages and disadvantages of more far-reaching limitations on technology transfers to the Soviet Union must be carefully balanced.

Consequences for Western Policy

A control system directed at only militarily relevant high technology is more easily defined and applied than broad controls on technology exports. There remain open questions about the effects, on both the USSR and the Western Alliance, of broader controls aimed at the Soviet economy as a whole. The more comprehensive the controls, the more difficult it becomes to solve the problems of coordination and/or political acceptance within the Western Alliance. This was clearly illustrated by the controversies in the West surrounding the 'natural gas deal' with the Soviet Union. U.S. sanctions against Western European firms that were party to the 'gas pipeline deal' with the Soviet Union, shattered existing confidence in trade between Western industrialized countries.

What would a compromise between the interests of the United States and Western Europe look like? In particular, how would West German interests be taken into account? Recent trends in the various areas of economic cooperation with the Soviet Union – credits, energy, agriculture and technology – have favored American interests. When it comes to granting loans West Germany is in any case the country most rigidly guided by what are strictly commercial considerations. At present, there is also no need for new joint energy projects with the Soviet Union because of reduced expenditures on technology, the effects of higher oil prices in the 1970s, the exploitation of other energy sources, the recent global recession and uncertainties about economic growth. In the agricultural sector American export and Soviet import needs suggest there will be long-term cooperation between the two countries in this sector. Equally one must continue to expect West German interest in exporting technology to CMEA countries.

If only militarily relevant technology as more narrowly defined were included in the CoCom list, West Germany would retain a reasonable degree of freedom in shaping its economic relations with the CMEA countries. But in revising the CoCom list, differing views on the role of the Soviet Union in the world order could once again become a problem. In the United States the prevailing opinion is that the Soviet Union is, by nature, an expansionistic power which must therefore be "contained". There is, however, an alternative view that "containment" is a necessary but insufficient means of stabilizing relations with the Soviet Union. These contrasting views ultimately reflect different images of the Soviet Union. There are also different views on economic relations with the USSR stemming from divergent interpretations of Soviet foreign policy behaviour. Political assessments of the problems of technology transfer to the Soviet Union are therefore, unlikely to change no matter how much information on their volume and significance is available. In conclusion, it is necessary to indicate why the assessment of the Soviet Union presented here differs from the present American assessment. Today, both Soviet ideology and Soviet international law emphasize the theory and politics of peaceful coexistence which has determined relations with countries of antagonistic political and economic order since the beginning of the Soviet state. The USSR — in contrast to official American interpretations — does not see itself as an expansionist power. All the same, Soviet foreign policy is by no means unidimensional and exploits various options. The strategy of class conflict and the establishment of socialist systems outside the Soviet Union, i. e. a socialist community of states, are essential elements of the Soviet self-image. But this is only one option. Since the coming into being of the Soviet state, Soviet foreign policy has tended to oscillate between a revolutionary, expansionistic, political course and a policy of coexistence. The general interest in security and foreign trade relations with the West, which is deemed desirable for economic development, has, for the most part, tipped the balance in favor of coexistence as the most important component of Soviet foreign policy.

It goes almost without saying that a change in Soviet conduct would alter expectations of its future behaviour. For this to happen, however, assumptions about Soviet behaviour must recognize its multi-dimensional nature if changes in conduct are to be perceived. Technology transfer was one important reason why the Eastern side entered into détente. Without question, the flow of technology from the West has increased Soviet economic capacities, such as in vehicle construction, synthetic materials and fertilizers, and the consumer goods and energy sectors. All imports intended for use in the underdeveloped area of civilian technology can relieve the strain on the Soviet arms sector. But economic relations are, however, also an important element in confidence-building. If this cooperative component is missing from East-West relations the Soviet Union will emphasize its military threat potential more strongly than would otherwise be the case. Confidence-building can only improve the climate for solutions to security related problems. "Economic ties alone cannot, of course, prevent political and strategic rivalry ... But compatible international contacts are surely a prerequisite for reasonably stable political relations."[10]

62

Notes

1 For a typical view, see M. Costick, "Soviet Military Posture and Strategic Trade," in W.S. Thompson (Ed.) *From Weakness to Strength*, (San Francisco, Calif. 1980), pp. 189-213.

2 See, for instance, R.V. Roosa and W.M. Reichert, "East-West-Relations — Economic Ties are a Needed First Step to Détente," *International Herald Tribune*, 17. April 1983.

3 As representative of this view, see H.D. Genscher, "Toward an Overall Strategy for Peace, Freedom and Progress," *Foreign Affairs*, vol. 61, no. 1, 1982, pp. 42 ff.

4 See, for example, A.E. Stent, *"Technology Transfer to the Soviet Union. A Challenge for the Cohesiveness of the Western Alliance"*, Working papers on international politics of the Deutsche Gesellschaft für Auswärtige Politik e. V., Bonn 1983.

5 See H. Kravalis et al., 'Quantification of Western Export of High Technology Products to Communist Countries', *Issues in East-West-Commercial Relations. A Compendium of Papers submitted to the Joint Economic Committee* (Washington, D.C.: Congress of the United States, 1979), pp. 34 ff.

6 See B. Pičugin, in: Meždunarodnaja žizn, no. 7, Moscow 1979.

7 For details, see R. Campbell, 'Soviet Technology Imports: The Gas Pipeline Case', *The California Seminar on International Security and Foreign Policy*, no. 91 (Santa Monica, Calif., Feb. 1981)

8 See C. Röthlingshöfer, *Die Absorption westlicher Technologien für die Sowjetunion. Bericht über Erfahrungen deutscher Exporteure* (Munich: Ifo-Institut für Wirtschaftsforschung, 1978), pp. 18-19.

9 See R.S. Randolph, 'Technology Transfer and East-West Trade, Strategic Perspectives for the 80s', *Comparative Strategy*, vol. 3, no. 2, 1981, pp. 117 ff.

10 R.V. Roosa and W.M. Reichert, 'East-West Relations', *International Herald Tribune*, 17. April 1983.

5
Industrial Cooperation
Klaus Bolz

In parallel with the volatile growth in East-West trade in the first half of the 1970s the new forms of cooperation between Western firms and socialist enterprises in Eastern Europe became increasingly important. By the end of the 1970s, however, the expansion of industrial East-West cooperation had already lost its impetus. During that single decade the Federal Republic of Germany was able to increase the number of cooperation agreements with partners from the Comecon nations from around 300 to more than 500, although the structure of its agreements with the individual nations underwent a marked change. The proportion of Hungarian projects grew from one-third to well over one-half,[1] and the proportion of Polish projects fell from just under one-third to around one-fifth of all the cooperation arrangements involving German concerns due to the limited growth of new German-Polish cooperation projects and the termination of many existing agreements by the end of the decade. In this same period there was probably little change in the total number of agreements with Rumania, Czechoslovakia, the USSR, Bulgaria and the German Democratic Republic but within this group there was a clear shift towards the Soviet Union and Bulgaria.

Signs of stagnation

In the early 1980s there were also signs of stagnation in East-West cooperation in the case of Hungary despite that country's comparatively satisfactory economic development and the fact that it has successfully pushed ahead with economic reform. Hungary's political relations with all the Western industrialized nations have been fairly good despite the general deterioration in the climate between East and West. Although growth in the number of cooperation projects could be satisfactory-to-good even as late as 1982 experts in Hungarian cooperation now see a downward trend in this sector of Hungarian economic relations.[2] The most recent figures provided by the Hungarian Ministry for Foreign Trade and covering the period to the end of 1982, indicate that the trend may have reached its turning-point during 1982. The development in the total number of cooperation agreements in the previous years had shown considerable interannual growth. Yet, when interpreting these figures, we must bear in mind that they also include cooperation with Yugoslavia and, possibly, other countries which cannot be counted as Western nations. In other words, if the total number of cooperation agreements with the West, for which unfortunately no data is available, is considered in isolation, one would probably also find a downward trend before 1982. When the cooperation projects with Yugoslavia and other countries are included, cooperation was virtually stagnant in 1982, i.e. in absolute terms the number of contracts increased by only 4 to 508.

If one considers the total number of agreements (see table 1) and the number of new agreements concluded each year (1978, 53; 1979, 54; 1980, 79; 1981, 56; 1982, 74) it appears that quite a number of agreements expire each year, and that in 1982 the number expiring must have been almost as high as the number of new agreements. In 1982 there were 224 German-Hungarian cooperation agreements compared to 63 with Austria, Yugoslavia 38, France 33, Switzerland 27, Sweden 22, USA 21, Great Britain 20, Italy 17 and the Netherlands 8.

Hungary's foreign trade generated by cooperation

Developments in imports and exports linked with cooperation have not been in proportion with the total number of cooperation agreements. In most years the growth in trade was below growth in the number of cooperation agreements. In 1982, however, when the total number of cooperation agreements stagnated despite a relatively large number of new agreements, Hungary had no real reason to complain because it managed to increase the exports generated by cooperation by some 600 m. Forint while imports from the West actually fell by some 150 m. Forint. This shows that new cooperation agreements concluded in previous years did not produce exports until 1982. It also provides some evidence about the functioning of cooperation agreements even during a period of economic recession, as well as reflecting Hungary's efficiency in domestic and foreign trade.

As mentioned above, the Federal Republic of Germany was Hungary's leading partner country in cooperation agreements in 1982 with 224 agreements.[3] If one considers the trade generated by cooperation as the criteria however, Yugoslavia, with a turnover of 3.9 bn. Forint, outstrips the Federal Republic as Hungary's main partner in industrial cooperation. The large Hungarian imports from Yugoslavia can probably be explained by the Yugoslav-Hungarian cooperation projects on Yugoslav territory which mainly supply consumer products, such as cosmetics, of high quality owing to Yugoslavia's cooperation with Western countries in that sector.

Although Hungarian expectations of increased exports from the cooperation may not always have been fulfilled, it has registered a surplus in trade associated with cooperation agreements, especially those with the Federal Republic of Germany, in every year except for 1982. When considered in isolation, however, the development of imports and exports shows rather clearly that Hungary has so far been unable to achieve any real breakthrough in its exports to the West on the basis of cooperation agreements. The figures also show that the Western nations have also set their own export targets much too high. This is particularly the case for the Federal Republic of Germany where German exports reached 1.3 bn. Forint compared to imports of 2.4 bn. Forint from Hungary. These trends help to explain the present greatly diminished interest in concluding further cooperation agreements.

Table 1: *Development of the total number of Hungarian cooperation agreements and cooperation-related trade*

Year	Imports		Exports		No. of Agreements	
	Ft.m.	% of previous year	Ft.m.	% of previous year	No.	% of previous year
1978	4.546,1		5.149,7		363	
1979	4.615,3	101,5	6.559,1	127,4	390	107,4
1980	4.310,5	93,4	6.421,9	97,9	451	115,6
1981	5.606,7	130,1	6.469,8	100,7	504	111,8
1982	5.454,2	97,3	7.057,6	109,1	508	100,8

Source: Hungarian Ministry for Foreign Trade (taken from *Nachrichten für Außenhandel* (NfA), 11.11.1983, p. 5); author's calculations.

Table 2: *Hungary's cooperation-linked turnover with its principal partner nation in convertible clearances, 1982*
— in Mio. Ft —

Country	Imports	Exports
Yugoslavia	2.048,7	1.835,8
FRG	1.305,1	2.410,4
France	394,1	470,1
USA	448,1	386,1
Sweden	379,7	389,6
Great Britain	369,1	296,5
Austria	210,3	332,3
Italy	71,5	379,6

Source: Hungarian Ministry for Foreign trade (taken from *Nachrichten für Außenhandel* (NfA), 11.11.1983, p. 5).

Other countries' imports and exports generated by cooperation are well behind those of the Federal Republic (see Table 2) and their rankings differ from those based on the number of cooperation agreements.

The importance of cooperation for the national economies involved becomes more evident if the cooperation-generated revenue is expressed as a proportion of the countries' bilateral trade. These figures show pronounced fluctuations in the early 1970s and, in the last analysis, the range of fluctuation makes them almost meaningless. The data are more reliable at the beginning of the 1980s. Transactions resulting from cooperation now account for 10 per cent of German-Hungarian exchanges of goods with Hungarian exports slightly exceeding imports. The data permits estimates to be made for the other partner nations and in most cases the proportions are somewhat smaller.

If one differentiates between the various sectors, one finds that cooperation agreements are now of vital importance for Hungarian exports in certain sectors, such as mechanical engineering (30 per cent), machine tools (as much as 50 per cent) and agricultural machinery (almost 100 per cent). Compared with the total volume of trade generated by cooperation, no single cooperation project accounts for any really large volume of trade, and in the case of many cooperation projects the initial imports required are succeeded by hardly any movements of goods.

A serious crisis in Poland's cooperation

Whereas for the time being at least, there are only indications of stagnation in Hungary's industrial cooperation with the West, Polish cooperation is now undergoing a serious crisis, and may be threatened with complete collapse in the near future. For example, only a few of the 100 or so German-Polish cooperation agreements that existed in the late 1970s are likely to have survived until 1984. This is due to the termination of the cooperation agreements concluded before 1979 and the fact that virtually no new cooperation agreements have been concluded, and only a few of the former agreements extended beyond their agreed terms. This is equally the case with cooperation between Polish enterprises and both Germany and the other Western nations because, on the whole, the arrangement and timing of agreements with the latter are similar to the German-Polish cooperation arrangements. According to an unpublished Polish analysis, only 51 cooperation agreements still existed with the entire Western World in 1981, a figure which actually fell to 41 in 1982. In this connection it is interesting to note that the number of specialization and cooperation agreements between Poland and its Comecon partners has also been greatly reduced as a result of the Polish economic crisis, from 190 in 1981 to only 156 in 1982, because many agreements have not been extended.

In addition to the general deterioration in East West cooperation due to the worldwide economic and political conditions, Poland also suffered from a domestic economic crisis in 1980, and from political instability and martial law in December 1981. Consequently, almost all the economic and the political preconditions necessary for beneficial cooperation with Poland are lacking.[4] If there is to be any recovery in cooperation with the West, Poland will have to work hard to convince Western firms that cooperation can be profitable in a relatively short term and does not involve unreasonable economic and political risks. It is a tragedy for Poland that while it now needs the benefits of cooperation with the West more urgently than ever before, it must also offer greater concessions than before in order to attract potential Western partners in the private sector. These concessions will however, affect the subsequent financial return from such cooperation. It is impossible to foresee how Poland will escape from this vicious circle.

The marked downward trend in industrial cooperation has further increased the overall significance of the cooperation project with Fiat of Italy which was in any case the largest project between Poland and the West. In 1982 the Polish exports generated by the Fiat project, which, unlike most of the other agreements, is certainly not expected to be broken off, accounted for 73 per cent of all industrial cooperation related exports. The fact that all the other cooperation projects with Western firms produced only 27 per cent of the cooperation exports graphically underlines the minor importance of other projects for exports.

Table 3, based on unpublished Polish material, shows a rather different picture as regards the diminishing significance of Western cooperation for exports and thus for foreign exchange earnings, and imports, especially for supplies of inputs for the Polish economy. Figures are available for the first half of 1981 and the first half of 1982. During that period the total Polish cooperation-linked exports to the West fell from 6.5 bn. Zł to 4.7 bn Zł, i.e. to only 72 per cent of the volume achieved in the first half of 1981. In the first six months of 1982 Polish exports to its major trading partners were only about half the level of the equivalent period of 1981. Cooperation exports to Italy fell by only 25 per cent owing to the continued comparative success of cooperation with Fiat.

In the first half of 1981 Poland's cooperation-linked imports of 1.8 bn. Zł were already extremely low, but they fell even further in the first half of 1982 to less than 30 per cent of the 1981 figures. The figures in Table 3 clearly indicate the drop in the total number of cooperation agreements. They also show that despite the fall in cooperation-linked exports there would have been an even greater fall had special efforts not been made in the sector. The drop in cooperation-linked imports reflects Poland's desperate attempts to reduce imports in order to conserve hard currency despite the detrimental consequences for Poland's industrial output and export capacity. These figures also show Poland's hopeless position in solving its economic problems. While cooperation was formerly accompanied by a certain degree of euphoria in Poland as regards the objectives it was to achieve, for the time being it is impossible to attach any hopes whatsoever to cooperation as a means of developing the Polish economy.

Table 3: *Poland's cooperation-linked exports and imports from/to its partner countries*

	Cooperation Exports			Cooperation Imports		
	1st half 1981 Zł bn.	1st half 1982 Zł bn.	1st half 1982 % of 1st half 1981	1st half 1981 Zł bn.	1st half 1982 Zł bn.	1st half 1982 % of 1st half 1981
All capitalist countries	6,5	4,7	72	1,8	0,5	28
Italy	4,0	3,0	75	0,9	0,4	44
FRG	0,9	0,5	56	0,1	0,07	70
Switzerland	0,4	0,2	50	—	—	—
USA	0,4	0,3	75	0,5	—	—
France	0,3	0,2	67	0,05	0,006	12
Austria	0,1	0,09	90	0,2	—	—
Great Britain	0,09	0,3	333	0,02	—	—

Source: Foreign Cooperation and Specialization of Industry in 1st half of 1982, Head Office of Statistics, Warsaw, 1982, unpublished.

Growth prospects

Political conditions in the 1970s certainly favoured the expansion and intensification of East-West industrial cooperation. If, however, the real breakthrough in cooperation has not been achieved, and this is true even for Hungary, the reasons must be sought in the economic sector in general and in the serious problems of entrepreneurial cooperation between two different systems in particular. As in the case of East-West trade, the stagnation in East-West cooperation towards the end of the 1970s was primarily caused by unfavourable general economic conditions in both East and West. The downward trend of East-West cooperation, heralded at the beginning of the 1980s, can also be partly attributed to the major deterioration in political relations, but this did not itself initiate the trend. This view is shared, inter alia, by the experts on Hungary's cooperation, both theorists and practitioners, who cite economic factors as the principal cause of the unsatisfactory development and see political factors only as a secondary cause.[5]

Even former keen advocates of East-West cooperation now have to resign themselves to the fact that no great advances have been made in the field despite years of experience. Indeed this experience has taught both sides that the objectives of cooperation cannot often be fully achieved. For example the Western partners have not often expanded their markets in Comecon or reduced costs, and Eastern partners have not benefitted from Western technology or strengthened their competitive position in the West as they had envisaged, or saved foreign exchange and increased exchange earnings. Moreover, even after more than ten years' practical experience the well documented fundamental problems, most of which are inherent in the systems are still an everyday part of cooperation, with constant detrimental effects. It is not surprising therefore that, in view of the deterioration in the general economic and political climate responsible parties in both East and West are increasingly questioning the benefits and risks of collaboration.

Prosperous East-West entrepreneurial cooperation requires stability and predictability in the general economic and political conditions. Because neither can be expected in the foreseeable future, and also because certain processes are inducing a change in the world's economic and political priorities, it is at present impossible to foresee any serious growth prospects for East-West cooperation.

In order to offer more than just an overall view of the growth prospects of East-West cooperation we shall examine some hypotheses which help us to understand the present situation and/or draw conclusions concerning future trends.

- In view of the manifold problems and risks facing East-West cooperation it is no longer surprising that the forms of cooperation have been only slightly intensified since it was established in the late 1960s. It can be shown that firms from the OECD countries have so far preferred forms of cooperation which involve only a small degree of commitment to the Eastern partner. Licensing agreements are particularly still employed essentially as a means of acquiring better access to the socialist markets. Since the low growth-rates and the problems of indebtedness in the socialist countries give little hope of any real expansion of Western exports to that region in the foreseeable future, Western firms' interest in cooperation is also bound to remain very limited in the medium-term.

- We are all too well aware that, for reasons inherent in the system and the markets, a large number of socialist firms had little interest in cooperating with the West. Nor can this be expected to change in the future, particularly since even those socialist firms with many years' experience of cooperation are now questioning its benefits.

  Like the Western firms, they too often conclude that the risks and the difficulties to be overcome before cooperation can succeed outweigh the potential benefits. As long as Western firms continue to give their Eastern cooperating partners access to only second-class technology, the prospects of exporting to the West, and thus of earning more foreign exchange are hardly likely to improve. In addition, cooperation agreements frequently include market restrictions which prevent or impede the Eastern partner's access to Western markets. Even if the socialist enterprise is able to improve its market position in its own or other Comecon markets as a result of technology transfer effected as part of cooperation, this certainly does not satisfy all its expectations. In the last analysis, satisfaction of these expectations will depend first and foremost upon the net inflow of foreign exchange, because cooperation is usually contingent upon the use of a hard currency and only in special cases can foreign exchange be earned from Comecon sales.

- Whereas over-employment in the Federal Republic and other countries formerly encouraged cooperation agreements with the socialist states, the labour market is now unequivocally acting as a brake upon cooperation. A quite significant effect is that cooperation is now seen as a risk to jobs which are in short supply in any case. Furthermore, the existence of unused production capacities should, in principle, discourage cooperation. It is, for example, very improbable that firms which postpone investment at home, because of unused capacities and unfavourable assessment of the market, will enter into cooperation arrangements with Eastern countries. Moreover, industrial cooperation in socialist countries no longer necessarily produces substantial cost reductions, especially if in earlier years this was contingent upon low prices for raw materials.

- At times of fully utilized capacity Western firms transferred the production of certain items in their own range of products, such as lathes of a specific size and capacity, to enterprises in Eastern Europe and used their own equipment for higher value-added production. It may now once again be profitable to manufacture such lower value-added products at home in order to increase capacity utilization and thus reduce overhead costs per production unit.

- The socialist nations must also have realized by now that other economies, such as the industrialized countries in the Far East, are more attractive to Western firms, especially since some socialist countries are themselves now endeavouring to take advantage of the same low cost countries.

- The constant references to economic conditions in this paper are not directed solely towards the cyclical movements and growth tendencies of international trade, but also towards the radical restructuring processes which have long been taking place. Mention has already been made of the way in which the newly industrialized countries are developing as part of the world economy. Nor will East-West cooperation remain unaffected if the growing tendency to transfer first-class technology only in conjunction with capital continues;[6] in other words, such transfers are increasingly taking place as part of the interlinked system of the multinational firms.

Competition often makes it impossible to allow others a share in the benefits gained from modern technologies which have been developed in return for a high capital outlay. If modern technology is in fact employed in other countries, this is not by way of licensing arrangements but increasingly through direct investment, i.e. the technology is accompanied by the firm's own capital. Only in this way can the firms retain full control.

Although several socialist nations now offer the possibility of setting up joint ventures, the vast majority of Western firms prefer to invest their technology and capital in other countries, especially in South-East Asia, which offer a base for investment with far fewer strings attached than do the Comecon nations. If they retain their existing conditions on foreign capital, the socialist countries will in the not too distant future, find it almost impossible to ensure an inflow of the most modern technology by way of co-operation agreements. As long as Western firms can employ their capital and technology in countries with comparatively liberal investment laws and with better prospects of profits, they will shun the cumbersome and restrictive socialist economies. In future the socialist countries will only stand a chance of being chosen as a partner in cooperation when it is a question of utilizing and marketing second-class technologies.

— One vital factor affecting the prospects of developing East-West-cooperation has not yet been mentioned: CoCom. No matter how long the lists of embargoes eventually become or how the controls are strengthened, one thing is certain; the precautions taken by the West, led by the U.S.A., on the grounds of security will be more detrimental than ever to industrial cooperation with many countries and especially with the socialist states.

Notes

1   This is based on some 350 German-Hungarian agreements, a number given by the Hungarian Chamber of Commerce, Intercooperations AG and other sources.
2   For information on this point and the following comments see: *Nachrichten für Außenhandel*, No. 219, 11.11.1983, p. 5.
3   These figures are lower than those employed earlier in the paper because the Ministry for Foreign Trade applies stricter criteria when defining cooperation.
4   See K. Bolz, P. Pissula: *Die Erfahrungen deutscher Unternehmen aus der Kooperation mit polnischen Wirtschaftsorganisationen*, Hamburg 1981, pp. 133 ff.
5   See B. Kádár: Formen und Motivationen der industriellen Kooperation, in: *Marketing in Ungarn*, Vol. 4, 1983, and *Nachrichten für Außenhandel*, No. 219 of 11.11.1983.
6   See B. Kádár, op. cit. pp. 20 ff.

6
Energy

Friedemann Müller

Introduction

Although the Atlantic partners have for the most part ceased to argue about whether the natural gas transaction between Western Europe and the Soviet Union is mutually beneficial or threatens the security of the West a resentment remains. Trade in energy and the resultant East-West projects have become quantitatively the most important factor in East-West economic relations. The sheer scale of energy trade means that it enhances the political salience of East-West economic relations.

Certainly energy is not a traded good in the usual sense of the word. Rather, it is a kind of strategic commodity whose sensitivity became obvious to everyone during the crises in the mid- and late-1970s. Energy is the product in economic relations between East and West to which both camps ascribe the greatest importance. On the one hand they perceive energy relations as a medium of détente policy and on the other as a dangerous instrument of appeasement and thus, potentially, a particularly suitable object of economic warfare. In order to assess the arguments of both sides, it is necessary first to describe the magnitude of East-West energy relations.

The Magnitude of Energy Relations

In 1974, at a time when détente policy was rapidly taking shape, Otto Wolff von Amerongen wrote at the end of an essay: "The assumption (seems) justified that in the near future Europe will have at its disposal an alliance system which can make a contribution toward meeting West European energy needs in the form of oil, gas and electricity."[1] The reality of such an all-European alliance system came nowhere near meeting these expectations. Political setbacks, impediments posed by Eastern economic systems and the depressed economic outlook in the West significantly constrained growth of East-West relations during 1974 and 1975.

Of all the CMEA countries, only the Soviet Union's energy relations with the West can be considered to be of any real political relevance. To be sure, energy plays a significant role in the export structure of many East European countries vis-à-vis the Western industrialized countries (Rumania 39 per cent of total exports, Poland 25 per cent, GDR 20 per cent, CSSR 17 per cent);[2] but compared to total Western imports, these volumes are politically insignificant and are also unlikely to become more important. Poland's coal exports decreased drastically in 1981, and cannot be expected to reach more than the 1979 level before the 1990s.

Soviet energy exports, however, thanks primarily to price developments, have become the main product of East-West trade. In 1980 energy comprised 71 per cent of total Soviet exports to the West. In 1981 this share grew to 75 per cent, and continued to increase in 1982, with the Soviet Union able to significantly expand its oil exports to the West, particularly by selling on the spot market. This counteracted the decline evident since 1979, although in 1983 the trend seemed to reverse once again. At any rate, in 1982 the Federal Republic imported 8 per cent of its oil and 20 per cent of its natural gas from the Soviet Union.

For the Soviet Union energy relations with Western Europe are of major importance not only because they are one of its main sources of foreign exchange. The development of the Soviet infrastructure necessary for exploiting its energy resources, for the main part natural gas, is also considerably dependent on Western investment goods.[3] The primary import commodity is pipes. Without questioning the ability of Soviet research and development to produce technologically advanced products such as large-diameter pipes, it clearly has severe difficulty producing the desired quality in sufficient quantities. But procuring an adequate number of pipes is an essential part of Soviet economic growth. With stagnating coal production and only negligible growth rates in oil production, growth in the production of energy depends almost exclusively on increasing natural gas production. In the Soviet Union, economic growth is also far more dependent on increases in available energy than is the case in the Western industrialized countries. According Campbell, Soviet energy consumption in the second half of the 1970s grew 1.3 times more than economic growth.[4] Since natural gas can only be transported via pipelines within the Soviet Union, there is a very direct connection between the availability of transport capacities for the natural gas, the output of which is growing at an annual rate of seven to eight per cent, and Soviet economic growth. In a somewhat more moderate form this is as true for compressors as it is for pipes. As is often the case in the Soviet economy, however, the problem of compressors has demonstrated that a substitute can be found even for imported high technology products when a high enough priority is ascribed to the task.

In the Soviet Union, energy *exports*, far more than energy *production* are in a state of upheaval. In production, natural gas must assume the largest share of growth; in exports, natural gas must substitute for oil completely. In 1980 oil comprised 55 per cent of exports to the West, natural gas 12 per cent. Regardless of which estimate one choses for the Soviet export balance at the end of the 1980s, natural gas will have to account for more foreign exchange earnings than oil by the year 1990. The CIA, like the OECD, assumes that by 1990 the Soviet Union will no longer be able to deliver oil to Western Europe;[5] the ECE (United

Nations Economic Commission for Europe) expects oil exports to reach a level of 25 billion tons compared to 58 billion tons in 1980.[6]

Where natural gas is concerned, the export possibilities through 1990 will depend less on available production than on West European demand. During the past years, estimates of West European demand have continuously had to be revised downward, so that for 1990 one can expect trade levels between the Soviet Union and Western Europe of only 55-60 billion cubic meters (compared to 28 billion cubic meters in 1981).[7] This is approximately a doubling of natural gas trade and an increase of about 30 billion cubic meters over the figures for the early 1980s.

Measured in energy units, 30 billion cubic meters of natural gas are equivalent to approximately 24 million tons of oil. It is highly probable that the decrease in oil deliveries from 1980 (50 million tons) to 1990 will be more than 24 million tons. Since there is no reason to expect any significant change in the amount of coal or electricity the Soviet Union will be able to deliver, one can assume that in 1990 the Soviet Union will be supplying less energy to Western Europe than it has done during the 1980s. But as the use of energy by Western Europe is expected to increase during this decade,[8] it can be assumed that the Soviet share of West European energy supplies will decrease significantly.

This decrease in the dependence of Europe on the Soviet Union is particularly true for oil; not, however, for gas. According to a study by the European Community, the share of Soviet natural gas deliveries to the countries of the EC will increase from 12 per cent in 1981 to 14-17 per cent in 1990.[9] These figures vary of course from country to country. According to the study, the Federal Republic will reach a level of dependence of 29 per cent, France 28 per cent, and Italy up to 33 per cent, whereas all other EC countries could possibly remain completely independent of Soviet gas. Outside the European community, only two West European countries receive Soviet gas, namely Austria and Finland. In 1981 Austria already got 62 per cent of its natural gas supplies from the Soviet Union, and this share could grow.[10] Finland imports all of its natural gas (one billion cubic meters) from the Soviet Union. This will not change during the 1980s. The high level of dependency of these two countries on Soviet supplies raises the dependency of Western Europe as a whole to above the average for the European Community, namely to 15 per cent (1981).

For purposes of thoroughness, coal deliveries are included here even though the Soviet Union has never delivered significant amounts of coal to Western countries. There is no tendency for this to change since Soviet coal production has stagnated since 1978. In 1978 and 1979 coal exports to the West amounted to four million tons; in 1981 exports reached only one million tons.[11] East European deliveries on the other hand, which came almost exclusively from Poland, reached 25 million tons in both 1978 and 1979. They fell to 18 million tons in 1981 due to a decrease in Polish production. Compared to an OECD coal consumption of 1,160 million tons or a West European consumption of over 400 million tons (1980), these exports are relatively insignificant. CMEA electricity deliveries to West European countries, which reached 3.7 terawatt hours (1980), half of which came from the Soviet Union, are also of no importance.

Energy Relations and Détente

During détente energy relations excited the imaginations of politicians and experts alike. This is seen not only in the above quote by Otto Wolff on an all-European energy alliance, but also in Prime Minister Kosygin's speech at the 24th Party Congress of the Communist Party of the Soviet Union in which he called for a European security conference, which later resulted in the CSCE (Conference on Security and Cooperation in Europe). In this speech he also described a vision of such an alliance system.[12] As shown by the phraseology, cooperation was afforded the same importance as security during preparations for this conference.

In the formulated text of Basket II of the Final Act, energy relations ranked extremely high within the framework of the CSCE. The following text demonstrates this: "The participating states... are of the opinion that the fields of energy resources, in particular oil, natural gas and coal ... are suitable for strengthening long-term economic cooperation and for developing trade, to the extent to which it ensues."[13]

The Soviet Union was obviously of the opinion that there were great possibilities for the expansion of economic cooperation in the field of energy. Thus at the end of 1975 Brezhnev suggested that an all-European energy conference be convened. The West received this suggestion rather cautiously, although the Federal Republic repeatedly promoted the idea to its own alliance partners. Consequently before the first CSCE follow-up conference in Belgrade (from October 1977 until March 1978) the Federal Republic encouraged the participants to consider this suggestion seriously, and in the process clearly placed greater emphasis on détente considerations than on energy needs.[14] In May 1978, after the failure of the Belgrade conference, General Secretary Brezhnev visited Bonn. During this visit, the Soviet Union and the Federal Republic signed a 25-year economic agreement. Here, too, energy relations are recognized as having not only an economic impact but also, more importantly, an effect on the policy of détente. Article 1 states:

> The treaty parties have as their goal the advancement of economic, industrial and technical cooperation between both states as an important and necessary element for the strengthening of bilateral relations on a more stable and long-term basis. Given the long-term nature of the...projects, in particular in the fields of raw materials and energy, the treaty parties strive for further intensification of cooperation for the mutual advantage of both parties."[15]

This is expressed even more precisely in the "Long-Term Program" which was worked out by the summer of 1980 in order to complete Article 6 of the German-Soviet economic agreement, and signed during Chancellor Schmidt's visit to Moscow on July 1, 1980.

On June 30, 1980, Helmut Schmidt gave an after-dinner speech in Moscow which created somewhat of a sensation because of its very critical remarks about the Afghanistan invasion. The only section of that speech which dealt with economic policy is, however, of particular interest:

> Our first priority must be to attempt to establish an internationally secure and adequate supply of energy. Otherwise we will be risking a world-wide conflict over the distribution of energy resources which would have a devastating effect... We can achieve much through the cooperation of our two countries. From the beginning, Mr. General Secretary, I have welcomed your ideas on an all-European energy conference and will continue to advocate such a conference.[16]

Here too, then, was a clear call for détente through the medium of cooperation in the field of energy policy, in spite of the tension which had developed between the two countries.

The change of government in Bonn in October 1982 plainly demonstrated that the efforts to introduce, by means of energy relations, a long-term stabilizing element into the relations between the Soviet Union and the Federal Republic cannot be attributed to any one governing coalition but rather are supported by all parties. The findings of a report delivered to the OECD (or IEA International Energy Agency) in November 1982 on the problems of supply security in energy cooperation with the Soviet Union, do not indicate that the new federal government is willing to curtail the previous policy. On the contrary there is a remarkable tendency to plead for a greater use of economic cooperation in order to ease the difficult situation surrounding security policy. Thus Richard von Weizäcker writes:

> If we succeed, in the field of science, technology, nutrition, environment, transportation, economics, energy and development policy, in gradually building cooperation, then in the end arms control and even unrestricted borders will also move into the realm of the possible.

And in the next paragraph he summarizes: "It is the task of us Germans to make Basket II the focal point of East-West relations."[17]

On this point, however, the Federal Republic's continuity stands relatively alone within the Western alliance, although many smaller West European states have hidden behind the Federal Republic in the past few years. Until the United States imposed sanctions in June 1982, Great Britain had shown little interest in economic relations with the Soviet Union, and France has had problems formulating a consistent policy. Thus, for the most part a bilateral conflict developed between the United States and the Federal Republic focusing primarily on the natural gas pipeline agreement.

The Special Case of Natural Gas

In 1970, due to the confluence of various factors, natural gas assumed a special role in East-West economic relations.
- With approximately 40 per cent of the world's exploitable reserves, the Soviet Union has at its disposal the greatest potential in natural gas of any region of the world.
- Projected future costs of exploitation are lower than for any other source of energy. While the marginal costs for exploiting oil in the Soviet Union increased seven-fold between 1970 and 1983, for natural gas they increased only two and a half times, and this from a lower base in 1970. Thus, for 1985, one must expect costs five times higher for additional oil exploitation than for the same number of calories from natural gas.[18]
- Since the oil crisis in 1973/74, there has been a world-wide attempt to substitute gas for oil. In the Federal Republic, for example, five percent of the energy used in 1970 came from natural gas; in 1981 it was 16 per cent.[19] Conversely, the share of energy supplied by oil dropped from 53 per cent to 45 per cent during the same period.
- Western Europe can be far more self sufficient in gas than in oil. In 1980 it produced 88 per cent of its own natural gas.[20] Even though there is a clear trend away from self sufficiency, Western Europe cannot reach the same level of dependence on imported gas as it has on oil.
- The transport of natural gas is far more dependent on pipelines than is any other source of energy. Inland distribution of natural gas presupposes a pipeline infrastructure, thus severely limiting the number of potential buyers. In international transport also, there is seldom an alternative to the pipeline-dependent, and therefore investment-intensive, form of transport. Eighty percent of international natural gas trade is carried over pipelines. It is economically infeasible for the Soviet Union, as a gas exporter, to transport liquid gas. Therefore the number of potential buyers who can pay in convertible currency is for all intents and purposes reduced to several West European countries where the pipeline infrastructure already exists. Naturally, the Federal Republic assumes a special role because it can hardly be bypassed as a country of transit and itself offers the largest market for natural gas.
- Since pipelines must be used for decades in order to amortize the original investment, once the decision to build a pipeline has been made, a virtual bilateral monopoly between supplier and purchaser is created. As the Soviet Union must provide the largest share of the investment for Soviet-West

European natural gas trade, the market position of the West European side is especially strong if the Soviet Union does not succeed in playing-off the West Europeans against one another.

Because trade in natural gas as a rule requires large investments, treaties must also be concluded which bind the contracting parties over large periods. During the course of the 1970s, the Soviet Union and the Federal Republic therefore signed four natural gas pipeline agreements, each of which also included a credit agreement.

The first natural gas pipeline agreement was signed in February 1970, even before the Moscow Treaty. This agreement officially documented the recommendment of cooperation in the field of energy following the pipeline embargo of 1962/63. In 1969 Thyssen and the Soviet Union had already signed a $ 25 million contract for the mutual production of pipelines,[21] but the first (1970) agreement between the governments of the Federal Republic and the Soviet Union became a model which has been used into the 1980s. The delivery of pipes from Mannesmann to the Soviet Union was covered by a 12-year credit guaranteed by a bank consortium under the leadership of the Deutsche Bank. Later the natural gas deliveries should make it possible for the Soviet Union to repay the credits. This model was again used in 1972 and 1974. Finally, in 1975, the IGAT II Project, with a volume of 11 billion cubic meters of natural gas, was negotiated. IGAT II was a triangular transaction with Iran supplying gas, the Soviet Union both buying and supplying, and the Federal Republic, as well as other West European countries, just buying. Iran cancelled the agreement in 1979.

For the above reasons and by the nature of natural gas, these pipeline transactions were the largest individual bilateral projects between the Soviet Union and the Federal Republic. The well-known natural gas pipeline agreement which caused such a heated discussion in the early 1980s once again completely altered the dimensions of East-West trade.

The Natural Gas Pipeline Agreement

The preliminary negotiations for this agreement began in 1978. At that time it was already becoming evident that Soviet oil production would not continue to grow at its normal rate so that the main source of Soviet hard currency earnings would no longer continue to expand. At the same time, new discoveries of natural gas suggested a shift from oil to gas. In addition, the North Star Project, which should have brought approximately 20 billion cubic meters of Soviet natural gas to the United States, Japan and France, failed in 1977. The Soviet Union was therefore extremely interested in expanding its "natural" market in Western Europe. Actual negotiations began in 1980, at a time when the Afghanistan invasion already overshadowed East-West relations.

Originally, the total volume of the agreement was projected at 40 billion cubic meters. However, due to both declining demand for energy and political considerations, the West reduced the deal to approximately 25 billion cubic meters. The volume of Western investment goods for the transport of the gas shrank by an even greater extent. The original $ 15 billion credit the Soviet Union had expected to receive was reduced to the same extent. Nevertheless, the deal became the largest East-West project in history, and this in spite of the fact that negotiations were carried out during a time of disenchantment with détente. In early 1980 the United States had tried to apply pressure on the West Europeans to keep them from signing the agreement. At the beginning of 1980 the American firm Armco also withdrew from the preliminary negotiations.[22]

Because of its size, the agreement became a symbol for the German (or European) -American difference of opinion over how to react to Soviet behavior in Afghanistan and Poland. The Americans had long since taken a different position on détente than the West Europeans. The 1974 Jackson-Vanik Amendment, and the ensuing failure of the Americans and Soviets to sign a trade agreement, was an early sign of American disenchantment with détente. American impotence (after Vietnam and Watergate) in dealing with the shifts of power in Africa (Angola 1975), Soviet human rights policy following the CSCE and finally, the permanent arms build-up in the Soviet Union all prepared the groundwork in the United States for a movement which turned the détente euphoria of the early 1970s into a deep mistrust of any policy of cooperation with the other superpower. Given the intensity of this reaction, Western Europe's interest in a continuation of détente, and some positive experiences with détente in Europe during the 1970s, carried little weight in the United States.

After the Carter Administration failed, in January 1980, in its first attempt to formulate a common embargo policy including the natural gas agreement, the Americans unfortunately began to argue that the transaction was directed against the Europeans' own best interests. In the first phase, the Americans emphasized the dependency argument. Regardless of the degree of sophistication of the European argument, that they had given special attention to the problem of dependence on natural gas imports and had neutralized it by counter-measures,[23] opponents of the transaction continued to use simplistic slogans and disregarded such assurances. In addition however, a foreign exchange argument was later introduced which claimed that the Soviet Union would accumulate a surplus of foreign currency through the sale of natural gas. The counter-argument stated that even according to American estimates,[24] the Soviet Union would be able to deliver less energy to the West in 1990 than it had in 1980, and that the United States could surely have nothing against Western Europe maintaining the 1980 import levels.

After the natural gas treaty was signed, the United States argued that the agreement had been poorly negotiated. Since, however, the other West European treaty partners had made their negotiations dependent on the outcome of the

Ruhrgas AG negotiations, Ruhrgas had effectively negotiated as a monopsonist, that is, from the best-possible market position. Finally, the United States offered the slave-labor argument, according to which political prisoners in the Soviet Union were being forced to work on the construction of the pipeline. But there was little solid evidence in support of this latter argument, and it also raised uncomfortable questions about the human rights practices of other international trading partners.

In all these cases it was clear that at issue was not the particular issue raised by the United States but the deep-felt cleft which had opened between the Americans and Western Europe after the Afghanistan crisis over how to deal with the Soviet Union.

During Chancellor Schmidt's visit to Moscow at the end of June and the beginning of July 1980, the starting shot was fired for the opening of negotiations on the natural gas agreement. This visit clearly demonstrated that the Federal Republic would continue to pursue its own self-interest, even at the risk of conflict with the United States. In the spring of 1981 the negotiations on the natural gas supplies were separated from the negotiations on the delivery of construction equipment and the extension of credit. In the summer of 1981, as a result of this decoupling, it appeared that the Federal Republic and the Soviet Union would soon reach an agreement on the natural gas transaction. The United States then made a last-ditch effort at the economic summit meeting in Ottawa in June 1981, to prevent an agreement by offering the prospect of American coal and Canadian natural gas as alternatives. This offer was not very well-prepared however, and thus not considered ready for serious consideration. As a result the Europeans flatly rejected it thereby further intensifying the Atlantic dissonance. On November 21, 1981, the natural gas contract was signed. It was not published, but all the paragraphs affecting either security or international economic interests were made public. The agreed-upon volumes and the pricing formula reflected a compromise between the supplier's need for long-term purchase and price security, and the purchaser's need for flexibility in adjusting to other energy prices and changes in demand.

The United States continued to fight the project even after the contract had been signed and during negotiations on construction equipment and credits. The June 1982 economic summit meeting in Versailles was a disappointment because of dissension over the credit agreements. Immediately following, on June 18, 1982, the American government imposed sanctions on firms in Western Europe which could be reached through their American licenses or capital and which were supplying equipment for the pipeline. The United State's European alliance partners bitterly contested these sanctions which they saw as a violation of their sovereignty. In addition, European subsidiaries of American companies suffered such a loss of confidence that the US government, in the form of Secretary of State Shultz, was very interested in ending these sanctions by reaching some kind of understanding with Western Europe. This was accomplished on November 13,

1982 without the Europeans making any concessions. They agreed only to conduct studies, prior to the economic summit meeting in Williamsburg, to analyze the security implications of economic relations with the Soviet Union. The energy study determined that, for the most part, the natural gas deal would have little adverse effect on the security policies of the West, but it did point out that Western Europe could experience a gap in self-sufficiency in the 1990s which, accompanied by an economically attractive Soviet offer, could lead to an increase in the share of Soviet gas in West European supplies. If such a situation is to be avoided it will therefore be necessary, in the next few years, to consider the question of a guarantee for Norwegian investments in the new Troll Field to ensure full security of supply.

The Future of Energy Relations

The economic scope for the development of energy relations between Western Europe and the Soviet Union or the whole CMEA is, as has already been shown, severely limited. The oil deliveries of the Soviet Union will shrink by at least a half during the course of the next decade and the demand for Soviet gas will not keep pace with the available supply, so that the Soviet Union will not be able to compensate for its loss of oil revenues.

There are new considerations in the field of coal exploitation and refining. In a certain sense the circumstances in the Soviet Union which would make sense of converting coal into a gas or liquid are unique. There are huge, largely unexploited coal basins, particularly in Kansk-Achinsk which would provide a supply of energy so low in specific calorific value that its transportation in a solid form seems relatively unprofitable. Furthermore, the necessary transport capacities for coal do not yet exist, so that the possibility of transportation in a liquid or gaseous form via pipelines is still an alternative.

Finally, there is a much greater demand for liquid fuels than for solid fuels particularly given stagnating oil production. The environmental effects of a coal-liquification plant would also be felt far less in the Soviet Union than in the West European urban areas where this technique is considered economically unjustifiable. Certainly it will take a long time to negotiate a comprehensive cooperation project, but in the long term the possibility of such an agreement should not be underestimated.

The possibilities for cooperation in the field of electricity have also by no means been exhausted. For various reasons efforts, in the mid-1970s, to cooperate in the construction of a nuclear plant in the Soviet Union and then to transfer a share of the electricity produced to Western Europe were unsuccessful. Here the problem of guaranteeing that the quality of the electricity supplied would remain constant, and the investment costs played a role. There is little reason to expect that a new attempt will be made during the 1980s to cooperate in the establishment of an electricity alliance.

Energy equipment will continue to be in great demand in the Soviet Union and Eastern Europe. The limits to cooperation here will be determined primarily by monetary limits on import capacities. There still exists a tendency in the import structure of the CMEA as a whole to import more raw materials and fewer investment goods, and there is no indication that this trend will soon be reversed.

The West Europeans are obviously determined to adhere to the basic philosophy of the CSCE process in spite of crises in Afghanistan, Poland, the arms build-up, and American pressure. This is politically far more important than the quantitative development of East-West relations in the field of energy. The long-term stability which was indicated not only in Basket II of the CSCE but also in the German-Soviet economic agreement of 1978 has proved itself both feasible and productive. The argument that only the Soviet Union profited from the natural gas transaction at the expense of the Atlantic Alliance because of disunity within the Alliance over East-West relations is hardly valid. The West has in fact kept open the option of either reviving the policy of détente, or reacting to Soviet behaviour which is detrimental to détente. The accusation that the Europeans have conducted all their economic relations as "business as usual" is also unjustified. It is in fact easier to find a direct correlation between disappointment in the détente process and a reduction in East-West trade by looking at figures for Western Europe's trade with the East than it is looking at U.S. figures.[25] The Western Alliance would only be damaged if it persistently followed the model of recent US policy in response to the Soviet Union. The evolution of the Atlantic debate since early 1983 indicates however that here too a détente could prove very productive.

Notes

1 Otto Wolff von Amerongen: Möglichkeiten und Grenzen der West-Ost-Zu-sammenarbeit, in: *Europäische Rundschau*, Vol. 2, No. 2, 1974, p. 18.
2 OECD: *Statistics of Foreign Trade*, Series C, 1980, Paris: 1982.
3 Compare Robert Campbell: *Soviet Technology Imports: The Gas Pipeline Case.* California Seminar on International Security and Foreign Policy. Working Paper, Nov. 6, 1980.
4 Compare Robert Campbell: 'Energy', in: Bergson, H.S. Levine: *The Soviet Economy: Toward the Year 2000*, London: 1983, (pp. 191-217), p. 192.
5 Sources: OECD: *World Energy Outlook*, Paris: 1982, pp. 177, 184 and 188; Joseph Licari: 'Linkages Between Soviet Energy and Growth Prospects for the 1980s', in: NATO Economics Directorate, *CMEA: Energy 1980-1990*, Brussels: 1981, pp. 265-276.
6 Compare John B. Hannigan and Carl H. McMillan: *The Soviet-West European Energy Relationship: Implications of the Shift from Oil to Gas*, Research Report 20, Carleton University, Ottawa: May 1983, pp. 37 ff; and Gregory Grossmann, Ronald L. Solberg: *The Soviet Union's Hard Currency Balance of Payments and Creditworthiness in 1985*, R-2956-USDP. The RAND Corporation, Santa Monica: April 1983.
7 Compare John B. Hannigan and Carl H. McMillan, loc. cit., p. 62; Jonathan P. Stern: *East European Energy and East-West Trade in Energy*, Energy Paper No. 2, Royal Institute of International Affairs, London: 1982, p. 70; OECD: *World Energy Outlook*, Paris: 1982, p. 192; Europäische Gemeinschaften: *Mitteilungen der Kommission an den Rat, Zur Erdgasversorgung der Gemeinschaft*, Brussels: Oct. 5, 1982; UN ECE: *Economic Bulletin for Europe*, Vol. 33, No. 2, June 1981.
8 According to the OECD, energy use in Western Europe during the 1980s will increase 17 per cent. Source: World Energy Outlook, Paris: 1982, p. 429.
9 Mitteilungen der Kommission an den Rat (see Note 7).
10 Jonathan Stern believes that Austrian natural gas purchases will increase from 2.9 billion cubic meters in 1980 to six billion cubic meters in 1990. Compare J. Stern, East European Energy (see Note 8), p. 70.
11 OECD: *World Energy Outlook*, Paris: 1982, p. 176.
12 See *Pravda*, April 17, 1971, p. 5.
13 CSCE Final Act, Basket II.
14 See Günther van Well, Belgrad 1977, Das KSZE-Folgetreffen und seine Bedeutung für den Entspannungsprozeß, *Europa Archiv*, Vol. 32, No. 18, 1977, p. 577.
15 See Deutscher Bundestag *Drucksache* 8/2143 from May 27, 1978.
16 See Presse- und Informationsamt der Bundesregierung, *Bulletin* No. 79 from July 3, 1980, p. 663.
17 *DIE ZEIT*, No. 40, from Sept. 30, 1983, p. 3.
18 See Wharton Econometric Forecasting Associates: *Centrally Planned Economies Current Analysis*, Washington, Oct. 27. 1982.

19 Compare Klaus Liesen: *Der internationale Erdgashandel und die Bedeutung des Erdgases für ein ressourcenarmes Land*. Essen: 1982, p. 24.

20 OECD, *World Energy Outlook*, Paris: 1982, p. 402.

21 Compare Angela Stent, *Soviet Energy and Western Europe*, The Washington Papers, No. 90, Washington: 1982, p. 23.

22 Compare Axel Lebahn, Die "Jamal-Erdgasleitung," UdSSR-Westeuropa im Ost-West Konflikt. *Außenpolitik* III/1983, p. 266.

23 For example short-term capacities to increase production in Holland and the Federal Republic, interruptible treaties with industrial buyers, expansion of the pipeline network, reduction of use through regulation.

24 The CIA expects that by 1990 the Soviet Union will no longer be able to deliver oil to the West. At the most, 25 million tons of oil equivalent (31 billion cubic meters of gas) would be available to compensate for the drop from 58 million tons of oil to zero tons. Compare Joseph Licari: 'Linkages, Between Soviet Energy and Growth Prospects for the 1980s,' in: NATO Economics Directorate: *CMEA: Energy 1980-1990*. Brussels: 1981, pp. 265-276.

25 Compare Friedemann Müller: 'Der Zusammenhang von politischem Klima und Wirtschaftskooperation', in: Friedemann Müller et al.: *Zur Frage von Wirtschaftssanktionen in den Ost-West-Beziehungen: Rahmenbedingungen und Modalitäten*. Baden-Baden: 1983.

7
Summary of Economic Relations
Peter Knirsch

Introduction

The general public, as well as policymakers and scholars, frequently sees a close correlation between East-West economic relations and political relations in this area. It is often felt that these economic relations significantly influence political relations between the two systems — both positively and negatively. Thus, on the one hand there is the view that more intensive economic relations should lead to improved East-West relations on the political front and that they can contribute significantly to détente and make conflict less likely, thereby reducing the danger of war.[1] On the other hand, East-West economic relations are also often viewed as an instrument which may be used by one side to influence political conduct on the other side. In this case, the measures considered can range all the way from economic aid to economic sanctions, even to "economic warfare."

If my assessment is correct, both sides often more or less take it for granted that East-West economic relations contribute to an easing of tensions between the two blocs. This can be seen in the Final Act of the CSCE, where the participating countries express their conviction that "their efforts to develop cooperation in the fields of trade, industry, science and technology, and the environment, as well as in other economic areas, strengthen peace and security in Europe and throughout the world."[2] By contrast, as far as we know only on the Western side has there been discussion of employing East-West relations as an instrument to help realize Western policy goals. In this context, for the most part encouraging, or imposing restrictions on, East-West economic relations is expected to have direct political effects on the other side.

This paper will attempt a reassessment of these views — which are of great importance for the current world political situation and are frequently the subject of controversial discussion — by examining the realities from an economic point of view.

The Findings of an Empirically-Based Assessment

The preceding contributions provide a fairly comprehensive assessment of the state of East-West economic relations during the first half of the 1980s. *Trade relations* undoubtedly represent the most significant aspect of these overall economic relations. In his contribution, Dr. Bethkenhagen gives little reason to view East-West trade as an element which could help maintain peace or provide opportunity to exert political influence. He emphasizes that the significance of trade relations for the political situation is frequently overestimated as well, and that the reverse is also true, i.e. that the significance of East-West political relations for trade relations between the two political systems may also be overemphasized.

He sees the main reason for the current stagnation of East-West trade relations as lying in the extreme imbalances which characterize this trade: As a result of rapid expansion during the first half of the 1970s it was necessary for the CMEA countries to reduce their burden of indebtedness by cutting back on imports from the West. Despite these measures, most of the smaller CMEA countries are still confronted with an extremely strained balance of payments situation. With regard to commodity structure, Bethkenhagen points out that crude oil and natural gas represent an exceedingly large share of Soviet exports to the West (a sort of "one-crop" export structure), which implies a correspondingly high degree of dependence on world market developments for the Soviet Union. In the case of Soviet and East European imports from the West, it is clear that agricultural products are claiming an increasingly large share of these imports. The observed decline in imports of finished goods from the West is important for any discussion about the opportunities of exerting political influence. In this connection, technology-intensive goods by no means play as important a role as is often assumed.

Dr. Bethkenhagen is quite justified in devoting a large part of his article to describing the economic significance of East-West trade. While trade with the East is clearly of only marginal importance for the Western trading partners, at least in macroeconomic terms, it is apparently not possible to state this as definitively with reference to the CMEA states. At least in the case of the smaller East European countries, imports from the West represent an important supplement to their own economic potential, and such imports are probably of rather great significance for all the CMEA nations when it is necessary for them to overcome shortages in the short and the medium term. However, in Bethkenhagen's opinion, the countries give absolute priority to the political system and external security. Consequently when Western policy toward trade with the East is restrictive, it is primarily the standard of living for the general population in the CMEA area which suffers from this dependence on Western imports. This could possibly lead to a hardening of domestic and foreign policy in the CMEA countries, which is not the objective of Western policymakers, as well as to closer ties between the smaller East European states and the Soviet Union.

The other contributions deal with more specific aspects of East-West economic relations. Of these, Dr. Schröder's essay on *financial relations* between East and West is of far-reaching significance because the accumulated debt of the CMEA states represents a heavy burden on East-West economic relations. Schröder emphasizes that Poland's grave financial problems have created an unjustifiably negative assessment of CMEA credit-worthiness, especially when the ability of CMEA countries to repay their debts is compared to that of most newly industrializing and developing nations. Schröder contends that, with the exception of Poland, the CMEA countries have shown their ability to come to terms with their problems as soon as they were — or presently are — experiencing more serious balance of payments difficulties. They did so by making fairly rapid changes in their economic policy, and for the most part by reducing their imports from the West. For political reasons he pleads for a more discriminating, and on the whole again more liberal, Western policy with regard to granting loans to CMEA countries.

The contributions by Dr. Nötzold concerning *technology transfer* and by Dr. Müller on *energy relations* deal with special aspects of East-West economic relations which have been the subject of intensive Western discussion on both sides of the Atlantic in recent years. Their discriminating and balanced presentations, carefully documented with details, come to the conclusion that the political significance of both these areas, and also their importance in terms of military strategy, is often overestimated by the West. Nötzold states that, in contrast to the view often held in the West, imports of technology by the CMEA countries represent only a relatively small share of their total imports from the West, and that this share has been declining in recent years, while that of food imports has been increasing. He also finds that imports of capital goods, which represent by far the most important form of technology transfer, by no means include only particularly advanced Western technology. He argues above all that there is no guarantee this foreign technology will be applied efficiently in the CMEA countries and provide economic benefits, let alone be developed further. The well-known difficulties of the Soviet economic system with regard to implementing technical progress also apply to employing imported technology. With a few exceptions Nötzold views technology transfer from West to East as being of relatively minor importance for the economies of the CMEA states, which naturally greatly reduces its significance as a starting point for exerting political influence.

Dr. Müller assigns a rather important role to energy relations, consisting of mainly Soviet oil and gas exports to Western Europe as part of East-West trade. If we compare this view with Bethkenhagen's earlier comments about the relatively slight overall significance of East-West trade, what Müller says must be qualified considerably, also with regard to energy deliveries by the Soviet Union. This is all the more true because Müller, on the basis of estimates made in the United States, believes that the share of West European energy supplied by the Soviet Union will drop considerably by 1990 as an expected decline in oil deliveries is not compensated by increased natural gas deliveries. In Müller's opinion, the pipelines-for-gas transactions which have been so controversial in the West attracted so much attention mainly because of their large-volume, long-term nature. Müller believes that the objections raised by opponents of these deals, especially the last and biggest deal in 1981, lack a rational foundation, both in economic terms (the argument that the Soviet Union would have an additional source of hard currency) and in political terms (the fear of excessive European dependence on Soviet deliveries).

The last contribution by Dr. Bolz examines *industrial cooperation* as a special form of East-West economic relations. Viewed in its narrower sense as referring strictly to cooperation between firms, industrial cooperation must be examined from a historical point of view. At the beginning of the 1970s, policymakers and economic experts had high hopes of expanding East-West economic relations by means of this qualitatively new form of direct cooperation on company level. Industrial cooperation projects were carried out in a few CMEA countries on a fairly limited basis. Actual experience, together with economic developments in the West, kept this form of cooperation from spreading further, and in recent years it has been in precisely those CMEA countries where this form of cooperation was employed more extensively (Hungary, Rumania, Poland) that a decrease in the number of cooperation agreements can be observed. So far industrial cooperation has only resulted in a very mild stimulation of East-West trade, and on the whole it is of only minor significance.

The Economic Significance of East-West Economic Relations

All these rather comprehensive and detailed empirical assessments come to the conclusion, with only slight differences in emphasis, that the significance of East-West economic relations for the national economies involved should not be overestimated. This clearly applies to the industrial nations of the West and to the Soviet Union, but is also generally true for the smaller CMEA countries if we take the limitations on formulating domestic and economic policy into account. These studies come to the conclusion that no strong global dependencies exist between East and West. There is some degree of dependence on both sides, but the interdependence which results is only of limited significance. Basically the East European countries tend to be more dependent on the West, due to the frequent shortages which occur on East Europe's domestic markets. This is clearly the case when one considers the level of import dependency on each side. At the very worst Western economies would experience temporary adjustment difficulties but are in a position to obtain alternative Western sources of supply for most, usually all, of their former imports from the East. If we accept the expertise presented in the preceding contributions, this possibility of substitution also applies to the only strategically sensitive area of energy imports.

For Eastern Europe imports from the West are not only more important in terms of overall foreign trade, but it is also much more difficult for these countries to find adequate substitutes. It is not possible to arrange alternative sources of supply in the CMEA, the "socialist world market," because the other countries concerned are usually experiencing equally significant shortages of the same goods. The lack of hard currency also precludes the possibility of substituting imports from third countries for those that previously came from the West. If East-West economic relations were interrupted, the countries on the Eastern side could not expect to find substitutes for what they formerly imported from the West. With the current pattern of trade such imports consist mainly of food-stuffs and capital goods, but also include considerable quantities of raw materials and semifinished products.

The fact that these products cannot be obtained elsewhere[3] could be inter-preted as representing a fairly significant degree of dependence. There is much to be said for the assumption that the resulting shortages would generally be passed on to the population in the form of a lowered standard of living, so that the area of security is hardly affected at all. There is no denying that central planning as the system of economic control in these countries makes it possible to take such steps fairly directly and quickly. Whether or not it is feasible to actually imple-ment such measures depends on how one assesses the internal political stability of the various CMEA countries. Since such an extensive "breakdown" would be accompanied by dramatically worsened political relations between East and West, it is necessary to consider not only the rigidity of the system of political control but also the possibility that patriotic feelings may be aroused. One would assume that the greater dependence of the CMEA states on imports from the West is largely, perhaps even completely, compensated for by the greater economic and domestic control it is possible to maintain in these countries.

This mutual interdependence of both sides on imports,[4] which is slight in terms of actual import volume or is limited by political factors, looks quite different when viewed from the export side. In the first place, one should proceed from the assumption that the CMEA states have no autonomous interest in exporting to the West. On the contrary, if we leave aside certain adjustment problems, the domestic market situation, which is clearly characterized by demand for almost all goods that exceeds available supplies, would be less strained. As a rule, goods are only exported to the West in order to earn the foreign currency needed to pay for necessary imports from the West.

In the West the situation is different. In overall economic terms exports to Eastern Europe are of little importance. In certain sectors however they are definitely of significance in maintaining income, such as for US grain exporters or for making use of existing capacity and thereby preserving jobs, as in Western European steel and machine-tool industries, especially in the Federal Republic of Germany. In the event of a "breakdown", the limited macroeconomic impact of these exports makes it economically and politically feasible to compensate those affected for their export losses. Furthermore, the effect that exports to the East have on employment is often overestimated (Bethkenhagen). At any rate, in view of the West's considerably greater economic potential and the relatively small volume of exports to the East, it does seem unlikely that this dependence would have a very strong influence on Western policy toward Eastern Europe.

East-West Economic Relations and the Process of Détente

The limited significance of East-West economic relations for national economies on both sides makes it seem doubtful from the outset that they are of fundamental significance for the political process of détente.[5] The mutual economic dependence between East and West is not as great as is often assumed. To put it concretely, this means that the need to maintain or develop these economic relations is not so great that it takes precedence over political antagonisms.

This fundamental statement must however be understood in perspective. Here it is understood to mean that there is no reason to assume East-West economic relations automatically result in improved political relations between these two power blocs. This clearly applies to the current state of East-West economic relations, because both sides obviously did not regard them as important enough to keep the political relations between East and West from worsening between 1980 and 1983.

However, this view fails to take into account the possibility that this worsening of relations could have been much more dramatic, had there been no concern about preserving East-West economic relations. Even though there is no direct proof, there is a great deal to be said for the assumption that East-West economic relations are among those factors which help moderate and stabilize East-West political relations, despite the clear priority given to political considerations. Indeed, in concrete terms, such economic relations probably represent the most important of these stabilizing factors. As naive as it may seem when we look back at history to expect East-West economic relations to overcome political differences, it is all the more important not to underestimate their influence and to realize that they are included in political calculations on both sides and thereby do contribute to maintaining peaceful relations. Their contribution is, of course, only limited and corresponds to their limited importance.

The concrete significance of the limited role played by East-West economic relations in the overall relationship apparently depends to a large extent on the state of East-West political relations. The assumption often made on this issue is questionable, namely that the political significance of East-West economic relations is particularly great during a period of political détente. During such a phase, it is certainly easier to emphasize the positive aspects of these economic relations, and they may provide support for efforts to ease tensions. If we consider the role played by East-West economic relations in maintaining world peace however, the limited importance of East-West economic relations can increase when political relations are poor. This is the very time at which their ability to keep conflicts from expanding can be of great, and in some cases even of very great, importance. Furthermore, when political relations between East and West are curtailed sharply, economic relations, as a more stable link between the antagonistic blocs, can attain a political importance far beyond their actual economic significance.

For the purposes of this discussion it will be assumed that, at the present time, economic relations between East and West can no longer be negatively affected by worsened political relations as they were at the beginning of the 1950s. One reason for this is that, despite what we have said about their limited importance, economic relations have become much more intense. Both sides would consider it disadvantageous to curtail them sharply and would try to avoid this if at all possible. In contrast to the late 1940s however, it is no longer possible simply to speak of "antagonistic blocs". East-West antagonism exists primarily between the two major powers, the Soviet Union and the United States of America. Immediately after World War II, the predominance of these two powers in their respective spheres of influence was uncontested. During the three to four decades since then, the economic and political significance of their smaller allies has grown. This is obviously true for the West European industrial states and Japan, with all that it implies for their relations to the United States. It also applies, though perhaps not as noticeably due to differences in publication practices, to most of the Warsaw Pact and CMEA countries in Eastern and Southeastern Europe who have close ties to the Soviet Union.

In contrast to both great powers, these smaller nations on both sides are, due to their greater dependence on foreign trade, comparatively more interested in continuing and expanding East-West economic relations with as little interference as possible. Even if they identify with the basic political stands taken by the great power in their alliance, they still try as much as possible to avoid confrontation that negatively affects their economic relations. In the 1980s, the greater importance of these countries within their respective alliances now gives them many more opportunities to continue trading than they had during the "cold war" of the 1950s. This situation contributes to continued economic relations with little change even during periods of political tension.

If we accept the primacy of political concerns, then it seems that East-West economic relations are capable of promoting the process of détente, but that they are hardly able to establish it in the first place. They are probably also not important enough to prevent serious disturbances in the détente process, and certainly cannot eliminate the danger of a major conflict between the two systems. It does still seem possible that they might set limits to such disturbances and possibly raise the threshold for conflict. However, at the present time their most important function is probably to serve as a stabilizing factor in the face of East-West political tensions, to ensure a minimum degree of contact between the two sides, including opportunities for political contacts,[6] and thereby to help preserve the foundation for more favorable political relations between East and West in the future.

East-West Economic Relations as an Instrument of Policy

Both in the past and the present there have been, and still are, rather frequent attempts to influence the political conduct of a country or group of countries by measures intended to affect their external economic relations. Such attempts to exert influence may be positive as in the form of economic aid, reduction of trade barriers, etc., or negative as in the form of economic blockades which completely break off trade relations, possibly also with third countries, or a partial embargo, or establishing trade barriers, etc. Because of the nature of such measures, they can only be imposed by the side which has more economic power. If the measures are expected to have negative effects, it is assumed that the country targeted is in a state of one-sided economic dependence on the world economy as a whole or on the trading partner imposing the sanctions.

In considering this question it may be useful to look more closely at these elementary prerequisites for economic intervention. In the case of East-West economic relations, only the economically more powerful side, i.e. the Western industrial nations under the leadership of the United States, have tried to use economic intervention as an instrument to achieve political aims. Today it is easy to forget that, during the 1960s and 1970s, intervention by Western governments was aimed primarily at promoting trade. This took the form of concluding trade agreements, reducing quantitative restrictions and other trade barriers, and government backing for CMEA credit by means of subsidies and loan guarantees. However, both the public and the academic world are more aware of the restraints on trade imposed by the West. The course of events has always followed a rather similar pattern. Political moves by the Soviet Union such as on the Berlin blockade, in Angola, with the invasion of Afghanistan, and Soviet actions to counteract tendencies toward liberalization in Poland, were considered by the United States as clear indications of expansionist tendencies. Military confrontation or even the threat of war were inconceivable as rational policy instruments, and political countermeasures such as those possible within the framework of the United Nations could not be expected to have much, if any, real effect. Many policymakers therefore viewed economic sanctions as the only possible countermeasures they had at their disposal.

In this case Western sanctions against East-West trade represented, on the one hand, a direct reaction to concrete political actions by the Soviet Union. On the other hand, Western willingness to impose such sanctions also stemmed from the more general fear of many Western policymakers, and among the public at large, that the threat posed by the Soviet Union was of a more fundamental nature. According to this view, the political and ideological differences between the systems, which neither side denies, represent the basis for a threat which must be confronted in all areas. In the area of economics this means avoiding any strengthening of the "enemy" through foreign trade. When carried to its extreme, this approach leads to the conclusion that the Western industrial nations should not conduct any trade at all with socialist nations.

Clearly at least the second, more extreme, point of view is not completely rational. The fear of a Soviet threat may still be understandable, or at least cannot be disproved. However, internal developments in the Soviet Union and in the Soviet system of alliances make it seem likely that its original expansionist tendencies and interest in world revolution no longer play as significant a role, if any at all. The fear of the Soviet threat is irrational as far as the comparative strength of East and West is concerned, at least in terms of economic potential, where Western superiority is very clear and very great.[7] In view of this fact, the fear that only the socialist countries might be strengthened as a result of East-West trade is probably also exaggerated and illogical. It is exaggerated because the huge difference in potential between the two blocs could only be reduced over a very long period of time, if at all, given the relatively small volume of East-West trade. It is illogical because this trade certainly does not result in one-sided advantages for the East, but rather also contributes to the prosperity of national economies in the West. On the contrary, the generally poor market position of the CMEA countries in East-West trade[8] suggests that the West probably derives relatively greater advantages.

As for Western sanctions as a reaction to concrete Soviet moves, the only question that can really be asked is whether Western policy in such cases is effective and likely to be successful. Here one is essentially concerned with embargo measures to block Western supplies of so-called "strategic goods." Past experience has shown that these sanctions were unpleasant for the Soviet Union, which was the target of most of the measures, in view of its already difficult economic situation, but these sanctions by no means led to a change in the Soviet Union's political conduct. One reason is because these sanctions were of only limited effectiveness. Lack of unity in the West or deliveries routed through third countries usually made it possible to obtain embargoed goods anyway, though they may have been more expensive. There is also the basic fact that East-West economic relations are relatively insignificant in terms of trade volume, which is particularly true for the Soviet Union, and this greatly limits the effectiveness of any such measures.

In connection with negative sanctions there is also discussion in many quarters about whether using the "carrot and stick" approach with the West offering trade benefits would be more likely to result in desirable political response from the Soviet Union. As is well known, this approach has brought about some fairly significant humanitarian improvements in relations between the two German states during the past decades. However, it does not seem very realistic to apply this to the entire complex of East-West economic relations. The relative insignificance of East-West economic relations for the Soviet Union, but also for all CMEA states, probably means any modest economic concessions by the West are not likely to be very effective either. But, in view of the profound differences between the two systems, there is no reason to expect any more extensive Western "economic aid" to the socialist countries. Despite their considerable economic problems, the CMEA nations would probably refuse to accept such aid, as they already rejected the Marshall Plan in 1947, because of what the West wanted in return and because they fear becoming dependent on the West (both economically and politically). On the Western side the argument against strengthening the enemy would be much more convincing and justifiable than in the case of normal East-West trade. Only in very special cases may it be possible for the West to "buy" limited political concessions from the East in return for certain goods and services.

On the whole, the experience gained so far in East-West economic relations indicates that these relations are not very suitable for use as instruments of Western policy; they do not function well for blackmail or bribery, because the gap between the two systems is simply too great compared to the significance of the economic relations. It would be a good idea for policymakers on both sides to put East-West economic relations in proper perspective and no longer burden them with damaging and exaggerated hopes and expectations.

The Influence of Politics on East-West Economic Relations

To warn about political damage to East-West economic relations is to touch upon the question of how much East-West economic relations are affected by political factors.[9] There would appear to be no way of denying the influence exerted by political factors. For example the sharp decline in economic relations between 1949 and 1955 can probably only be explained by the desolate state of East-West relations during the "Cold War." However, history also shows that political factors have not always played a decisive role. East-West economic relations had already begun to improve in the 1960s, before both sides became proponents of détente. Indeed some very unpleasant political incidents, such as Kruschev's Berlin ultimatum of 1959, the construction of the Berlin wall in 1961, and the Soviet invasion of Czechoslovakia, all occurred during a period when East-West trade was expanding. Conversely, East-West economic relations were already beginning to stagnate in 1975 following the European Security Conference, at a time when the concept of détente still permeated the political climate.

The examples cited above should at least indicate that it is not always easy to predict how economic and political factors will influence each other. The common assumption that East-West economic relations are largely or even totally determined by political factors is certainly not tenable. At the present time (1983) however, there are frequent attempts to explain the problems which have arisen in East-West economic relations in precisely this way. In particular, Eastern Europe is seen as attaching a great deal of importance to the American sanctions. But this line of reasoning fails to take proper account of the fact that current economic conditions are themselves quite unfavorable. The extremely poor economic situation in the West, at least until the second half of 1983, the extensive indebtedness of the CMEA countries with the complicated debt restructuring problems of Poland and Rumania, which almost exclude the granting of any further credit, and the difficult economic situation in all the CMEA states are more than sufficient to explain the poor state of East-West economic relations. It could be that the unfavorable political climate contributes to these unsatisfactory relations, but in reality it cannot make things much worse than they already are.

It now appears that in the summer of 1984, when political relations between East and West are at a low point, things will be improving somewhat for East-West economic relations, although perhaps in the rather distant future. The economic situation in the Western industrial nations, especially in the United States, is showing clear signs of improvement, which will probably have an effect on the export opportunities of the CMEA countries as well. In addition, the problem of CMEA debt is now viewed in a much more positive light than it was even a year ago. Western banks have now been confronted with much greater debt problems in Latin America and many developing countries. Except for Poland, the East European debtor countries, with their policy of achieving an active balance of trade at any cost, are now again considered to be fairly acceptable clients, who will probably have access to larger credits in the foreseeable future. It is too early to know whether the individual CMEA countries will try to obtain new credits, but it no longer seems out of the question that this type of transaction could, in principle, again stimulate East-West economic relations.

This newest development also gives the impression that East-West economic relations are determined more by economic than by political factors. In the future it would probably be best for economic relations if policymakers did not overestimate their significance, if they realized that such relations are too weak to serve as active instruments of policy, but that they nevertheless play an indispensable stabilizing role in overall relations between East and West.

Notes

1 Ideas like these were particularly widespread at the beginning of the 1970s and were expressed most concisely in catchphrases such as "Wandel durch Handel" (change through trade) or "Annäherung durch Handel" (coming closer through trade).

2 "Schlußakte der Konferenz über Sicherheit und Zusammenarbeit in Europa vom 1. August 1975," *Bulletin des Presse- und Informationsamtes der Bundesregierung* (August 15, 1975), No. 102, pp. 975-980. English translation based on *Phraseologie der KSZE-Schlußakte* (Phraseology of the Final Act of the CSCE), compiled by the Translating and Interpreting Service of the Foreign Ministry (Bonn: 1977).

3 This is definitely true in the short run, because one important reason these products are imported from the West is that they are not available in the CMEA area, at least not in sufficient quantities. Even in the short run, such a "breakdown" provides some relief for domestic markets in the CMEA to the extent that what had previously been exported to the West now remains in the country and increases domestic supplies — although naturally it is probably *not* the formerly imported products which are now more readily available. In the longer run (in the case of food imports it will probably be quite a long time), changes in domestic production structure can be expected to help replace part of what was formerly imported from the West.

4 For the first development of this concept of politically limited interdependence between East and West see Peter Knirsch, 'Interdependence in East-West Economic Relations,' in Organization for Economic Cooperation and Development, *From Marshall Plan to Global Interdependence* (Paris: OECD, 1978), p. 161 f.

5 The significance of economic relations for détente is heavily emphasized by the Soviets. Cf. Georgij Arbatov, W. Oltmans, Der sowjetische Standpunkt (The Soviet Viewpoint) (Munich: 1981), p. 193 ff.

6 To a certain extent, East-West economic relations have paved the way for efforts to improve political relations in the past as well. Sometimes this was done in a very direct manner, as when Western businessmen and East European economic functionaries made arrangements for political contacts. During the 1960s, for example, this role was attributed to the head of the Krupp company in West Germany, Beitz, and to the chairman of the Soviet Union's State Committee for Science and Technology, Gvishiani.

7 As difficult as it is to make international comparisons of gross national products, it can be assumed that Soviet GNP amounts to between 50 % and 60 % of United States GNP. On the whole, the Soviet Union and the smaller European CMEA countries have gross national products equal to about 20 - 25 % of GNP in the more important OECD nations. See The World Bank, ed., *World Development Report 1981* (New York: 1981), p. 131 f; National Foreign Assessment Center, ed., *Handbook of Economic Statistics 1981* (Washington: 1980), p. 10 f.

8 This is due in part to the ponderousness of their foreign trade organisations,

but most importantly to the fact that the quality and appearance of their export production often falls short of international standards, as well as to inadequate marketing and service.

9   For a more detailed and systematic discussion of how political and economic factors interact, see my contribution: Peter Knirsch, 'Political and Economic Determinants of East-West Economic Relations,' in *Acta Oeconomica* (Budapest: forthcoming).

PART III

WESTERN POLICIES

8
The Federal Republic of Germany

Angela E. Stent

Introduction

The Federal Republic of Germany's economic relations with Eastern Europe and the Soviet Union have been determined by its special geographical and political place in Europe. One half of a divided nation, West Germany depends on the United States for its security and on the USSR for its continued relationship with the German Democratic Republic. This complex and at times contradictory political framework has shaped the development of Germany's postwar economic contacts with a region with which it had close historical trade ties, closer than those of any other West European nation. Today's CMEA nations are Germany's traditional trading partners, and this legacy of economic interdependence has predisposed Bonn toward encouraging economic relations with the East for purely economic reasons. Yet political factors — particularly the need to comply with U.S. policy — for twenty years limited the degree to which Bonn could pursue these commercial ties.

Germany has, since 1949, been more beholden to United States policy on East-West economic relations than have its European partners because of its political dependence on Washington; yet at the same time, it has a greater political stake in these economic ties than do any of its allies because of the division of Germany and the presence of ethnic Germans in most CMEA nations. More than any other Western nation, Germany has sought to use its economic ties with CMEA for political purposes, and has to some degree succeeded. While Bonn has eschewed the use of economic sanctions since 1969, it continues to believe in the efficacy of trade incentives to elicit certain political concessions in the humanitarian field. Moreover, it has become clear since the fall of the Social Democrat/Free Democrat coalition government that the Christian Democrats share their predecessors' commitment to a stable East-West economic relationship. A positive political and economic attitude toward Osthandel (trade with the East) has been the hallmark of continuity in German policy over the last fifteen years. This policy has been productive for Germany's Ostpolitik (policy towards the East), but has become increasingly problematic in Bonn's relations with Washington.

Germany has for centuries been trading with Russia and Eastern Europe. These economic relations have flourished even in times of tense political contacts, because neither side was willing to jeopardize its economic gains. Thus, history suggests no automatic correlation between economic and political relations. After the end of the war, however, the Western part of Germany was cut off from its traditional economic hinterland and was forced to reorient its trade almost exclusively toward the West. During the Cold War era, Chancellor Adenauer stressed Westpolitik over Ostpolitik, and tailored his policy on economic relations with the East to fit American policy. Thus, the German government took a restrictive view of trade with the East, and discouraged it actively until 1963. It also tied economic relations with Moscow specifically to issues such as the status of Berlin and to reunification. It was the only West European nation to comply with the U.S.-imposed NATO ban on the export of large-diameter pipe to the USSR during the 1962-63 pipe embargo.[1] Moreover, until 1964, it followed a restrictive policy on credits for the East.[2] When it became clear that its West European competitors were gaining the lion's share of the business with the East, and after the retirement of Adenauer, the German government relaxed its East-West trade and credit policy and began to use it as a political incentive for Eastern Europe to develop somewhat more independent ties with Bonn.

Before the reorientation and liberalization of German Osthandel in the mid-1960s, there was no domestic consensus on economic relations with the East. The CDU-CSU, although it represented business interests, felt constrained, for political reasons, to follow the American line in restricting trade with communist countries. The SPD and most of the FDP favored encouraging commercial ties with the East for political and economic reasons. Within the government, the Foreign Ministry, was more opposed to East-West trade than was the Economics Ministry, and there were periodic bureaucratic rivalries over who determined East-West commercial policy. All this changed with the advent of the SPD-FDP government in 1969.

The Brandt-Scheel government ushered in a new era in Bonn's economic relations with the East, introducing a policy that has been followed by all succeeding governments. Some have argued that Brandt pursued his new Ostpolitik partly under pressure from business interests, as a precondition for increasing economic ties with CMEA.[3] Others see the growth in economic relations as a welcome consequence, although not a determinant, of the 1969-72 rapprochement with the Soviet Union and Eastern Europe.[4] Brandt altered Germany's Ostpolitik and Westpolitik, and as part of his new détente policy, he rejected the use of economic sanctions, since these had never brought the Federal Republic any political benefits from the East. He was willing to use trade as a political incentive; indeed the first Soviet-German gas-pipe agreement of 1970, with substantial Hermes government-backed credit guarantees, was partly concluded to encourage the USSR to reach agreement with Germany during the difficult negotiations preceding the Renunciation of Force Treaty.[5] It must also be remembered that at this juncture, American policy under Nixon and Kissinger followed a similar line in that it sought to use commercial ties as an incentive toward modifying Soviet behavior.[6]

Brandt's new policy on East-West economic ties had three main components. He encouraged the growth of German economic ties with the East, including long-term trade agreements with all CMEA nations and the granting of government-backed credit guarantees. Henceforth a consensus developed that commercial ties with the East were a stabilizing factor for the German economy. Secondly, he eschewed the use of sanctions as a form of political linkage. Henceforth positive, not negative linkage was to prevail. Thirdly, he viewed economic relations with the East as a part of Germany's overall rapprochement with the CMEA nations — a détente that was designed to facilitate closer ties between West and East Germany. Thus, economics and politics were supposed to reinforce each other. This view of German economic ties with CMEA was multilateralized in the Helsinki Final Act of the Conference on Security and Cooperation in Europe, where Baskets One, Two and Three were linked. Another feature of the new Osthandelspolitik (policy on trade with the East) was that there was a domestic consensus on this issue. Despite the CDU-CSU's opposition to the treaties with the East, there was no significant opposition to the policy of encouraging greater economic ties with CMEA by the mid-1970s.

East-West Commercial Policy under Schmidt and Genscher

Economic Interests. Since 1975, Germany's trade with CMEA (excluding the GDR) has increased from DM 24 billion to DM 37 billion (see Table One). In 1975, trade with CMEA represented 7.2 per cent of exports and 4.3 per cent of imports; in 1982, the figures were 4.3 per cent and 5.1 per cent respectively (Table One). Although trade with CMEA forms a rather small percentage of total German foreign trade, it is disproportionately important for certain sectors of the German economy. For instance, 25 per cent of steel pipe, 20 per cent of sheet iron and 17 per cent of machine-tools and rolling mill plant exports go to CMEA. On the import side, 25 per cent of gas and coal imports, 13 per cent of platinum, 56 per cent of palladium and 25 per cent of asbestos come from the East.[7] German exports to CMEA are mainly of finished goods, whereas its imports are largely of raw materials and industrial materials (see Tables Two and Three). There has, thus been a steady expansion of German economic relations with the East since 1974. In 1981, the USSR accounted for 43.4 per cent of Germany's trade with the East, and the next most important country was Hungary, with a share of 12 per cent (Figure 1).

The German economic interest in commercial relations with the CMEA nations derives both from the export and the import side. In the early Schmidt-Genscher years, the economic situation within the Federal Republic was stronger than it is today and, as a trade-dependent economy, Germany has always been vitally interested in a healthy export sector. As the problems with the steel industry grew toward the end of the 1970s, orders from CMEA became even more important. In 1976, during the election campaign, the SPD printed a political advertisement claiming that Osthandel provided 300,000 jobs for people, and that economic relations with the East were vital for Germany's continued economic health. By the late 1970s, for instance, Mannesmann was exporting 60 per cent of its production of large-diameter pipe to the USSR. Experts now claim that trade with the USSR employs 92,000 people, but that one should not exaggerate the overall employment effects.[8] Germany has a long-term interest in stable export markets in the East and would be loath to jeopardize them.

The Schmidt-Genscher government gave an institutional boost to economic ties with the USSR when Brezhnev visited Germany in 1978. The two sides signed a 25-year Agreement on Long-Term Cooperation (since the European Community forbids its members to conclude bilateral trade treaties with CMEA nations, this was called a cooperation and not a trade agreement) which was a broad agreement covering a variety of areas. The accord stressed bilateral cooperation in fields such as energy and marketing, and commited both sides to grant medium and long-term credits.[9] Although this was only a framework agreement, it encouraged the development of general economic ties. Interestingly enough, a spokesman for Schmidt described this treaty as "a political act without parallel in the recent history of the world."[10]

The expansion of East-West economic relations took place without subsidized credits. Unlike its E.C. partners, Germany does not officially subsidize rates of interest on credits to CMEA nations. The subject was debated within the government before Brandt resigned, but opposition to subsidies prevailed. The Germans claim that this puts them at a competitive disadvantage vis-à-vis their European competitors. Other West European nations claim that they remain at a disadvantage because of the strength of the Deutschmark. The United States, while chastizing Britain, France and Italy for subsidizing credits, criticizes the German government for Hermes guarantees. According to Washington, Hermes guarantees represent an indirect subsidy, because they make the cost of guarantees cheaper than they would be on the open market. The German government disagrees, claiming that private credit guarantees would be so expensive as to be unaffordable. The debates continue, but Germany's credit policy does not so far appear to have put it at a commercial disadvantage in comparison to its European competitors.

Since the 1973 Middle East War and the ensuing energy crisis, Germany has become increasingly interested in the import side of East-West economic relations. Germany lacks indigenous energy resources, and seeks to diversify its sources of energy. It supplies 60 per cent of its energy demand from imports, and will continue to be dependent on these imports. The Soviet Union, which is the world's largest producer of oil, its second most important oil exporter, and possesses the world's largest natural gas reserves, appears a promising and reliable supplier of energy.

The most promising area of East-West cooperation since 1975 has been the energy field. As economic problems in Eastern and Western Europe grew, this field — where compensation agreements predominate — became the most attractive. Germany could sell its superior steel products in return for Soviet gas, and financing was made easier by the fact that this was partly a compensation deal. The first triangular gas-pipe deal was signed in 1970, the second in 1972, the third in 1974 and the fourth in 1975. However, this last one involved Iran, and was torpedoed when the Shah fell in 1979.[11] The biggest deal, however, was the Urengoy natural gas pipeline, which will be discussed below. The agreement was of considerable long-term economic importance to Germany, but its political significance as a source of West-West tension arguably overshadowed its immediate East-West economic significance, and contributed to the Schmidt government's difficulties with the United States.

Foreign Policy Interests: Ostpolitik vs. Westpolitik. Before détente, Germany, like the United States, accepted that there was a conflict between welfare and security interests in its economic ties with CMEA. Whereas concern for economic welfare suggested promoting commercial relations with Eastern Europe and the USSR, security considerations dictated a restrictive policy, since trade was presumed to strengthen the Soviet economy. Indeed, when President Kennedy decided to liberalize aspects of U.S. policy and export grain to the Soviets in 1963, Adenauer complained that this was wrong, because the exports fortified the Soviet economy and were not tied to specific political concessions.[12] Since 1969, however, the German view has changed. The German government has stressed that economic relations with CMEA are not a one-way street, but mutually beneficial.[13] Instead of threatening German security by building up the Soviet antagonist, they strengthen security by providing employment and contributing to economic stability. There is, from the German point of view, no contradiction between welfare and security interests any more, because the USSR and Eastern Europe have signed treaties with the Federal Republic that have stabilized the political situation in Europe, and thus Germany can enjoy the economic fruits of commercial relations without being unduly concerned about the danger of strengthening a potential enemy. This view is shared by Germany's E.C. partners, who also reject the notion of a conflict between welfare and security interests.

Until the mid-1970s, the official U.S. view was roughly concordant with that of Germany. Once Nixon and Kissinger came into office, they revised traditional American views of the security dangers of East-West exports and were more willing to accept their welfare benefits. The American view has, however, changed since the beginning of the disillusionment with détente in 1975. Today, American policy stresses traditional concerns: that all non-agricultural exports to the East, especially to the USSR, represent a security threat because they build up the Soviet economy and make Moscow a more formidable military antagonist. German policy has, however, not changed. It has remained consistent, and thus Bonn has increasingly come into conflict with Washington over the politics of East-West trade. Germany claims that the economic benefits of East-West exports are arguably equal to, if not perhaps greater than, the benefits that CMEA nations gain from imports from Germany. On the import side, the German government has perhaps been more willing to consider American arguments — namely that dependence on raw materials, especially Soviet energy, could represent security risk, but has stressed that partial dependence on the Soviets is preferable from a security perspective to almost total dependence on unpredictable OPEC nations. Apart from agreement that exports that have direct military application must be controlled in CoCom, Germany believes that the welfare benefits of commercial ties with CMEA far outweigh potential security threats.

East-West economic ties have, therefore, become a major problem in German relations with the United States, whereas they have become a normal and desirable element of German Ostpolitik. One cannot discuss the foreign policy implications of German Osthandel without examining its two dimensions — its impact on Bonn's ties with the USSR and Eastern Europe, and its impact on Bonn's relations with Washington. The U.S. has determined a security agenda for East-West commercial ties, seeking to restrict the export of civilian high technology, that none of its European partners share. However, given Germany's special place in the Western alliance, it is required to take the U.S. position into account more than France or even Britain.

What have been the political benefits from East-West commercial ties? These have been tangible in the humanitarian field, and have brought a considerable easing of travel restrictions and a liberalization of emigration policies from Eastern Europe and the USSR. The German government learned in the 1950s and 1960s that the USSR would not make major political concessions on issues such as Berlin or the nature of its control over the GDR in response to restrictive economic measures. However, Bonn has come to believe that trade incentives, when judiciously offered, can be productive on issues that are not considered of vital importance to the USSR and Eastern Europe. The Germans consider that economic and political relations reinforce each other and even that, in times of political strain, economic relations are one channel of cooperation that can exist even when other aspects of the relationship are strained.[14] Since the USSR has traditionally sought to separate its economic and political relations with Western countries and to avoid being the object of Western linkage, in order to maximize the benefits of these economic ties, it too has sought to sustain the economic relationship with the Federal Republic during times of political tension. For instance, the German-Soviet Economic Commission met in November 1983 just before the U.S. was scheduled to deploy the first Pershing missiles in Germany. New agreements were signed, despite differences over the stationing of U.S. missiles.

Beyond this general level of mutually reinforcing political and economic levels, there have been some concrete political payoffs from trade with the USSR. Perhaps the most tangible one has been the increased emigration of ethnic German from the USSR. However, although the numbers rose to a high of 10,000 per year in 1976 they fell to 2000 in 1982. It appears that emigration may be as much determined by Soviet domestic politics as by political relations with Germany. Of far greater importance, although one cannot measure it, are the indirect benefits that Bonn has gained from its commercial relations with the USSR — namely Moscow's willingness to stabilize the situation in Berlin and its agreement to permit closer intra-German ties. The USSR has been willing to permit a rapprochement between the GDR and the Federal Republic because it has wanted to maintain Bonn's interest in détente, irrespective of American policy. Clearly, the economic aspects of German-Soviet ties have served as an incentive to Moscow to encourage closer ties between the two Germanies, although they are not the only factor influencing Soviet policy. Indeed, the prospect of continued economic relations made the Kremlin reluctant to jeopardize the state of intra-German contacts even after new U.S. missiles were deployed. The Federal Republic's political stake in its economic ties with the USSR is therefore largely determined by its commitment to a rapprochement with East Germany.

Bonn may have gained more direct political benefits from its economic relationship with the other CMEA members. Emigration of ethnic Germans from Poland, Rumania, and Czechoslovakia continues, although the figures for Poland have declined from 36,000 in 1979 to 30,000 in 1982. Moreover, it became increasingly clear in the late 1970s that as a result of détente — both bilateral German relations with individual Eastern European nations and the multilateral CSCE process — Eastern Europe was able to use its increasing economic interdependence with Western Europe to assert a greater degree of independence from Moscow. The most striking case was undoubtably Poland, and Schmidt's personal friendship with Polish leader Gierek undoubtedly reinforced the German government's conviction that closer economic ties would promote greater flexibility for smaller CMEA nations. The fate of Poland — its initial ability to follow an unexpectedly independent domestic policy, and then the ultimate failure of this policy with the imposition of martial law and the accumulation of a huge hard currency debt — revealed both the benefits of and pitfalls of encouraging diversity in Eastern Europe and using economic means to promote political independence. Nevertheless, the Hungarian case also demonstrates that, within limits, greater economic ties with Western Europe have enabled some CMEA nations to pursue a more autonomous path.

Bonn has therefore had considerable reason to believe that economic ties can contribute to an improved political climate in relations with CMEA nations and can even produce some concrete results in the humanitarian field. Certainly, it has seen little reason since the early 1970s to change this positive evaluation. However, the United States has changed its attitude toward the desirability and advisability of maintaining détente, and this has caused difficulties for the Federal Republic in seeking to promote East-West commercial relations. Under the Carter administration the United States began to revert to its traditional policy of using negative economic linkage to respond to Soviet behavior which it considers unacceptable, and this tendency has been sharpened under the Reagan administration.

Initially, the German government sought not to undermine U.S. sanctions against the USSR, as long as they remained limited. For instance, after President Carter forbade Sperry-Univac to sell the USSR a computer for use by Tass (in response to imprisonment of human rights activist Anatoly Shcharansky), Siemens did not try to gain the contract, unlike its French counterpart Cll-Honeywell Bull SA which eventually took over the deal. After the Soviet invasion of Afghanistan, the Federal Republic was the only major ally to support the U.S. boycott of the Olympic Games in Moscow. German athletes could not compete, although many German firms supplied the equipment for the games.[15]

The Federal Republic has found it increasingly difficult to support U.S. policy on expanded sanctions toward the USSR and Poland. The German government has argued that the invasion of Afghanistan, however reprehensible, should have been viewed primarily as a problem between the USSR and the less developed nations and not as essentially an East-West conflict. With its European allies, Bonn has stressed that détente can and must be divisible, applying to Europe if not to extra-European areas. Moreover, Germany has a significant enough stake in economic ties with CMEA — and particularly with the USSR — that it will not jeopardize these interests for what it considers to be questionable political results. Germany pledged not to undercut U.S. sanctions, but refused to introduce its own after the invasion of Afghanistan or after the imposition of martial law in Poland. Thus, by 1979, the Schmidt government had made it clear that it would give higher priority to maintaining its economic ties with CMEA than to complying with the U.S. East-West trade policy.

The most controversial aspect of this Germany policy was, of course, Bonn's refusal to support American attempts to cancel the mammoth Urengoy natural gas pipeline project with the USSR. Like some of its European partners, Germany was interested in this pipeline for two compelling economic reasons — its ailing steel industry welcomed the exports of pipe and it sought to diversify its sources of energy imports. Moreover, this long-term agreement promised to intensify the cooperative aspects of German-Soviet relations at a time when the prospects of deployment of new U.S. missiles in Germany had heightened tensions between Bonn and Moscow. The inclusion of West Berlin in the gas agreement was a major breakthrough. When the United States introduced extraterritorial sanctions, forbidding the export of European rotors under U.S. licenses, the German government did not order its companies to comply with the U.S., and AEG-Kanis shipped rotors to the USSR before the U.S. lifted the extra-territorial sanctions. Unlike the British and French, the German government did not tell its firms to disobey the U.S. either, but it maintained a neutral position. Again, its interest in the pipeline overrode its perceived obligations to the United States.

Since the lifting of the pipeline sanctions, the German government has been cooperating with the U.S. on the various multilateral studies designed to improve allied coordination on East-West economic relations. It has supported the general desire to strengthen CoCom, but has been skeptical about the extent to which the U.S. concept of militarily critical technology can be applied in practice to export control lists.[16] Germany, like its European allies, does not believe that CoCom should become a political instrument for restricting all East-West economic relations. Bonn believes CoCom should remain a limited, technical organization. While agreeing with the U.S. position against subsidizing credits, it is unwilling to accept the principle of restricting volume of credits. Thus, although it supports the current allied initiatives, there is little prospect that Bonn will permit the U.S. to restrict its economic ties with CMEA – particularly when American grain exports to the USSR continue to expand.

Domestic Policies. There is a basic consensus within West Germany over East-West economic relations. All major political and economic groups favor these ties, and there is no debate any more as to whether they should indeed be encouraged. Since 1975, this consensus has grown to the point where only a few minority fringe groups oppose East-West commercial ties. The major political parties agree that economic ties with the East are economically beneficial and can be politically productive. The German exporters, especially those in the steel industry, machine-tool and chemical industry, favor expanding East-West economic ties, and, since 1954 have had an effective lobbying organization in the Ostausschuß der deutschen Wirtschaft (Eastern Committee of the Federation of German Industrialists). Likewise, energy importers have become increasingly interested in trade with the USSR and Eastern Europe. Most German banks are closely tied to industry, and have been willing to grant credits to finance these trade deals, sometimes charging lower interest rates for cosmetic purposes, and subsequently being reimbursed by the manufacturers in Germany for the difference between the market rate and the interest rate charged, as in the various gas-pipe deals.[17] The consensus on encouraging East-West commercial ties includes the major trade unions, who favor these exports for the jobs they create.

There is no significant opposition to East-West commerce in Germany. This may partly be a result of the fact that opponents there can utilize American views instead of their own. Given Germany's special ties with the U.S., it is more acceptable for a German to cite with approval American opposition to East-West commerce than it is for a French or British citizen. Basically, most opposition tends to be tactical and short-lived. For instance, the *Frankfurter Allgemeine Zeitung*, supported by parts of the CDU-CSU, carried on a campaign against the Urengoy pipeline when Schmidt was in power, but this arguably had as much to do with electoral politics in Germany than with any major stand on East-West commerce. There are some economic interest groups that have protested against unfair competition from the smaller Eastern European nations in the textile and clothing area, but these groups are relatively unimportant.[18] Since the bulk of imports from the USSR is not competitive with German products, these concerns are more relevant to relations with Eastern Europe. Thus, there is no national German debate any more over the desirability of economic ties with the East. If there is any discussion over East-West trade, it is about how far to follow American policies on these issues.

East-West Commercial Policy Under Kohl and Genscher

As soon as Helmut Kohl replaced Helmut Schmidt in September 1982, he stressed his party's commitment to continuity in German foreign policy.[19] Despite the CDU-CSU's intermittent criticisms of the SPD's Osthandel policy, as soon as it came into office, the new government followed the policies of its predecessors. Discussions for future large-scale projects have continued, including the giant project for coal liquefaction at Kansk-Achinsk.[20] The German-Soviet economic commission has met and discussed new agricultural projects. Moreover, the Federal Republic has been no more willing to support a more restrictive U.S. policy than was its predecessor.[21] Indeed, the Kohl government was willing to guarantee an unprecedented DM 1 billion credit to the GDR in 1983 followed by a DM 950 m in 1984, largely for political reasons. The West German Commerzbank also arranged a DM 500 m loan to the Soviet Union in 1984. There is no sign that this government will alter its policy on East-West trade, despite its greater rhetorical support for the security policies of the Reagan administration.

The prospects for intensified East-West commercial relations are limited, however, because of the economic problems in Western and Eastern Europe. Since 1979, Germany has begun to incur a balance of trade deficit with some of its CMEA partners, most notably the USSR, and in 1982 imported more from CMEA than it exported (Table One). Moreover, some CMEA nations, notably Poland, owe Germany large amounts of money (Table Four) and there is little sign that the debt problems of East European nations will be resolved that quickly. The debt problem inhibits East European import capacity from the West and acts as a dampener on expansion of trade.[22] Future prospects will, therefore, be determined more by economic than by political factors.

The Political/Economic Balance Sheet

The German evaluation of the interconnection between economics and politics in East-West relations is more positive and more complicated than that of its European allies and that of the United States. Certainly, since Germany's economic relations with CMEA began to expand in the early 1970s, political relations have also improved and there has been increased emigration from Eastern countries. Yet one must be careful not to confuse cause and effect in any discussion of the links between politics and economics. There clearly is a general connection between détente and East-West economic relations, but it is difficult to say much that is definitive about specific links.

One difficulty in establishing the linkage between politics and economics is because the stakes are so asymmetrical. The political stakes involved in German-Soviet relations are enormous, literally matters of life and death. The Federal Republic's political agenda with the USSR concerns the survival of Germany — both East and West — and a whole range of other security issues. The agenda vis à vis the rest of Eastern Europe is on a different level of magnitude, but is still involved with basic security issues. The economic agenda, is of a totally different order of magnitude. Trade with the USSR and Eastern Europe, as we have seen, forms a relatively limited percentage of total German foreign trade, and is not a life-and-death matter. Germany could survive without Osthandel. Thus, a fundamental asymmetry in political and economic stakes makes it difficult to establish a rate of exchange between politics and economics. This asymmetry suggests two basic results: sanctions will not work when a relatively insignificant level of trade is interrupted in order to produce some change in Soviet foreign policy, particularly in areas considered of vital importance to Soviet national security. Conversely, the functionalist hypothesis that economic interdependence somehow produces less conflictual political relations is also impossible to prove in an environment with such disparities in the stakes.

How can one then explain the temporal coincidence between détente and increased East-West economic relations in the 1970s? Firstly, politics did have a restricting impact on economic relations in the pre-Brandt era. The removal of political limits facilitated the growth of economic ties. Secondly, because the political and economic aspects of Germany's relations with the USSR and Eastern Europe are perceived in both Bonn and Moscow to be interconnected, in that way they can reinforce each other. However, there is also a commitment on both sides to seek to insulate economic relations from the vagaries of East-West political relations. That is, Germany encourages a positive interconnection between trade and politics, and uses trade as an incentive for improved political ties. However, it prefers to separate politics and economics when political relations deteriorate, and the same is true for the Soviets and East Europeans. Germany, in short, would prefer to have Pershings *and* pipelines, if the alternative is to forego the latter. Thus, Germany has a dual approach toward the politics of East-West economic relations. It links politics and economics in a positive sense whenever possible. However, it rejects linkage whenever that linkage threatens to impede economic relations.

The other side of this question is the impact of economics on politics. Has increasing economic interdependence had any effect on stabilizing political relations? Again, the answers are elusive. Certainly, some sectors of the German economy – steel, machine-tools, chemicals, gas importers – have developed a long-term stake in the CMEA market. These industries, plus the major banks, generally identified as being linked to the CDU-CSU have, in the 1970s, adopted a fairly hardline position on political relations with the USSR and Eastern Europe despite their interest in economic relations with the CMEA. However, these representatives of industry do not favor sanctions, or any political actions that might have a detrimental impact on economic ties. Their organization, the Ostausschuß der deutschen Wirtschaft – has only sought to influence East-West economic policies, and has had little or no say on issues such as arms control.[23] Thus, the business community has accepted that security interests take priority over economic interests, and has not lobbied against measures, particularly under the Kohl government, that have led to tenser Soviet-German relations.

Ultimately, however, the future of German economic ties with CMEA will be determined by economic factors, and the indications are that the political goodwill in the world cannot overcome the basic problems of largely complementary economic relations between an advanced capitalist country and less developed East European nations who face major hard currency shortages.

One result of the experience of the 1970s is that Germany has eschewed the use of sanctions and all restrictive measures, apart from the activities of CoCom. German government and industry representatives argue that sanctions do not produce political concessions from the USSR and Eastern Europe, and moreover they damage Germany's reputation as a reliable economic partner and impede its economic ties with CMEA. Since sanctions are usually retroactive -- responding to Soviet actions already taken (i.e. Afghanistan) – rather than forward-looking, they are indeed bound to be unproductive because they are not specifically designed to modify future behavior. The U.S. argument, however, is that sanctions may act as a deterrent to future Soviet and East European behavior. Moreover, the American administration has claimed that sanctions are an important form of political symbolism, showing the USSR or Poland that the U.S. is willing to incur some economic sacrifices in return for asserting political principles.

Germany rejects these arguments and also points to the hypocrisy involved in U.S. grain exports at a time when the U.S. is pressing its allies to cut back on industrial trade. The reasons behind this rejection are twofold. First, the Federal Republic knows that it might jeopardize the humanitarian gains from détente by imposing economic sanctions on its CMEA partners. Moreover – and perhaps more important – its economic stake in both East-West exports and imports is not worth threatening for the sake of dubious symbolism.

Since there is, for Germany, a definite connection between politics and economics in East-West relations, it is highly unlikely that the Federal Republic will reorient its policy on these issues for some time to come. Thus, it faces the prospect of recurrent difficulties with the U.S. over these issues, although it will always have the support of its European allies. Unless American policy reverts to that of the 1969-74 period, transatlantic disputes over these issues will remain. The current multilateral exercise in producing a consensus on East-West trade and security via the use of studies may deflect the tension for some time. But the basic differences of interest will remain. Given Germany's complex position in the world, and its inevitable conflict over the demands of Westpolitik versus Ostpolitik, Bonn will probably continue to pursue the compromise it developed in the 1970s — cooperation with the U.S. on security matters related to East-West issues and basic agreement on strategy; but the assertion of an independent position on East-West economic relations, permitting Germany to reap the economic and political benefits of commercial ties with CMEA and maintaining one important channel of cooperation with the East while it follows U.S. policy on matters of high politics. In short, Germany will continue to pursue a two-track détente policy[24] whether or not the United States reverts to a single track in dealing with the East.

112

NOTES

1 Angela Stent, *From Embargo to Ostpolitik. The Political Economy of West German-Soviet Relations, 1955-1980* (New York: Cambridge University Press, 1981) Chapter 5.

2 *Ibid*, pp. 145-151.

3 See Claudia von Braunmuehl, "Ist die "Ostpolitik" Ostpolitik?" in ed. Egbert Jahn und Volker Rittberger, *Die Ostpolitik der Bundesrepublik: Triebkräfte, Widerstände, Konsequenzen.* (Opladen: Westdeutscher Verlag, 1974) pp. 13-28.

4 Michael Kreile, *Osthandel und Ostpolitik* (Baden-Baden: Nomos Verlag, 1978) pp. 115-117.

5 Stent, *From Embargo to Ostpolitik*, 163-169.

6 See Henry Kissinger, *Years of Upheaval* (Boston: Little, Brown 1982) pp. 985-986.

7 Der Bundesminister für Wirtschaft, *Der Deutsche Osthandel 1982* (Bonn, 1982), p. 4.

8 Jochen Bethkenhagen, Heinrich Machowski, "Entwicklung und Struktur des deutsch-sowjetischen Handels und seine Bedeutung für die Volkswirtschaft der Bundesrepublik und der Sowjetunion" (Berlin, May 1982).

9 For text, see *Deutschland Archiv*, 1978, p. 650.

10 *New York Times*, May 7, 1978.

11 For details of these agreements, see Angela E. Stent, *Soviet Energy and Western Europe*. The Washington Papers no. 90 (New York: Praeger, 1982) pp. 22-31.

12 Stent, *From Embargo to Ostpolitik*, p. 122.

13 See for instance Hans Dietrich Genscher, "Toward An Overall Western Strategy for Peace, Freedom and Progress," *Foreign Affairs*, Fall 1982, Vol. 61, no. 1. Section IV.

14 Indeed, Schmidt, replying to questions about Germany's reactions to the Soviet invasion of Afghanistan said "Our economic relations with the Soviet Union have been built up through many years of cooperation, and primarily for political reasons." Quoted in Der Bundesminister für Wirtschaft, *Der Deutsche Osthandel 1980* (Bonn: 1980) p. 61.

15 The Germans also built a new international airport at Sheremetyevo in Moscow in time for the games.

16 This concept is a product of a 1976 Defense Science Board report, entitled "An Analysis of Export Control of U.S. Technology – A D o D perspective," otherwise known as the Bucy Report. The concept is embodied in U.S. law.

17 Joachim Jahnke, "The East Bloc and Western Credit," *The German Tribune Political Affairs Review* September 19, 1982. Axel Lebahn, "The Yamal Gas Pipeline from the USSR to Western Europe in the East-West conflict" *Außenpolitik*, no. 111, 1983.

18 For a discussion of the impact of imports from CMEA on the German textile and clothing industry, see Claudia Woermann, *Der Osthandel der Bun-*

desrepublik Deutschland: Politische Rahmenbedingungen und ökonomische Bedeutung (Frankfurt: Campus Verlag 1982) pp. 203-210.

19 See reports of Kohl's speech in *New York Times*, October 5, 1982. Kohl said West Germany would be a "reliable partner in relations with Eastern Countries, both economically and politically".

20 *Der Spiegel*, April 25, 1983 pp. 70-71.

21 *Der Spiegel*, April 18, 1983 pp. 28-30.

22 For a fuller discussion, see Jochen Bethkenhagen, "Handelsverflechtung mit den kleineren RGW-Ländern auf neuem Tiefstand." Deutsches Institut für Wirtschaftsforschung, *Wochenbericht* no. 12, 1983, pp. 163-170.

23 However, they have supported closer ties for political reasons. The head of the Ostausschuß has written that East-West economic cooperation serves to improve the political climate because it is less concerned with conflicting ideologies than are more strictly political ties. See Otto Wolff von Amerongen, "Wirtschaftsstrategie der RGW-Länder: Geschlossener Markt oder Weltwirtschaftliche Arbeitsteilung," lecture to Deutsche Gesellschaft für Osteuropakunde, October 13, 1983, Berlin.

24 For a reassertion of the German commitments to the two-track philosophy of the Harmel Report, see Genscher, *op. cit.*

114

Table 1: *West Germany's trade with the East[1], 1970 to 1982*

DM million

Country, group of countries[2]	Exports (fob) 1970	1975	1979	1980	1981	1982	Imports (cif) 1970	1975	1979	1980	1981	1982
Bulgaria	240	1.023	722	872	1.131	1.220	237	232	358	324	466	472
Czechoslovakia	1.058	1.678	1.982	1.892	2.007	1.953	727	1.158	1.600	1.901	2.069	2.051
Poland	658	3.213	2.464	2.661	2.160	2.142	744	1.436	2.207	2.495	2.128	2.137
Rumania	722	1.607	1.978	1.623	1.508	912	580	994	1.631	1.599	1.496	1.358
Hungary	522	1.417	2.140	2.194	2.657	2.628	490	906	1.687	1.819	1.995	1.848
CMEA (5)	3.201	8.937	9.286	9.242	9.463	8.856	2.778	4.725	7.483	8.138	8.155	7.865
USSR	1.546	6.948	6.624	7.943	7.621	9.398	1.254	3.240	7.381	7.517	9.225	11.357
CMEA (6)	4.748	15.885	15.910	17.185	17.085	18.253	4.031	7.965	14.864	15.655	17.379	19.222

Change on previous year in per cent

Country, group of countries[2]	Exports 1970	1975	1979	1980	1981	1982	Imports 1970	1975	1979	1980	1981	1982
Bulgaria	— 2.6	33.5	0.6	20.9	— 29.6	7.9	14.6	— 1.1	13.6	— 9.4	43.9	1.1
Czechoslovakia	28.6	— 5.9	8.8	— 4.5	6.1	— 2.7	5.4	11.8	18.0	18.8	8.9	— 0.9
Poland	7.6	— 11.1	— 6.9	8.0	— 18.8	0.8	39.8	0.7	5.8	13.1	— 4.7	0.4
Rumania	— 1.0	— 12.5	11.8	— 17.9	— 7.1	— 39.5	25.0	3.1	34.3	— 2.0	6.4	9.2
Hungary	47.6	19.8	— 2.4	2.5	21.1	— 1.1	21.6	— 0.2	30.4	7.8	— 9.7	— 7.4
CMEA (5)	15.3	— 8.5	1.5	— 0.5	2.4	— 6.4	21.1	3.5	19.4	8.8	9.7	— 3.6
USSR	— 2.3	45.6	5.1	19.9	— 4.1	23.3	— 4.0	— 0.9	35.7	1.8	0.2	23.1
CMEA (6)	9.2	9.3	3.0	8.0	— 0.6	6.8	12.0	1.7	27.0	5.3	11.0	10.6

Share in West Germany's total foreign trade in per cent

Country, group of countries[2]	Exports 1970	1975	1979	1980	1981	1982	Imports 1975	1979	1980	1981	1982
CMEA (5)	— 2.6	4.0	3.0	2.6	2.4	2.1	2.6	2.6	2.4	2.2	2.1
USSR	1.2	3.1	2.1	2.3	1.9	2.2	1.8	2.5	2.2	2.5	3.0
CMEA (6)	3.8	7.2	5.1	4.9	4.3	4.3	4.3	5.1	4.6	4.7	5.1

(continued)

West Germany's share in the CMEA countries' trade with the West in per cent[3]

CMEA (5)	23.4	21.8	24.7	24.8	25.9	26	19.2	22.3	23.8	24.3	23.4	26
USSR	10.5	15.0	17.3	19.1	20.7	20	13.2	20.0	17.1	18.9	14.8	15
CMEA (6)	17.9	18.4	20.6	21.6	22.7	22	16.5	21.2	20.4	20.7	18.2	18

Annual balance in DM billion   **Cumulative balance in DM billion[4]**

	Annual balance in DM billion						Cumulative balance in DM billion[4]				
Bulgaria	0.8	0.4	0.5	0.7	0.7	0.0	1.6	3.3	3.8	4.5	5.3
Czechoslovakia	0.5	0.4	— 0.0	— 0.1	0.1	0.3	2.9	5.1	5.1	5.1	5.0
Poland	1.8	0.3	0.2	0.0	0.0	— 0.1	5.8	8.7	8.8	8.9	8.9
Rumania	0.6	0.3	0.0	0.0	0.4	0.1	2.0	3.5	3.5	3.5	3.0
Hungary	0.5	0.5	0.4	0.7	0.8	0.0	2.0	4.4	4.7	5.4	6.2
CMEA (5)	4.2	1.8	1.1	1.3	1.0	0.4	14.3	24.9	26.0	27.4	28.3
USSR	3.7	— 0.8	0.4	— 1.6	— 2.0	0.3	7.9	12.3	12.7	11.1	9.1
CMEA (6)	7.9	1.0	1.5	— 0.3	— 1.0	0.7	22.1	37.2	38.7	38.4	37.5

Import-export ratio in West Germany's trade with the East

	Annual figures						Cumulative figures[4]				
Bulgaria	99	23	50	37	41	39	48	45	44	44	43
Czechoslovakia	69	69	81	100	103	105	66	68	72	75	78
Poland	113	45	90	94	99	100	53	63	66	69	71
Rumania	80	62	82	98	99	149	71	74	77	79	83
Hungary	94	64	79	83	75	70	68	69	71	72	71
CMEA (5)	87	53	81	88	86	89	62	66	69	70	72
USSR	81	47	111	95	121	121	61	74	77	82	87
CMEA (6)	85	50	93	91	102	105	62	69	72	75	78

[1] European CMEA countries, excluding the GDR. – [2] Producer and consumer countries. – [3] Based on CMEA statistics (CMEA countries = reporting countries). i.e., West Germany's export shares in the reporting countries' trade with the West are shown on the left, import shares on the right. 1982 estimated. [4] Minus = West German deficit. – [5] Cumulated from 1970. – Variations in total due to rounding.
Sources: Federal Statistical Office, Wiesbaden, Technical Series 7, set 1, various years; CMEA countries' statistical yearbooks and monthly statistics; DIW estimates.

Table 2:   *West Germany's exports to the CMEA (5)[1] by category of goods,*
            1981[2]

Goods or categories of goods	Exports	Change[3]	Composition of exports	Export weights[4]
	DM million		per cent	
Exports, total of which:[5]	9.463	+ 221	100	2.4
Food	874	+ 294	9.2	3.9
Raw materials	204	— 34	2.2	2.7
Semimanufactures	909	— 35	9.6	2.7
Finished manufactures of which:	7.413	— 80	78.3	2.3
Primary products	2.555	— 254	27.0	3.7
Finished products	4.858	+ 174	51.3	1.9
Selected sub-categories[6]				
Meat and meat products	179	+ 29	1.9	6.4
Grain	119	— 31	1.3	17.1
Chemical semimanufactures	234	— 45	2.5	6.2
Woven goods	465	+ 40	4.9	6.5
Chemical primary products	1.212	— 95	12.8	3.9
Tubes	132	— 64	1.4	3.2
Hardware	587	— 251	6.2	2.2
Machinery	2.448	+ 178	25.9	3.5
of which: machine tools and rolling mills	486	+ 69	5.1	5.3
Electrical engineering products	663	— 20	7.0	1.8
Precision mechanical and optical products	129	+ 9	1.4	1.8
Chemical finished products	565	+ 3	6.0	2.7
Motor vehicles	277	+ 5	2.9	0.5

Table 3: *West German imports from the CMEA (5)[1] by category of goods, 1981[2]*

Goods or categories of goods	Exports	Change[3]	Composition of exports	Export weights[4]
	DM million		per cent	
Imports, total	8.159	+ 21	100	2.2
of which:[5]				
Food	1.222	+ 114	15.0	2.6
Raw materials	731	+ 56	9.0	1.1
Semimanufactures	2.081	— 91	25.5	3.1
Finished manufactures	4.004	— 29	49.1	2.2
of which:				
Primary products	1.246	+ 18	15.3	2.7
Finished products	2.758	— 47	33.8	2.0
Selected sub-categories[6]				
Meat and meat products	518	+ 61	6.3	9.7
Fruit and vegetables	295	+ 29	3.6	2.7
Wood and wood products	566	— 126	6.9	9.3
Coal	332	+ 27	4.1	19.0
Tar and tar distillation products	129	+ 47	1.6	6.4
Copper, crude	335	— 62	4.1	14.1
Fuels, lubricants, natural gas	924	— 83	11.3	2.6
Chemical semimanufactures	155	+ 15	1.9	5.2
Woven goods	128	— 22	1.6	1.8
Knitted goods	328	+ 3	4.0	5.5
Chemical primary products	351	+ 28	4.3	2.0
Hardware	721	+ 3	8.8	5.2
Clothing	735	+ 31	9.0	8.1
Leather goods, including shoes	188	+ 3	2.3	3.9
Machinery	303	— 25	3.7	1.3
Electrical engineering products	198	— 2	2.4	0.9

1 Bulgaria, Czechoslovakia, Poland, Rumania, Hungary. — 2 Provisional figures. —
3 Change on previous year. — 4 Share in respective total West German imports. —
5 Excluding returns and replacements. — 6 The categories of goods cover 76 per cent of
total imports from the CMEA (5).
Source: Federal Statistical Office. Wiesbaden. Foreign Trade. Technical Series A, Sets 1
1 and 3.

Table 4: *Net claims of banks*[1] *based in West Germany against the European CMEA countries*[2] *in DM million*

in DM million

	1976	1978	1979	1980	1981	1982
Poland	3.066	3.959	5.126	5.591	6.527	6.313
USSR	4.891	3.998	2.586	2.619	2.955	2.544
Hungary	820	1.702	1.432	1.461	1.107	844
Bulgaria	669	1.042	966	905	765	692
Rumania	314	322	502	484	334	337
Czechoslovakia	123	168	17	164	138	210
CMEA (6)	9.883	11.191	10.629	11.224	11.826	10.940
CMEA (5)[3]	4.992	7.193	8.043	8.605	8.871	8.396

1 Excluding claims of domestic banks foreign branches.
2 Excluding the GDR; year-end figures. – 3 CMEA (6) excluding the USSR.
Source: German Bundesbank: Statistical Supplements to the German Bundesbank's Monthly Reports, Series 3, balance of payments statistics.

Figure 1: *Trade with the East for the Federal Republic of Germany in 1981, by region (Turnover in %)*

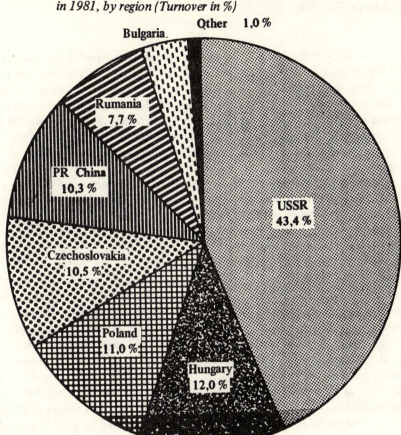

Source: Der Bundesminister für Wirtschaft, Der Deutsche Osthandel, 1982

9

The Special Case of Inter-German Relations

Hanns-D. Jacobsen

The ties between both German states have always played a specific role in East-West relations. During the Cold War they reflected the break between both blocs most dramatically, but they also reflected very clearly the successes which could be achieved through the détente process. This contribution considers the means employed by the Federal Republic of Germany in its dealings with the German Democratic Republic to the end of achieving its goal of "keeping the German question open" and the successes and failures the Federal Republic of Germany had to accept.

When the GDR was founded in Fall 1949 the government of the FRG had to strike a difficult balance, between disapproval on the one hand and a desire to maintain intra-German relations on the other. It therefore reacted to what it considered to be the illegitimate creation of the GDR by imposing sanctions, the most important of which was the refusal to grant diplomatic recognition to this "Soviet occupied state". This position was supported by the Western allies which also accepted that the "German option" should be kept open, at least theoretically, because of the domestic political situation in the FRG. This policy fit perfectly into the general Western strategy of containing the Soviet threat. West Germany had highly offensive instruments at its disposal in the form of refusing to recognize the GDR and, beginning in 1955, by employing the "Hallstein-Doktrin", according to which the FRG would suspend economic aid to countries granting diplomatic recognition to the GDR.[1] Rather than imposing economic sanctions in response to the foundation of the GDR however, the FRG used inter-German trade, at that time called inter-zonal trade, as a means of keeping the German question open. Inter-German trade was therefore given a particular status which meant that it never reached the level of "high politics" in East-West controversies.

As the East-West conflict worsened the Western allies agreed to grant the GDR special status, not only because of the FRG's pressure for domestic reasons, but because it was also in their own interests. The "Berlin Agreement of 1951" confirmed, once again, the rights of the victory powers (particularly concerning the status of Berlin), the continuous validity of the foreign currency laws, the particular involvement of Berlin in the Berlin Agreement and, finally, the link between the free access to and from Berlin and the inter-zonal trade.[2] The FRG and the Western allies recognized that this special status would enable the GDR to realize certain material advantages, but they left no doubt that a deterioration in the status of Berlin would result in a reduction of economic concessions.

According to the Berlin Agreement on inter-zonal trade of September 20, 1951,[3] which retained its validity even after the conclusion of the basic treaty between the FRG and the GDR in 1973, inter-German trade is the exchange of goods between two currency areas (thus including Berlin-West) within a joint customs region. For the FRG therefore it does not constitute foreign trade. Trade between both German countries is conducted by a clearing process so that no foreign currency crosses the border.[4]

Although the GDR has always been eager to stress its national sovereignty, particularly vis-à-vis the FRG, it has never expressed a desire to renounce the benefits accruing from this special kind of treatment. The benefits are numerous. From an additional protocol to the 1957 Treaty of Rome establishing the EEC for instance, it follows that GDR supplies of agricultural and manufactured products enter the FRG duty free, i.e. inter-German trade is excluded from the provisions of the EC's trade with third countries. Furthermore the GDR is able to enjoy certain benefits from what is in theory a mutual interest-free credit line ("swing"), but which has in fact only been used by the GDR.[5] Finally, East German foreign trade agencies have benefited by adjusting their exports to Western Germany to the preference structure provided by the FRG.[6]

It is difficult, if not impossible, to quantify the benefits the GDR has been able to realize from these concessions.[7] But without doubt part of what the West German fiscus renounces by way of revenue in its trade with East Germany benefits the GDR. In credit relations also the GDR is able to save several millions of Deutschmarks per year by using the "swing". By the same token West German exporters have better access to GDR markets than to other member countries of the "Council for Mutual Economic Assistance" (CMEA), so that these advantages should be balanced. In addition to such advantages in trade the GDR stands to benefit far more from all the other economic relations with the FRG. These include transit fees paid by the West German government for traffic between the FRG and West-Berlin, and payments for improvement of roads to and from West-Berlin. The GDR also earns West German marks from such sources as the minimum obligatory currency exchanges and its foreign currency shops (Intershop, Intertank, Genex). All such earnings unconnected with inter-German trade account for about 2 to 2.5 billion Deutschmarks per year.[8]

These examples clearly show that the GDR pursues a foreign economic policy aimed at realizing economic benefits, even when it cannot achieve basic political goals, such as rejection of being treated as a non-foreign country by the FRG. Nevertheless the GDR tries to reduce the economic influence the FRG has or could have on its policies. The GDR views inter-German trade, and all the other specific advantages the FRG is granting, as a lever against itself. This is especially the case with respect to the free access to Berlin, the provisions concerning the visits of citizens from West Germany and West-Berlin to the GDR and, most of all, to the openness of the German question. Accordingly, the GDR not only tries to limit inter-German trade to a level which it considers economically and politically acceptable, but also seeks to diminish all the other direct and indirect sources of influence on its economy and society which originate in the Federal Republic.

Since the early 1980s however, the GDR has changed its emphasis, and the economic relations with the FRG have gained in importance as part of its overall economic relations with the West. There are many signs that − at least for the foreseeable future − the GDR is even more prepared than before to accept certain additional political risks simply in order to exploit the economic benefits it can derive from inter-German trade. This position is particularly surprising, given that the GDR has, since its foundation but also after the conclusion of the basic treaty with the FRG, always emphasized the need to limit its economic dependency on the FRG.[9]

It is certainly easy to understand that the GDR should try to use the opportunities offered by the FRG more extensively when domestic economic strains and external pressures are increasing.[10] It is very unlikely however, that this represents a long term shift in the foreign economic policies of the GDR, because it is always alert to the potential increase in importance of certain political groups in the FRG which tend to politicize the trade ties even more. Such an approach would, by imposing sanctions or by conducting an explicit linkage-policy, pursue the ultimate aim of destabilizing of the GDR's relations with its CMEA partners and the Soviet Union in particular. In 1982/83 the GDR's interest in an above average increase in inter-German trade was accompanied by a preparedness to accept a "balanced give and take" which without doubt implied that the FRG's granting of economic benefits would be honored politically by the GDR. If the GDR had not stood to benefit economically from inter-German trade etc.[11] it would not have exhibited its readiness to respond favorably in political terms to West German offers of economic cooperation. This however, left the question of which form the GDR response would take.

This question gained in importance against the background of an untied financial credit of 1 bn Deutschmarks, provided in the summer of 1983 by a West German bank consortium and guaranteed by the West German government.[12] The credit was not directly tied to any reciprocal measures by the GDR, but there were expectations on the West German side concerning some kind of humanitarian gestures such as a general lowering of the minimum obligatory currency exchanges for visits in the GDR. These expectations remained largely unfulfilled. A few weeks after the credit the GDR announced a lowering of the obligatory exchanges but only for teenagers, as well as several other measures such as the return of families. Furthermore the GDR accepted new negotiations on a cultural agreement with the FRG which had been interrupted in 1975, and East German border guards began dismantling the automatic firing devices on the border with the West.

There can be no doubt that it has been primarily economic considerations, particularly the chance to get credits on favorable terms, which have led the

GDR to moderate its stance vis-à-vis the FRG and point out that a return to the Cold War would be disadvantageous for both countries especially after the failure of the INF-talks in Geneva. Whilst it may be correct when GDR vigorously emphasizes that it is "not to be blackmailed,"[13] this is unlikely to prevent any favorable reaction to economic offers of the Federal Republic. As the historical experience has shown, this has always been the case. Such behavior confirms the old, though much disputed, wisdom that carrots as an ingredient of West German policies vis-à-vis the GDR tend to be more effective than sticks which can only lead to more confrontation in the relationship between the two Germanys.

Such a policy certainly entails some risks, because the GDR could openly disregard the political expectations of the other side. The GDR must, however, also be cogniszant of the fact that if it did so, it would forfeit future economic benefits such as large credits. Therefore it seems very likely that the GDR will tend to accept economic carrots offered by the FRG within the undoubtedly pretty narrow range of choices, set by the U.S.S.R. and its own basic political and security interests. In doing so the GDR will try to trade certain humanitarian measures for a maximum of economic advantage provided there is no direct linkage, and the national prestige of the GDR is not at stake.

The FRG could quite easily follow another strategy in its dealing with the GDR. In view of the GDR's recent and enduring economic difficulties the FRG could explicitly and officially link its granting of economic benefits to political and humanitarian concessions. This would however, overburden the economic relations between both German states and would turn out to be ineffective for the FRG. It could indeed even be counterproductive because, due to political and prestige reasons, the GDR would be obliged to reject such offers. One result would be that those people in the GDR who should be helped would not be better off, and those responsible for formulating such a linkage policy in the FRG could be accused of being weak because their concept failed.[14] Such reproaches were made during the discussions on the extension of the "swing" agreement in the spring and summer of 1982. The Federal Government's effort to link the new arrangement of the "swing", within a "political-psychological context", to a reduction of the obligatory currency exchanges by the GDR failed because the GDR refused to accept the two were connected. However, the GDR granted several humanitarian improvements which had been sought for a long time,[15] so that the Federal Government did not persist with its policy of a sudden diminution of the "swing" from 850 mill. to 200 mill. accounting units, a step which would have been consistent with the original "swing" agreement but accepted a gradual reduction down to 600 mill. accounting units by the end of 1985. Nevertheless, the intense public debate of the link between the extension of the "swing" and the reduction of the obligatory exchange led to harsh criticism of the government's behavior, because it had raised expectations which it could not fulfill.[16]

Economic relations between the two Germanys are determined by the particular political considerations of both sides. The GDR leadership seems to be well aware that an improvement in economic relations with the FRG depends, to a large extent, on its own efforts to improve the political atmosphere. On the other side even the more conservative circles in the FRG seem to accept that "if we succeed in developing cooperation step by step in the areas of science, technology, nutrition, pollution, transportation, energy and development policy, ultimately even arms control and the free movement of people could be possible."[17] Whilst it would be overoptimistic to assume that this statement indicates a functional connection between progress in the different issue areas and East-West relations as a whole, it shows a continuity and consistency in the FRG's dealings with East Germany. Within the framework of such a strategy the Federal Government could offer the GDR certain joint projects, such as the electrification of the transit railroads between the FRG and Berlin (West), which would be economically very attractive for the GDR. By a multiplication of the levels of interaction, and by the involvement of the GDR in a network of bi- and multilateral relations, a further reduction of tensions could be achieved or at least the effects of increased tensions in other parts of the world on the inter-German relationship could be reduced.

All in all the experience of inter-German relations has shown that it is possible to link economic concessions of the FRG with politically desirable conduct of the GDR. It has also been shown, however, that an overburdening of such links with overambitious demands by the FRG may well be counterproductive, because the GDR is likely to reject any linkage if it sees its economic and political sovereignty threatened or even just to save face.

NOTES

1 See H. End, *Zweimal deutsche Außenpolitik. Internationale Dimensionen des innerdeutschen Konflikts 1949-1972* (Köln: Verlag Wissenschaft und Politik, 1973), pp. 23-25, and J. Kuppe, "Phasen", in H.A. Jacobsen/G. Leptin/ U. Scheuner/E. Schulz, eds., *Drei Jahrzehnte Außenpolitik der DDR* (München - Wien: Oldenbourg, 1979), pp. 173-176.

2 See H. Lambrecht, *'Die Entwicklung des Interzonenhandels von seinen Anfängen bis zur Gegenwart'*, Sonderheft des DIW No. 72 (Berlin: Deutsches Institut für Wirtschaftsforschung, 1965). Inter-German trade is currently conducted on the basis of the renewed "Berlin Agreement" of June 18, 1960. This status confirmed internationally when the member states of the European Economic Community accepted the particular rules in inter-German trade in a specific protocol. As far as trade policy is concerned the FRG can act autonomously in its dealings with the GDR where Art. 113 of the EEC treaty does not apply.

3 The legal basis of FRG's trade with the GDR is the allied "Devisenwirtschaftsgesetze" (foreign exchange laws). These provisions were replaced by the "Außenwirtschaftsgesetz" (foreign trade law) of April 22, 1961, with the exception of the trade with the GDR. See G. Ollig, 'Rechtliche Grundlagen des innerdeutschen Handels', in C. D. Ehlermann et al., *Handelspartner DDR – Innerdeutsche Wirtschaftsbeziehungen* (Baden Baden - Wien: Nomos, 1975), pp. 149-152.

4 For the development of inter-German trade see table 1.

5 From 1974 until the end of 1981 this credit ("swing") had a ceiling of 850 mill. accounting units (i. e. West German marks). By the end of 1985 this credit line is supposed to be reduced to 600 mill. accounting units.

6 Empirical studies have shown that the composition of GDR exports to the FRG began to diverge from that of comparable countries in the mid-1960s. This is a direct result of the specific rules of inter-German trade. See S. Nehring, 'Präferenzen und DDR-Exportstruktur im Innerdeutschen Handel', *Weltwirtschaftliches Archiv*, Vol. 114, No. 2, p. 339 (1978).

7 There have been some doubtful efforts to quantify these advantages; see R. Biskup, *Deutschlands offene Handelsgrenze* (Berlin: 1975); S. Nehring, 'Einnahmenverzichte der BRD – Handelsvorteile der DDR', *Die Weltwirtschaft*, Tübingen, No. 2, pp. 76-88 (1974); S. Kupper/H. Lambrecht, 'Die Vorteile der DDR aus dem innerdeutschen Handel', *Deutschland Archiv*, Vol. 10, No. 11 (1977).

8 See H. Lambrecht, 'Der innerdeutsche Handel – ein Güteraustausch im Spannungsfeld von Politik und Wirtschaft', *Aus Politik und Zeitgeschichte*, B 40/82, October 9, 1982, p. 8.

9 This subject has been elaborated in H. D. Jacobsen, 'Foreign trade relations of the GDR', in K. V. Beyme/H. Zimmermann, eds., *Policymaking in the German Democratic Republic* (New York: St. Martin's Press, 1984), pp. 144-169.

10 The declining growth rates in the GDR in the early 1980s have been mainly

caused by foreign economic pressures. Import needs could not be financed by increased exports, so that additional credits had to be taken in the West. At the end of 1981 the gross indebtedness of the GDR in the West reached a peak of nearly 15 billions of US-dollars. See OECD, *Financial Market Trends*, March 1983, Table 12.

11 Because inter-German trade is conducted on a clearing basis in which no hard currency crosses the border, the GDR is able to use it, at least in part, as a substitute for trade with other hard currency areas.

12 *Neue Zürcher Zeitung*, July 1, 1983, p. 13.

13 *Neues Deutschland*, May 3, 1983, p. 2.

14 This was the experience of the U.S. administration when it lifted the grain embargo, imposed after the Soviet invasion in Afghanistan, at the end of December 1979. The lifting of the embargo took place even though the cause of the U.S. measure had not been removed.

15 These measures included: the raising of certain monetary transfers; the assurance that people who had left the GDR "illegally" before 1980 (except deserters) should not be prosecuted; the possibility of West Germans to stay until 2 a.m. when visiting East Berlin; the assurance that a new transfer point for pedestrians would be created in Berlin-Heiligensee; and, finally: the possibility for East Germans to visit the FRG in cases of urgent family matters.

16 In 1974, however, the linking of economic concessions of the FRG and politically desirable behavior on the part of GDR led to a remarkable result: The West German government was tying the granting of a high ceiling for the swing with the demand that the obligatory exchanges, which had been unilaterally increased by the GDR in November 1973, should be reduced. The GDR gave in, at least partially, but made it clear at the same time that a link between both incidents did not exist. See H. Lambrecht, 'The Development of Economic Relations with the GDR', in E. Schulz/H.-A. Jacobsen/ G. Leptin/U. Scheuner, eds., *GDR Foreign Policy* (Armonk, New York/ London: M. E. Sharpe Inc., 1982), p. 345.

17 R. v. Weizsaecker, 'Nur Zusammenarbeit schafft Frieden', *Die Zeit*, No. 40, August 30, 1983, p. 3.

Table 1.
*Trade between the Federal Republic of Germany and the German
Democratic Republic, 1950–1983* (million accounting units)

	From East to West	From West to East	turnover	balance
1950	414,6	330,0	744,6	— 84,6
1951	145,3	141,4	286,7	— 3,9
1952	220,3	178,4	398,8	— 41,9
1953	306,9	271,3	578,1	— 35,6
1954	449,7	454,4	904,2	+ 4,7
1955	587,9	562,6	1.150,5	— 24,7
1956	653,4	699,2	1.352,7	+ 45,8
1957	817,3	845,9	1.663,3	+ 48.6
1958	858,2	800,4	1.658,6	— 57,8
1959	891,7	1.078,6	1.970,3	+ 186,9
1960	1.122,4	959,5	2.082,2	— 162,9
1961	940,9	872,9	1.813,8	— 68,0
1962	914,4	852,7	1.767,1	— 61,7
1963	1.022,3	859,6	1.881,9	— 162,7
1964	1.027,4	1.151,0	2.178,4	+ 123,6
1965	1.260,4	1.206,1	2.466,5	— 54,3
1966	1.345,4	1.625,3	2.970,7	+ 279,9
1967	1.263,9	1.483,0	2.746,9	+ 219,1
1968	1.439,5	1.422,2	2.861,7	— 17,3
1969	1.656,3	2.271,8	3.928,1	+ 615,5
1970	1.996,0	2.415,5	4.411,5	+ 419,5
1971	2.318,7	2.498,6	4.817,3	+ 179,9
1972	2.380,9	2.927,4	5.303,3	+ 546,5
1973	2.659,5	2.998,4	5.657,9	+ 338,9
1974	3.252,4	3.670,8	6.923,3	+ 418,4
1975	3.342,3	3.921,5	7.263,9	+ 579,2
1976	3.876,7	4.268,7	8.145,4	+ 292,0
1977	3.960,4	4.343,3	8.308,8	+ 382,9
1978	3.899,9	4.253,9	8.423,8	+ 624,0
1979	4.589,0	4.720,0	9.309,0	+ 131,0
1980	5.579,0	5.293,0	10.872,0	— 286,0
1981	6.051,0	5.576,0	11.626,0	— 475,0
1982	6.639,0	6.382,0	13.021,0	— 257,0
1983	6.878,0	6.947,0	13.825,0	+ 69,0

Sources: Bundesministerium für Innerdeutsche Beziehungen (Ed.), *DDR-
Handbuch*, Köln 1979, S. 531; 1978–1981; H. Lambrecht, *Der
Innerdeutsche Handel*, S. 13; 1982–1983: Data from the DIW
(Deutsches Institut für Wirtschaftsforschung), Berlin.

10
France

Renata Fritsch-Bournazel

Historical Background

France considers itself a power which seeks, with all available means, to preserve or expand its freedom to act. This desire for independence was certainly stated particularly forcefully by General de Gaulle, but it has also been of central importance to his successors. It is expressed above all in an aversion to any unconditional alliance solidarity, because a consolidation of the postwar power structures is considered equivalent to a restriction on the national freedom of action.

By virtue of the exemplary nature of its political relations with the USSR, France was able, during the 1960s, to upgrade its international position, at least in Europe. De Gaulle's policy to limit America's predominance with the help of the Soviet Union and vice versa, served the goal of establishing Europe as a third force. Europe was to find its own independent identity between the two superpowers by providing the link between sovereign and voluntarily cooperating nations. De Gaulle believed that his concept of East-West communication and cooperation between all European countries would bring about a liberalization of the Eastern European regimes and the existing bloc structures.

The expansion of trade relations with the state trading countries assumed a key role in this policy. During the Fifth Republic, France was the first West European country to embark on the road of détente with all of Eastern Europe. It did so partly to help promote France's economic development. Improved relations with the state trading countries were to lead to increased exports by reducing political confrontation and increasing cooperation across the East-West divide. Faithful to the motto "détente – understanding – cooperation" de Gaulle hoped to achieve his own "Wandel durch Annäherung" (change by rapprochement). In de Gaulle's view stable foundations and a suitable institutional framework for economic cooperation were required for such a policy to progress from détente via understanding to cooperation. There was a small volume of trade between France and Eastern Europe as early as the 1950s, but it was only with the political opening to the East that a solid basis was created in the form of longer-term trade arrangements. The first five-year trade agreement with the Soviet Union was signed in 1964, and the first production cooperation agreement (for color TV) dates from the year 1965. This was followed by the first general agreement on scientific, technical, and economic cooperation signed on 30 June 1966 on the occasion of de Gaulle's state visit. This set out the spheres of cooperation and determined the functions of the permanent mixed commissions which were to be created. A similar model was followed in economic relations with the smaller East European countries, such as Poland and Rumania which, after the Soviet Union, were France's two most important trade partners in the East. At the same time, France worked toward a liberalization of all EC trade with the state trading countries. The Fifth Republic opened its markets to CMEA exports as early as 1966 by autonomously lifting export restrictions on about 960 items.

After the end of the period of major policy initiatives towards the East, marked by the intervention of five Warsaw Pact powers in Czechoslovakia and de Gaulle's resignation, there was also a relative decline, under President Pompidou, in France's economic engagement with the CMEA. While the political overtures to Moscow between 1966 and 1970 had also paid off in economic terms, the Soviet Union was clearly able, during the 1970s, to better satisfy its needs for economic cooperation, by dealing with other industrial countries, such as the Federal Republic of Germany, as political relations allowed. It was therefore no longer prepared simply to subordinate economic interests to political intentions.[1] Although France was no longer Eastern Europe's exclusive Western partner in détente, and although the West's policy towards the East became increasingly multilateral after 1970-1971, France nevertheless continued to play a pioneering role in the search for new forms of economic, industrial and scientific cooperation with the CMEA countries. During Pompidou's term, economic questions turned up for the first time in consultations at the very highest level. Both Pompidou's state visit to the USSR in 1970 and the working summit in Rambouillet in 1973 ended with the conclusion of 10-year agreements on economic and industrial cooperation. These first and foremost secured the basis for long-term cooperation, but also contained spectacular innovations, such as, for example, Soviet participation in industrial projects in France. Between 1972 and 1975 France entered into long-term, 10-year agreements with all CMEA countries and formed permanent mixed commissions on government and administrative levels.

Interests

The Eastern trade policy pursued by General de Gaulle and his successor Pompidou caused very little controversy in France. When the economic expert Valéry Giscard d'Estaing became President in 1974 however, after an extremely slim election victory over his socialist opponent François Mitterrand, economic cooperation assumed a higher priority then the other aspects of détente policy. For France, as the world's fourth-largest exporting country and fifth-largest importing country, the radical changes in world trade which occurred after the October 1973 Yom-Kippur War, were bound to have as much an effect on foreign policy as in the other raw-material dependent industrial countries. In contrast to what had happened under de Gaulle and Pompidou, France was now forced to pursue a foreign policy aimed at securing the supply of energy and raw materials as well as maintaining employment levels. The nation's independence and economic security — described by Giscard d'Estaing as the two fundamental principles of its global (mondialiste) policy — could only be guaranteed through further growth in France's foreign trade.

Advocates of Economic Relations with the East. Trade with the CMEA countries was to play a role in this overall strategy even though its share in total foreign trade remained fairly modest (about 4.5 per cent of exports and 3 per cent of imports in 1978). In 1975, for example, it was possible to make up for the stagnating demand in the Western industrialized countries by expanding exports to Eastern Europe and thus considerably reducing the French foreign deficit. Between 1970 and 1977 the contribution of trade with the East to the upswing of French capital goods exports was by no means insignificant. Finally, the heavy concentration of France's trade with the East in large, partly public-owned enterprises also helped to ensure that its qualitative significance would far exceed its quantitative value.[2]

One can assume that French industry has a strong interest in continuity in economic relations with the East, even under more difficult political conditions. During the 1970s companies such as Péchiney, Rhône-Poulenc, Creusot-Loire, Renault, and Thomson-C.S.F. profited considerably from big orders awarded by the state trading countries. Creusot-Loire — which in 1976 exported two-thirds of its output amounting to Ffr 10 bn. — recorded a sales volume of Ffr 3 bn. with the CMEA, while orders from the Urengoi Project amounted to more than Ffr 8 bn. in contracts for Dresser-France, Alsthom-Atlantique, Thomson-C.S.F., Creusot-Loire, and Vallourec.[3]

Up to 1975 the USSR was France's biggest export market for machine tools and equipment for the chemical industry, until, starting in the middle of the 1970s, semi-finished products from the smelter industry began to play a bigger role. In connection with the long-term contracts on deliveries of Soviet natural gas since 1971, France, along with the Federal Republic of Germany, increasingly participated in the delivery of plants for the gas-extracting and gas-processing industry. The pattern of trade with the CMEA shows that some specific industry branches are much more dependent on exports to the East than the overall statistics might suggest. According to data from C.E.P.I.I. (Centre d'études prospectives et d'informations internationales), the CMEA accounted for 50.4 per cent of total steel pipe exports in 1980, 41.3 per cent for compressors, 30 per cent for steel strips, and as much as 75.6 per cent for metalurgical testing machines.[4]

Another area of considerable dependence is the essential foods industry and the entire agricultural sector. In 1980 the East accounted for 18.7 per cent of wheat exports, 15.7 per cent of sugar (with a considerably higher share in the case of cane sugar), 39.6 per cent of butter, 45 per cent of frozen meat, and as much as 50.9 per cent of veal exports. The French are hoping the tremendous Soviet needs in the agricultural sector will enable them to further increase exports in order to at least partly balance increased French imports of natural gas. In November 1983 Jean-Baptiste Doumeng, the influential French Communist Party member and general manager of Interagra, negotiated an agreement with the USSR on the delivery of about 1.5 million tons of cereal crops. Soviet agreement to such a deal must be interpreted as a political gesture because the "red billionaire" had previously been criticized for his allegedly non-transparent business practices. The signing of an exclusive contract with Interagra is contrary to usual Soviet negotiating methods, and clearly signals the fact that Moscow considers the committed Communist Doumeng a privileged future business partner.[5]

East-West trade relations therefore, created partial interdependence which led to a kind of "Flucht nach vorne" (an attempt to escape contradictions by pressing forward)[6] in dealing with the USSR. While France had always achieved an export surplus with the East before 1979, it suffered a deficit of Ffr. 4.7 bn. in 1980 and Ffr. 8.4 bn. in 1981. The economic need to expand trade with the Soviet Union, therefore, grew as France's foreign trade position declined. Although trade with the USSR only accounted for about 2 per cent of exports and 3 per cent of imports in 1981, it accounted for 10 per cent of France's foreign trade deficit. The conclusion of a Ffr. 2.7 bn. contract with the firms Technip and Creusot-Loire for a desulfurization plant in the development of the big natural gas deposits at Astrakhan, was clearly a reflection of Soviet readiness to help reduce the French balance of trade deficit and its ability to get around ticklish financing problems by paying cash.

Negotiations on this financial problem, which dragged on for 4 years, become a test[7] for OECD arrangements regulating the granting of export credit guarantees for the USSR. After the OECD agreed on a minimum interest rate of 12.5 per cent in June 1982, French representatives faced the problem of reconciling this with the 7.8 per cent they had offered, and which the USSR wished to keep for other contracts in the energy sector. There is no denying that the growth in France's exports to the USSR, Poland, and Rumania, which account for 80 per cent of France's total CMEA trade, was partly due to France's generous loan policy of the 1970s. For example, one study shows that for the year 1975 37 per cent of the long-term customer loans and 32 per cent of the supplier loans involved state trading countries.[8] According to 1982 estimates France accounts for 15 per cent of the CMEA's debt to the West; this was Ffr. 70 bn. in 1982, 10 per cent of France's foreign lending.[9]

The banks involved, which have in the meantime almost without exception been nationalized, are certainly interested in the continued payment capability of the state trading countries; but do not promote, unconditionally, more loans to the smaller CMEA countries because of the recent traumatic experiences with Poland and Rumania. In 1982 alone, COFACE, the semi-official credit insurance company, had to pay out over Ffr. 5 bn. in claims, half of which were due to Poland's insolvency.[10]

The fact that such services are, in the final analysis, provided at the cost of the entire population, necessitates some qualification of the anticipated economic benefit from business with the East. While the USSR is undoubtedly among the "good" debtors, it is very difficult for French agencies to reflect this in preferential terms for credit, subsidized by the French taxpayer because, in the opinion of many Frenchmen, it is the Soviet Union which represents the biggest threat to France's independence. On the other hand, the employment policy argument, according to which trade with the East guarantees about 200.000 jobs, cannot be dismissed outright especially during a phase of increased unemployment and reduced economic growth.[11] Foreign Minister Cheysson reduced this dilemma to a simple formula: Economic warfare against Moscow — he commented in a speech to the National Assembly on 6 July 1982 — "would be conducted with our own forces, with our own unemployed."

Opponents of Trade with the East. The fact that the costs of economic sanctions must be borne by constituencies other than those that derive political benefit from them, explains the absence of any clearly defined lobbies opposed to trade with the East. In France, as in other Western industrial countries, there are certainly a number of politicians, as well as military and economic experts, who warn against the risks of East-West relations. Recent international crises have also led to a greater emphasis on the strategic dimension of trade with the East and a lively public debate ensued on the advantages and disadvantages of "cooperation" and "economic warfare".[12]

There is no firmly established group supporting U.S. sanction and embargo measures, apart from a few intellectuals or representatives of the security establishment, who are fundamentally opposed to trade with the Soviet Union.[13] Vulnerability to blackmail and economic security was, however, the focus of discussions on the risk of unilateral dependence in the energy sector[14], while the Polish crises provided, among other things, an occasion to criticize government export loan subsidies.[15] In addition, the significance of technology transfer via research cooperation, licenses and industrial cooperation, which has played a by no means minor role in France's trade relations with the East since de Gaulle, is being questioned in an increasingly critical vein.[16]

With the change of administrations in the spring of 1981, the debate between the advocates and opponents of trade with the East assumed an additional domestic-policy dimension inasmuch as the former president was made co-responsible for the "illusions" of the advocates of functionalist or convergence-theory approaches. The international lawyer Samuel Pisar — who lives in Paris and whose book "Commerce and Coexistence" was largely written on the country estate of the Giscard d'Estaing family — provided food for thought for the détente concept of the early 1970s with his theses about the "weapons of peace" and about "transideological exchange". The economic expert Giscard d'Estaing – who in his capacity as de Gaulle's finance minister was the co-author of France's Eastern trade policy during the 1960s – revealed a considerable commitment in support of the new "lex mercatoria" (law of trade) in his foreword to the French edition of Pisar's book.[17] As Willy Brandt had done in his memorandum to Dean Rusk in 1964,[18] Giscard d'Estaing also pleaded for the expansion of across-system energy cooperation and an in-depth development of economic, humanitarian, and cultural exchange between the two parts of Europe. After he was elected president, Giscard d'Estaing continued to maintain close contact with Pisar whose theories became the target of general criticism directed against détente policy, especially after the Soviet intervention in Afghanistan.[19] In a recently published book, Pisar once again affirmed his fundamental commitment to the peace-promoting effects of East-West trade relations. But this time, in contrast to his work during the 1970s, he found hardly any positive resonance among the public. His plea to make an "anti-Berlin-Wall" out of the European gas grid[20] also found very little support given the hardening of French policy towards the East under Mitterrand.

Decisions

The ideological and power stuggle with Soviet-style communism has indeed caused the cooperative elements of French policy towards the East to fade into the background since Mitterrand took office. The deterioration of the political climate between Moscow and Paris produced, for the first time since de Gaulle, a situation in which relations with the Soviet Union no longer play a supportive key role in France's claim to independence. The socialist dominated left-wing administration is presently more interested in the dialogue with the United States than in any preferential relations with the Communist superpower.

French policy towards the East was always primarily an instrument of global diplomacy with which France tried to upgrade its own position in the East-West power play and, at the same time, tie up Germany's potential. In contrast to the Federal Republic of Germany, France had to settle neither boundary questions nor other major problems with the CMEA countries. As a nonintegrated member of NATO and as a nuclear power, France has its own deterrence which is simultaneously a means and a symbol of its independent posture. In the French view, the nuclear risk is indivisible and any automatic approach to participation in NATO strategy is strictly rejected. Nevertheless, when it comes to the question of stationing American medium-range missiles in the FRG and in other NATO countries, France clearly advocates the Alliance position.

This set of interests has had a number of effects on François Mitterrand's policy toward the East since 1981. For security reasons, there has been a move toward the U.S. positions on all issues concerning the problem of a balance of forces in Europe. The resumption of a normal political dialogue with Moscow on the government level is considered to be opportune only if an outline solution to the East-West crises emerges. During the 1981 election campaign, presidential candidate Mitterrand charged his opponent Valéry Giscard d'Estaing with great complacency with regard to the USSR particularly on the Afghanistan issue.

This abstinence of the socialists from any active policy towards the East is certainly not supported by the communists or by elements of the opposition who continue to consider the direct line to Moscow an absolutely indispensable part of Paris' diplomacy.[21] Such differences between the socialists and the communists and between the old and new administrations, show how much the general domestic climate for French policy towards the East has changed since 1981. While de Gaulle and his successors hoped to get a certain amount of support from the French Communist Party, especially in the field of economic and social policy, through their open-minded attitude toward the Soviet Union, Mitterrand included the communists in the government. He was therefore able to get along with Moscow's disciplining role on the communists, but is also forced to prove to the Western Alliance partners that his policy towards Eastern Europe is not determined by the "Moscow faction" in the coalition. In contrast to his predecessor Giscard d'Estaing, who, for example, deliberately refrained from emphasizing the "totalitarian threat" issuing from the USSR during the 1974 election campaign, Mitterrand made dissociation from communism a basic feature of his policy.

The hardening of the French position on all the explosive issues of East-West relations such as Afghanistan, Poland, or the missile basing problem, has clearly brought it closer to that of the Reagan administration. But this convergence of French-American interests has had no major impact on the trans-Atlantic controversy over trade relations with the East. Although trade with the East is no longer considered the nucleus of détente policy, as it was under Giscard d'Estaing, its continuation has nevertheless remained an important element of government policy also under Mitterrand.

Giscard d'Estaing: Economic Cooperation as the Nucleus of Détente Policy.
Valéry Giscard d'Estaing had been known to the Soviets as a pragmatic economic expert since the beginning of Gaullist policy towards the East. In his capacity as minister of economics and finance, he visited the USSR in 1964 and prepared the first five-year Franco-Soviet trade agreement. In January 1967, he presided over the first regular meeting of the "Grande Commission" which was created in 1966. He also had a special interest in Poland, with which France maintained traditionally good relations, and whose economic program under Gierek had provided the impetus for a further deepening of cooperation between both countries. Like Federal Chancellor Schmidt, Giscard d'Estaing also overestimated the significance of good personal contacts with the Polish leadership. Between 1975 and Gierek's ouster in September 1979, both statesmen had met

Gierek no less than six times, and it was certainly no accident that Warsaw of all places was the scene of the controversial meeting between Giscard and Breshnev in the spring of 1980. A year after his election defeat in 1981, Giscard d'Estaing, in a highly informative essay in "Le Figaro", gave the real reason for sticking to the objective of maintaining a privileged dialogue with Moscow even after Afghanistan. This was that France was very much concerned with "preventing the predominance of the Federal Republic of Germany in Europe because we know that West Germany will not renounce an open or concealed dialogue with the Soviet Union but will, on the contrary, continue to stick to it in the future".[22]

Latent competition with the FRG also had a certain significance in France's economic policy decisions even after the institution of the Afghanistan sanctions, because of the desire to promote exports in spite of more difficult general political conditions. Only two and a half months after the Soviet invasion of Afghanistan, France signed a new general credit agreement with the Soviet Union which guaranteed fixed interest rates and other terms of credit that were below the levels set by 1978 OECD export credit arrangements. France was able to increase its exports to the East by 20.8 per cent in 1980, only 2 per cent below the West German growth rate.[23] In 1980, both countries accepted contracts for projects which previously involved U.S. firms who had cancelled in the wake of the U.S. Afghanistan sanctions. In response to U.S. complaints after the conclusion of a $ US 300 million order for a steel mill in Novolipetsk, the French foreign ministry announced that it would not supply technology as sophisticated as that in the U.S. contract. In November 1980, however, the Carter administration reacted to the French move by issuing an import ban on steel from Creusot-Loire under the pretext that it contained nickel from Cuba.[24]

To be sure, France, together with its EC partners, had condemned Soviet action and voted against the USSR on the corresponding resolutions in the United Nations. From the very beginning however, it displayed no great readiness to support the unilateral measures of the United States. These had been taken without consulting the EC countries, who considered them to be somewhat excessive. In a statement on 6 January 1982, French Foreign Minister Jean-François Poncet declared that France was sticking to détente, especially in the field of trade relations, and was not ready to risk political relations with the Soviet Union by ordering sanctions.[25] A month later, a joint commission was already meeting in Moscow, and at the end of April Soviet Foreign Minister Gromyko was received in Paris on his first trip to the West after Afghanistan. In contrast to the FRG, France did not participate in the U.S. initiated boycott of the Moscow Olympic Games.

François Mitterrand: Ideological Confrontation and Economic Pragmatism.
At a time of stagnating East-West trade and deteriorating general political relations – two French economic experts recently commented – a French chief
of state faces the following choice in economic relations with the East: He can
either try, through political overtures and especially economic incentives vis-à-vis
the Soviet Union, to improve the French foreign trade position, or he can use
the disappointing economic balance as an opportunity to defy the Soviet Union
politically. Giscard d'Estaing, they argued, opted for the first option in order to
limit economic loss through the acceptance of "political sin", whereas his successor supposedly prefers the politically more attractive second option.[26]

Indeed Mitterrand's opposition to Giscard's allegedly exaggerated concilia-
tory attitude towards Moscow made him look particularly good to the French
public in the presidential campaign of 1981 because the Soviets, as in the West
German election campaign in the spring of 1983, were trying to make sure,
through ostentatious "election aid", that one of the rivals would be suspected as
being "Moscow's candidate". When on 13 March 1981 "Pravda" signalled
cautious but unmistakable sympathy for Giscard d'Estaing and aversion to
Mitterrand, the socialist, who had sharply condemned Giscard's meeting with
Brezhnev – referred to the "reward for Warsaw" on television.[27]

The "withdrawal treatment",[28] which François Mitterrand ordered for
France after his election, is however coming-up against the limitations set, even
among socialists, by material interests. When it comes to foreign trade relations
with CMEA countries, the union of the left assumes "realistic positions" similar
to these observed by an East-German expert at the time of the Afghanistan
crisis.[29] The French delegation, led by Trade Minister Michel Jobert, did not
think of cancelling the 16th meeting of the Grand Commission, held in Moscow
on 13th December 1981, and justified the conclusion of a Ffr. 1.4 bn. order for
the firm Creusot-Loire with the explanation that the planned five refrigeration
plants for the Urengoy project represented 4 to 7 million working hours.[30] At a
time when Federal Chancellor Schmidt was being attacked by large segments of
the French press, including those sympathetic to his government because he did
not immediately break off his visit with Honecker following the declaration of
martial law in Poland, Jobert in Leningrad argued that "the world of business is
not the world of moral condemnations".[31]

As in the case of Afghanistan, the French were not inclined to follow the
U.S. sanctions in the case of Poland. It was therefore, only consistent for the
Mitterrand administration to sign the agreement on delivery of Soviet natural gas
which had been initiated by predecessor Giscard, barely a month later in spite of
the Polish crisis. There was a strong emotional commitment to support the
Polish people and the fate of Solidarity. This rendered the left-wing administration incapable of finding a credible course between ideological confrontation and
economic compulsion, as was evidenced by Premier Mauroy's attempt to justify
the agreement by questioning whether one should add "a drama of the French",

in the form of a natural gas shortage following a renunciation of Soviet deliveries, to the "drama of the Poles".[32] To the great surprise of the public, Socialist Party Chairman Lionel Jospin displayed an unexpected sense of political continuity when he commented, on the topic of ethics and politics, that one must "separate the logic of human rights from the logic of the economy".[33]

The French President stated that "France's independence is based on its ability to manage its economy and its own defense efforts, to abide by its alliances, and organize collective security in Europe".[34] As the U.S.-West European conflict over the Urengoy project and subsidized credit escalated in the ensuing weeks and months, Mitterrand categorically rejected any French participation in economic warfare against the Soviet Union but also argued that it "would not do anything to strengthen the Soviet military potential unnecessarily".[35] France therefore, vehemently rejected the U.S. measures of 18 June 1983 which tried to prevent non-American firms, affiliates of American enterprises or French firms licenced to use U.S. technology from complying with existing contracts. In a statement on France's basic position in the fall of 1982 Foreign Minister Cheysson observed that such measures not only undermine confidence in international commerce between free economies, but also directly violate the sovereignty of the Western country concerned.[36]

The victims of the extra-territorial reach of American sanctions in France included the firm of Creusot-Loire, Dresser-France, Alsthom-Atlantique, and Thomson-C.S.F. The French administration's first reaction came on 22 July 1982 when it placed a compulsory order upon the firms involved to make delivery. This came immediately after Foreign Minister Cheysson had even spoken of a "progressive divorce" in French-U.S. relations.[37] When President Reagan finally lifted the pipeline embargo in November, it once again became clear just how far Marianne (France) and Uncle Sam had drifted apart in their views on trade with the Soviet Union. While the United States talked of a compromise between the Western industrial countries regarding economic policy toward the CMEA countries, the French government emphasized that no agreement had been reached.[38]

France in no way opposes export controls which are in the interests of the Western Alliance.[39] In order to implement such controls a committee on the transfer of "sensitive" technology was created by order of the Prime Minister dated 29 October 1981, which, in addition to representatives of the foreign and industry ministries, also includes military personnel and arms experts. This body, as a legal national agency, is responsible for all questions discussed within Cocom. France is not ready to support, unconditionally, U.S. demands for tighter controls on exports of dual-use technology, but sees it in its own interest to restrict those exports which jeopardize national French security or which could strengthen the Soviet offensive potential.[40] The spectacular expulsion, on 5 April 1983, of 47 Soviet citizens suspected of industrial espionage, showed how serious France is about protecting its security interests.

Balancing Security and Economic Interests

In contrast to the United States, which sought to solve the dilemma of security or lost exports by trying to get its West European allies to carry most of the costs of sanctions, France sought to resolve this dilemma almost exclusively within the national context. While the Giscard administration saw trade as a means of moderating the Soviet behavior and, in the long term, liberalizing the Eastern regimes, the socialists are trying to implement a strict separation between politics and economics. On questions of security, such as industrial espionage, "sensitive" technologies, or national defense, the political-military viewpoints clearly prevail and result in positions close to those of the U.S. administration. There was of course, strong support for Alliance positions in only special cases, such as the U.S. initiated declaration on security policy at the 1983 Williamsburgh summit. As a rule France sidesteps such American demands with reference to France's independent national security posture. When West European cohesion was tested after Afghanistan and during the Polish crisis, France acted in keeping with its national economic interest, but was also able to welcome the fact that it no longer stood alone in rejecting U.S. guardianship as it had in the past. On the issue of subsidized export credit, and in its general reluctance to seek compromises with the United States, France inhibited agreement on a common Western policy on trade with the East. However, French firmness on the pipeline issue helped the FRG by ensuring stronger European backing.[41]

Mitterrand's handling of relations in the Western Alliance and with the Soviet Union showed how difficult it has become to maintain the Gaullist line in a completely new international and domestic policy environment. On the question of the "Euro-strategic" balance, ties with the main Western partner have again become closer, whereas the political dialogue with Moscow has been kept to a minimum since 1981. Conversely, economic realities and the deterioration of France's foreign trade position, make France appear as a "petitioner" in business with the East because only the Soviet Union can make a decisive contritribution to its deficit in East-West trade. In the long term the Fifth Republic will only be able to retain flexibility in its political and economic relations with the East if it can achieve domestic economic and social stability.

NOTES

1 Sokoloff, Georges: *L'économie de la détente. L'URSS et le capital occidental*. Paris: 1983, p. 84-88.
2 Lemoine, Françoise: 'Les échanges commerciaux de la France avec les pays de l'Est'. In: *Notes et études documentaires*. No. 4569–70. 30. April 1980. p. 93–101.
3 Les Echos. 23. 7. 1982.
4 Wild, Gérard: Les dépendances de la France dans ses relations économiques avec l'Europe de l'Est. *Le Courrier des pays de L'Est*. October 1981. p. 3–11.
5 *Le Monde*. 16. 11. 1983.
6 Boyer, Michel: France: Le piège de la dépendance. *Le Monde*. 6. 4. 1982.
7 Lavigne, Marie: Développer les échanges franco-soviétiques. *L'Humanité*. 10. 1. 1983.
8 Lemoine, Françoise. op.cit. p. 94
9 Boyer, Michel. op.cit.
10 Lachaux, Claude: Les problèmes de financement du commerce Est-Ouest. In: Banque. October 1983. p. 1101.
11 Des échanges sous surveillance. *La vie française*, 21.–27.2.1983.
12 Compare RAMSES 1981 (Rapport annuel mondial sur le système économique et les stratégies). *Coopération ou guerre économique*. Paris: 1981.
13 See for example: Equivoques du commerce avec l'URSS. *Le Figaro*, 29.–30. November 1980.
14 See RAMSES 1982. Paris: 1982. p. 91–102.
15 See XXX: La Corde et le pendu: *Géopolitique*. No. 1. 1983. p. 46–51.
16 See Association des Auditeurs de l'Institut des Hautes Etudes de Défense Nationale: *Enjeux dans les relations économiques Est-Ouest*. Paris: 1983.
17 Pisar, Samuel: *Transactions entre l'Est et l'Ouest*. Paris: 1982. Part 1 of the French edition appeared in 1970 under the title 'Les armes de la paix', and played a part in the French debate similar to 'Wandel durch Handel' (change through trade) in the German debate.
18 Compare Fritsch-Bournazel, Renata: *L'Union sovietique et les Allemagnes*. Paris: 1979, p. 172.
19 See Dumoulin, Jérôme: Les Kremlinologues du Président. In: *L'Express*, 24.–30.5.1980.
20 Pisar, Samuel: *La Ressource humaine*, Paris: 1983. p. 210.
21 See Tatu, Michel: 'Das Ende jeden Flirts? Paris – Moskau seit dem Regierungswechsel vom Mai 1981'. *Dokumente*. No. 3, Vol. 39. September 1983. p. 213–223.
22 Giscard d'Estaing, Valéry: Où va la France? Le recul. *Le Figaro*. 21.6.1982.
23 RAMSES 1982. op.cit. p. 97.
24 RAMSES 1981. op.cit. p. 25.
25 *Le Monde*. 8. 1. 1980.
26 Sokoloff, Georges and Wild, Gérard: *Les relations économiques de la France avec l'Est. La Période giscardienne*. Paris: 1983. p. 21. (Colloque sur la politique extérieure de Valéry Giscard d'Estaing.).

140

27 *Le Monde*. 18. 3. 1981.
28 Tatu, Michel: Les rapports franco-soviétiques: la fin d'une "cure de désintoxication". Le Monde. 25. 12. 1982.
29 Freiberg, Paul: 'Realistische Positionen Frankreichs in den Außenwirtschaftsbeziehungen zu den RGW-Staaten'. *IPW-Berichte*, Heft 9. September 1980. S. 34—40.
30 *Libération*. 17. 12. 1981.
31 *Le Monde*. 16. 12. 1981.
32 *Le Monde*. 27. 1. 1982. See satirical treatment by Jean-François Kahn: La morale est-elle soluble dans le gaz? *Les Nouvelles littéraires*. 28. 1.—4. 2. 1982.
33 *Le Quotidien* de Paris. 26. 1. 1982.
34 *Le Monde*. 29. 1. 1982.
35 Haagland, Jim: Mitterrand Rejects U.S. Campaign for Economic War against Russia. *International Herald Tribune*. 16. 6. 1982.
36 Cheysson, Claude: The Pipeline Spat, Viewed from France. *International Herald Tribune*. 18.—19. 9. 1982.
37 Evening news 'Antenne 2'. Also Fontaine, André: C'était trop beau ... *Le Monde*. 24. 7. 1982.
38 Kergolay, Henri de: Paris: Il n'y a pas d'accord sur le commerce Est-Ouest. *Le Figaro*. 15. 11. 1982.
39 See Zaleski, Eugène and Wienert, Helgard: *Transferts de techniques entre l'Est et l'Ouest*. Paris: 1980.
40 Fredet, Jean-Gabriel: Reprise des négociations à Paris sur les exportations stratégiques. *Le Matin*. 8. 10. 1982.
41 See Fritsch-Bournazel, Renata: *Germany's Role in Europe: Historical and Psychological Dimensions*. Washington: 1982. p. 19—29. (The Wilson Center, International Security Studies Program. Working Paper. No. 44.)

11
Great Britain
*Stephen Woolcock**

Introduction

British policy on East-West economic relations has been influenced by the existence of a broad, stable consensus that trade with the CMEA countries should be maintained or promoted. This consensus, which has encompassed all government departments, major political parties and interest groups, first developed when Britain was among the leading trading nations. In the 1950s and 1960s it was supported by the fact that Britain took a major share of CMEA markets. As Britain's share of these markets declined in the late 1960s and throughout the 1970s, the desire to compete with other OECD countries helped ensure that Britain continued to favour East-West trade. As the "post-détente" period of the 1980s progresses this consensus is likely to survive but with more qualified support for East-West economic links. In the Atlantic debate on the strategic importance of trade, which is likely to characterize the 1980s as it did the previous 30 years, Britain will adopt the centre ground between restrictive, strategic concepts of the United States and the pro-trade approach of the Federal Republic of Germany (FRG).

With a relatively small stake in East-West trade, British policy is also likely to be influenced by policies of other Western governments. It will in particular seek to avoid transatlantic conflicts which damage US-European economic and political relations. If pushed to decide between an American strategic approach and a "European" commercial approach to East-West trade as it was over the 1982 pipeline embargo Britain's position is likely to remain closer to the broad West-European consensus it helped to create in the 1960s.

The Legacy of Leadership

British policy towards economic relations with the USSR and later with the CMEA countries has been influenced by its past role as a leading trading nation. In March 1921 Britain led in concluding a trade agreement with the Soviet Union. This agreement, which granted de facto recognition of the Soviet Union,[1] encouraged other European countries to follow suit, and was based on the view that all potential markets had to be exploited if Britain was to maintain its leading position in world trade. The decision was also influenced by a belief that trade would help moderate revolutionary fervor in Soviet Russia.

141

In the late 1940s Britain was no longer able to exercise leadership in trade with the USSR and the other European CMEA countries. Along with other Western governments Britain supported a policy of security export controls on items of military importance to the USSR, but together with France it also wanted national rather than multinational controls under American leadership.

American military and economic dominance of the West enabled it to assume leadership of Western policy and establish multinational controls in the form of CoCom (The Coordinating Committee on East-West trade).[2] Under U.S. leadership CoCom was used as an instrument of economic containment of the Soviet Union. In the 1950s and with more success in the 1960s, Britain and France pressed for a normalization of economic relations and the limitation of controls to items of military as opposed to economic importance to the Soviet Union. Britain's interest in normalizing trade relations during this period was primarily economic. Indeed until the mid 1960s Britain was the CMEA's leading trading partner in the West.

In the 1960s, the consensus in favour of East-West Trade was therefore based on the legacy of leadership in trade policy, and immediate economic interests. Direct experience with economic embargoes also had an important influence on the British approach. Past experience with sanctions, from Abyssinia to Rhodesia created a profound scepticism of their effectiveness. If sanctions were less than effective against a small land-locked country in Africa, they could not be expected to have much effect on a superpower far more capable of economic autarchy. This scepticism has been carried over into current policy analysis thanks to the continuity of the British foreign policy establishment. The legacies and experiences of the past therefore helped ensure that the consensus in favour of trade survived the 1970s, despite a decline in Britain's share of CMEA markets. These were, however, augmented by the pressures to compete with other countries.

Competition in the 1970s

Britain's role as a leading trading partner for the CMEA countries faded from the mid-1960s. By the end of the 1960s it also faced more intense competition from other European countries, and, at least for the first few years of the 1970s, from the United States. The U.S.-Soviet détente and 'Ostpolitik' of the FRG meant that whatever economic advantage Britain and France had previously held on CMEA markets, due to the relative absence of the US and FRG, no longer existed. Britain responded with a more vigorous promotion of East-West trade by seeking further liberalization of CoCom controls, by matching credit conditions and by collaborating in joint East-West trade commissions.

During the 1960s Britain gained some slight advantage from the fact that American national export controls were more restrictive than either the British or CoCom controls. British exporters of certain high technology products were therefore able to gain CMEA orders. For example, Britain developed markets for computers, and a British company, English Electric Computers,[3] was first to export computers to the Soviet Union in 1966. By 1970, pressure was mounting for a liberalization of export controls in the United States. More liberal controls would have meant competition from U.S. computer giants such as IBM. In order to retain their CMEA market share British exporters therefore sought a further liberalization of British national controls. This created tensions with the United States, such as in the case of ICL orders for computers in the USSR.

In 1970-71, the United States blocked the granting of a licence for the export of certain ICL computers in CoCom for nearly two years. This led to speculation that the United States was motivated by commercial considerations, such as allowing IBM to build-up its marketing position in Vienna in order to enter CMEA markets. In the summer of 1970 the United States finally lifted its veto in CoCom but only after Britain had threatened to veto all U.S. requests for exemption from CoCom controls. The Nixon Administration however then used its powers under the 1969 Export Administration Act (EAA) to prevent reexportation of US components used in the ICL computers. The dispute was finally resolved in early 1971, but only after the intervention of Prime Minister Heath, and a long interdepartmental debate within the US Administration. Such experience with the use of US legislation to bypass multilateral negotiations on controls helps explain the strength of British opposition to the extraterritorial application of the 1979 EAA in the 1982 pipeline dispute. The issue faded in the early 1970s because U.S. and European interests converged when the Nixon Administration finally moved toward greater liberalization of East-West trade controls.

Britain's desire to compete with other Western exporters also affected its policy on credit. This was particularly important with regard to France, but also some other European countries, such as Italy. Credit lines for the Soviet Union were granted by both Conservative and Labour governments during the 1970s. In 1972 the Conservative government offered £ 200 m[4] in an effort to boost British exports with the Soviet Union. Britain experienced a deteriorating trade deficit with the USSR during the 1970s, but generally had a small surplus with the other CMEA countries.[5] In 1975, another credit line was arranged, the so-called "Wilson" credit after the Labour prime minister, for £ 950 m.[6] Again this credit line failed to redress the trade deficit with the USSR, which increased in the period 1976-1979, and by the end of the Labour government in 1979 only half the £ 950 m had been taken up. In 1977 the Conservative opposition came out against continuation of credit line on the grounds that it was ineffective, but this opposition was also the result of a shift towards a more ideological stance vis-à-vis the Soviet Union in the Conservative party led by Margaret Thatcher.[7]

In early 1977, the Conservative opposition also criticized the apparent willingness of the government to license aerospace exports for the Soviet supersonic airliner, the TU 144.[8] The government was seen as trying to boost exports in order to avoid embarrassment over the fact that the credit line was not being taken up.

Throughout the 1970s and indeed into the 1980s, Britain continued to provide official export credit guarantees for trade with the CMEA. British policy was to match, as best as possible, the terms offered by competing countries. As France and Italy subsidized, Britain also provided guarantees at perferential rates and was only prepared to reduce subsidization if other countries did likewise. A desire to compete also led Britain to collaborate in joint intergovernmental commissions with CMEA countries, and to conclude long term trade and cooperation agreements. In 1968 it signed an agreement with the Soviet Union on cooperation in the field of science and technology, followed by a long term trade agreement in 1969. The UK thus matched the French 'Grande Commission' established in 1966, and also set-up joint bodies such as the Permanent Soviet-UK Intergovernmental Joint Commission for Cooperation in the Fields of Science, Technology, Trade and Economic Relations (Joint Commission) in 1971. In an effort to provide a counterbalance for the benefits West German industry gained from market proximity and traditional trading links, a whole series of working groups for a range of industries were also established under the auspices of the Joint Commission. With the possible exception of one working group on automation and electronics, these all became moribund as potential British exporters found them to be mainly talking shops from which few orders materialized. The Joint Commissions with each CMEA country have of course survived.

While Britain has been keen to increase exports, this has not stopped it from adopting relatively tough political postures. In 1968 Britain suspended formal trade contacts with the Soviet Union following Czechoslovakia for longer than many countries. This had some effect on trade talks. In 1970 and 1971, efforts were made to boost Anglo-Soviet trade, but the day before the arrival of a high level trade delegation from Moscow, the government expelled 105 Soviet trade officials on grounds that they were engaging in industrial espionage.[9] In 1980 the British government was also first to support the U.S. position and sanctions against the Soviet Union following the invasion of Afghanistan, and did so by ending the 'Wilson' credit agreement. As noted above, the Conservative government was already committed to allowing this 1975 credit line to lapse. Consequently, Britain's position on sanctions must be seen as motivated more by a desire for Western solidarity than belief in the effectiveness of the economic sanctions. Trade considerations have not therefore constrained British governments from signaling strong condemnation of Soviet actions, or taking measures, such as expelling Soviet diplomats, which might damage the political atmosphere within which trade is conducted. Past experience has, however, created a body of opinion highly sceptical of the effectiveness of sanctions. If sanctions were ineffective against Rhodesia, it is argued, economic warfare against the Soviet Union will have a negligible effect. There is also a firm consensus that selective sanctions will also have little effect, and certainly should not be introduced if they damage the West more than the East.

Economic Interests

Before discussing whether this consensus in favour of trade and against sanction is likely to survive the 1980s, it is necessary to consider Britain's economic interests in greater depth.

The structure of Britain's trade with the CMEA is similar to most other West European countries. Exports of machinery and manufactured goods account for the bulk of British exports to both the Soviet Union and the other East European economies. Together with chemicals these account for more than 80 per cent of British exports (see table 3).[10] On the import side, Britain's pattern of trade with the East is again similar to the rest of Western Europe, with energy and raw materials accounting for about 80 per cent of imports from the Soviet Union but with a broader spread of products from the CMEA six. Anglo-Soviet trade is peculiar in the sense that diamonds account for a very high percentage of British imports. In 1980, diamonds, many of which are subsequently reexported, accounted for no less than 47 per cent of imports from the USSR. This has tended to distort trade figures and in 1982, diamonds were removed from the trade statistics.[11] Despite North Sea oil, Britain still imports a significant volume of oil from the USSR. Indeed, oil, diamonds and wood accounted for more than three quarters of British imports from the USSR throughout the 1970s, the figures for 1980 being 23 per cent, 47 per cent and 13 per cent respectively.[12] Britain is, however, distinctive from the other major West European economies in that is has less need to diversify energy supplies and was not importing Soviet natural gas in the mid-1980s.

Whilst the structure of Britain's trade is "European", the overall importance of CMEA markets for Britain is more in line with the importance of such trade for the United States. In 1981 CMEA trade accounted for only 2.5 per cent of Britain's trade.[13] The trend appears to be towards a slight decline in the importance of East-West trade for Britain (see table 2). It is important to bear in mind, however, that even during the 1960s, the share of CMEA trade in total trade seldom increased above 3 per cent.

Compared with Britain's general trade performance there were no signs of a decline in performance on Eastern markets in the 1970s.[14] Relative to other West European exporters however, Britain's share of CMEA markets has declined, By 1980, Britain accounted for only 6.7 per cent of OECD exports to the CMEA, compared to 25 per cent for the FRG and 12 per cent for France and Italy. The reasons for this decline are numerous. An important contributing factor is that

Eastern Europe is not a natural market for Britain. A fairly small number of larger companies have invested time and effort in developing CMEA markets, but for most companies Britain's "natural" markets in the English-speaking world offer the prospect of quicker returns on marketing investment. In addition to the linguistic and bureaucratic problems posed by CMEA markets, there is also a general waryness of Eastern trade ministries. It is indicative that the USSR ranks only 25th in Britain's top 100 export markets (1982 figures), a long way behind countries such as Nigeria, Australia, India and Hong Kong and even behind Singapore. Poland, the next CMEA country ranks 53rd behind Kenya and Trinidad and Tobago. Romania is next at 55th, followed by Hungary 66th, behind Zimbabwe, Czechoslovakia after Malta and the GDR 73rd behind Ghana. Other factors often quoted as reasons for the loss of CMEA market shares, are a general reluctance to enter into long term counter-trading agreements, or to form joint ventures with other Western consortia. Finally, a general lack of competitiveness on the part of British industry during the 1970s must be seen as a contributing factor. Political events, such as the expulsion of trade officials, are not thought to have had a significant effect as industry has generally maintained contacts during periods of political tension.[15]

Whilst of no major importance to the economy as a whole, exports are clearly of significance at the margin, and for a number of industries. It is also believed that there is a floor to any decline in Britain's share of CMEA markets because Eastern trade ministries will always want to diversify their sources of supply. Table 4 shows a breakdown of major exports by sector and country. In a number of sectors, Britain appears to have retained a competitive edge. In textile fibers and yarns, power generating equipment, office equipment and data processing for example, British exports to the USSR exceed West German exports.[16] There is also a broad strength in chemicals, although the chemical industries' share of total British exports has declined in recent years (see table 3). For these sectors it is not difficult to identify the major British companies which account for most trade.[17] Although there are some 620 companies affiliated to the Anglo-Soviet chamber of commerce, most trade only irregularly if at all.

Lobbying by the major companies on policy issues such as export controls or credit is fairly easily facilitated thanks to informal contacts with government departments. As in other European countries, open conflicts with government are rare, and the companies do not employ the media in lobbying. A number of trade bodies have sought to promote trade. The Anglo-Soviet chamber of commerce, along with regional chambers of commerce organize trips to CMEA countries, but tend to provide only a framework for individual sales efforts. The London Chamber of Commerce has been important in that it has helped maintain business contacts during and after periods of political tension. The Confederation of British Industry (CBI) has also organized round tables for the so-called captains of British industry, including one in March 1983. Finally the East-European Trade Council provides logistic support and advice on a more continuous basis.

Although East-West trade is not significant for the British economy, these organizations, and the major companies involved, continue to maintain a presence, as is indicated by the creation of two new Anglo-Soviet working parties on machinery and equipment and agro-industries following the May 1983 Anglo-Soviet Joint Commission meeting in London.

In addition to the interests of exporters there is also a banking lobby with a substantial interest in the stability of East-West economic relations. London banks including the bank of England took an active part in trying to prevent the Polish financial crisis causing a chain reaction in Eastern Europe and beyond. The City is also concerned that credit should not be used as an instrument of foreign policy, because of the damage this could do to London's position as a world financial centre. The interests of the London banking community were certainly an important factor influencing British policy on Polish debt, in particular its opposition to the calls, from parts of the US administration, for a declaration of default on Poland's debts. In late 1983, Britain along with other West European countries took a lead in favouring a rescheduling of Poland's official debt.

Of the other important interest groups trade unions are if anything neutral on East-West economic relations. There has been some concern, especially in the petro-chemical industry, about the effects of buyback agreements on jobs.[18] The National Union of Seamen (NUS) is also sharply critical of Soviet and Polish ships carrying cargo at "dumping" rates. But whilst the NUS opposed subsidies for the construction of ships for Poland in British shipyards in the late 1970s, other shipbuilding unions were strongly in favour. Only on very rare occasions have unions made an issue of export controls. Such a case was when shop stewards at a Lucas factory opposed the sale of sophisticated fuel systems for the Soviet TU 144 supersonic airliner (see above).[19] The interests in favour of trade are important, but probably less important than the existence of a broad and stable consensus within Whitehall which favours trade and is sceptical of the effectiveness of using economic relations as an instrument of foreign policy. This consensus helps to explain why Britain has consistently pursued a policy in favour of trade, despite the relative decline in its share of CMEA markets and low level of East-West trade. The cohesion of this consensus has, to date, not been challenged by any effective anti-trade lobby.

Major Policy Decisions

As noted above, the Labour government of 1974-1979 actively sought to promote trade. In 1978 it did not therefore support the U.S. 'human rights' sanctions against the Soviet Union. Indeed when U.S. exports of computers for use in the Moscow Olympics were embargoed, the British company ICL picked up part of the contract. As in the 1963 pipe embargo therefore, Britain not only failed to support U.S. embargo policy, it actively undermined it. In 1978 Britain did, however, make a number of gestures, such as the cancelling of ministerial contacts with the USSR, but this was done more to show the Americans it was doing something rather than in a belief that it would have the slightest effect on human rights in Russia. Britain's response to the Soviet invasion of Afghanistan in December 1979 was far tougher. The Conservative government, under the leadership of Mrs. Thatcher, who was not coy about her anti-Soviet views, was first to give verbal support to the U.S. sanctions policy. The United States consequently saw Britain as evidence of some support for the U.S. position,[20] a fact which may have encouraged the United States into believing it could gain wider European support.[21] When it came to more concrete support for U.S. sanctions, however, the government still saw itself constrained by the need not to act unilaterally, that is without equivalent measures by other West European governments. This was reflected in the British sanctions announced on January 25th 1980. The Soviet credit line was discontinued, a move which brought pressure on France to do likewise, but a tightening of credit guarantees was made conditional to general West European agreement. As there were no major British contracts pending, and the government was already committed to ending the Soviet credit line, support for the U.S. sanctions policy was not very costly. Furthermore it was emphasized that no measures would be taken which would be more costly for Britain then the Soviet Union.[22] Failure to end credit guarantees as a sanction was criticized by sections of the Conservative party, but the older generation of Conservative politicians and business lobbies felt the government went too far in cancelling the 1980 meeting of the Anglo-Soviet Joint Commission.[23]

On Poland, the British consensus was that actions of the West were unlikely to have much effect on what happened in the country. Britain again appeared to be more receptive to U.S. arguments on the need for sanctions, but it wished to avoid precipitative action, such as forcing a default on Polish debt.[24] Once it became clear that martial law excluded a return to progressive political liberalization in Poland Britain adopted a position of wishing to signal disapproval, but not in such a way that the costs to Britain and the West were greater than the costs to the Soviet Union. There was also a widespread view that martial law at least meant a return of some semblance of stability and that this had some positive aspects.[25] When Britain pressed for an emergency meeting of the European Council before the end of Britain's presidency, there was some concern that it would use its position to push the European Community into adopting a tough line.[26] But the meeting was not held and as 1982 progressed it became clear that the UK was not prepared to get too far out of line with its European partners. Indeed, Britain's policy on Poland and the pipeline embargo, was influenced more by relations within the West, than convictions about the importance of economic relations with the East. Britain's analysis of West European energy dependency was at odds with American arguments about the dangers of growing dependency. There was also no support for American neo-economic containment or economic warfare policies, which were seen to be the motivation behind the pipeline embargo. There was also unqualified opposition to the retroactive use of U.S. reexport controls as an instrument of U.S. policy. Thanks to past experience with the extraterritorial application of U.S. legislation, the danger of a major clash with the United States over extraterritoriality was identified, at any early stage, as a major concern of the British government.

In the spring of 1982 Britain hoped for a compromise in which the United States would end its pipeline embargo, the extraterritorial implications of which were already alarming the UK, in return for European agreement to do something about the provision of subsidized credit for the Soviet Union. When the United States proposed setting quotas on the amount of export credit covered by guarantees however, there was a split in the UK between those who wished to pursue a tough anti-Soviet line, and those who wished to continue to conduct economic relations along purely commercial lines. This was a particularly sensitive time because it came in the midst of the Falklands crisis when Britain needed U.S. support for its actions against Argentina.

In the talks in CoCom, which had been initiated at the Ottawa Western economic summit, Britain was uncertain about U.S. objectives. If the American desire was to make CoCom more effective and close loopholes in existing controls, British policy was supportive. If, however, the U.S. was seeking to use CoCom as an instrument of economic containment, which the British argue would undermine its effectiveness in controlling the transfer of militarily relevant security goods, British policy was to retain the status quo, and to oppose a broadening of controls. Uncertainty about US objectives therefore, led the UK to move only very cautiously on US proposals in CoCom.

The US dissatisfaction with progress in talks on credit and CoCom culminated at the Versailles western economic summit. British policymakers were dismayed by the U.S. decision to escalate sanctions following the summit meeting. It was felt that significant progress had been made, with British help,[27] towards a tighter policy on export credits.[28] The British took the view that, owing to the complexities of the negotiations, and the need to reach agreement with all OECD countries, the US could not possibly have expected all their objectives to be achieved quickly. The extraterritorial nature of the extended embargo policy of June 1982, guaranteed that Britain would move off any mid-atlantic fence and firmly into the arms of its European Community partners. British legislation in the form of the Protection of Trading Interests Act was employed to counter what was seen as a direct challenge to British sovereignty. Britain also coordinated its defiance of U.S. policy with its European partners, and appeared to fall back into its traditional pro-trade stance.[29]

150

Current British Policy

Following the lifting of the pipeline embargo by the United States, British policy remains one of maintaining or even promoting 'mutually beneficial' trade. This is not quite business as usual however, and the broad consensus in Britain on East-West economic relations is not as firm as it was. First, 'mutually beneficial' trade means that Britain will not seek to buy trade by means of financial or political favours. Following the lack of success in competing for CMEA markets in the 1970s, and under a Conservative government it is less likely that Britain will compete, at the margin, for CMEA markets. If other West European countries offer credit or other trade inducements therefore, there may well be a further decline in Britain's relative share of CMEA markets.

The combination of a Conservative government which shares President Reagan's ideological stance vis-à-vis the Soviet Union, if not his tactics on East-West trade,[30] and a further decline in Britain's stake in trade will ensure Britain remains at the restrictive end of the European policy spectrum. Indeed there is already some evidence that Britain is now more prepared to accept the U.S. case that CoCom and national security export controls are ineffective in preventing the Soviet Union from obtaining important Western technologies. Whilst the UK still wants decisions on export controls taken in national capitals, and therefore opposes a radical strengthening of CoCom as an institution, it is less sceptical of, and more prepared to support the U.S. case than in the 1970s. On credit, Britain has also shifted from a position of matching other countries' subsidies to one of greater support for effective common norms which minimize subsidies.

There are, however, a number of qualifications to Britain's tougher stance on East-West trade. First and foremost it will not entertain any extraterritorial use of the U.S. export control legislation or retroactive measures to reduce trade or break contract sanctity. In the field of CoCom controls, there are also problems concerning the U.S. objective of introducing broad controls on electronic equipment such as those used in automation and data processing, sectors in which Britain retains some interest in CMEA markets. Finally, Britain can only move as far as its European Community partners move. It may exert pressure for more effective export controls or credit norms but will always act within the context of what its European partners do. In short, Britain's stance on the interplay between East-West political and economic relations will depend as much on the policies of its Western allies as on any deep convictions about the role of economic relations in East-West political relations.

NOTES

* This chapter is based on research work conducted whilst the author was a research fellow at The Royal Institute of International Affairs (Chatham House), London.

1 Formal recognition followed in March 1924.

2 CoCom represented a compromise in the sense that it was not a single set of multinational controls, but a means of coordinating national controls.

3 Following a merger with International Computer and Tabulations in 1968 this became I.C.L.

4 The credit covered 80 per cent of costs of British exports and was offered at an interest rate of 5.8 per cent. *Financial Times* 21 July 1972.

5 Britain had in fact run a deficit with the USSR throughout the 1960s. See table 1.

6 Interest rates were set at 7.5 per cent and 7.2 per cent for large projects.

7 See *Daily Telegraph* 13 June 1977.

8 The licence for fuel systems was finally turned down.

9 The Foreign Office gave electronics, computers and related circuits as targets for the KGB. *Financial Times* 29 September 1971.

10 This contrasts with US exports in which agricultural products predominate.

11 It is indicative of Britain's poor export performance with the USSR that despite the removal of diamonds, worth £ 367 m in 1980, Britain still runs a trade deficit. (See Table 1).

12 The 62 per cent share for oil given for 1982 in table 3 is due to the removal of diamonds from the trade figures and an unusually high figure, 422 m for oil imports in that year.

13 This compares with 6-7 per cent for the FRG and 5 per cent for France.

14 UK Department of Trade, *A Review of UK-Soviet Trade*, 1969-1978, London, 1980, pg. 11.

15 See however, Anglo-Soviet Trade, *Financial Times Survey*, 22 July 1975.

16 Figures from 1982 only.

17 ICI (in chemicals) and along with Courtaulds (textile fibres and yarn), Shell and BP (oil and gas equipment and oil imports) Rolls Royce and John Brown (Power generation) ICL, Ferranti and Plessey (Automation and data processing), etc.

18 British firms have signed long term trade agreements, such as ICI in 1976, partly to avoid problems caused by opposition to bilateral UK-CMEA agreements from the EC Commission. *The Times*, 11 May 1976.

19 *The Times*, 23 April 1976.

20 *New York Times*, 6 January 1980.

21 *Guardian*, 17 January 1980.

22 This principle was also employed in the sanctions against Argentina during the Falklands war in 1982.

23 The more moderate Conservative party view was expressed by ex-Prime Minister Heath who saw the British response as empty rhetoric and the sanctions as ineffective.

24 See for example the Governor of the Bank of England on the need for caution. *Financial Times*, 15 December 1981.
25 The view was perhaps most evident in the financial community.
26 *Financial Times*, 2 January 1982.
27 Prime Minister Thatcher is reported to have supported President Reagan at the summit, against President Mitterrand's and Chancellor Schmidt's opposition to tighter credit. *International Herald Tribune*, 24 June 1982.
28 As late as June 1982, Britain was confident a trade-off between ending the embargo and credit tightening could be reached. *Financial Times*, 7 June 1982.
29 Foreign Secretary Pym spoke of the need to maintain "political, commercial and cultural...links between the two halves of Europe"... and that "we are convinced that as long as these exchanges and contacts are on a reciprocal basis we have nothing to lose and much to gain". *Financial Times*, 29 September 1982.
30 See statement of the Trade Secretary Parkinson, *Financial Times*, 16 September 1982.

Table 1: *UK Trade balances with CMEA: £ m*
exports fob – imports cif

	1963	1966	1969	1971	1973	1975	1977	1979	1980	1982
USSR	− 27	− 75	− 100	− 117	− 233	− 198	− 434	− 409	− 331	− 289
CMEA	− 40	− 90	− 104	− 91	− 226	− 106	− 411	− 427	− 150	− 268

Source: East European Trade Council

Table 2: *Exports to CMEA (Europe) as a Percentage of Total British*
Exports

	1975	1976	1977	1978	1979	1980	1982	1983
USSR (exports)	1.1	0.9	1.0	1.1	1.0	0.9	0.6	0.8
(imports)	o. A.	2.1	2.1	1.7	1.7	1.5	1.1	1.0
Total CMEA (Europe)								
(exports)	3.0	2.5	2.5	2.6	2.2	2.2	1.5	1.6
(imports)	o. A.	3.3	3.4	2.9	2.9	2.4	1.9	1.9

Source: East European Trade Council

154

Table 3:   *Trends in the Structure of Britain's Trade With CMEA Countries (percentages)*

Soviet Union	1977	1980	1982	CMEA total	1977	1980	1982
Exports:				Exports only:			
Chemicals	36	19	16	Machinery	37	34.	34
				Manufactured			
Machinery	31	33	40	Goods	23	24	16
Manufactured							
Goods	21	33	20	Chemicals	26	17	19
Misc. Manufac-							
tures	5	4	7	Crude Materials	6	5	5
				Misc. Manufac-			
Others	7	11	7	tures	6	5	6
				Foodstuffs	–	8	6
				Other	2	7	14
Imports:							
Petroleum	33	23	65**				
Non-metalic							
minerals*	30	47	–				
Wood and							
cork	14	13	13				
Road vehicles	2	2	4				
Other	17	15	18				

* Almost exclusively diamonds
** Diamonds excluded from trade figures in 1982; and exceptional oil imports
Source: EETC data

Table 4: *Study of Principal Products Exported from U. K. to U.S.S.R. & E. Europe for Twelve Months of 1982*

Items under main headings show principal contributions to that heading. (Figures in brackets are values for same period 1980 in £ m)

USSR	GDR	POLAND
1. MACHINERY £140 (152)	1. MACHINERY £22m (12)	1. CHEMICALS £36m (41)
Power Generating 37	Metalworking 9	Artificial Resins 8
Industrial 37	Industrial 6	Chemical Matl's 7
Specialised 32	Electrical 4	Medicinal 6
Office & Data 15	Specialised 2	Organic 5
Electrical 8		Dyeing Matl's 3
2. MANF'D GOODS £70m(149)	2. FOODSTUFFS £19m (13)	2. MACHINERY £28m (122)
	Cereals 9	Industrial 10
Textile Yarn 26	Meat 7	Specialised 5
Iron & Steel 20		Electrical 4
Non-Ferrous Metls 13	3. MANF'D GOODS £8m (34)	Power Generating 4
Metal Manf's 6		Metalworking 2
	Textile Yarn 3	3. FOODSTUFFS £24m (63)
3. CHEMICALS £60m (87)	Non-metallic Minls 3	Cereals 20
		Meat 2
Organic 15	4. CHEMICALS £7 (8)	4. MANF'D GOODS £22m(33)
Chemical Matl's 14	Artificial Resins 2	Non-Metallic Min Manf 5
Inorganic 12	Organic 2	Textile Yarn 4
Artificial Resins 11	Medicinal 1	Iron & Steel 4
4. CRUDE MATL'S £28m(25)		Metal Manf's 3
	5. MISC. MANF'S £3m (4)	Non-Ferrous Metals 2
Textile Fibres 16		5. CRUDE MATL'S £8m(12)
Crude Rubber 9	Scientific	Crude Fertilisers 3
5. MISC. MANF'S £26m(20)	Instruments 1	Textile Fibres 3
Scif'ic Instruments 15	Photographic Eqpt. 1	
Clothing 6		
*£356m(455)	*£64m(94)	*£133m(296)

STUDY OF PRINCIPAL PRODUCTS IMPORTED BY U.K. FROM U.S.S.R. & E. EUROPE FOR TWELVE MONTHS OF 1982

1. Petroleum etc. £422m (179)	1. Non-Ferrous £49m Metals (12)	1. Cork & Wood £23m (23)
2. Cork & Wood £84m (106)	2. Furniture £9m (22)	2. Crude Fertilisers £22m (17)
3. Road Vehicles £24m (16)	3. General Industrial £14m Machinery (0.46)	3. Hides & Skins £15m (22)
4. Hides & Skins £23m (22)	4. Fertilisers £14m (12)	4. Coal & Coke £13m (13)
5. Cork & Wood £11m Manf's (11)	5. Misc Manf's £5m (5)	5. Iron & Steel £10m (12)
**£645m(786)	**£134m (88)	**£152m(195)

* Total UK Exports
** Total UK Imports

NOTE: For this table product groups are necessarily broad and approximate, detailed information is available in the 'Overseas Trade Statistics of the United Kingdom' publication.

(continued)

CZECHOSLOVAKIA	HUNGARY	ROMANIA	BULGARIA
1. MACHINERY £20m (22)	1. CHEMICALS £26m (20)	1. MACHINERY £45m (43)	1. MACHINERY £15m (12)
Specialised 7	Organic 11	Transport Eqpt 26	
Office & Data 4	Chemical Matl's 6	Power Generating 12	Specialised 5
Industrial 3	Medicinal 2	Industrial 3	Industrial 3
Metalworking 2	Artificial Resins 2	Electrical 2	Office & Data 3
Electrical 2	Dyeing Matl's 2		Electrical 2
2. CHEMICALS £19m (19)	2. MACHINERY £21m (20)	2. MINERAL FUELS £31m(9)	
Artificial Resins 5	Industrial 6		2. CHEMICALS £12m (10)
Organic 5	Specialised 6	Coal & Coke 31	
Chemical Matl's 2	Electrical 4		Chemical Matl's 3
Inorganic 2	Office & Data 2	3. FOODSTUFFS £12m (10)	Organic 3
3. MANF'D GOODS £11m(18)	Vehicles 1	Cereals 10	Inorganic 2
Textile Yarn 4	3. MANF'D GOODS £16m(16)	Meat 1	Artificial Resins 2
Non-Ferrous Metls 3	Textile Yarn 4		
Rubber Manf's 1	Metal Manf's 4	4. CHEMICALS £8m (10)	3. BEVERAGES & £5m(3)
Paper & Board 1	Paper & Board 2		TOBACCO
Metal Manf's 1	Non-Ferrous Min Manf 1	Chemical Matl's 3	Beverages 5
4. MISC M/NF'S £10m(11)	Non-Ferrous Metl 1	Artificial Resins 2	
Scientific	4. MISC MANF'S £7m (6)	Organic 1	4. MISC MANF'S £4m (2)
Instruments 5	Misc 3	5. MANF'D GOODS £8m(14)	Scientific
Photographic Eqpt 2	Scientific		Instruments 3
Clothing 2	Instruments 3	Non-Metallic Mins 2	5. MANF'D GOODS £4 (4)
5. CRUDE MATL'S £7m (9)	5. CRUDE MATL'S £4m (3)	Iron & Steel 2	Textile Yarn 1
Textile Fibres 5	Textile Fibres 3	Textile Yarn 2	Non-Ferrous Metls 1.
Hides & Skins 1			
•£70 m(81)	•£77m(69)	•£115m (99)	•£46m(35)

CZECHOSLOVAKIA		HUNGARY		ROMANIA		BULGARIA	
1. Cork & Wood	£10 m (14)	1. Electrical Machinery	£6 m (5)	1. Clothing	£12m (9)	1. Petroleum etc.	£7m (-)
2. Road Vehicles	£9m (8)	2. Clothing	£5m (5)	2. Petroleum etc.	£4m (22)	2. Iron & Steel	£5m (6)
3. Misc. Manf's	£7m (6)	3. Organic Chemicals	£4m (0.7)	3 Furniture	£4m (4)	3. Fruit & Vegetables	£2m (1)
4. Footwear	£6m (8)	4. Fruit & Vegetables	£4m (3)	4 Non-metallic Mineral Manf's	£4m (1)	4. Cork & Wood	£1 m (0.3)
5. Non-Metallic Mineral Manf's	£5m (6)	5. Textile Yarn	£3m (3)	5. Power Generating Machinery	£3m (2)	5. Non-Ferrous Metals	£1 m (0.6)
••£82m(88)		••£44m(43)		••£52m(65)		••£21m(0.4)	

Source: East European Trade Council

12
Italy

Giuseppe Schiavone

The alternative between economic warfare and détente in regard to relations with the USSR and Eastern European countries has been neither a subject of heated ideological debate nor a cause of serious conflicts of interest on Italy's political, economic and business scene. As a matter of fact, it hardly needs emphasizing that, within the framework of the Western defense and alliance structure, Italy is in a class of its own. Although it is near to impossible, in a short paper, to do justice to such a complex issue and to provide a thorough briefing on the strengths and weaknesses of the Italian position on East-West issues, it seems only fair to state from the very beginning that Italy clearly favors détente and does not regard economic warfare as a suitable foreign policy tool. This basic stand can be viewed as the outcome of the interaction of several factors.

On the economic side, foreign trade — consisting to a large extent of imports of raw materials and exports of finished and semifinished products — makes a major contribution (around 30 per cent) to Italy's gross national product, and has been a factor of paramount importance in the rapid economic growth of the country in the postwar period. A high level of international trade is, therefore, generally considered to work to Italy's advantage. Besides giving consistent support to international efforts aimed at removing tariff and nontariff barriers and promoting trade, Italy has played a prominent role in the setting up and expansion of the European Economic Community (EEC), and has also been a pioneer of East-West trade and industrial cooperation.

On the political side, the electoral strength and the remarkable influence on quite a number of aspects of public life of the Communist Party (Partito Comunista Italiano/PCI) — the second-largest party in the country and by far the largest Communist party in Western Europe — represent an important factor which should not be underestimated in any discussion on the basic political and socio-economic trends in Italy. It should be added that the non-Communist-voting electorate, with the exception of a tiny minority of dyed-in-the-wool anti-Communists on the far right, has never advocated a tough anti-Soviet posture. It is widely believed in Italy that peaceful methods should be used to settle differences among nations thereby excluding the use of force and economic warfare as basic elements in foreign policy. Recent anti-missile demonstrations have evidenced, *inter alia*, that pacifist-oriented factions exist within the two non-Communist mass parties — that is the Christian Democrats (Democrazia Cristiana/DC) and the Socialists (Partito Socialista Italiano/PSI) — as well as in the small parties that have emerged on the Communists' extreme left. Given the fact that what the French call *anticommunisme primaire* is virtually nonexistent in Italy's economic and business environment, the pros and cons of trading and entering into cooperation and joint-venture agreements with the USSR and East European countries are usually assessed from an economic and financial standpoint rather than on a basis of ideological priorities or national security considerations. In short, resorting to economic warfare has never been considered in Italy as a major means of putting pressure on the USSR and its allies in Eastern Europe or elsewhere in the world. Moreover, there seems to be a widespread scepticism about the effectiveness and practicability of economic countermeasures – such as trade sanctions and embargoes – which are inevitably double-edged.

Whatever the wisdom of this matter-of-fact attitude, there can be no doubt that the basic systemic constraints involved in dealing with centrally planned economies have played a far greater role in the evolution of Italy's relations with the socialist countries than the vagaries of the international climate and the changing prospects of détente. A quick overview of Italy's trade patterns in the last decade shows important deficits with the centrally planned economies (European as well as non-European) for the whole period, with the exception of a surplus in 1975. Between 1973 and 1982, the East's global share of Italian foreign trade did not undergo radical changes and accounted for a fraction well below 7 per cent of total trade even in the halcyon days of détente; the share of European members of CMEA averaged less than 4 per cent.

Trade between Italy and its most important partner in the socialist camp – the USSR – climbed from 462.7 billion lire in 1973 to 6830.9 billion in 1982. However, Italy has proved unable to generate sufficient exports to pay for the growing level of imports from the USSR. Annual trade deficits, again with the exception of a small surplus in 1975, rose from 52.5 billion lire in 1973 to an all-time record of 2746.1 billion in 1982, primarily because of huge outlays for imports of energy. The latest available figures suggest that Italy's struggle to gradually reduce its heavy trade deficit vis-à-vis the USSR has met with limited success; however, no major change in traditional patterns is to be expected in the short term.

On the Soviet side, official statistics show quite clearly the marked shift towards trade with the West over the last decade, and Italy's position among the USSR's top trading partners. In 1982 Italy represented a 3.4 per cent share of total Soviet trade and was preceded, among EEC countries, only by the Federal Republic of Germany which accounted for 5.8 per cent of the turnover. According to Soviet sources, the Italian trade deficit amounted in 1982 to nearly 1.6 billion roubles.

In the early 1980s Italian trade has been also characterized by deficits with the countries of Eastern Europe, with the partial exception of Bulgaria. Hungary as well as Poland, despite recurring tensions, remain Italy's major partners in Eastern Europe. The era of massive turnkey project purchases in Italy is over, and the Eastern European countries now concentrate on imports of semifinished products and spare parts. On the whole, it seems likely that hardcurrency liquidity and commercial considerations rather than political and ideological commitments will shape the trade outlook with Eastern Europe throughout the first half of the 1980s.

Despite the variety of multi-party coalitions which have governed the country since the end of World War II, the fundamental options of Italian foreign policy have remained remarkably constant. Italy's commitment to Western democratic principles and values and the pro-American orientation of Italian governments have never been called into question.

After the ejection of the Communists from the Cabinet in 1947, Italy was governed by several versions of 'center' coalitions – made up by the three small lay parties, Liberal, Social Democratic and Republican, under the leadership of the DC – until the early 1960s when the 'opening to the left' eventually materialized. The PSI abandoned the opposition and formally entered the 'center-left' coalition in 1963. After a series of governmental crises – including the return to a center coalition, the subsequent reestablishment of center-left and finally the formation of a minority government – the domination of political life by Christian Democrats was seriously challenged by the PCI in the 1976 general elections. Although the DC still led the poll, the Communists received over one-third of the popular vote and pressed for a 'historic compromise' with Catholic forces. The PCI, which had successfully resisted Soviet pressures, advocated an independent policy leading to an original road to socialism in keeping with the principles of 'Eurocommunism'.

As a consequence of the failure of non-Communist coalitions, the Christian Democrats had to rely on the parliamentary support of the PCI which, however, was allowed no direct participation in the 'national solidarity' government. The subsequent return to a clear-cut opposition role did not prevent the PCI from suffering unprecedented losses in the 1979 general elections. The invasion of Afghanistan made the PCI's differences with Moscow even more explicit but no strong anti-Soviet attitudes actually emerged either among the Communist rank and file or on the Italian political scene. Although a detailed examination of the key actors in the government and the main political parties would certainly evidence a diversity of positions, it can be said that U.S. economic sanctions against the USSR have never enjoyed a widespread support in Italy.

The deterioration of political relations between Italy and the USSR after the Soviet occupation of Afghanistan impaired the development of bilateral economic and trade links only to a fairly limited extent. The Italian government was, however, adamant in the refusal to enter into new agreements with the USSR for the concession of fresh credit lines, although supplier credits continued to be extended.

The Polish crisis of mid-1980, and the threat of a military intervention on the part of the USSR to restore 'order' in Warsaw, were actively discussed by the Italian political parties. The PCI openly criticized the 'model' of political organization existing in Eastern Europe and especially in Poland and urged the Polish

United Workers' Party to continue its efforts for 'renewal' and to undertake a far-reaching reform of the 'system' without yielding to any foreign pressure and interference in the internal affairs of the country. With respect to relations with the Soviet Party, the PCI managed to avoid dramatizing the differences with Moscow and repeatedly stated its readiness to seek constructive ways for re-establishing a climate of 'mutual understanding'. The other Italian parties stressed the gravity and complexity of the Polish events; parties directly support-ing the government coalition advocated a united reaction of Western European, and especially EEC countries, in order to substantially assist the Polish people without unduly strengthening the Warsaw régime.

The Christian Democrats' monopoly of the premiership terminated in June 1981 when the leader of the small Republican Party formed a five-party govern-ment including Christian Democrat, Socialist, Social Democratic, Liberal and Republican ministers. The markedly pro-American stand characterizing the three small lay parties participating in the coalition did not result in any hardline ap-proach to the USSR and its Eastern European allies, despite mounting East-West tensions.

In 1981, Italy, along with other Western European countries, announced its willingness to participate in the construction of the Urengoy pipeline project for delivering Soviet natural gas to Western Europe by the mid-1980s, and to buy substantial amounts of such gas.

The imposition of martial law in Poland in December 1981 further strained relations between the PCI and its Soviet counterpart. The PCI's Secretary called into question the 'Soviet model' and denounced the exhaustion of the 'propul-sive forces' which had instigated the October Revolution. The clash between the Italian and Soviet parties created quite a stir both inside and outside the PCI, but no complete breach with Moscow was ever envisaged by the Italian Communist leadership.

In early 1982 Italy, together with the other EEC member-countries, con-demned the Warsaw régime, but refused to endorse the U.S. economic sanctions imposed against both Poland and the USSR. Besides precluding the participation of American companies in the trans-Siberian pipeline, the Reagan Administra-tion barred the use of American technology by Western European firms working on the controversial project. The U.S. ban directly affected Nuovo Pignone, a firm which was manufacturing American-licensed turbine compressors in Italy and was forced to slow production. According to Italian and Western European views, U.S. restrictions hurt exporters far more than they helped national securi-ty. Moreover, the Italian government — as well as nearly all of Italy's political forces — did not share the U.S. concern that Western Europe might become over-ly dependent on the USSR for energy supplies.

As a riposte to Soviet behavior, however, the Italian government declared that participation in the pipeline would be deferred and that a 'pause for reflec-tion' would be necessary before arriving at a final decision on the subject. Furthermore, sessions of Joint Commissions involving Soviet or Polish participation were adjourned while meetings of foreign trade or economic ministers were cancelled. It must be stressed that such countermeasures had no significant impact on the bulk of Italian economic relations with the USSR and Eastern Europe.

The 'pause for reflection' concerning Italian participation in the Soviet-West European gas deals was repeatedly extended well beyond the original deadline. In fact the pause gradually assumed an essentially economic character as a result of Italy's decreasing interest in Soviet gas. It is a well-known fact that Italy is heavily dependent on imported energy; in 1982 roughly two-thirds of the country's energy requirements came from abroad and a large trade deficit was incurred because of oil imports. For several years the Italian State Electrical Board (Ente Nazionale per l'Energia Elettrica/ENEL) has been pressing for increased use of alternative energy sources such as nuclear power and coal. In order to avoid a chronic national energy shortage, legislation has recently been passed to allow construction of eight nuclear and sixteen coal-fired power stations.

With a view to diversifying its energy sources, the Italian government also signed a long-term agreement with Algeria for the supply of gas through an undersea pipeline between North Africa and Sicily in 1982; when this pipeline went into operation in mid-1983, Algeria became Italy's largest foreign source of natural gas. Despite its much-disputed cost to the Italian taxpayer, the trans-Mediterranean pipeline now provides more than adequate amounts of gas, thus significantly reducing the importance of future deliveries from Siberia. Moreover, the purchase of substantial quantities of Siberian gas would further aggravate Italy's already large trade deficit with the USSR, unless a serious effort is made on the Soviet side to increase imports of Italian goods. But the USSR is apparently unable to increase its purchases unless Italy extends fresh credit facilities. Italy for its part is only willing to grant supplier credits for specific deals.

In November 1982, the second government in Italy's postwar history to be led by a Republican premier, actually a carbon copy of its predecessor, resigned. A new coalition was then established under a Christian Democrat prime minister with the participation of the parties of the former coalition with the exception of the Republicans. When the Socialists eventually withdrew their wavering support for the four-party coalition, new parliamentary elections were held in June 1983.

The unexpected electoral setback suffered by the DC, which lost a sizeable share of the popular vote, favored the strategy of the PSI's Secretary who succeeded in setting up a five-party coalition government in August 1983. The Socialist premiership brought about no radical alteration in either the tone or substance of Italy's foreign policy vis-à-vis the socialist countries and was not expected to. Given the magnitude of the domestic issues confronting the Socialist-led coalition, especially the basic concern with Italy's economic health, there is precious little scope for the formulation of an articulate foreign policy that adequately meets the challenges of the 1980s, both in Europe and the rest of the world.

The Italian government shares the Western European view that the reduction of East-West tension, and genuine improvements in relations with the other half of the continent, should be based on undiminished security and continued dialogue. All of the parties represented in the government coalition back NATO's 'two-track' strategy for countering the growing arsenal of SS-20 missiles targeted on Western Europe. Italy's decision to allow nuclear missiles to be based at Comiso, Sicily, if a settlement is not reached at the U.S.-USSR talks in Geneva, should not adversely affect economic and trade ties with the USSR. According to the Italian view, such relations should be governed primarily by economic considerations, without the inordinate fear that any expansion of trade would, by itself, assist the Soviet Union in enlarging its war potential. This also applies to CoCom lists of strategic materials which should not be unduly expanded; Italy is unlikely to back moves for further CoCom constraints on the transfer of technology and related sales to CMEA member-countries.

The episode of the South Korean civil airliner, which strayed into the airspace of the USSR and was eventually shot down over Sakhalin by Soviet fighters, aroused strong emotion and outraged public opinion in Italy. However, it was clear from the start that the airliner incident was unlikely, on its own, to become an issue in Italian-Soviet relations. When it comes to taking countermeasures, Italy, like other Western European countries and the U.S. itself, has to select practical responses that do not harm its own interests. Moreover, it should be kept in mind that, in Italy, there has never been public pressure for, nor identifiable lobbies favouring the application of sanctions against the socialist countries. On the one hand therefore, there is practically no need for an Italian government to impose sanctions for 'internal use' that is for domestic policy considerations, in order to meet the demands of specific groups asking for the 'punishment' of the Soviet Union. On the other hand, the adoption of sanctions for 'external' use – that are really intended to hamper a foreign partner's development – would be quite unrealistic and would hardly have any crippling effect in the case of the USSR. Such measures would meet with the opposition of Italian economic and business interests who have always shown their fundamental willingness to stay on good enough terms with the USSR and its allies in Eastern Europe.

The Western countries should emphasize plans for a mutually coordinated trade and financing policy vis-à-vis the USSR and Eastern Europe, rather than attempt erratic and ill-fated experiments in economic and financial warfare. An important step towards bringing the West's diverging policies into comparative harmony could be the radical changes recently agreed upon by OECD member-countries with respect to export credit rates; that is the interest rates on long-term loans granted to mainly third-world importers but also including the USSR.

With a view to strengthening the competitive position of their respective exporters and boosting trade, some countries, notably Italy and France, have for a number of years been providing heavy government subsidies so as to allow their banks to offer cheaper export credits. In conformity with the recent 'gentlemen's agreement' concluded between OECD member-countries after heated debate, 'consensus rates', which have been fixed since 1976 within the OECD framework, will be periodically adjusted by means of an automatic mechanism closely reflecting the evolution of market interest rates. This complicated compromise, besides reducing the cost to Italian and French taxpayers of subsidizing the difference between market rates and consensus rates, will strengthen Western solidarity on a vital issue of East-West economic relations.

The unwillingness of the Italian government to deal with the Soviet Union and the other socialist countries by means – such as far-reaching economic and financial sanctions and boycott measures – that would ultimately hurt the nation's economic interests without appreciable gains in other fields is generally shared by economic and business circles.

Italy's industrial sector is characterized by a handful of large, and fairly rigid, private and publicly owned groups, and a multitude of small and medium sized companies, which are generally flexible and able to react quickly to changing demands, and have developed a fairly high degree of expertise. The largest private groups such as Fiat have been quite active in establishing ties with the Eastern half of Europe and have consistently advocated the full normalization of economic relations. The major state-owned holding companies, notably the Istituto per la Ricostruzione Industriale (IRI) and the Ente Nazionale Idrocarburi (ENI), have made an outstanding contribution to the progress of relations with the USSR and Eastern European countries. IRI, which controls Italy's largest industrial holding company, is responsible for much of Italy's public enterprise, from steelmaking, plant engineering, energy, public works and shipbuilding to electronics, communications, shipping and air transport and banking. Finsider and Finmeccanica are among the IRI Group companies which have most intensely participated in carrying out programs and projects in the USSR and Eastern Europe. The leader of Italy's energy industry, and the third-largest enterprise outside the U.S. is the ENI Group, which is involved in all aspects of oil and gas from exploration to distribution and has gained first-hand experience in constructing natural-gas pipelines from work in the Netherlands, the USSR and Algeria. ENI Group companies are also present in the chemical industry, engineering and services, textile machinery and textiles, along with mining and metallurgy.

The principal employers' body in Italy is Confindustria (General Confederation of Italian Industry) which comprises territorial and trade associations, regional federations and branch groupings, and has traditionally played a significant role in Italy's economic and political life. Over the past decade Confindustria has repeatedly stressed the importance of public support for small and medium-sized enterprises striving to preserve and/or increase their share of the Soviet and Eastern European market. This especially applies to conventional forms of payment (cash payments and supplier credits) and medium- and long-term credit, as well as to countertrade and buy-back transactions. According to Confindustria, coproduction and specialization agreements also deserve special consideration despite their limited impact on the bulk of Italian relations with the socialist countries.

The basically favorable attitude of the industrial and business community towards the development of East-West relations is shared, albeit for different reasons, by major labor unions which are traditionally characterized by fairly strong political overtones. The biggest union is the General Confederation of Labor (Confederazione Generale Italiana del Lavoro/CGIL) which remained very closely linked to the PCI until the last decade and still is, at least in part, under heavy Communist influence. Dissatisfaction with the excessive politicization of the CGIL in the early postwar period led to the formation of two rival unions – the Italian Confederation of Workers' Unions (Confederazione Italiana Sindacati Lavoratori/CISL), mostly influenced by Christian Democrats, and the Italian Union of Labor (Unione Italiana del Lavoro/UIL), controlled by Socialists, Social Democrats and Republicans. In the 1970s these three confederations gradually extended their intervention well beyond the traditional sphere of labor relations. Despite their forthright condemnation of the Soviet Union's invasion of Afghanistan and of the Polish government's crackdown on 'Solidarity', the confederations have not advocated an economic boycott against any socialist country.

The steadily deteriorating economic climate in the late 1970s and early 1980s has weakened the bargaining power of the three main unions which have thus far proved unable to forge an effective unity of action of the labor movement, though some of their affiliated unions have combined.

As far as the agricultural sector is concerned, neither employers' nor workers' organizations have ever requested the reduction of economic and trade ties with the USSR and its allies.

Besides the widespread consensus among political and economic forces, the prospects for Italy's improved cooperation with the socialist countries are obviously dependent on several other factors. Over the past few years Italy has been plagued by inflation and recession and has not begun to recover; the poor performance of the domestic economy is a source of serious concern to the Socialist-led coalition government and threatens the maintenance of Italy's strong position in world markets. Moreover, continuing economic difficulties could, in the long term, cause an imbalance in the institutional structures of a country which continues to serve as a testing-ground in the ideological struggle between East and West. Despite its many weaknesses, Italy remains strongly involved in the Atlantic Alliance and West European integration and has often expressed its willingness to cooperate in establishing more rational guidelines for conducting East-West relations, while keeping trade and foreign policy separate. A long-standing advocate of the elimination of artificial barriers to trade and economic relations, Italy does not favor the imposition of sanctions for political and ideological reasons. Nor does the Italian government approve of restrictive methods such as extraterritoriality (the control of the re-export of goods once they have left the national territory) and retroactivity (the prohibition of exports of goods or technology even after a contract has been signed), that are likely to cause major strains in the Western alliance without improving the West's security.

In a world of escalating interdependencies, the overriding interests of both world camps lie in cooperation. The existence of stable trade and economic ties between East and West while not promoting by itself international security and goodwill would make a substantial contribution towards rebuilding détente.

13
The European Community

Mathias Jopp

Introduction

From the end of the 2nd World War until well into the 1960s trade with the East was, despite a growing interest on the part of West European industry in the markets of Eastern Europe, greatly impeded by security and political differences. However, beginning with détente between the superpowers and continuing with the rapprochement evident in the Helsinki process, there was a huge expansion of East-West trade relations within Europe, and the political value of trade assumed a totally different importance. Just as the Cold War years of the 1950s and 1960s were dominated by the belief that trade with one's political enemies would strengthen them, the subsequent intensification of trade, industrial and scientific cooperation was linked with the hope of a secure peace, increased mutual prosperity and the dismantling of societal differences. Economic interdependency has even been seen as a possible means of raising the cost of military conflict and thus making the likelihood of conflict itself a little more remote.[1]

Expectations pinned on the development of economic cooperation between East and West have been considerably damped in recent years, by both the difficult economic climate and, in particular, by recurring political tensions between the Super Powers. The European Community still stresses its interest in developing East-West trade on the basis of the Helsinki Final Act, but it also emphazises the – more status quo oriented – need for a normalisation of its economic relationship with Eastern Europe, subject to factors of economic risk and security needs.

As opposed to the USA, Western Europe has rejected using its economic strength as a means of political confrontation with Eastern Europe. This is not only because of the geographical proximity to – and the historical and cultural ties with – its Eastern neighbours, but also because a complex set of economic relations has grown up between the two areas which is linked with significant industrial interests.

The importance of EEC trade with Eastern Europe

Since the middle of the 70s, approximately 7 per cent of the Community's entire external trade has been with CMEA countries. As a result it is Eastern Europe's most important economic partner. Almost two thirds of the CMEA countries' total exports to the West go to the Community, while 50 per cent of the

CMEA countries' total imports from the West are of EEC origin. There was a noticeable acceleration in the growth of trade between Eastern and Western Europe throughout the 70s. In this period, the volume of trade between the two showed almost a five fold increase, even when we take into account the perceptible leveling off of the rates of increase in the 2nd half of the decade (see Table 1).[2]

The structure of this trade has, in comparison to its volume, changed relatively little (see Table 2). Energy and raw materials, as well as semi-finished and agricultural products still form the bulk of the EEC's imports from Eastern Europe. Despite this, the EEC is still the largest Western customer for Eastern Bloc manufactured products. Machinery and capital goods dominate the EEC exports to the CMEA area, but in recent years the percentage of consumer goods, especially agriculture and food products has also increased. In certain branches of industry, such as mechanical engineering and iron and steel, CMEA countries have become important customers for the EEC. A fifth of all the EEC exports of tubular and sheet steel, as well as entire metal processing plants are shipped to Eastern Europe. In return, the Community's needs in natural gas, uranium, and oil as well as other important natural resources are supplied in growing quantity by the USSR and other European CMEA countries.

The EEC balance of trade with Eastern Europe (see Table 1) deteriorated significantly between 1979 and 1982. In this period, the Community faced growing imports from its CMEA partners, while EEC exports to Eastern Europe showed a tendency to stagnate. There was little change in this trend in 1983 despite the fact that the Community was able to reduce its deficit due mainly to an increase in exports to the USSR. Total exports to the other East European countries continued to stagnate. One reason for the continued large deficit of 8 billion ECU in 1983, is the unequal trading situation with the USSR, which, through its exports of raw materials and energy, has been able to build up a very large surplus with the Community. Another important reason is the fact that most of the state trading countries are attempting to overcome their balance of payments crises by trying to increase their exports to the West while at the same time cutting their hard currency imports (see Table 3). This strategy enabled the smaller European CMEA countries to achieve their first ever trade surplus with the EEC, of about 1 billion ECU's, in 1982.

The evolution of trade from the beginning of the 70s to the present has followed the pattern of "expansion", "consolidation", and "stagnation" (see Bethkenhagen in this volume). The cause of this must, first and foremost, be sought in economics. EEC trade barriers and cyclical weaknesses, together with the CMEA countries' foreign exchange and debt difficulties are the central problems of East-West trade. Unless they are solved trade will continue to stagnate. This is especially so in the area of trade relations with the smaller European CMEA countries. This state of affairs could have been ameliorated had the EEC and CMEA been able to agree on trade promoting measures such as adequate credit (guarantee) facilities and reciprocal dismantling of tariff and non tariff barriers. The fact that such an amicable regulation of relations has been and remains so far from reach has ultimately to do with political factors.

The EEC's trade policy

Since 1975, when the Community assumed jurisdiction in matters related to trade with the state trading countries, there have been no official treaties between the EEC and CMEA or between most of its Member States and individual CMEA countries.

In order to safeguard the continuation of the trade relations the EEC offered bilateral trade agreements with each of the CMEA countries at the end of 1974, shortly before the agreements between the individual states in the two economic areas lapsed. At that time, none of the CMEA countries responded to the offer. This was largely due to the extremely rigid position of the Soviet Union in refusing to have normal dealings with the Community. Since 1975, the Community has therefore adopted a so called "autonomous trade policy" in relation to imports from CMEA countries. This mainly consists of a list of import quotas which are changed yearly by a decision of the European Council of Ministers. The EEC Commission has established contact with individual CMEA states on a number of multilateral levels through GATT, ECE (the UN Economic Commission for Europe) and the CSCE (Conference on Security and Cooperation in Europe) process following the Helsinki agreement. Bulgaria, Czechoslovakia, Poland, Rumania and Hungary have opted for sectoral agreements with the EEC in textiles and steel in which these countries agreed to an auto-limitation of their exports. In 1980 a five year agreement between the EEC and Rumania concerning trade in industrial products was signed. There is also an agreement on the establishment of a permanent bilateral Joint Committee with Rumania which is the only case so far of a CMEA country taking up the EEC's 1974 offer and entering into a legally binding bilateral trade agreement.

In the most intense phase of détente it was the CMEA which took the initiative in intensifying contact between the economic organizations in Eastern and Western Europe. This was done in order to effect a change in the unsatisfactory legal relationship that existed between the CMEA and the EEC. But progress has not been great. Indeed, it would not be too unfair to describe the negotiations since their inception as "the Dialogue of the Deaf and Dumb".[3] Since 1976 both sides have presented totally differing blueprints for an agreement, and it has been impossible to obtain a real advance despite small concessions on both sides. While the Community does not recognize the CMEA as a partner in formal trade agreements, it is prepared, at the very least, to enter into an agreement in order to normalize its relationship with the Eastern economic organization in areas such as the exchange of statistical information, standardization, environmental issues and the comparing of economic forecasts. Only in the preamble of such an agreement would it deal with the importance of trade between the two economic organizations. The East European side has suggested a mixed agreement, between both the organizations and the individual Member States, covering trade related questions such as most favoured nation treatment and credit policies, as well as the setting up of a Joint Committee.[4]

On three occasions in 1980, a group of experts met in Geneva to discuss the possibility of a compromise between the different concepts, but no real progress was made. In 1981 commissioner Haferkamp sent a communication to the President of the Executive Committee of CMEA which probably confirmed the existing EEC position. This letter was never answered, and since then there have been no contacts with the CMEA as an organization. Both sides now have considerable reservations about the possibility of establishing a contractual framework. The recent deterioration in East-West political relations have made it even more difficult for either side to formally recognize the other.

The Community's competence

The EEC reservations about a skeleton agreement with CMEA are not entirely plausible. It is argued that the CMEA has no supra-national authority to enter into binding agreements. But this ignores the fact that CMEA has already signed economic, technical and scientific cooperation treaties with Finland (1973), Iraq (1975) and Mexico (1975).[5] West European criticism of CMEA's incomplete integration also glosses over the fact that the EEC's own position in relation to trade policy with CMEA countries is full of gaps and inadequacies.

Since the individual trade agreements between EEC countries and CMEA countries expired in the first half of the 1970s, the Community's Member States have entered into binding cooperation agreements in trade and commerce with their Eastern counterparts.[6] Through these agreements, which are designed to promote trade, the Community's legal competence in the area of trade policy has been undermined. The individual Member States are thus able to avail themselves of a legal precedent which does not appear in article 113 (EEC-Common Commercial Policy) of the Treaty of Rome. Most of the individual Member States have the ability to offer special conditions, such as in the form of public backing for credit or industrial cooperation, in order to increase their share of East European markets. The rules of the Community are essentially limited to restrictive measures concerned with imports, such as customs, anti-dumping and countervailing duties etc., and do not extend to the area of trade promotion.

In its decision 1/78, handed down on October 4 1979, the European Court of Justices decided that the above-mentioned cooperation agreements fall within the jurisdiction of the Community according to article 113 (EEC). In other words, the resistance of the Member States has frustrated attempts to enlarge the

Community's legal powers in this field. There is a consultation procedure within the Community which has existed since 1974, but this has unfortunately seldom functioned properly. The European Parliament has repeatedly criticized this state of affairs, and, in a 1982 Resolution it recommended that the Community itself ratify economic cooperation agreements.[7] In the early 1970s the emphasis in East-West economic relations shifted towards the areas of credit and industrial cooperation. Consequently the European Parliament wished to see the relevant components of foreign economic policy in these areas transferred to Community jurisdiction.

Given the competition for Eastern markets EEC Member States have concentrated on consolidating their trading positions with the individual CMEA nations. The Member States wish to expand trade and not to sacrifice potential markets on the altar of Community solidarity.[8] From a national point of view therefore, the prospect of a well regulated and orderly formal relationship between the economic blocs seems remote and of almost no practical benefit.

The Council of Ministers, faced with the individual interests of Member States, has never shown much enthusiasm for the developing trade relations between the EEC and Eastern Europe. It is evident that the Council only took the first measures towards the formulation of an East-West trade policy – such as the establishment of the committee for the examination of the individual cooperation agreements, the scheme of bilateral trade agreements between the EEC and individual CMEA countries, and the anouncement of the autonomous import policy – because of pressure created by expiration of the older trade agreements of EEC's Member States with their East European partners.[9] As long as the majority of Member States pursue national policies and try to influence the development of East-West trade relationships by offering special credit facilities and individual cooperation agreements, very little change can be expected.

Some EC officials believe that trade with the East could be intensified if the Community's full jurisdiction were established in areas of economic and industrial cooperation.[10] But the Commission has only concentrated on trying to improve, on a Community level, the consultative machinery for the cooperation agreements by the Member States. If it is recognized that CMEA is capable of entering into treaties on economic, industrial and technological cooperation, then the Community could also enlarge its responsibility in the area of cooperation agreements which could provide a catalyst for resolving the deadlocked relationship between the EEC and CMEA.

The Community's political objectives

The EEC's commercial policy is not only of economic importance, it also involves a vital political element. By maintaining the position that trade agreements can only be drawn up between the EEC and individual CMEA states, and not recognizing the CMEA as a full partner, the Commission is signalling its intention to prevent increased Soviet domination in Eastern Europe. The European Parliament also concurs with this policy as indicated in its July 1982 report. This argued that an agreement with the CMEA as an institution would be neither legally possible, because CMEA has no supra-national powers, nor politically desirable, because "it would help to strengthen the Soviet Union's grip on the East European countries, and that is not our aim".[11]

Through its encouragement of bilateral trade agreements with individual East European countries, the Community is also trying to cultivate a kind of "decoupling strategy", through which it would at least stand a chance of evolving special relationships with several different CMEA countries. This coincides with the interests of those smaller East European countries seeking foreign and external trade policies which have some independence from Soviet influence. It must be stressed, however, that these countries have also said that a basic agreement setting out the principles of economic relations between the EEC and CMEA could provide the ground work for bilateral agreements between the EEC and themselves.[12]

In the past the European Parliament has recommended greater political flexibility in this area and criticized the Commission on its uncompromising stance.[13] Today it no longer warns of the consequences of the EEC's rigidity, however, but clearly identifies with the Commission's position which is that it is, in principle, impossible to make a formal agreement with the CMEA on matters related to trade policy. This change of attitude on the part of the Parliament can be understood as a reflex to the cooling of East-West relations following Afghanistan and the events in Poland.

The unified stance within the Community may also have something to do with recent progress in the EEC's relationship with several CMEA countries. In the summer of 1983 the USSR brought an action against an EEC antidumping tariff in the European Court of Justices, thus indirectly recognizing the Community's jurisdiction in the area of trade.[14] Since the signing of the agreement between the EEC and Rumania in 1980, Hungary has also shown interest in drawing up a trade agreement with the Community. Czechoslovakia has furthermore expressed a wish to enter into additional sectoral agreements with the Community in glass and ceramics. Developments have strengthened the widely held notion within the EEC that by evading a framework agreement with the CMEA itself for as long as possible, the individual CMEA countries will "capitulate" one after the other in "domino fashion" and accept the Community's offer of bilateral trade agreements.[15]

One could be forgiven for questioning whether it was the EEC which brought about the above mentioned events. Towards the end of the Breshnev era and during Andropov's short term of office, the USSR probably moved away from its rigid position vis-à-vis the EEC. Given the problems of East-West trade the

USSR seemed to show a greater tolerance of the smaller European CMEA countries' wishes to establish bilateral relationships with the Community. Euphoria would, however, be inappropriate at this stage. The discussions between the EEC and Hungary on the possibility of a trade agreement have, up until now, been fruitless. The reasons for this failure lie in the nature of the Hungarian demands and the more or less uninteresting nature of the EEC's proposals. At the beginning of 1984 each side seemed to be prepared to compromise, but after the 1984 round of bilateral talks it was still uncertain if and when a trade agreement would be signed.[16]

One of the central problems is the oversensitivity of the West Europeans to import competition from the East. In its strategy towards the CMEA countries the EEC therefore, finds itself torn between political demands and economic realism. It is no longer just a question of the EEC seeking bilateral agreements with individual CMEA countries without having to deal with CMEA itself.[17] It is now also a question of whether the realization of bilateral trade agreements, in which the East European countries are now showing an interest, will come about given the Community's difficulty in liberalizing its import policy.

Trade with damage limitation

Despite the great interest shown by export oriented West European industries in the markets of Eastern Europe, the need has been felt within the EEC to seek some form of protection against the negative consequences of East-West trade. The European Parliament has shown much concern about the problems of counter-trade, the dumping practices of state trading countries and agricultural exports to Eastern Europe.

Because of their trade deficits, debt and chronic shortages of hard currency, the Socialist countries have, in the last few years, become extremely interested in barter as one basis of their trade with the West. In contrast to complementary barter practices, substitute compensation trade, through which Eastern Europe is able to compete the EEC products, is seen as a constant danger to Community markets and as an extra hindrance to the growth of employment. The European Parliament has, therefore suggested a possibility of implementing better controls at a Community level in order to reduce the negative impact of compensation trade.[18] The background of this parliamentary initiative is the need to protect weaker industries, as well as concern about small and medium sized enterprises. The latter see themselves as particularly disadvantaged by the increased importance of barter in trade relations with Eastern Europe, because, among other things, smaller companies are less able to engage in countertrade than large concerns with flexible sales organizations.

On account of the EEC's difficult economic climate, the dumping practices of state trading countries have become a subject of passionate interest within the European Parliament. As recently as October 1982, the Parliament expressed its apprehension about "the increasing cases of dumping by the CMEA countries which mainly affect a number of economically sensitive sectors in the Community . . . and which are also increasingly impeding the transport and services sectors".[19] It is extremely difficult to prove whether there has in fact been an increase in dumping by East European countries, or whether Western industries have just become more sensitive in this area. The economic significance of dumping has always been relatively small. Between January 1978 and July 1980, the Commission enacted antidumping procedures against State trading countries in iron and steel (strip and sheet), chemical products, artificial fibres, electrical motors and mechanical watches.[20] Given the complicated pricing policies of the East Europeans, it is not easy to prove dumping against them. A large proportion of the anti-dumping actions are therefore terminated by suitable price undertakings by the exporters.

The EEC's agricultural exports to Eastern Europe are a definite bone of contention within the European Parliament.[21] The sale of subsidized butter to the USSR has, in particular, caused great controversy. The stormy Parliamentary debates are even more astonishing when one considers that the EEC has actually increased its agricultural exports to CMEA countries, while CMEA access to EEC markets has been limited due to the protectionist character of the Common Agricultural Policy. The Parliamentary controversy can, however, be explained by the fact that the problems of financing agricultural exports are completely intertwined with the problems of quantifying the political value of trading with Eastern Europe and the USSR. Under pressure from the Parliament the Commission has limited the exports of butter to Russia for some time. Generally, however, it follows the Council's line which is to regard agricultural exports to the East as "normal trade" and thus pay the usual export restitutions.[22] In so doing, the Commission assumes a non-ideological position in which it subsidizes the exports of farm products regardless of destination, especially if this means saving storage costs or the disposal of old stocks.

Conflict in Transatlantic Relations

Sanction Politics. Since the beginning of the 1980s when the U.S.A. reintroduced trade into the East-West conflict and sought support for this approach from its allies, the European Community and its Member States have faced a latent conflict between their obligations as allies and their economic interests in Eastern Europe. The West Europeans were of the opinion that they should not stand idly by during the Soviet intervention in Afghanistan and the development of events in Eastern Europe. But contrary to U.S.A., they considered diplomatic and political action, not economics as the main means of expressing Western displeasure.[23] Despite a great deal of American pressure, the Member States and the Community itself, showed very little enthusiasm for the proposed economic sanctions against the USSR. In the end the EEC sanctions were of only symbolic value, proved difficult to apply and, as expected, had very little influence on events.

Import sanctions against the Soviet Union were agreed upon by the Council of Economic and Financial Ministers on the 15th of March 1982, in retaliation for the imposition of martial law in Poland.[24] Member States, however, insisted on some exemptions. Greece refused to ratify the Council's decision and Denmark later distanced itself from an extension of the measures.

The ministerial pronouncement of the 15th of January 1980,[25] made after the Soviet intervention in Afghanistan, promised not to replace the grain deliveries embargoed by the United States. Ultimately, however, it had wide parliamentary consequences: EEC agricultural exporters quite obviously profited from the American embargo and, contrary to the Council's intentions, EEC deliveries to the USSR were far above their traditional quotas. Between July 1979 and June 1980 alone the exports of corn quadrupled and, according to European Parliamentary sources, exports of prepared animal feed rose 44-fold in 1980 and wheat exports were 340 times greater than the year before.[26]

The two "sanctions agreements" of the Council of Ministers can be seen as the maximum attainable within a Community consensus. While wishing to express solidarity with the U.S.A. and demonstrate Europe's disapproval to the Soviet actions, the Member States did not wish to jeopardize their commercial relations with CMEA countries. Thus on the 29th/30th of March 1982 the European Council (the EEC heads of government) within the framework of the EPC (European Political Cooperation) stated that economic ties between the EEC and CMEA countries have been a stabilizing factor in "East-West relations as a whole" and pleaded for their continuation.[27] This was only three and a half months after the introduction of martial law in Poland. In a number of resolutions in the summer and fall of 1982, the European Parliament recommended the continuation of détente and the promotion of East-West trade. In response to a report by MEP (Member of the European Parliament) Seeler, the Parliament also stressed that the Community should refrain from engaging in any form of economic sanctions.[28]

In taking this line most West European governments and political parties were motivated by a common interest in maintaining the economic and political status quo in Europe. The consolidation of agreed areas of understanding between East and West was also behind the EEC/EPC state's successful effort to prevent the CSCE follow up conference in Madrid breaking down after the introduction of martial law in Poland. The threshold of European moderation and conciliation would have been crossed had the Soviet Union invaded Poland. In this case not only political, but also massive economic measures were ready as part of NATO's contingency plan in the event of a direct Soviet intervention.[29]

Western Europe's lack of enthusiasm for the use of sanctions can also be explained by a decisive structural difference within the Atlantic Alliance itself. The division of the costs of sanctions among the Western Allies is unequal. Because Western Europe has more commercial links with Eastern Europe than the U.S.A. the costs of sanctions for Europe would have been higher. According to estimates the Community would also have suffered much greater damage than the Soviet Union.[30] On top of this was the fact that grain exports, which form the main part of the U.S.A.'s trade with Socialist countries, would have been more easily discontinued than the delivery of machinery and processing plants which form the main part of West European exports to the CMEA area. The European reticence towards American sanction politics can therefore be largely explained by the fact that Europe was being asked to pay a higher price than the U.S.A. for the disruption of its economic relations with Eastern Europe. The Reagan Administration's termination of President Carter's grain embargo and the new long-term U.S.-USSR wheat agreement illustrates that important economic interests take precedence over the political objectives of sanctions on both sides of the Atlantic.

The Siberian Gas Pipeline as an example of Dependency? The Community adopted a clear position several times during the transatlantic conflict over the gas pipeline (see chapter 6 in this volume), even though the issues concerned mainly national interests and did not really fall within the EC's jurisdiction. The project did, however, complement the EC's concept of energy diversification, both in terms of the sources of supply and the mix of energy products. The EC has concerned itself with the problems of Western European dependency on Soviet energy more than ever before. In its August 1982 memorandum to the U.S.-government, the EC showed that, at its peak in 1990, the import of Soviet natural gas will account for no more than 4 per cent of the Community's total energy consumption, and argued that this in no way constituted a dangerous level of dependency.[31] The Commission has also concerned itself, in detail, with the security of the Community's energy supply.[32] It has shown that Soviet natural gas will in the future account for about 19 per cent of the Community's needs, and would represent no more than a third of the natural gas requirements of any Member State. Based on this research the Commission also concluded that the Community could suffer a 25 per cent cut in gas supplies for 6 months without any great inconvenience to the end user. However, it did recommend a further diversification of imports and the development of indigenous gas production and synthetic substitutes in order to avoid problems in "extreme circumstances".

After initial hesitation, the EC reacted to the extension of the U.S. pipeline sanctions against the Soviets with two protest notes. These stated that the claims to extraterritorial jurisdiction of American law were in contravention of the basic principles of international trade and an unacceptable interference in businesses which were located in Europe and thus under the jurisdiction of European law.[33] Just before the U.S. lifted its sanctions the EC Commission was, through its delegation in Washington, involved in the attempt to formulate a set of guide lines for East-West trade policy within the Alliance. Among other things, it was agreed not to engage in new natural gas projects with the Soviet Union until the possibility of alternatives had been properly researched. This did not clash with Europe's actual interests, because demand had fallen in the wake of the recession and energy saving policies. Further spectacular natural gas deals with the USSR were therefore not on the cards.

Export Credit Policy. In 1982 during the increasingly contentious transatlantic differences over subsidized credit for the East, the Community was only involved in the OECD talks on officially guaranteed export credits (OECD-Consensus). On the 30th of June 1982 the Council of Economic and Financial Ministers, after some internal controversy, accepted the OECD proposals that the USSR, Czechoslovakia and GDR be effectively reclassified as advanced industrial countries (category I), as they had a per capita GNP of over $4 000, thus attracting the maximum level of minimum interest rates set by the OECD.[34] These countries had to accept a twofold rise of interest rates, the first because of the reclassification and the second because of a general increase in minimum interest rates for the category I.

For the EC, the reclassification of certain CMEA countries was a compromise strategy. On the one hand, it accommodated some of the American demands for higher interest rates and tougher conditions on loans to CMEA countries. On the other hand, it avoided the possibility of a too dramatic rise in the minimum interest rates. A number of EEC Member States also saw the new arrangements as a means of adjusting to the then world wide spiralling interest rates which were making the provision of subsidized credit on competitive terms more and more costly for the public exchequers.

Reactions to the U.S. Export Control Policy. Following its experience with the extension of the American pipeline embargo to include affiliates and licenses of American cooperations in Europe, the EC was quick to respond to the U.S.-Administration's attempt to tighten export controls unilaterally (see chapter 16 in this volume).

In communications in March and April 1983 the EC clearly spelled out its reservations on the U.S.-Administration's proposal for updating the Export Administration Act of 1979. It criticized above all the continuation of the provisions for extraterritorial use of controls in this law. It also expressed disapproval of the retroactive application of export controls and provisions which would grant presidential authority to impose import bans on foreign firms contravening American export controls.[35]

The EC complained that the U.S.A. was seeking to use controls not only for security reasons, but also as a means of pursuing its foreign policy objectives. The EC does not consider the latter exempted, under article 20 and 21 of the GATT, from the general ban on trade restrictions and therefore reserves the right under GATT to retaliate against such measures if they have the effect of limiting EC trade. Despite suggesting possible counter measures, it is in the Community's interest to avoid direct conflicts over export controls because, as the pipeline case showed, these incur political and economic costs.

The Community has actively lobbied in Washington on the planned revision of the Export Administration Act in the hope that "the comments and suggestions made by the Community and its Member States would be taken into account during the legislative process in the United States".[36] If this law passes through Congress without some accommodation of the EC's wishes, it will be a permanent source of dispute between the U.S.A. and the EC.

Conclusions

After the lifting of the U.S. pipeline embargo there has been a reduction in U.S.-EC tensions over trade with the East, except in the area of export control policy. But there has been no change in the structure of West-European and the U.S. interests which were the fundamental cause of the transatlantic conflict. The West Europeans are as little interested in reducing their economic cooperation with the East, as America is in changing its position on East-West economic relations which is shaped by rivalry with the Soviet Union. It seems that the relevant bureaucracies and policy-makers on both sides of the Atlantic have learned to come to terms with different conceptions of the East-West economic relations.

The recent controversies concerning East-West trade have had the side effect of encouraging the Community members to unite in the face of American pressure. But the EC has not yet succeeded in moving from this "reactive" position into the realm of political activity. To date there has been a lack of sufficient legal or practical competence to implement a common EC policy on credit and cooperation agreements with the CMEA countries. The EC's policy on consultation with the CMEA as an organization is, after a short period of successful rapprochement on both sides, still without positive results. Only in trade diplomacy with individual CMEA countries could the Community become more successful provided it manages to sign an agreement with Hungary. The Community must develop a policy which can both solve the problems inherent in economic relations with the East, and, at the same time, stimulate trade. Given the relevance of East-West trade for the economic and political stability of Europe, policies are needed which can not only regulate the long term commercial relations between Eastern and Western Europe, but also, in particular, deal with crises.

178

NOTES

1   See Klepsch-Report (Committee on External Economic Relations), *EP (European Parliament)-Document*, No 425/74, January 9th 1975, p.p. 10-11 and Annex of this Report: Opinion of the Political Affairs Committee, p.p. 36-37; Schmidt-Report (Committee on External Economic Relations), *EP-Document, No 89/78*, May 11th 1978.

2   Here and for the following see: Irmer-Report (Committee on External Economic Relations), *EP-Document*, No 1-531/82, July 28th 1982, p.p. 32-35; Schmidt-Report (Note 1); statistical explanation by EC Vice-President Haferkamp, *EP-Debates*, No 1-288, September 16th 1982, p. 280; *Monthly External Trade Bulletin*, Special Number, 1958-1982, Eurostat, Luxembourg 1983, p. 6.

3   Lebahn, Axel: Alternativen in den EG-RGW-Beziehungen, *Außenpolitik*, Issue No 2/1980, p. 147; for the legal and historical aspects of EEC's commercial policy towards Eastern Europe see in general the very balanced analysis by J.W. Maslen, *Developments in the European Community's relations with the State-trading countries 1981-1983*, Yearbook of European Law, 3, 1983, Oxford 1984, pp. 323-346.

4   See: Irmer-Report (Note 2), p.p. 39-44; *14th General Report on the Activities of the European Communities in 1980*, Brussels-Luxembourg 1981, p.p. 297-298; EP-Debates, Sitting of Thursday, January 18th 1979, p.p. 201-207; explanations by EC Vice-President Haferkamp, EP-Debates, No 1-288, September 16th 1982, p. 300.

5   See: Machowski, Heinrich: Zur politischen Ökonomie der Beziehungen zwischen dem RGW und der EWG: *Aus Politik und Zeitgeschichte*, B 12/1982, Beilage zur Wochenzeitung Das Parlament, p.p. 33-34.

6   See: Maslen, The European... (Note 3); Sachs, Klaus Michael: *EG-Handelspolitik und zwischenstaatliche Kooperationsabkommen*, Baden-Baden 1976.

7   Compare EP-Resolution, October 11th 1982, *Official Journal of the EC*, No C 292, November 8th 1982, p.p. 15-20.

8   Concerning this general problem see also: Pinder, John: Integration in Western and Eastern Europe. Relations between the EC and CMEA, *Journal of Common Market Studies*, Vol 8-1979/80, p.p. 114-134.

9   Compare Klepsch-Report (Note 1), p.p. 7-8.

10 See: Response of EC Vice-President Haferkamp to a question of MEP Martinet, *Official Journal of the EC*, No C 156, June 25th 1980, p.p. 13-14.

11 Irmer-Report (Note 2), p. 37.

12 See: Machowski (Note 5), p. 39. The efforts of the smaller CMEA countries to become more autonomous in their external trade politics are also stressed by: Baumer, Max and Jacobsen, Hanns-Dieter 'CMEA's Economic 'Westpolitik' Between Global Limitations and All-European Potentials', in *East European Economic Assessment, Part 2 – Regional Assessments. A Compendium of Papers Submitted to the Joint Economic Committee*, U.S. Congress, Washington, D.C. 1981, pp. 872-886.

13 Compare Schmidt-Report (Note 1), p.p. 29-30.
14 Here and for the following see: Maslen (Note 3); *Handelsblatt*, July 11th and July 27th 1983 and *Frankfurter Rundschau*, July 19th 1983.
15 Concerning this interpretation see also: Machowski (Note 5), p. 40.
16 *Handelsblatt*, January 25th 1984; Agence internationale d'information pour la presse, *general information*, No 3859, 28/29 May 1984, p. 5.
17 See, for example, Machowski (Note 5), p. 38.
18 EP-Resolution, October 11th 1982 (Note 7); see also: EP-Resolution, October 15th 1980, *Official Journal of the EC*, No C 291, November 10th 1980, p.p. 24-29.
19 EP-Resolution, October 11th 1982 (Note 7); see also: Hoffmann-Report (Committee on Transport), *EP-Doc*, No 1-203/82, May 28th 1982.
20 See: Irmer-Report (Note 2), p.p. 22-25 and p.p. 56-59.
21 See, for example: *EP-Debates*, Sitting of Tuesday, September 15th 1979, p. p. 69-90; *EP-Resolution*, Oct. 11th 1982 (Note 7); *EP-Resolution* March 8th 1982, *Official Journal of the EC*; No C 87, April 5th 1982, p.p. 19-21; Aigner-Report (Committee on Budgetary Control), *EP-Doc.*, No 1-846/81, January 8th 1982.
22 See the explanations of EC Commissioner Gundelach, *EP-Debates*, Sitting of Monday, March 10th 1980, p. 30.
23 On 29/30th June 1981 for example the European Council made the proposal to establish a two phase international conference to find a political solution to the Afghanistan problem (see: Europa Archiv, Vol. 14/1981, p.Z 147). After the announcement of martial law in Poland the Council of Foreign Ministers demanded an earlier summoning of the CSCE Follow Up Conference in Madrid at foreign ministerial level to discuss developments in Poland (see: *Europa Archiv*, Vol. 3/1982, p. Z 31).
24 Council Regulation (EEC) No 596/82, March 15th 1982, *Official Journal of the EC*, No L 72, March 16th 1982, p.p. 15-18; *Bulletin EC*, No 2/82, p. 49; *Bulletin EC*, No 3/82, p. 66.
25 *Official Journal of the EC*, No C 93, April 23th 1981, p. 6; *14th General Report* (Note 4), p. 22.
26 *Official Journal of the EC*, No C 60, March 19th 1981, p. 16; EP-Resolution, March 8th 1982, *Official Journal of the EC*, No C 87, April 5th 1982, p.p. 19-21.
27 Agence internationale d'information pour la presse, *general information*, No 3341, March 31th 1982, p. 5.
28 EP-Resolution, July 9th 1982, *Official Journal of the EC*, No C 238, Sept. 13th 1982, p.p. 96-98; EP-Resolution, Oct. 11th 1982 (Note 7); Seeler-Report (Committee on External Economic Relations), *EP-Doc.*, No 1-83/82, April 8th 1982.
29 See in this connection. Schlotter, Peter. 'Linkage—Politik und KSZE. Eine Zwischenbilanz des Madrider Folgetreffens', in: *Deutsche Studien*, 21. Jahrgang, Issue 81/March 1983, p.p.69-84; Rummel, Reinhardt. *Zusammengesetzte Außenpolitik. Westeuropa als internationaler Akteur*, Kehl am Rhein/Straßburg 1982, p. 78.

180

30 Compare Jopp, Mathias. 'Friedenssicherung durch wirtschaftliche Zusammenarbeit? Die europäisch-amerikanische Kontroverse über die Rolle des Handels in den Ost-West-Beziehungen, in: Vogt, Wolfgang R. (ed.): *Streitfall Frieden*, Heidelberg 1984, pp. 120-132.

31 See: Reprint of the Memorandum of August 12th 1982: *Europe documents*, agence internationale d'information pour la presse, Luxembourg-Brussels, No 1216, Aug. 12th 1982, pp. 1-3.

32 See: the Commission's reports to the Council of Ministers on natural gas: COM (81) 530, Oct. 1st 1981; COM (82) 45, Feb. 15th 1982; COM (82) 653, Oct. 15th 1982; COM (84) 120, April 9th 1984, Commission of the European Communities, Brussels.

33 See: *Memorandum* (Note 31), p.p. 3-14; *Bulletin EC*, No 7-8/82, p. 9; see also: EP-Resolution, Sept. 16th 1982, *Official Journal of the EC*, No 267, Oct. 11th 1982, p. 42.

34 *16th General Report on the Activities of the EC in 1982*, Brussels-Luxembourg 1983, p. 238; Bulletin EC, No 7-8/82, p. 58.

35 Here and for the following c.f.: Aidemémoire of March 11th 1983 (8p.) and Aidemémoire of April 28th 1983 (4p.); *Memorandum* (Note 31); relevant press reports in: *Handelsblatt, Frankfurter Allgemeine Zeitung* und *Süddeutsche Zeitung*, March-May 1983.

36 *Bulletin EC*, No 4/83, p. 52.

Table 1: *Community trade with Eastern Europe, 1958-1983*
Value in Mio ECU (excluding inter-German trade)

Year	I Export	II Import	III Balance	IV Total - Trade (I+II)	V increase of IV in %.
1958	922	1.067	— 145	1.989	—
1960	1.367	1.504	— 137	1.871	—
1963	1.604	2.014	— 410	3.618	—
1970	3.890	3.907	— 17	7.797	—
1972	4.929	4.699	230	9.628	—
1973	6.642	6.057	585	12.699	31,9
1974	10.110	8.257	1.853	18.367	44,6
1975	11.942	8.695	3.247	20.637	12,4
1976	12.808	11.659	1.149	24.467	18,6
1977	13.530	12.646	884	26.176	7,0
1978	13.734	13.382	352	27.166	3,8
1979	14.946	16.582	— 1.636	31.528	16,0
1980	16.773	20.068	— 3.295	36.841	16,9
1981	17.321	22.257	— 4.936	39.578	7,4
1982	17.298	26.330	— 9.032	43.628	10,2
1983	20.376	28.416	— 8.040	48.792	11,8

Sources. *Monthly External Trade Bulletin*, Special Number, 1958-1982, pp. 50-52 and Special Number, 1958-1983, pp. 78-80, Eurostat, Luxembourg, 1983 and 1984.

182

Table 2: *Community trade with State-trading countries, 1972–1982*
Value in Mio ECU by SITC sections

				IMPORT			
Year	0—9	0 + 1	3	2 + 4	5	7	6 + 8
1972	5.198	1.012	773	1.037	246	· 340	1.413
1973	6.748	1.219	1.048	1.330	312	481	1.839
1974	9.149	1.095	2.138	1.729	557	551	2.309
1975	9.609	1.151	2.878	1.503	530	813	2.558
1976	12.733	1.136	4.318	1.999	700	882	3.344
1977	13.674	1.273	4.400	2.029	989	996	3.693
1978	14.536	1.388	4.859	1.846	1.012	1.155	3.851
1979	18.175	1.487	6.890	2.092	1.364	1.214	4.738
1980	22.414	1.600	9.887	2.294	1.443	1.275	5.532
1981	24.793	1.577	10.475	2.384	1.614	1.216	4.751
1982	29.058	1.637	14.168	2.493	1.607	1.223	5.455
				EXPORT			
1972	5.433	462	59	224	724	2.054	1.754
1973	7.476	658	71	313	909	2.603	2.738
1974	11.488	697	79	421	1.773	3.713	4.240
1975	14.104	551	106	365	1.752	5.413	4.916
1976	14.504	814	117	426	2.031	5.900	5.033
1977	14.852	804	114	493	2.415	5.933	4.913
1978	15.751	940	152	520	2.550	5.845	5.569
1979	17.564	1.299	279	589	2.929	6.068	6.223
1980	19.159	2.383	380	771	3.623	5.950	5.878
1981	19.855	3.601	373	732	2.989	5.459	5.379
1982	19.910	2.757	360	662	2.860	5.923	6.136

Source: Monthly External Trade Bulletin, Special Number, 1958-1982,
Eurostat (Statistical Office of the European Communities), Luxembourg 1983, p. 93.

0+1 Food, beverages and tobacco
3   Mineral fuels, lubric. and related materials
2+4 Raw materials
5   Chemicals and related products
7   Machinery and transport equipment
6+8 Manufactured goods (classified) and miscellaneous manufact. articles
9   Commodities and transactions not classified elsewhere in the SITC
0—9 Total trade

Table 3: *Community trade with East European countries (excl. inner-German trade), 1970-1982, Value in Mio ECU*

		1970	1972	1973	1974	1975	1976	1977	1978	1979	1980	1981	1982
USSR	Ex	1.410	1.573	2.195	3.405	4.989	5.239	5.942	5.705	6.353	7.583	7.886	8.984
	Imp.	1.543	1.683	2.310	3.626	3.899	5.679	6.300	6.671	8.568	11.214	13.541	17.045
	Bal.	— 133	— 110	— 115	— 221	1.090	— 440	— 358	— 966	— 2.215	— 3.631	— 5.655	— 8.061
GDR	Ex.	211	317	312	448	479	583	507	565	779	842	1.048	710
	Imp.	225	284	327	482	494	615	631	724	765	911	1.158	1.293
	Bal.	— 14	33	— 15	— 34	— 15	— 32	— 124	— 159	14	— 69	— 110	— 583
Poland	Ex.	586	986	1.658	2.479	2.677	2.876	2.586	2.546	2.523	2.841	2.307	2.051
	Imp.	667	885	1.149	1.493	1.624	2.008	2.173	2.310	2.485	2.723	2.062	2.256
	Bal.	— 81	101	509	986	1.053	868	413	236	38	118	245	— 205
Czecho-slovakia	Ex.	551	648	759	1.030	1.045	1.262	1.275	1.256	1.312	1.368	1.385	1.399
	Imp.	466	575	696	816	851	1.017	1.105	1.131	1.325	1.505	1.564	1.751
	Bal.	85	73	63	214	194	245	170	125	— 13	— 137	— 179	— 352
Hungary	Ex.	406	543	642	1.081	968	1.071	1.361	1.572	1.506	1.592	1.959	1.962
	Imp.	366	514	647	713	702	870	1.043	1.058	1.307	1.415	1.461	1.534
	Bal.	40	29	— 5	368	266	201	318	514	199	177	498	428
Rumania	Ex.	487	628	776	1.127	1.070	1.143	1.233	1.471	1.781	1.708	1.699	1.060
	Imp.	449	562	684	861	892	1.150	1.055	1.131	1.616	1.767	1.829	1.770
	Bal.	38	66	92	266	178	— 7	178	340	165	— 59	— 130	— 710
Bulgaria	Ex.	224	219	284	507	678	604	579	578	643	774	963	1.023
	Imp.	185	186	228	238	204	294	308	331	463	478	555	589
	Bal.	39	33	56	269	474	310	271	247	180	296	408	434

Source: Monthly External Trade Bulletin, Special Number, 1958-1982, Eurostat, Luxembourg 1983, p.p. 50-51.

14
The United States
Reinhard Rode*

Introduction

During the Cold War there was little controversy about East-West economic policy in the United States. It was seen mainly as an instrument in the East-West conflict which should deny communist countries the benefits of access to Western goods and capital. The key word was export control, which meant refusal to trade. East-West trade policy stood at the service of security interests. Furthermore, it was an instrument for containment. The embargo policy of the United States during the post-war era was rightly characterized by Adler-Karlsson[1] as economic warfare.

Relations with communist countries were excluded from the tradition of the United States as a trading nation which explicitly grants its business community the right to realize profits from foreign trade. This meant a double restriction. On the one hand communist countries, especially the Eastern hegemon, the Soviet Union, was refused the benefits of trade, on the other hand, the U.S. economy was also denied the chances to benefit from such trade. The latter was no cause for complaint as long as Western Europe also held back from trade with the East. When, at the end of the 1950s, West European countries reestablished their traditional trade relations with the East, and expanded them throughout the 1960s, the United States was confronted with a conflict between political and security considerations favoring continued controls and welfare-oriented business interests favoring liberalization. As early as under the Kennedy administration there had been the first unsuccessful attempts to liberalize export controls, or in other words to adapt to the West European level of controls.[2]

This conflict of interests lasted until the beginning of the 1970s when President Nixon and Henry Kissinger pushed through a policy of liberalization. Under pressure for a reduction in control in favor of exports from the business community and Congress the Nixon administration, after some hesitation, pursued a determined liberalization policy. But at no time was the administration, with the exception of some voices in the Department of Commerce, ready to allow a policy of free trade towards communist countries solely geared to business interests. Henry Kissinger saw East-West trade policy as part of his linkage policy, and liberalization was perceived as a concession to the East which had to result in reciprocal political concessions. East-West trade policy was to satisfy American interests by forming one part of the network of relations which was to moderate the Soviet Union by making it more dependent.[3]

184

The Nixon-Kissinger policy of détente, which encompassed East-West trade policy, allowed for a previously unknown degree of cooperation with the Soviet Union and was under pressure from conservative opponents of détente as early as 1973. Under the leadership of Senator Henry Jackson these succeeded in forming a large congressional coalition of both conservatives and liberals under the umbrella of human rights policy. This managed to obstruct Kissinger's policy of linkage but not the expansion of trade relations for which East-West traders in the business community continued to lobby.

Interests

The Pro-Traders: Agriculture, Industry and the Pro-Détente Lobby. During the 1970s U.S. agriculture became the biggest beneficiary of the trade with the East. Chronic overproduction meant that producers and exporters of grain had a major interest in the large Soviet market. In 1972 there was a tenfold increase in U.S. agricultural exports to the Soviet Union and in 1973 there was a further doubling (see table 2). A glance at the statistics of U.S. exports to the Soviet Union, which show that grain accounted for between 42 and 78 per cent during the 1970s, clearly illustrates the importance of this trade. The agricultural lobby not only used its chance to export but also pressed strongly for the new business. On every occasion farm lobbies, such as the American Farm Bureau Federation, the National Farmers' Union, and the National Association of Wheat Growers, demanded unrestricted export of agricultural products to the East. Despite their conservatism on domestic issues these lobbies became proponents of détente because of their export interests.

Neither the executive branch nor the Congress challenged the farm lobby's interest in exporting to the East until 1980, when President Carter's grain embargo tried to undermine the "right" to export to the Soviet Union which had been consolidated over a period of eight years. Carter provoked the whole agricultural lobby with this embargo including the farming community as well as the multinational grain trading companies, the latter ensuring that the embargo was inefficient at an international level. Under Ronald Reagan, the farm lobby succeeded with its main demand of having the grain embargo lifted, as Reagan had indeed promised during his election campaign. Under the Reagan administration the farm community also managed to preserve its special role by gaining the domestic acceptance of agricultural exports to the Soviet Union. Agriculture was excluded from all economic sanctions against the Soviet Union and Poland at the beginning of the 1980s, and the U.S.-Soviet grain agreement was extended in 1981 and 1982, and finally renewed in 1983.

The second large group of East-West traders, manufacturing industry and especially the transnational corporations, were overoptimistic in their estimates of the growth in East-West trade in the early 1970s. This exaggerated view of the prospects for trade was based on the generally low level of U.S. exports to the East (see table 1) and the East's tremendous demand for modern Western technology. As the United States led both West European and Japanese competitors in high technology, U.S. industry saw a good chance to increase exports at the expense of its well established competitors on Eastern markets.

The interest in East-West trade within U.S. industry was demonstrated by the foundation of new lobbying organizations and various joint cooperation councils as well as general public support for liberalization. In 1972, the East-West Trade Council was established in Washington, and by 1974 it had 150 members including 100 companies engaged in business with the East. In 1973, inspired by the administration, the U.S.-USSR Trade and Economic Council, functioning as a Soviet-American Chamber of Commerce, was established. In 1974 this had a membership of 168 U.S. companies. The membership on the U.S. side was dominated by transnational corporations. The American co-chairman Donald Kendall, the president of Pepsi Cola, worked as an active advocate of East-West trade and détente. As stated before the Senate Commerce Committee hearings in 1975/76, the main demands of U.S. transnational corporations, banks and trade organizations were, most favored nation treatment for communist countries, Export-Import Bank credits for trade with the East, and thus a lifting of the Jackson/Vanik amendment restrictions on both.[4]

As the euphoria of détente faded in both the administration and the U.S. society as a whole, the business community also became more circumspect in its demands. In 1979, during the debate on the extension of the Export Administration Act, the main demand consisted of a liberalization of the U.S. export licensing procedures. But there was no longer the enthusiasm of the first half of the decade. In contrast to the opposition of agricultural lobbies, President Carter's sanctions in 1980 provoked no major resistance from the producers of oil and gas equipment and computers. The U.S. business community also seemed resigned to the increased restrictions on East-West industrial trade, which came during the first year of the Reagan administration. However, no sooner had the hardliners within the administration gained ground with their concept of economic warfare, when the industry responded. The embargo of the Soviet-West European gas deal and the sanctions against West European companies provoked business groups. They perceived this as undermining the U.S. reputation as a reliable source of supply, which would jeopardize the participation of U.S. companies in future international industrial cooperation. Now business openly opposed the hardliners and supported the moderate line, and in 1982 the presidents of the Chamber of Commerce and of the National Association of Manufacturers made dramatic appeals to President Reagan and the public at large.[5]

In comparison with the successes of agriculture, industry has a remarkably bad record in East-West trade. Industrial East-West trade remains largely a domain of Western Europe. In the domestic debate, industry's ability to trade was drastically reduced by the fact that politics prevailed over the profit motive.

In this sense agriculture was interpreted as an exception, not as an example for the industrial sector. The industrial lobbies were also more reluctant to press for a liberalization of East-West trade than were the agricultural lobbies. There are a number of possible reasons for this. First of all, a big share of the business with the East is conducted through the West European subsidiaries of U.S. transnational corporations. The exact share is unknown but this nevertheless provides an alternative means of trading whilst avoiding the necessity of intensive lobbying in the United States itself. Second, exports to the East remained a marginal factor for U.S. business, at no more than 3 per cent of total exports of finished products in both 1970 and 1980.

Furthermore the Reagan administration had the political support of the business community because of its wide neglect of trade union demands and generally pro-business stance in domestic policy. As Eastern markets were of marginal interest there was no readiness to oppose the administration until the government went too far by precipitating the gas deal controversy.

Agriculture and industry promoted détente only indirectly because it provided the necessary framework for trade. As there is no broad societal support for détente in the United States, such lobbies only acted in a defensive role. The pro-détente American Committee on East-West Accord had prominent liberal scholars and businessmen among its membership, but it lacked the general public support of its opponents.

The Opponents: The Conservative Security Establishment, Ethnics, AFL-CIO. For the conservative wing of the U.S. security establishment the "no trade with the enemy" motto of the Cold War was still valid. The main interest of this group was to block military détente. The fear of American inferiority and the demand for a restoration of superiority consequently led to efforts to stop the SALT II agreement in the Senate. In this context East-West trade was of only indirect importance. It was perceived as a one-way street favoring only the East by granting it access to the Western technology it needed to increase the economic and military efficiency of the Eastern system. These positions gained support with the general growth in influence of conservative thought in the second half of the 1970s, as the American Security Council, the Coalition for Peace Through Strength, the National Strategy Information Center and the Committee on the Present Danger, all sought to influence American public opinion. The discussion of trade restrictions and economic warfare towards the Soviet Union, however, remained within expert groups. The lobbying activities of the Institute on Strategic Trade[6] had no significant public impact.

More sophisticated criticism of increased East-West trade was to be found among the ethnic East European and the Jewish lobbies. These were not fundamentally opposed to trade as such, but favored the use of leverage on communist governments. They demanded that all economic concessions be linked to significant political concessions favoring their constituencies in the East. They were thus potential supporters of a linkage policy but regularly raised such excessive political demands that the linkage policy was very unlikely to have any effect. For example, on the question of Jewish emigration the Soviet Union made considerable concessions, but, for reasons of prestige, was not prepared to be seen to yield to American pressure. This was precisely what Senator Jackson tried to do with his famous amendment to the Trade Act of 1974 which was vigorously supported by the Jewish lobby. In retrospect the Jewish lobby played mainly an instrumental role in the anti-détente policy of Senator Jackson.[7]

The American Federation of Labor – Congress of Industrial Organizations (AFL-CIO) has traditionally been one of the opponents of East-West trade. In contrast to West European trade unions that stress the jobs created by trade with the East, the AFL-CIO has adopted a tough anti-communist position. The AFL-CIO was therefore one of the most important supporters of the Jackson/ Vanik amendment. The only prominent exception among U.S. trade unions was the United Electrical, Radio and Machine Workers of America (UE). The AFL-CIO has consistently opposed most favored nation treatment, technology transfer and credits and was thus in line with the Reagan administration on East-West trade even though the latter pursued policies hostile to trade union demands on domestic issues. The AFL-CIO saw the proponents of détente and pro-traders as part of an unholy alliance between U.S. multinationals and communism.[8]

The U.S. debate on East-West trade therefore equated security with control and economic welfare with business interests. There was, of course, a range of views from the economics-oriented demands for freedom to export with the farm lobby, to the security-oriented demands for economic warfare by the conservative wing of the security establishment. In the early 1970s moderate attempts to accomodate security and trade interests predominated. During the second half of the 1970s however, there was a political tide flowing in favour of the security-oriented approach.

Decisions

The Carter Administration. The Nixon and Ford initiatives liberalizing East-West trade policy provoked resistance from a broad coalition of congressional advocates of human rights policy. As a result the realist, linkage policy approach of Henry Kissinger was extended to include the objective of influencing Soviet domestic policy, i. e. on Jewish emigration. From the outset the Carter administration emphasized human rights and therefore placated the congressional human rights advocates enough to regain a freedom of movement on East-West trade policy which had been lost by its predecessors. This irritated the Soviet Union because such an ideological offensive was bound to displease given the Soviet Union's undisputed systemic failures in the field of human rights. But it was precisely this human rights offensive which offered Carter the chance to gain freedom of action at home and thus liberalize East-West economic relations.

At the beginning the Carter administration was even ready to give up the linkage between human rights and East-West trade. Economic relations with the East were to be freed from congressional restrictions, which would mean Congress lifting the Jackson/Vanik amendment and facilitating most favored nation treatment and credits. The President, the Secretary of State, the Secretary of Commerce and the Secretary of Treasury jointly proposed steps to expand trade. The Sixth Meeting of the U.S.-Soviet Trade Commission in June 1977, held in Washington, and a meeting of the U.S.-USSR Trade and Economic Council provided the framework in which to coordinate the initiatives of the administration and the business community aimed at stimulating both East-West trade policy and trade itself. The 1977 amendments to the Export Administration Act also served the purpose of liberalization, by simplifying and speeding-up procedures for granting export licences on trade with the East.

In practice, export licensing procedures under the Carter administration then followed "foreign policy" criteria which were often contrary to business interests. The Department of Defense, under Secretary Brown, tried to implement the liberalizing recommendations of the Bucy Report,[9] but faced tremendous practical difficulties. These centred on the fact that liberal export control procedures were dependent on the definition of "critical technologies" which were not available before 1979 by which time the political trend in the administration had already changed. Although Brown as Secretary of Defense was more liberal than either his predecessor or successor, his interests as the defender of the U.S.A.'s security interests still resulted in a conflict with U.S. economic objectives. This is a dilemma which Carter like other American presidents could not escape and was underlined by the attempts to harmonize the liberalization of the CoCom control list with the European allies. The United States still practiced more restrictions than the Western European countries, so that even at a time of U.S. liberalization it still failed to adopt the lower Western European levels of control.[10]

The initial enthusiasm for liberalization in the Carter administration was dampened by foreign policy considerations as well as by the security interests in export control. Security Advisor Brzezinski, for example, opposed the détente policy of Secretary of State Cyrus Vance. Brzezinski articulated fears that the Soviet Union would win worldwide influence at the cost of the United States, and especially exemplified these fears with respect to Africa. As a counterstrategy he proposed a return to linkage policies. Instructed by Brzezinski, Samuel Huntington undertook a study of the U.S.-Soviet power relationship (PRM 10) which came up with the proposal of using economic diplomacy in relations with the Soviet Union. President Carter indeed signed a corresponding presidential directive (PD-18), but delegated coordination and implementation to the State Department. This was not yet a real decision for economic diplomacy because the State Department was dominated by opponents of such a policy such as Marshall Shulman. It was not until 1978 that the implementation of Huntington's recommendation was taken up at the National Security Council. Although Huntington indicated that leverage works most effectively when applied in the form of a carrot, the decision in favor of economic diplomacy in effect supplied the foundation for the use of leverage in the form of a stick.[11]

The subsequent decisions of the administration oscillated between the hardline of the National Security Council and the pro-détente and pro-trade position of the Departments of State and Commerce. In July 1978 President Carter ordered technology and equipment used for exploration and production of oil and gas to be put on the Commodity Control List, after just one year earlier Secretary of Commerce Juanita Kreps had still sought cooperation with the Soviet Union in the energy sector. Linkage policy first became evident in the summer of 1978. The decision on energy equipment, and a presidential recommendation to the Department of Commerce to reject the application of Sperry Rand to sell a Sperry Univac System computer to the Soviet news agency TASS, were both linked to the conviction of the Soviet dissidents Ginzburg and Scharanski and the American newsmen Whitney and Piper. In August the administration surprisingly approved the sale of oil-drilling equipment to the USSR by Dresser Industries, but three weeks later the President himself called for a review of this decision. On 7th September 1978 Carter finally approved the sale. This vacillation was a reflection of the infighting going on within the White House; linkage policy was in an experimental stage.

In the last quarter of 1978 the State Department's line prevailed because of progress in the SALT II negotiations. Simultaneously Security Advisor Brzezinski played the "China card" by following diplomatic recognition with a liberalization of U.S.-Chinese economic relations and a July 1979 trade agreement granting the People's Republic of China most-favored nation treatment still denied the Soviet Union. The Department of State failed in its efforts to maintain a balance in the U.S. treatment of the Soviet Union and the People's Republic of China, i. e. by also granting the former most-favored nation treatment. The debate over the presence of a Soviet brigade in Cuba gave Brzezinski the opportunity to use some kind of Cuba-brigade-trade linkage. This concept of economic diplomacy was, in principle, more refined than Kissinger's linkage policy, but a refined application was impossible given the infighting within the administration.

After the Soviet Union had sent troops to Afghanistan on 24th December 1979, the Carter administration looked for a tough and immediate response and came up with economic sanctions. In the inner circle of presidential councilors everybody, including Secretary of State Vance but with the exception of Vice President Mondale, opted for the "grain weapon". On 4th January 1980 the United States imposed economic sanctions on the Soviet Union. Apart from a halt to license approvals for high technology and strategic exports, the partial grain embargo formed the core of the U.S. catalogue of sanctions. In accordance with the U.S.-Soviet bilateral grain agreement grain supplies in excess of 8 million metric tonnes were embargoed. In February 1980 there was also an indefinite embargo on phosphates which followed the decision to boycott the 1980 Summer Olympic Games in Moscow.

The effectiveness of the Carter administration's economic sanctions in punishing the Soviet Union relied on the assumption of American "food power". It was believed that the USSR would not be able to diversify its sources of supply in the short term because of its tremendous requirements for grain imports. For the grain embargo to be effective, however, it required more than American food power; it also required international support and a domestic consensus in favour of such action. These latter conditions for an effective embargo were not sufficiently satisfied.

Despite the attempts of the Carter administration to prove otherwise the sanctions were a failure.[12] The economic price for the Soviet Union remained low. Indeed the USSR would only have been seriously affected had there been a sustained grain embargo but this was made difficult by political factors. The initial domestic support for the embargo gave way to increased criticism from the spring of 1980 onwards. The farm lobby opposed the embargo and Carter's political opponent, Ronald Reagan, promised to lift the embargo if elected. The attempt to build international support for the embargo also failed. The Soviet Union showed no readiness to compromise over Afghanistan. The West European allies only half-heartedly joined the sanctions, and together with U.S. grain trade multinationals they were involved in a circumvention of the embargo. The grain embargo turned out to be a bad decision for the luckless Jimmy Carter and contributed to his election defeat. For the United States as a whole it proved the weapon of U.S. food power to be ineffective and thus damaged U.S. prestige.

The Reagan Administration. Ronald Reagan and his administration started with a resolute conservative policy towards communist countries. The aim to preserve or to restore U.S. superiority over the Soviet Union in all areas was also decisive for East-West trade policy. Although the general approach was far more to the right of the political spectrum there was, as under Carter, a split between a moderate and a hardline position. The State Department under Haig and Shultz tried, in cooperation with Western Europe, to restrict trade with the East by concentrating mainly on the export of technology. The hardliners in the Pentagon and the National Security Council were influenced by the Cold War concept of economic warfare, and believed that the United States should, if necessary, take unilateral action and oblige the allies to follow this line. There was infighting within the administration in the first year over whether a hardline approach was consistent with ending the grain embargo. However, the President very soon had to face the demands of the farm lobby and his own election promise to lift the grain embargo. On 24th of April 1981 he did so, thus signaling a triumph of the farm lobby.[13]

After ceding to the interests of grain exporters the administration adopted a double-track approach in which the restrictive approach to East-West industrial trade was accentuated. The Pentagon developed its concept of economically weakening the Soviet Union in order to mitigate the arms race.[14] Economic warfare, however, did not become an official policy because the Departments of State and Commerce and their supporters blocked a clear commitment to such a policy. Those who assumed that the lifting of the grain embargo meant the administration was following a fundamentally pro-trade policy, despite all tough rhetoric, did so too hastily. The administration simply excluded the agricultural sector as a special case, and set about tightening controls on technology transfer with new vigor. This provoked the 1982 gas deal conflict with Western Europe, when the United States attempted to stop the deal retroactively.[15]

The U.S. complaints about the gas deal focused on three issues; the danger of dependence on Soviet gas imports, Soviet access to hard currency and the political implications of the deal. A high degree of dependence was seen as opening Western Europe to political blackmail. Soviet earnings of hard currency from the export of gas would mean additional funds for imports of technology. Finally, from the point of view of global power politics long-term East-West cooperation on this scale would be a striking example for business, but an example in the détente tradition symbolizing the failed policies of the 1970s.

The conflicting positions of the United States and in Western Europe surfaced in December 1981 in the discussion on the appropriate reaction to the declaration of martial law in Poland. The United States imposed economic sanctions on Poland and the USSR but the main sanction was the suspension of all licenses on oil and gas equipment. U.S. pressure on Western Europe to cancel the gas deal increased during the following months, and the United States also put the possibility of using credits as a lever against the East on the agenda. As the United States could not stop the pipeline project on its own, but only delay it, a general U.S.-European compromise was anticipated in which the United States would accept the gas deal in exchange for more restrictive conditions for credits. It appeared that such an understanding had been agreed upon at the Versailles summit in June 1982.

President Reagan, however, decided in favor of the U.S. hardliners and extended the sanctions to cover U.S. and European companies participating in the pipeline project in an extraterritorial measure which if anything reinforced European resistance to U.S. policies. This coup by the hardliners which excluded the Departments of State, Commerce and Treasury was later softened by their correcting influence. During the autumn of 1982 the new Secretary of State, George Shultz, made an effort to reach a transatlantic compromise, and in mid-November the President lifted the sanctions against West European companies. In return West European governments were to harmonize interest rates on credit to the East and enhance CoCom restrictions on the export of high technology. Detailed agreements were, however, postponed and given over to joint study groups, a reliable means of delaying any action. The U.S. government was able to save face but the details of new restrictions on East-West trade had still not been agreed upon.[16]

The U.S. attempts to restrict industrial exports, which hurt Europe more, whilst simultaneously excluding agricultural exports from restrictions and indeed even trying to increase grain exports, was a remarkably difficult policy to explain to the allies. The initial elegant answer was that this was an inevitable result of the dilemma between business and national security interests. But this was aimed exclusively at U.S. interest groups and was unacceptable in Western Europe, where the policy was mainly interpreted as an attempt to shift the cost of U.S. embargo policies onto the European allies.

1983 saw a further crumbling of the restrictive East-West trade policy. In August a new grain agreement with the Soviet Union was signed, and in September U.S. export control policy vis-à-vis China was liberalized to coincide with a visit of Secretary of Defense Weinberger. Communist China[17] was granted access to exactly the same important high technology refused the Soviet Union. By this step the Reagan administration returned to Brzezinski's approach with the "China card". The interpretation of U.S. security interests also differentiated between communism in general and the competitive world power i. e. the USSR. Here there are obviously contradictions between resolute conservative objectives and the tough anti-communist rhetoric on the one hand, and the somewhat less resolute actual decisions on the other. Whatever policy on imposing economic pressure on the Soviet Union may have been set out in the spring of 1983 in the secret National Security Decision Directive 75,[18] the concrete decisions of the administration have had to deal with the complex structure of U.S. domestic interests.

The Congress: Human Rights, National Security and Business. Congressional decisions have also responded to different requirements. In the first half of the decade when, under Nixon and Ford, business interests still held sway, the congressional majority moderated with the Jackson/Vanik amendment. The link between Jewish emigration and East-West trade represented above all an ideological offensive against the Soviet Union which challenged Kissinger's realistic approach. By desisting from blunt statements of U.S. moral superiority over the Soviet Union, Kissinger's policy of parity provoked both conservative and liberal members of Congress. This was largely limited to questions of nuclear strategy. But the slightest hint of treating the totalitarian Soviet Union as a world power of equal rights, even if this was not acceptable, in the last analysis, for Kissinger himself, touched a raw nerve in the American self-image. Security is not limited to its military elements but also concerns the fundamental self-perception of societies. In this perspective Jackson's obstruction of détente undoubtedly contained a security-related element.

The dualism of security and general economic interests can be clearly seen in the different versions of the Export Administration Act. During the 1970s legislation showed a trend towards liberalization, in other words a relative reduction in security interests in favor of business interests. This trend culminated in

194

1977. In 1979, the Export Administration Act amendments suggested that the trend towards further liberalization had stagnated, as, for the first time, there was no reduction in controls. Despite all that happened during the 1970s the fact that there were both economic and security interests remained, however, undisputed. Congressional reaction to executive policy on export controls has followed the general pattern of the American system of the division of power. If a specific administration leaned too far towards either economic or security interests Congress would correct the balance. This was especially the case in 1983 when the Reagan administration's draft for a new Export Administration Act concentrated too much on security interests, and, significantly for the executive-congressional system of checks and balances, also sought a considerable expansion of Presidential discretion in implementing export controls. (H.-D. Jacobsen, in chapter 17).

The Dilemma of Politics Between Business and World Power Interests

The dilemma of competing and conflicting demands has not been solved by any U.S. government. The different administrations have merely changed the balance between security and economic interests. The policies of administrations from the linkage policy of Nixon/Ford, through the economic diplomacy of Carter to Reagan, have used East-West trade policy as an instrument of power and security politics in relations with Communist countries and especially in relations with the USSR. East European countries have often received more carrot than stick in an effort to weaken the cohesion of the antagonistic alliance system. The United States has also granted trade concessions to the People's Republic of China which it refused the Soviet Union.

In general, security interests have prevailed over business interests. The initial policies of the Carter and Reagan administrations represent the two extremes of liberal or conservative policies, but both approaches were corrected by the political system and brought more into the mainstream. This was the case when the liberalism of the early Carter administration neglected security interests too much, and for the Reagan administration whose proponents of economic warfare tried to neglect business interests. Both were pushed towards mainstream policy, which is that East-West trade policy is primarily an instrument of power and security politics, but economic interests must be safeguarded, particularly agricultural interests.

Table 1: *U.S. Trade with the USSR, 1950-83*
(in million dollars)

Year	Exports to the USSR	Imports from the USSR
1950	0,6	40
1951	1	32
1952	0,0	17
1953	0,02	11
1954	0,2	12
1955	0,2	17
1956	4	25
1957	-,-	17
1958	3	17
1959	7	27
1960	38	23
1961	43	23
1962	15	16
1963	20	20
1964	145	21
1965	44	43
1966	42	49
1967	60	41
1968	57	57
1969	105	47
1970	119	64
1971	162	57
1972	542	96
1973	1.195	220
1974	607	350
1975	1.833	254
1976	2.306	221
1977	1.623	234
1978	2.249	540
1979	3.604	873
1980	1.510	431
1981	2.239	357
1982	2.589	229
1983	2.002	341

Source: U.S. Department of Commerce

TABLE 2.—U.S.-U.S.S.R. TRADE: 1971-82

[In millions of dollars]

	1971	1972	1973	1974	1975	1976	1977	1978	1979	1980	1981	1982 [1]
U.S. exports (FAS):												
Total......................	162	542	1,195	607	1,833	2,306	1,623	2,249	3,604	1,510	2,339	3,000
Agricultural................	45	430	921	300	1,133	1,487	1,037	1,687	2,855	1,047	1,665	2,300
Nonagricultural	117	112	274	307	700	819	586	562	749	463	674	700
U.S. imports (CV):												
Total......................	57	96	220	350	254	221	234	540	873	453	347	500
Agricultural................	3	4	5	10	7	8	11	13	14	8	13	15
Nonagricultural	54	92	215	340	247	213	223	527	859	445	334	485
Gold bullion [2]...........								287	549	88	22	100
U.S.-U.S.S.R. trade												
turnover.....................	219	638	1,415	957	2,087	2,527	1,857	2,789	4,477	1,963	2,686	3,500

[1] Projection.
[2] Gold bullion (nonmonetary gold) was not included in trade statistics until 1978.

Source: Highlights of U.S. Exports and Import Trade (FT-990), U.S. Census Bureau, U.S. Department of Commerce IM 450/455 Microfilm, IM 150/155 Microfilm. Annual data derived from sum of monthly data.

Table 3: *U.S. Trade With Communist Countries*
($ billions)

Year	Exports[1]			Imports[2]			Balance		
	USSR	PRC	Other[3]	USSR	PRC	Other[3]	USSR	PRC	Other[3]
1970	0,1	—	0,2	0,1	—	0,2	—	—	0,1
1971	0,2	—	0,2	0,1	—	0,1	0,1	—	0,1
1972	0,5	0,1	0,3	0,1	—	0,3	0,4	—	0,1
1973	1,2	0,7	0,6	0,2	0,1	0,3	1,0	0,6	0,3
1974	0,6	0,8	0,8	0,4	0,1	0,5	0,3	0,7	0,3
1975	1,8	0,3	1,0	0,3	0,2	0,5	1,6	0,1	0,5
1976	2,3	0,1	1,2	0,2	0,2	0,6	2,1	— 0,1	0,6
1977	1,6	0,2	0,9	0,5	0,2	0,7	1,2	—	0,2
1978	2,3	0,8	1,4	0,5	0,3	1,0	1,7	0,5	0,5
1979	3,6	1,7	2,1	0,9	0,6	1,0	2,7	1,1	1,1
1980	1,5	3,7	2,3	0,5	1,1	1,0	1,0	2,6	1,3

Totals may not add due to rounding
1   Exports valued on f.a.s basis. Total exports exclude military grant-aid.
2   Imports valued on f.a.s. basis for 1974-1980 and at Customs Value for 1970-73.
3   Includes German Democratic Republic, Czechoslovakia, Hungary, Estonia, Latvia, Lithuania, Poland, Albania, Rumania, Bulgaria, Mongolia and North Korea.
Source: U.S. Department of Commerce, Bureau of Census.

198

NOTES

* This article is based on the study by Reinhard Rode, *Sicherheit versus Wohlfahrt. Die Osthandelspolitik der USA von Nixon bis Carter*, Peace Research Institute Frankfurt, Frankfurt 1985.

1 Gunnar Adler-Karlsson, *Western Economic Warfare 1947-1967. A Case Study in Foreign Economic Policy*, Almquist & Wiksell, Uppsala 1968.

2 Edward Skloot, 'The Decision to Send East-West Trade Legislation to Congress, 1965-1977', in *Commission on the Organization of the Government for the Conduct of Foreign Policy*, vol. 3, Appendix H, Washington GPO 1974, pp. 72-85.

3 Henry A. Kissinger, *White House Years, 1968-1973*, Little, Brown and Company, German Edition, *Memoiren 1968-1973*, Bd. 1, München 1979, p. 172 ff.

4 95/1 U.S. Congress, Senate, Committee on Commerce, *American Role in East-West Trade*, Washington GPO 1977.

5 Letter of the President of the Chamber of Commerce of the United States of America, Richard L. Lesher, to President Reagan of Feb. 5, 1982, and letter of the President of NAM of Aug. 11, 1982. 97/2 U.S. Congress, Senate, Committee on Foreign Relations, Subcommittee on International Economic Policy, Hearings, *Economic Relations with the Soviet Union*, Washington GPO 1982, p. 197 ff.

6 Miles Costick/Mark Dean Millot, *The Soviet Gas Deal and Its Threat to the West*, Institute on Strategic Trade, Washington, D.C. 1980.

7 Paula Stern, Water's Edge. *Domestic Politics and the Making of American Foreign Policy*, Greenwood Press, Westport, Conn. 1979.

8 *AFL-CIO Free Trade Union News*, Department of International Affairs, American Federation of Labor and Congress of Industrial Organizations, vol. 32, 1977, no. 2, p. 1.

9 *An Analysis of Export Control of U.S. Technology – A DOD Perspective*, Defense Science Board Task Force on Export of U.S. Technology, Washington, D.C. Feb. 4, 1976.

10 95/2 U.S. Congress, House, Committee on International Relations, Subcommittee on International Economic Policy and Trade, *Export Licensing: CoCom List Review Proposals of the United States*, Washington GPO 1978.

11 Samuel P. Huntington, 'Trade, Technology, and Leverage', *Foreign Policy* no. 32, Autumn 1978, pp. 63-80; critical remarks of Franklyn Holzman/Richard Portes, 'The Limits of Pressure', *ibid.*, pp. 80-90; Raymond Vernon, 'The Fragile Foundations of East-West Trade', *Foreign Affairs*, Summer 1979, p. 1045 ff.

12 97/1 U.S. Congress, House, Committee on Foreign Affairs, Subcommittee on Europe and the Middle East, *Report, An Assessment of the Afghanistan Sanctions: Implications for Trade and Diplomacy in the 1980's*, Washington GPO 1981.

13 97/2 U.S. Congress, Joint Economic Committee, *East-West Commercial Policy: A Congressional Dialogue with the Reagan Administration*, Washing-

ton GPO 1982.

14 *Report of the Secretary of Defense, Caspar W. Weinberger, to the Congress on the FY 1983 Budget, FY 1984 Authorization Request and FY 1983/87 Defense Programs*, Washington, D.C. 1982.

15 Harald Müller/Reinhard Rode, *Osthandel oder Wirtschaftskrieg? Die USA und das Gas-Röhren-Geschäft*, Frankfurt 1982. 97/2 U.S. Congress, Senate, Committee on Banking, Housing, and Urban Affairs, Hearing, *Proposed Trans-Siberian Natural Gas Pipeline*, Washington GPO 1982.

16 *Wireless Bulletin from Washington*, no. 215, Nov. 15, 1982, pp. 1-6 and no. 218, Nov. 19, 1982, p. 25 f. Hanns-Dieter Jacobsen, *Die Ost-West-Wirtschaftsbeziehungen als deutsch-amerikanisches Problem*, Ebenhausen 1983, p. 173 ff.

17 *The Washington Post*, Sept. 28, 1983, D7, and Sept. 30, 1983, A27.

18 *The Washington Post*, March 21, 1983, A3.

15
U.S. Energy Policy

Harald Müller

Introduction: Functionalism versus Power Politics

International energy relations are widely viewed as a prime example of the "one world" image. If a strike of oil workers at the shores of the Persian Gulf and the dramatic deforestation in Nepal are factually related to each other, through a long chain of intermediate steps, then global interdependence is an evident reality. For the industrialized states of the West as well as of the East, energy policy has thus become a field of foreign policy with international relations of its own. The unique relevance of energy to the infrastructure of a modern economy, to transport, and to individual welfare, forces governments to treat energy policy as a specific area of action, connected to, but not identical with other issues of foreign economic policy.

In the United States, these facts are not disputed. How they are to be evaluated and translated into political action, however, is subject to considerable controversy. In this debate, one can distinguish between two competing models of interpretation and policy prescription:

- The *globalists*, in the tradition of classical idealism and functionalism, believe in an imperative for international cooperation. Resources and consumption are distributed extremely asymmetrically; OECD countries, particularly the continental Europeans and Japan, are inevitably forced to import. The advantageous reserve position of the USSR makes energy trade a sensible option. Since Comecon countries cannot match Western technology for the exploration, extraction, transport, refining and consumption of energy, Western and Eastern interests are fully complementary. If additional production capacity in the Soviet Union was available in case of emergencies, and if the volatile world energy market could be spared additional pressure by Eastern demand, this would serve the interests of both sides perfectly; East-West energy cooperation would thus not only make economic sense, but also contribute to global stability.

- The promoters of *power politics* use the old argument of the realist school of international relations. They view energy resources as instruments of national power. Import dependency indicates political weakness, vulnerability to blackmail, and military handicap in war. Asymmetry and interdependence are to be related, in the first place, to the superpowers' global struggle. They are to be scrutinized with a view to their potential for strengthening one's own position.

From the end of World War II until 1969, the latter view dominated American foreign energy policy. Defensive actions against Soviet oil exports in the late 1950s, and the famous pipe embargo of NATO of 1963 were examples of a policy of strict denial.[1] Détente brought the infusion of globalist elements into energy strategy towards the Soviets, but the power politics element never disappeared from the scene. Dreams of grand U.S.-Soviet projects in Siberia which came close to reality in the early 1970s faded with the Stevenson amendment to the Eximbank Authorization Act of 1974. A series of links had, however, been created which were carried over into the first years of the Carter administration. These included:

- bilateral energy research within the framework of the U.S.-Soviet energy agreement of 1974,
- multilateral cooperation in CSCE basket II and (as a means of implementing the CSCE) the Economic Commission for Europe (ECE) of the United Nations,
- trade with energy equipment and technology, and
- the continued attempts to bring the plans and negotiations on joint ventures in Siberia to fruition.[2]

These issues were dependent on political decisions, and therefore became subject to the demands of powerful interests.

The Interests

The Non-Committed. Energy policy is a policy area which has been furiously fought over, has divided American society for most of the 1970s, and has involved a multiplicity of interest groups. The foreign policy implications were missed in most of these debates, and left to oil companies and foreign policy makers. While political demands abounded concerning the domestic distributional problems in the energy sector, the public was indifferent as to foreign energy policy, particularly energy policy towards the Soviets.[3] One reason is certainly the marginal importance of Soviet energy exports to the United States. These never exeeded 1 per cent of U.S. consumption and their dollar value, with a maximum of $ 106 million (1974) and $ 112 million (1981) is peanuts compared with the multibillion U.S. oil import bills.[4]

The lack of commitment of the large oil companies is remarkable. If they considered participating in the Siberian ventures, they soon retreated after a short exploration phase because the conditions offered by the Soviets were not attractive enough compared to alternative investment opportunities. They did not, however, request an embargo policy, as they had 15 years earlier, but simply remained uncommitted.

Therefore, demands originated from two different corners: From those participating in the various types of cooperation; and from those whose foreign and security attitudes applied to energy relations as well.

Energy Companies, Equipment Industry and Scientists. Obviously most prominent among the supporters of East-West energy cooperation, were the companies with stakes in the large projects such as engineering firms like Bechtel, and Brown & Root, gas transmission companies like El Paso and Tenneco, and a few oil companies, particularly Occidental Oil Company. Occidental's chairman Hammer held impecable credentials in Eastern trade for almost 60 years.

From the late 1960s to the late 1970s, the natural gas companies feared an erosion of their domestic business due to shrinking American natural gas reserves. Their strategy of supply diversification led them to look to the large Soviet natural gas resources as a suitable source of imports. Those companies pleaded for an end of foreign credit restrictions in the Eximbank legislation. At least they needed a stable and predictable government policy which was a necessary prerequisite if private bankers were to be induced into financing such large, long-term projects.

The energy technology and equipment producers also hoped for the large Soviet market. The deficiencies of Soviet energy technology were well-known. But what, in the eyes of power politicians, was a welcome opportunity for exerting some leverage, was, for the businessman, a promising opening for export growth.[5] This group desired a governmental policy of non-intervention in East-West energy trade so that their own exports were not disrupted, but also to give the Soviet Union opportunities to earn much needed hard currency. Of course, even for these companies, the Soviet market remained a minor affair. The worldwide boom in energy equipment offered ample export opportunities, leaving the Soviet Union a welcome, but still marginal market. At no time did deliveries to the Soviet Union amount to more than 10 per cent of overall energy equipment exports. Furthermore only in 1976 were U.S. companies able to take more than 10 per cent of the Soviet orders for energy technology and hardware. The overall importance of the Russian market was therefore quite limited,[6] which consequently had a restraining effect on the lobbying effort.

The most important exception was the Caterpillar Tractor Company. Soviet plans for expanding oil and gas pipeline networks made it the largest prospective market for pipelaying equipment in the world. A large share of this market would therefore generate decisive economies of scale and strengthen a company's position in world markets. For this reason there was bitter competition between Caterpillar and the Japanese company Komatsu, and Caterpillar's lobbying campaign in 1982 far exceeded anything else displayed by other firms in the sector.[7] These business interests were supported and complemented by scientists and bureaucrats. Scientific cooperation had been disappointing in many energy areas, either because the Soviets were not up to the American state of the art, or because they refused to permit access to the most advanced laboratories. But in fusion, in elementary particle physics, and in magneto-hydro dynamics, the cooperation was fruitful and interesting enough to force the National Academy of Sciences to oppose any attempts by the government to use cooperation as a political instrument. Politicization was opposed even at a time when many scientists were expressing concern, dismay and anger at the treatment of dissidents by Soviet authorities. Apart from the immediate interest in continuing scientific exchanges, the scientists main objection was to state intervention in the freedom of scientific communication.[8]

The bureaucrats in the Department of Energy and, to some degree, at the technical desks of the Department of State, also worked infatigably for the continuation of the joint energy projects. Particularly in Department of Energy's Office for International Projects, project officers tried to undermine boycott policies by steadfastly continuing at least a minimum of routine exchanges.[9]

Finally the advocates of a détente policy (see chapter 14 by Reinhard Rode) also applied their general globalist policy principles to the area of energy.

The Opponents of Cooperation. The opponents of East-West energy cooperation did not consider economic interests. The only exception was the American Coal Association (ACA) which, during the 1982 debate, proposed U.S. coal as an alternative to Soviet gas for Europe. Here the ACA acted in a purely opportunistic manner without any conviction in the political objectives involved.

Opposition to energy cooperation came mainly from the security establishment as described by Rode. The only organization from the energy scene expressing similar demands was Americans for Energy Independence (AEI), a Washington based group on the conservative side of the energy debate and overlapping membership with groups like the Committee on the Present Danger. Within the AEI, a discussion emerged between politically hawkish members and representatives of the energy industry opposed to embargo policies. As a consequence, the group pleaded for a compromise with the Europeans in 1982, while continuing to oppose the Trans-siberian pipeline in principle.[10]

In accordance with its perceptions of the requirements of national security, the security establishment applies the principles of power politics to energy policy, which results in the following basic positions:

- Energy, particularly oil, is in itself seen as a military resource. The growth of Soviet energy production, therefore, directly strengthens the Soviet military posture.
- The supply of foreign energy technology and equipment also strengthens the Soviet military effort by substituting for Soviet investment in the energy sector and thus releasing resources for the military.
- Energy exports to the West are also seen as providing the Soviets with the hard currency earnings it needs to buy Western technology which in turn

contributes, either directly or indirectly, to the military effort.
— Western dependence on Soviet energy exports leads to creeping "Finlandization" and to an inability to act decisively in crises.
— Finally, the smoke screen of cooperation is seen as a distraction from the
 most meaningful aspect of international energy policy, namely the Soviet
 strategy of enhancing its influence on the oil-producing countries by military threats and thus aiming to control or deny the West's oil supplies.[11]

Decisions

Carter: Influencing Soviet Policies. In April 1977, President Carter published, with a big fanfare, the results of a CIA study showing that Soviet oil
production would stagnate in the short term and shrink significantly in the
medium-term. It was argued that the Soviet Union itself would most probably be
forced to import petroleum by 1985,[12] a forecast Carter wished to use to bolster
his own domestic energy policy. Among the linkage strategists within the National Security Council (see chapter 14 by Reinhard Rode), the idea of serious
deficiencies in the Soviet energy economy triggered new strategic considerations. Here was obviously an effective lever, if the threat of denying the Soviet
Union the technologies it needed to make good such deficiencies could be
used to gain tangible concessions by the Soviets. The dependency of the Soviet
energy infrastructure on Western, particularly American energy technology, was,
however, exaggerated. This resulted in a considerable misconception of the true
degree of leverage, which was carried over into the next administration.
 The State Department, under the leadership of Marshall Shulman, preferred
rather globalist positions. These emphasized the coincidence of interests with the
Soviets rather than power competition. In August 1977, the President accepted
PD-18 a framework concept shaped by the linkage strategists. But it was almost
a year before this was translated into political action, during which time energy
cooperation was left undisturbed.[13] Bilateral cooperation under the energy
agreement reached its highpoint when a U.S. superconducting magnet was flown
to a Soviet magneto-hydrodynamic pilot plant by two C-5A airplanes of the
Military Airlift Command, an unprecedented event in the relations between the
two countries.[14] There was even a revival of negotiations on the Yakutsk project
concerning the exploration and extraction of natural gas in the province of
Yakutia, which had been stalled since the Stevenson amendment of 1974. It was
apparently possible to arrive at a new financing agreement involving an Ameri-
can-European-Japanese bank consortium.[15] The progress of multilateral negotiations, however, came to a halt in the European Commission for Europe (ECE),
when, at the time of the CSCE follow-up conference in Belgrade, there were tactical battles over the Soviet proposal for an all-European energy conference. The
United States and some European countries believed this to be an attempt to

decouple Basket III of the CSCE from Basket II by means of a popular but politically irrelevant spectacle. Moreover, the United States sought to use the Soviet proposal as a vehicle for its own objectives, namely an enhanced flow of information on the Soviet energy economy and planning. For the time being, therefore, the United States exercised delaying tactics.[16]

The linkage strategy set out in PD-18 was used for the first time in the summer of 1978. The grounds for applying leverage were given as the trials of dissidents and the arrest of an American businessman accused of espionage. The American government reacted by subjecting all exports of oil and gas exploration and extraction technology and equipment to a licence procedure. This gave the administration the flexibility it needed to use the leverage provided by the alleged weakness and import dependency of the Soviet energy economy. At the same time two licences were revoked, for a drill bit factory to be constructed by Dresser Industries in the Soviet Union, and subject to a reevaluation. The licences were finally reissued in August, ostensibly in connection with the transfer of the businessman from Moscow to the U.S.A. Meanwhile the Department of Defense had initiated a major review of policy towards Soviet energy. Was the development of Soviet energy resources in America's interest or should one follow a policy of general denial? This debate was influenced by increasingly vocal but fairly contradicting calls from interest groups. The oil equipment industry lobbied energetically for a removal of energy equipment from the export control lists, but the AFL-CIO and conservative congressmen pressed for an end to energy cooperation.[17]

The policy decision, which finally emerged in December 1978 underlined the linkage strategy of PD-18. The licencing procedure was continued, but it was to be handled flexibly. In fact, not a single licence was denied until the end of 1979.

The crisis in Iran considerably changed the political climate of the energy cooperation. The Shah of Iran was a necessary pillar of the Nixon doctrine in the sense that he relieved the United States of the need for a massive military presence of its own in the crucial Gulf region. His fall, therefore, shed a new light on the geostrategic problems of the Persian Gulf, and in particular made the Soviet activities in Ethiopia, South Yemen and Afghanistan appear more threatening. The growing geopolitical rivalry of the superpowers over the control of Western oil supplies pushed the "globalists" back into a defensive position. If a power struggle over the Persian Gulf was really imminent, it became harder and harder to justify energy cooperation.[18] For the time being, however, the cooperation continued, and for the first time under the Carter administration exports of energy equipment exceeded the previous peak of 1976. The negotiations between El Paso Natural Gas, Occidental Oil, the Bank of America, and Japanese and European banks on the Yakutsk projects came close to maturity.[19] In the Economic Commission for Europe, the tactical infighting over the Soviet proposal for an energy conference ended with a compromise. This took the form of the Soviets' agreeing to provide more information on their own energy system, and the United States accepting the idea of institutionalizing the exchange of information in the form of the "Senior Advisers on Energy", a body similar to those already existing for economic questions and the environment. This group was, among other things, preparing a future high-level conference within the ECE, for which no date was fixed because it would have led to new quarrels.[20]

These positive developments could not, however, hide the fact that demands from the security establishment to change foreign energy policy were growing louder and louder, at a time when the political climate between both superpowers was not particularly good. The Soviet invasion of Afghanistan transformed what was already an identifiable tendency into an abrupt change of policy. There was an immediate stop on licenses for U.S. energy exports to the Soviet Union, existing licenses granted were revoked, and energy equipment exports fell by almost 50 per cent. Meetings of the bilateral energy commission were halted. In the ECE, the United States blocked any new project proposals, and the negotiations on the Yakutsk project agreement, which was virtually ready for signature, were delayed; El Paso finally retreated in the face of fierce government opposition to the project.[21]

While this series of events suggests a very dramatic change, there was a degree of continuity. There was already a worsening in the political climate in 1979, so that decisions of 1980 underlined this trend. But even the decisions of 1980 did not mean a complete end to cooperation. The United States consciously kept the organisational skeleton of a substantially reduced energy cooperation. They did not revoke the energy agreement and they participated in low-level routine meetings. They did not boycott the Economic Commission for Europe, and even played host for a working group of the ECE. While they granted no licenses for technology exports, they resumed licenses for energy equipment in the summer of 1980. The most prominent example of the latter was the export license for pipelayers granted to the Caterpillar Tractor Company. The strategy of PD-18 was thereby carefully adhered to, and technology exports which could enhance Soviet independence were blocked, while product exports which resulted in a continued and possibly enhanced Soviet dependence were allowed. In other words, Afghanistan helped to perfect the PD-18's strategy initiated in the decisions of August and December 1978. The American-Soviet energy relations were in a bad way by end of 1980, and they had been subject to a determined U.S. linkage policy, but a new start, even a future expansion was not at all impossible.

Reagan: Change the Soviet system. The conservative coalition which shapes the Reagan administration subordinated energy relations to its worldwide strategy of "global opposition" and enforced system change. According to this view, both power blocs were vulnerable in the sector of energy: The West because of its import dependency, which the Soviets were trying to exploit by an undeclared natural resources war; and the Soviet Union because of its inability to increase energy production without Western assistance. The Reagan administration retained the Carter judgement of the Soviet energy economy, based essentially on the CIA report of 1977, that it was facing major problems. It was convenient for Reagan's people to do so because it fitted well with their existing ideological position and political strategy. For the hardliners, Soviet expansionism rested on genuine attributes of the Soviet system. This was seen as a notoriously violent, powerhungry, expansionist social order. To end Soviet expansionism it was thought necessary to bring about an internal change of the system, including, in particular, a reorientation of priorities away from the military sector and a liberalization of the economy. The United States therefore, had to interdict the Soviets' attempts to expand by military strength, and force internal change by economic pressure.[22] The perceived weakness in the energy sector in the form of the Soviet dependency on Western technology, offered the leverage needed; agricultural exports were already excluded for domestic reasons (see chapter 14 by Reinhard Rode).

Seldom has the perception of developments been so evidently shaped by the dictates of a pre-conceived policy strategy rather than the other way round. In 1981, the famous CIA report was already four years old and contrary to its expectations Soviet oil production had grown, even if at drastically reduced rates. The reduction of coal production was neutralized by an enormous growth of natural gas production which exceeded even the targets of the economic plan. Nuclear energy also grew, though more slowly than envisaged by the plan. These developments could lead one to conclude there were certain difficulties, but they did not indicate an imminent breakdown. Moreover, various studies had already cast doubt on the belief in a decisive Soviet dependency on Western, namely U.S. energy technology exports.[23] Nevertheless, the National Security Council and the Department of Defense held firmly to their political line. They used the concern about the security implications of the European-Soviet natural gas agreement, which was already evident in other parts of the administration, as a means of promoting their more radical political aims. The State Department was inclined to compromise with Europe, provided more attention was attached to the security aspects of East-West trade and at least some symbolic changes could be achieved in Western policies on East-West economic relations. The Department of Defense, in contrast, insisted on a basic decision on how to deal with the Soviet energy economy, and in effect prepared measures for an "energy economy war". The zigzag movements of U.S. policy between the summit in 1981 and the compromise in the fall of 1982 cannot be understood without considering the competing perspectives. On the one hand there was a readiness for a transatlantic compromise, which subordinated strategic energy policy to symbolic-diplomatic gains; on the other hand there was a conscious, unilateral striving for measures aimed at decisively weakening the Soviet energy economy in order to induce Soviet authorities to make internal changes.

The military coup in Poland provided the opportunity to push ahead with the first set of the desired measures. These included an expansion of licensing requirements to cover refinery and energy transport technology and equipment, i. e. pipelines, and an immediate halt to all licensing like Caterpillar's application for a license for 200 pipelayers. These measures already contained elements of extraterritoriality, because foreign licensees and subsidiaries of U.S. firms were permitted to export oil and gas related items to the USSR only if they did not contain parts and materials produced in the U.S.A. or technology transferred from the U.S.A. after the 1st of August 1978.[24]

The State Department, faced with harsh criticism from the European allies, viewed the December decisions as a point of departure from which to reach a viable compromise. For the hawks in the Pentagon and the National Security Council, however, it was only the first step, and was to be followed by even more obtrusive measures. In June 1982, shortly after the Versailles summit had appeared to at least partly solve the problem, they used the absence of Secretary of State Haig from a national security meeting to persuade the President of the need for sanctions on all energy technology and equipment exports to the Soviet Union of foreign licensees and subsidiaries. There was no retroactive limit placed on these sanctions. The energy agreement due for renewal in 1982, was canceled, and the U.S. government simultaneously informed the ECE that it would no longer participate in the energy projects of the Commission. The last U.S.-Soviet channel for energy cooperation was thereby closed.

The June decision, however, went too far (see chapter 14). At first, the European companies concerned were denied all U.S. goods, data, and services. Following howls of protests from the EC commission and the individual governments, backed by a strong expression of their will to defy the U.S. embargo policy, the decision was modified in September 1982 to cover only the areas of oil and gas technology. Meanwhile, the domestic protest could no longer be overlooked. There were protests from the Chamber of Commerce and the National Association of Manufacturers. Even more energetically than these business associations, Caterpillar Tractor started a big lobbying campaign. Fortunately for the firm, the sanctions against Caterpillar affected work in the constituencies of two of the most important Republican members of Congress, the Chairman of the Senate Foreign Relations Committee, Senator Percy, and the minority leader in the House of Representatives, Michel. Michel, a faithful follower of Reagan, introduced a bill that would have suspended the President's authority to impose economic sanctions.[25] Before this bill could pass through Congress, the administration revoked the sanctions against European companies in November 1982. Caterpillar received an export license for pipelayers by early 1983, and the United States had already resumed participation in ECE energy seminars at the low level in the fall of 1982.[26] A positive final agreement of the Madrid CSCE conference in 1983, also implied a continuation of the multilateral energy cooperation.

The United States, led by the new Secretary of State Shultz, returned to a more moderate line, after a majority in the administration became convinced that the political costs of sticking to the hard line — both at home and abroad — exceeded the expected benefits. In the end, therefore, the progress of the pipeline construction could not be impeded, and whilst the hardliners did not give up their case, their influence on policy in the East-West energy sector was far less in early 1984 than it had been two years before.

Conclusions: The Dominance of Power Politics

The prognosis of the functionalists, that objective complementary interests exert an irresistable pressure on governments in the direction of cooperation and integration, has not come true in U.S.-Soviet energy relations. American foreign energy strategy has evolved from a selective linkage policy, through an extensive policy of punishment, to an open economic energy war aimed at system change.

The most important finding is that in all four areas of cooperation described above, there was a need for both routine exchanges such as private business negotiations, licensing, seminars etc. and fundamental political decisions. The more cooperation had to rely on basic decisions concerning "high politics", the more vulnerable it was to the influence of power politics. The large U.S.-Soviet cooperation projects required high level, legislative decisions, so they fell victim to power politics from 1974 onwards. Trade in energy equipment was also brought to the political forefront, and thus also suffered significantly at an early stage in the general debate on East-West technology transfer. The bilateral cooperation under the energy agreement was, however, never in the headlines. As a result it flourished, even in times of major tensions, and only failed when for formal reasons, namely the need to renew the agreement, it landed on the desks of the top decision-makers. The multilateral energy cooperation had suffered constant delay, when it became politicized through its coupling to the CSCE process. But in routine exchanges such as working groups, seminars etc. it managed to resist the influence of power politics even at the height of the energy-economic war policy. It did so, however, only because its practical relevance remained relatively minor.

The development of energy relations was, therefore, fully dependent on the state of general political relations between the superpowers, a deterioration in the latter being mirrored by the drying-up of energy cooperation. Even more important, however, than the factual state of the U.S.-Soviet relationship were misperceptions on the American side concerning:

— the political intentions of the Soviets as a whole: the more inimical and offensive the Soviet position was viewed as, the more difficult it became to justify energy cooperation;

- the assessment of the Soviet energy policy: the prevailing pessimism fed the belief in the utility of the energy sector for power politics;
- the analysis of the effects of Western energy technology on the Soviet Union: an extremely positive judgement of these effects led to an overstatement of American leverage;
- finally, the existance of a kind of U.S. techno-machismo, which leads to an overestimation of the uniqueness of U.S. technology. The speed of innovation-diffusion and the innovative capability of Western competitors were strongly underestimated. This again resulted in an overoptimistic assessment of the chances of success for the chosen strategy.

The interests of power politics dominated over Western economic interests and a global optimization of economic utility. But there are definite limits to the application of power politics, which occur whenever domestic and international opposition is powerful enough to prevail over ideology.

211

NOTES

Stent, Angela: *From Embargo to Ostpolitik. The Political Economy of West German-Soviet Relations. 1955-1980.* Cambridge, Mass.: 1981, p. 98 ff.
2 Müller, Harald: 'Von der Versorgungsallianz zur Sicherung des Persischen Golfes'. In: Czempiel, Ernst-Otto (ed.): *Amerikanische Außenpolitik im Wandel. Von der Entspannungspolitik Nixons zur Konfrontation unter Reagan.* Stuttgart, Kohlhammer: 1982. S. 120-144, esp. p. 134 ff.
3 *Op. cit.*, p. 121-124.
4 Brougher, Jack: 1979-82: 'The United States Uses Trade To Penalize Soviet Aggression and Seeks to Reorder Western Policy'. In: 96/2 U.S. Congress. Joint Economic Committee. *Soviet Economy in the 1980s. Problems and Prospects.* Selected Papers. Washington, D.C., GPO: 1982.
5 95/2 U.S. Congress. Senate. Committee on Government Operations. Permanent Subcommittee on Investigations. Hearings. *Transfer of Technology and the Dresser Industries Export Licensing Actions.* Washington, D.C., GPO: 1979, p. 172.
6 U.S. Congress. Office of Technology Assessment: *U.S. Technology and Soviet Energy Availability.* Washington, D.C.: GPO, 1981.
7 See the Statement of Caterpillar's Chairman Chapman before the Subcommittee on International Economic Policy of the Senate Foreign Relations Committee. In: Müller, Harald/Rode, Reinhard: *Osthandel oder Wirtschaftskrieg? Die USA und das Gas-Röhren-Geschäft,* Frankfurt/Main, Haag und Herchen: 1982, p. 63-65.
8 Rushing, Frances W./Ailes, Catherine P.: 'An Assessment of the USSR-U.S. Scientific and Technological Exchange Programs'. In: 96/1 U.S. Congress. Joint Economic Committee. *Soviet Economy in a Time of Change.* Compilation of Papers. Vol. 2. Washington, D.C., GPO: 1979, p. 605-624.
9 Interviews in the Department of Energy, Washington, D.C.: June 1982.
10 Interview with Dr. Bergman (Americans for Energy Independence). Washington, D.C.: June 1982.
11 Costick, Miles/Millot, Marc D.: The Soviet Gas Deal and its Threat to the West. *Current Analysis.* Institute on Strategic Trade. Vol. II, No. 11. Washington, D.C.: 1980.
12 Central Intelligence Agency: *The International Energy Situation.* Washington, D.C., GPO: 1977.
13 Huntington, Samuel P.: 'Trade, Technology and Leverage', *Foreign Policy* No. 32, Autumn 1978, p. 63-80.
14 U.S. Department of Energy: *U.S.-USSR Cooperative Program on MHD Power Generation,* Washington, D.C., DOE: 1978.
15 *Energy in Countries with Central Planned Economies,* Vol. 1. 1978. No. 13. p. 11, and Vol. 2, 1979. No. 3. p. 2-3.
16 United Nations: Economic Commission for Europe. *Annual Report.* 33rd session. New York, U.N.: 1978.
17 95/2 U.S. Congress. Senate. Committee on Government Operations *op. cit.*
18 Brzezinski, Zbigniew: 'Power and Principle'. *Memoirs of the National Secu-*

rity Adviser. 1977-1981. New York, Farrar/Straus/Giroux: 1983. p. 443-459.

19 Brougher (*op. cit.*). p. 446; Energy in Countries with Planned Economies, Vol. 3. 1979. No. 11. p. 13.

20 United Nations: Economic Commission for Europe. *Annual Report*. 34th session, New York, U.N.: 1979.

21 Brougher (*op. cit.*) p. 446: United Nations: Economic Commission for Europe. *Annual Report*. 35th session, New York, U.N.: 1980; *Energy in Countries with Planned Economies*,Vol. 4. 1980. No. 8. p. 4.

22 Czempiel, Ernst-Otto et al.: 'Eindämmung, Überlegenheit und erzwungener Systemwandel − die amerikanische Perzeption der Entspannungspolitik zu Beginn der 80er Jahre.' In: Deutsche Gesellschaft für Friedens- und Konfliktforschung (ed.): *DGFK-Jahrbuch 1982/83. Zur Lage Europa im globalen Spannungsfeld*. Baden-Baden, Nomos: 1983. p. 41-66.

23 Goldman, Marshall I.: 'The Role of Communist Countries'. In: Deese, David A./Nye, Joseph S. (eds.): *Energy and Security*. Cambridge, Mass., Balliager: 1981. p. 111-130.

24 U.S. Congress: Office of Technology Assessment. *Technology and East-West Trade. An Update*. Washington, D.C., GPO: 1983. p. 31.

25 ibid. p. 32.

26 Interview at the U.N. Economic Commission for Europe in Geneva, March 1983.

16
U.S. Export Control and Export Administration Legislation

Hanns-D. Jacobsen[1]

The debate within the United States over the revision of the Export Administration Act of 1979 which expired on September 30, 1983 and was thereafter repeatedly renewed, took on a particular significance in the wake of the disputes between Western Europe and the United States over economic strategy vis-à-vis Communist-ruled states. The disagreement over the act's renewal offers insights into the lessons the American administration and Congress learned from the controversies of the late 1970s and early 1980s. In this context the important issues to be addressed include the extraterritorial extension of American legislative controls, as well as the attempt by the United States to exert influence over multilateral export controls within the CoCom framework of NATO.

The fundamental problem of American export policy is rooted in the conflict between: on the one hand, the desire to promote U.S. export in order to reduce the rising trade deficit[2] and improve the American ability to compete on world markets; and, on the other hand, the use of export controls to realize a variety of economic, political, and national security objectives. In most cases there is no conflict between these two objectives, because most U.S. foreign trade is conducted with countries which either do not endanger U.S. national security or against which the United States has no inclination to export restrictions in the pursuit of economic or political objectives. The conflict arises however, in the case of East-West economic relations because the United States views the Communist-bloc countries, in particular the USSR, as countries that threaten its national security and that must therefore be handled accordingly.

The "Export Administration Act" provides a legislative foundation for the application of export controls. Discussions over the renewal of this act promoted a series of fundamental disagreements throughout 1983 and 1984; at issue was the essential rationale of American economic policy toward the East and the consequences of the revised law for relations between the United States and its allies.

The History of U.S. Export Controls[3]

There is a long tradition in the United States of export controls vis-à-vis Communist countries beginning with the Export Control Act of 1949.[4] This was formally designed to apply to all countries but was, in practice, above all directed against the USSR and its allies. The aim of the Export Control Act was to deny these countries all militarily relevant exports. The act was extended by the passage of the "Mutual Defense Assistance Act of 1951,"[5] in which explicit reference was made to the USSR and its satellites as the objects of the American trade denial policy. This law provided moreover, the means by which the United States could attempt to impose its own approach to trade with Communist countries upon the West Europeans. For one thing, this so-called "Battle Act" laid the legislative foundations for the "Coordinating Committee for Multilateral Export Controls" (CoCom) of NATO,[6] which had been in existence since November 1949. It also stipulated that all countries participating in American aid programs would either have to cease delivery of embargoed goods to Communist-bloc countries, or forgo American aid.

When it was introduced the "Battle Act of 1949" represented a culmination of measures and actions against the USSR and other Communist countries adopted by the United States in the course of the Cold War. All these measures served the same purpose of denying the potential enemy any economic advantage it might gain from trade with the West and, by so doing, containing the spread of communist power as manifested in Eastern Europe and displayed during the Berlin blockade and the Korean War. In addition, they were to help preserve American supremacy, above all in the military realm.

Although there had been substantial reductions in both the American and multilateral control lists by the mid-1950s, the U.S. Congress extended the lists' range of application through the passage of an amendment, first introduced in 1962, to the Export Control Act. According to this amendment, controls were to apply not only to exports with direct military application, but also to those that represented "a significant contribution to the military or economic potential"[7] of the target countries. This extension of U.S. controls was an explicit declaration of economic warfare against the Eastern bloc states.

Not long after the passage of this amendment a number of developments become apparent which would gradually undermine the use of economic warfare as an instrument in competition with the Communist countries. Western Europe and Japan had increased their trade with these countries. Even in the United States itself, voices from the ranks of industry and Congress demanding modifications in export trade legislation multiplied in the face of changing perceptions of relations between the two superpowers, of the increased export opportunities from which the United States was excluded, and of the upward trend in the U.S. trade deficit.[8]

Initiatives to change legislation eventually led to the "Export Administration Act of 1969."[9] This law's provision reflected an attempt to move away from a restrictive embargo policy and towards a cautious export-promotion policy which included the Communist countries. As a rationale for the change,[10] it was asserted that the Sino-Soviet bloc was no longer monolithic, that the USSR could obtain goods embargoed by the U.S. from other countries in the West, and that, in contrast to those of its allies, the more stringent controls of the United States had, in the final analysis, proved to be less effective or even ineffective.

The most significant departure from previous legislation was contained in a provision specifying that exports of both potential military *and* economic import would no longer be subject to control, but only those products that represented "a significant contribution to the military potential of any other nation or nations which would prove detrimental to the national security of the United States."[11] Unlike the "Export Control Act," the new law emphasized the need to expand exports in order to contribute to the growth of the American economy. Export controls were no longer regarded as the rule, but rather as the exception. They were only to be applied in defense of the national security, in order to avert shortages in supplies of vital commodities, or in support of foreign policy objectives.

A number of amendments were appended in 1972, 1974 and 1977 to the "Export Administration Act of 1969", but these left the essential intent of the act unchanged. In the ten year period in which it was in force, the act did indeed lead to a substantial reduction in export controls directed against communist countries and, correspondingly, to a notable expansion in American trade with the East.[12]

Whilst the Department of Commerce had overall responsibility for administering U.S. export controls a number of other government agencies and departments were engaged in the process of license allocation. Above all the Department of Defense (DoD) decided on the export of products and technologies affecting the national security of the United States. In the process of clarifying its criteria for license allocation, the DoD increasingly concentrated on the transfer of "critical technologies," that is those technologies in which the United States had captured the lead, and which, though essentially of civilian nature, could have military application.

The conclusion drawn in the "Bucy Report" of 1976 paved the way for the first measures in this direction. The report concluded that "design and manufacturing know-how are the principal elements of strategic technology control."[13] This point of view found expression in the "Export Administration Act (EAA) of 1979."[14] The most pronounced difference between the new law and the 1969 act lay in the greater importance assigned to the control of technologies in comparison to that of final products.[15]

The EAA of 1979 replaced the "Mutual Defense Assistance Act of 1951" ("Battle Act"), by which it had been possible to link American aid to compliance with U.S. policies vis-à-vis the Soviet Union, but which at the same time had placed value on arriving at a more integrated export control policy with the allies under the auspices of CoCom. Like its predecessor, the EAA of 1979 placed more emphasis on the promotion of trade, and only assigned a secondary role to export controls. The incorporation of the new "critical technologies" approach, aggravated the practical difficulties associated with enforcing export controls, since the Department of Defense failed to provide a "Militarily Critical Technologies List"[16] that could be practically applied.

The deterioration of East-West relations in the late 1970s and early 1980s was accompanied, in the United States, by ever more vigorous calls for an extension of export controls on strategically relevant products, and especially on high technology products. Critics asserted that both legal and illegal technology transfer from the West, and in particular from the United States,[17] had contributed to Soviet rearmament.[18]

The overall accuracy of this assertion, and above all the actual effect of technology transfer on the Soviet military potential, can only be tested with difficulty, since it is based on findings that are not generally accessible.[19] Advocates of expanded trade with the East in no way reject a tightening of controls that would limit Soviet access to technologies that have direct or indirect military relevance. They question, however,[20] whether an extension of controls to include, for example, personal computers offered by a large number of companies in the West, is appropriate. Advocates of trade question simple generalizations about the benefits of trade to the East because the USSR, as a military superpower, can simply not afford to base its long-term efforts in military research and development on more or less fortuitous technology imports from the West. The USSR doubtless exploits technological advances in the West as completely and profitably as it can for its own military expansion. It is doubtful, however, that, substantially tighter, U.S. and CoCom export controls could prevent the USSR and other east European countries from obtaining the technologies, that they not only want but could also absorb given their relatively limited high-tech capacity, from elsewhere in the West. After all, other technologically advanced, but neutral, countries such as Sweden, Austria and Switzerland belong to the West. There are in addition the newly-industrializing countries such as the ASEAN states.

The controversy in the United States over the renewal of the "Export Administration Act" evolved against the backdrop of these diverging viewpoints. The debate centered primarily on the potential military relevance of technology transfer to communist countries, as well as on the internal and external effects of export controls motivated by foreign policy considerations, such as the most recent 1980-81 grain embargo against the USSR and the 1982 export restrictions on natural gas and petroleum equipment.

The Controversy over the Revision of the "Export Administration Act of 1979"

When the administration bill "to amend and reauthorize the Export Administration Act (EAA) of 1979"[21] was introduced on April 5, 1983, a representative of the U.S. Department of Commerce, L. Olmer,[22] insisted that the transfer of sensitive equipment and technologies has had a direct impact on Soviet rearmament. He maintained that technology transfer had in turn led to the introduction of new weapons systems in the Soviet Union which compelled the West to make additional military expenditures. For reasons of national security it was therefore necessary both to tighten export controls and to allow the President the freedom to impose controls in the execution of foreign policy.

National Security Controls. According to the administration's proposal the tightening of export regulations would be accomplished primarily through provisions designed to improve the effectiveness of controls on technologies of strategic importance. More specifically, the Commerce Department was to be relieved of its obligation to provide a justification for its actions to a license applicant and there were to be restrictions placed on Congress's ability to intervene in the implementation of policy. The objective of the administration's bill was to broaden the base of goods subject to control and sharpen controls on "militarily critical technology and keystone equipment". Since the efficacy of controls depends essentially on multilateral cooperation, the bill also attached importance to improvements in international cooperation, in particular by enhancing the effectiveness of CoCom. The test as to the foreign availability of goods would no longer be satisfied if third countries merely possessed the capacity to produce certain goods or apply critical technologies, but rather whenever those countries did in fact apply them. In such cases, the administration hoped to restrict the availability of various comparable products and technologies from foreign countries (including those not in CoCom), through consultation with these countries. Finally, the bill recommended that international control lists be expanded, that the observance and enforcement of the regulations be more strictly applied, and the CoCom secretariat be upgraded politically and financially better equipped. In the event of a violation of the "National Security Controls", the administration bill provided for import restrictions or other penalties.

Foreign Policy Controls. In spite of intense domestic and foreign protests about more restrictive policies, and in particular about the Reagan administration's sanctions against the Urengoi pipeline, the administration's bill sought Presidential powers to impose economic sanctions for reasons of foreign policy, which would, in essence be in violation of internationally accepted rules of conduct. The steps taken in each application of foreign policy controls would depend on the specific situation and would serve the overall purpose of achieving political objectives by economic means. In this regard, "Foreign Policy Controls" were to provide a method of creating a degree of political room-to-maneuver for the administration below the threshold of military action. Furthermore, as Olmer stressed,[23] the success or failure of sanctions imposed should not be evaluated solely on whether or not the country against whom the sanctions were directed put an end to its objectionable behavior. Rather, such actions would be undertaken with other objectives in mind including:

— to discourage the targeted country from future actions;

- to mobilize international support against the behaviour of the targeted country;
- to impose economic costs on the targeted country as a consequence of its undesirable behavior;
  and finally,
- to express political disapproval of what was felt to be objectionable conduct.

In order to limit the economic disruption caused by export controls imposed for political reasons, the administration's bill, in contrast to earlier legislation, contained a "contract sanctity" clause, which held that contracts concluded prior to the issuing of sanctions could be honored, providing that deliveries could be arranged within 270 days.

An Appraisal of the Tighter Controls. Passage of the administration's bill would have enhanced the administration's ability to influence export policy, and granted it more power to realize foreign policy objectives than under the EAA of 1979. Both at home and abroad, the bill therefore, attracted some sharp criticism, and the House of Representatives and Senate consequently changed the administration's version on a number of essential points.

A brief discussion of the four most important areas of controversy follows:

Multilateral Export Controls. There are no fundamental disagreements among CoCom members with regard to both an understanding of the need for controls, and the willingness to restrict the export to Communist countries of militarily critical products and technology. There are, however, a number of transatlantic differences over the "what" and the "how".

The "what" concerns export control lists. Though it may not proceed directly from the administration bill, the export policy of the United States, which is by nature oriented toward national security, has departed significantly from the criteria previously used by CoCom, and now includes many additional items that were formerly excluded.[24] The United States is no longer inclined to base its export control policy solely on the military relevance of exports, as is the position of CoCom recently ratified at a high-ranking meeting in April 1983, but all products and technologies are to be included that are somehow "strategically important" (Olmer). This includes civilian technologies if their range of application cannot be precisely determined, or in other words, when they fall into certain "gray areas". The other members of CoCom have opposed the expansion of CoCom criteria beyond the currently accepted standard of "military relevance", because it could lead to undue restrictions of East-West trade, which, in their eyes, help stabilize East-West relations. They are by no means unwilling to broaden the CoCom lists to include, for example, technologies such as those used in the production of silicon, or laser-technology, etc., or any such instances involving militarily relevant technologies. Indeed between the end of 1982 and mid-1983 CoCom members, acting on the basis of approximately 100 recommendations from the United States, were able to reach agreement on tighter export controls on a variety of items. Despite this agreement, however, the West European countries have refused to acquiesce in the inclusion of items whose military significance is not directly apparent. This basic difference between the United States and other CoCom nations will not only remain a source of conflict, but will also limit the effectiveness of American controls if the United States, either through persuasion or the exertion of more direct pressure, does not succeed in getting other CoCom members to change their position on the issue of export controls.

The "how" is related to CoCom itself. The U.S. administration's bill contained an initiative to strengthen the Paris-based institution of CoCom. The response of the other members of CoCom to such an initiative would not be to raise any objections to improvements in the operation of CoCom, particularly with regard to equipping the secretariat and the inclusion of third countries. The long overdue conformation of CoCom to a more effective set of controls could thereby be put into effect. The other members would, however, reject any change in CoCom's informal status to create a formal international organization as some in the U.S. Congress want. In several countries parliamentary approval for new legislation would be needed for such a move, and the public debate thus generated could well lead to the exclusion of a number of countries from CoCom. This would, in turn, further limit the effectiveness of CoCom.

Economic Sanctions as Instruments of Foreign Policy.[25] In contrast to the U.S. administration, West European governments have proved to be much more cautious with regard to the use of economic sanctions as instrument of foreign policy. If necessary, they were prepared, as for example in the case of the Federal Republic of Germany, to offer economic inducements to encourage politically desirable conduct on the part of communist countries. This was done in relatively marginal and at the same time clearly defined cases such as the emigration of persons of German descent from the USSR, Poland or Rumania, and citizens from the GDR, or access to West Berlin. As a general principle, even if with certain nuances,[26] West European countries see economic relations as a means of stabilizing East-West relations. Economic relations are alternatively treated separately from political relations, and by no means used as an instrument to punish or discipline the USSR or other Eastern countries.

For this reason, "Foreign Policy Controls" will remain an important source of controversy in relations between the United States and its allies, especially since the U.S. is now on the defensive — following the unsuccessful experience of the grain embargo of 1980-81, and the European gas pipeline sanctions in 1982. In voicing his criticism of the sanctions Senator Mathias was quite correct in emphasizing that the imposition of export controls with the goal of expressing political condemnation of objectionable conduct on the part of the targeted country is, by definition, successful: "the question is whether the gesture is worth the cost."[27] Indeed, as the partial grain and pipeline embargoes clearly showed a sufficiently strong protest by U.S. farmers and of the U.S. firms affected can force a withdrawal of "Foreign Policy Controls", if the sacrifices are perceived as being too costly for the home country. In any case, the credibility of American foreign policy is not enhanced by such reversals, especially since the original grounds for sanctions continue to exist.

Contract Sanctity. In order to counter domestic political criticism of foreign policy export controls, coming predominantly from the group of industries involved in East-West trade,[28] the Reagan administration's draft bill provided for contract sanctity under which no existing order would be affected by sanctions for a period of 270 days. This was viewed as inadequate by domestic critics who feared it could possibly work in favor of "off-the-shelf" contracts such as for the delivery of foodstuffs or grain to the Soviet Union, but not in the case of long-term agreements, which are typically planned and completed in the ongoing process of continued international cooperation. For this reason, a number of bills in the House of Representatives and the Senate included unconditional guarantees of sanctity for legally concluded contracts and proposals for such guarantees were finally adopted in both houses of Congress.[29]

Extraterritoriality and American Legislation. The extraterritorial application of U.S. legislative controls had already acquired major significance following the European-U.S. controversy, in the summer of 1982, over the construction of the "Urengoy" pipeline from Siberia to Western Europe.[30] The EAA of 1979 permitted the extension of U.S. export controls to foreign companies under U.S. ownership, to subsidiaries of American firms, and also to foreign companies licenced to use U.S. technology. For some time these regulations have met with the opposition of West European countries and the Commission of the European Communities (EC) which considered that international law did not permit such an extension of U.S. legal jurisdiction to firms with headquarters in the EC.[31] Since the administration's bill, as well as the Senate's version passed on March 2, 1984,[32] provided for the first time in American export legislation for an import ban against any firms violating American controls, it was not surprising that the EC once again protested against the regulations, declaring them "unacceptable in the context of relations with friendly states"[33] and incompatible with the provisions of the GATT. This criticism was dismissed by representatives of the U.S. government on the grounds that the ability to use extraterritorial controls was necessary in order to prevent the circumvention of export controls by reexports of U.S. goods via third countries. The U.S. had little option but to defend this position, because to completely deny itself extraterritoriality would have been tantamount to acknowledging that the pipeline embargo of 1982 had been an error, and would have created an incentive for U.S. firms to transfer their production facilities abroad.[34]

New Sources of Conflict

At the time of writing (March 1984), it was unclear what final form the renewal of the EAA would take. There were still major differences between the administration's bill and the House and Senate bills. For this reason, there was the prospect of protracted negotiations between representatives of both houses and even a presidential veto. By mid-1984 moreover, it became clear that no new law on export controls would be passed before the presidential elections of 1984.

From all three bills it was clear that neither the administration nor Congress was prepared to draw any conclusions from the transatlantic disagreements of the previous few years that would move them to make concessions to the interests of the West Europeans. On the contrary, with the exception of the House bill, the original intent of legislative export controls at their liberally imbued inception in 1969 and 1979 had been abandoned in favor of a more stringent application of controls for reasons of national security and U.S. foreign relations. This not only affected domestic companies. Through the expansion of the government's powers to intervention such as in import restrictions in the case of a violation of export controls, foreign companies are also affected. For this reason, passage of the law in any of its three forms will have consequences for transatlantic economic and political relations. In all probability West European, Japanese and other companies such as in ASEAN, will endeavor to reduce their dependency on U.S. technology as much as possible. Otherwise they will risk falling victim to export controls that are viewed as necessary by the U.S., but not by other nations, in times of increasing East-West tension. Such developments hamper long-term cooperation with the United States and the evolution of an international division of labor that benefits all parties. Ultimately, reliability and predictability are part of the very foundation of economic and political cooperation.

In CoCom as well, new controversies may arise in relation to multilateral export controls if the United States insists on including products and technologies whose military relevance is not readily apparent. This dispute between the United States and the remaining CoCom members has really existed since 1949. Given the continued differences between the current underlying philosophies, there is no early end to the dispute in sight.

NOTES

1 This chapter is based on portions of the following work: H.D. Jacobsen, *Ost-West Wirtschaftsbeziehungen als deutsch-amerikanisches Problem*, Habilitation submitted to the Department of Political Science of the Free University of Berlin, Berlin, January, 1984.

2 *The Economic Report of the President*, Washington, D.C., February, 1984, p. 42. The report estimates the U.S. trade balance deficit for 1983 at $ 63 billion.

3 For a discussion of this issue, see G. Adler Karlsson, *Western Economic Warfare* (Uppsala: 1969); T.A. Wolf, *U.S. East-West Trade Policy: Economic Warfare versus Economic Welfare* (Boston: 1973); H.J. Berman and J.R. Garson, 'United States Export Controls--Past, Present, and Future,' *Columbia Law Review*, vol. 67 (1967); Office of Technology Assessment of the U.S. Congress, *Technology and East-West Trade* (Washington, D.C.: November, 1979).

4 Public Law 81-11.

5 Public Law 82-213.

6 Founding members were the United States, France, Great Britain, Italy, Belgium, The Netherlands, and Luxembourg. In spring of 1950 Denmark, Canada, Norway and the Federal Republic of Germany became members of the committee, followed in 1952 by Portugal and Japan, and in 1953 by Greece and Turkey. In short, members at present include all countries in NATO (with the exception of Iceland and Spain) and Japan.

7 Office of Technology Assessment, op. cit., p. 114.

8 On this issue, see, in particular, T.A. Wolf, *U.S. East-West Trade Policy*, pp. 84 ff.

9 Public Law 91-184.

10 See R. Morton, *The United States Role in East-West Trade: Problems and Prospects*, Washington, D.C., U.S. Department of Commerce, August, 1975, pp. A-6 ff.

11 Public Law 91-184, Section 23.

12 See chapter 14 by R. Rode in this volume.

13 *An Analysis of Export Control of U.S. Technology--A DOD Perspective. A Report of the Science Board Task Force on Export of U.S. Technology*, Office of the Director of Defense Research and Engineering, Washington, D.C., February 2, 1976 ("Bucy Report," named after its chairman, the President of Texas Instruments), p. xiii.

14 Public Law 96-72.

15 For a thorough discussion of this issue, see, in particular, J.W. Golan, 'U.S. Technology Transfers to the Soviet Union and the Protection of National Security,' *International Business*, vol. 11, no. 3 (1979), pp. 2037 ff.; J.F. Bucy, 'Technology Transfer and East-West Trade,' *International Security*, vol. 5, no. 3 (Winter 1980/81), pp. 132 ff.

16 A first draft of the bill produced an 'Initial List of Militarily Critical Technologies,' in *Federal Register*, vol. 45, no. 192, from October 1, 1980, pp.

65014 ff. The list included a register of almost all new technologies and was therefore so comprehensive that effective application of the controls could not be ensured. As of early 1984 a more satisfactory list had not yet been proposed.

17 To combat illegal technology transfer, the U.S. Customs Service launched "Operation Exodus," the implementation of which was to require coopera-tion with allied customs agencies. See 'Testimony of W. v. Raab,' Commis-sioner, U.S. Customs Service, in *Transfer of United States High Technology to the Soviet Union and Soviet Bloc Nations. Hearings Before the Perma-nent Subcommittee on Investigations of the Committee on Governmental Affairs, U.S. Senate*, Washington, D.C., 1982, pp. 193 ff. By the fall of 1983, U.S. Customs investigators, in collaboration with European customs officials, had been able to seize approximately 1400 illegal shipments valued at almost $ 200 million. See W. Hoffmann, 'Geheimclub COCOM,' *Die Zeit*, October 10, 1983, p. 34.

18 See, for example, M.M. Costick, 'Soviet Military Posture and Strategic Trade,' in W.S. Thompson, ed., *National Security in the 1980s: From Weak-ness to Strength* (San Francisco: 1980), pp. 189 ff.

19 A number of incidents were cited by the CIA which lead the authors of the study to draw the following conclusion: "Thus, the Soviets and their War-saw Pact allies have derived significant military gains from their acquisition of Western technology, particularly in the strategic, aircraft, naval, tactical, microelectronics, and computer areas. This multifaceted Soviet acquisition has allowed the Soviets to: − Save hundreds of millions of dollars in R & D costs, and years in R & D development lead time. − Modernize critical sec-tors of their military industry and reduce engineering risks by following or copying proven Western designs, thereby limiting the rise in their military production costs. − Achieve greater weapons performance than if they had to rely solely on their own technology. − Incorporate countermeasures to Western weapons early in the development of their own weapon programs." CIA, 'Soviet Acquisition of Western Technology,' in *Transfer of United States Technology*, pp. 7-23. For a summary of these hearings, see *Transfer of United States High Technology to the Soviet Union and Soviet Bloc na-tions*. Report of the Committee on Governmental Affairs, U.S. Senate, Washington, D.C., December 15, 1982.

20 This and other arguments were compiled by a research group of the Ameri-can Academy of Science (under the direction of D.R. Corson, President emeritus of Cornell University) and published on September 9, 1982. The report called attention to the fact that a restriction on the exchange of scientific information, as foreseen under the new controls, would be detri-mental to scientific progress in the United States itself. The committee re-commended, therefore, the adoption of a strategy of "security by achieve-ment," which would strive to improve American scientific research and not to institute controls on the exchange of information. See *Scientific Commu-nication and National Security* (Washington, D.C.: National Academy Press, 1982), p. 45.

21 See *U.S. Department of Commerce NEWS*, International Trade Administration, ITA 83-29 from April 5, 1983.
22 Prepared Statement of L. Olmer, Under Secretary for International Trade Administration, Before the Subcommittee on International Economic Policy and Trade, Committee on Foreign Affairs, House of Representatives, April 5, 1983.
23 See L. Olmer, Prepared Statement, pp. 9 ff.
24 For recent publications on the controversies surrounding COCOM, see, for example, J.P. Hardt and K. Tomlinson, 'COCOM's Operating Procedures and an Assessment of Its Effectiveness,' in A. Becker, ed., *Economic Relations with the USSR* (Lexington/Toronto: 1983), pp. 111-27; H.D. Jacobsen, 'Multilaterale Exportkontrollen in COCOM,' *Die Neue Gesellschaft*, vol. 30, no. 10 (1983), pp. 967-70; Office of Technology Assessment, *Technology and East-West Trade*, Washington, D.C., May 1983), pp. 44 ff; A. Stent, 'Technology Transfer to the Soviet Union,' *Arbeitspapiere zur Internationalen Politik* Nr. 24, Bonn, April 1983, pp. 80 ff.
25 See chapter 21 by G. Adler-Karlsson in this volume.
26 For a discussion of this issue, see the chapters 10, 11 and 12 by R. Fritsch-Bournazel, S. Woolcock and G. Schiavone in this volume.
27 See C. McC. Mathias, Jr., 'A New U.S. Export Control Policy,' *Washington Quarterly*, vol. 5, no. 2 (Spring 1982), p. 71.
28 See, for example, Letter from A.B. Trowbridge, President of the National Association of Manufacturers to the Secretary of Commerce, M. Baldrige, January 28, 1983, as well as the Statement of K.B. Jenkins of the Chamber of Commerce of the U.S. before the Subcommittee on International Economic Policy and Trade of the Committee on Foreign Affairs, U.S. House of Representatives, February 24, 1983, pp. 8 ff.
29 See S. Auerbach, "Senate Passes Bill Extending Export Administration Act," *Washington Post*, March 2, 1984, sec. D, pp. 8,10.
30 For a discussion of the difficulties surrounding the issue of extraterritoriality and the jurisdiction of national laws, see D.E. Knighton and W.M. Rosenthal, *National Laws and International Commerce. The Problems of Extraterritoriality*, London, 1982 (Chatham House Papers, No. 17).
31 For a discussion of this issue, see "Comments of the European Community on the Amendments of 22 June 1982 to the Export Administration Regulations," July 12, 1982. These amendments authorized the extension of the American sanctions against the construction of the gas-pipeline from Siberia to Western Europe to American firms in Europe and to licensees of American technologies. When nevertheless a number of West European firms continued their deliveries, they were placed on a "temporary denial list," which prohibited them from importing American goods, services or technology.
32 See C.H. Farnsworth, 'Senate Works on Export Bill,' *The New York Times*, March 2, 1984, sec. D, pp. 1 and 4.
33 Memorandum of the EC-Commission from April 27, 1983; Farnsworth, 'E.E.C. Protest America's View on Soviet Trade,' *The New York Times*, April 29, 1983, sec. D, pp. 1 and 9.

34 See 'Dam Outlines Problems with Export Control Bills,' *U.S. Wireless Bulletin*, no. 116, June 28, 1983, p. 10.

17
International Organizations
Petra Pissulla

The Western industrialized and CMEA countries faced grave economic problems as the 1980s began. These ultimately resulted in a relative or even an absolute decline in economic growth in both blocs. The Eastern economies in particular have registered a rapid deceleration in overall economic growth rates. Such domestic economic problems inevitably had an adverse effect upon world trade in general, and upon East-West trade in particular.

Not insignificant in the present phase of stagnation in East-West trade are the unsolved financial problems. The CMEA countries have as yet not achieved any significant improvement in their competitiveness on Western markets, with the result that there is little chance for them significantly increasing their exports in the future. At least the smaller East European countries will therefore have to continue to concentrate their efforts on consolidating their balance of payments positions, primarily by restricting imports from the West, and increasing the integration of the CMEA. In 1982, for example, East European imports from OECD countries (excluding the USSR and inter-German trade) were 24 per cent lower than in 1981.[1] The modest 8 per cent recovery in these imports in the first half of 1983 was not nearly enough to compensate for the slump which preceded it.[2]

In the early 1980s the existing economic problems restricting East-West economic relations were exacerbated by serious political problems. There can therefore be really little doubt that for the foreseeable future East-West trade will not begin to approach the levels it reached in the 1970s. Given that these trends are exacerbating divisions between the two economic blocs, it seems especially relevant to devote greater attention to some of the international organisations which might help prevent any further decline in East-West trade. The most important of these organisations include the United Nations Conference on Trade and Development (UNCTAD), the General Agreement on Tariffs and Trade (GATT), the International Monetary Fund (IMF), and the World Bank.

There are large differences in the extent to which CMEA countries participate in international economic and monetary organisations. Whereas all of them, for example, are members of UNCTAD, only four of the East European countries have joined GATT as full members, and only two have so far joined the International Monetary Fund and the World Bank. Differences in the CMEA countries' willingness to participate in international organisations are clearly determined by their different circumstances. The Soviet Union, which can be self-sufficient in a variety of fields, shows no willingness to join organisations like the IMF or the GATT, which bear the stamp of the Western industrialized countries. Over the past 20 years the smaller CMEA countries have, however, increasingly looked to integration in the international division of labor and a greater opening of their economies to trade and cooperation with the West. The smaller countries were therefore more interested in international organisations which, by institutionalising the cooperation between countries with differing economic systems and levels of development, provided a means for them to better represent their interests and reduce barriers to trade. Apart from the Soviet Union the country with the least interest in participating in the international organisations is the GDR, largely because of its special position resulting from its trade with the Federal Republic of Germany.

UNCTAD

The widest framework for an East-West dialogue on questions of world trade and international cooperation is undoubtedly offered by UNCTAD. As of February 1983 UNCTAD had 166 members, including all CMEA countries, and therefore has the biggest membership of all the international organisations considered below. When founded in 1964 as a permanent special organisation of the UN, UNCTAD was hailed by the socialist countries as a "rival organisation to GATT".[3]

During the IVth UNCTAD meeting in Nairobi in 1976 the CMEA countries — with the exception of Rumania — made a clear statement on the importance they attach to UNCTAD as an institution: "The socialist countries reaffirm their appreciation of this international organisation as a comprehensive, representative forum for the solution of world trade problems in which the unanimity of discussions and the participation of countries interested in these discussions are guaranteed".[4] Particular emphasis was also placed on the fact that, in comparison with the IMF, UNCTAD was regarded as a more suitable forum for the adoption of resolutions on the international monetary system. The CMEA countries see that by moving from gold, which is neutral in currency terms, — to a handful of Western currencies as official foreign reserves, the IMF gave these countries an unacceptable, dominant position in the international monetary system.[5] Hungary, which has been a member of the IMF since May 1982 and Poland, which applied in November 1981, have since joined Rumania in rejecting this position but the remaining CMEA countries have not moderated their basic criticism of the IMF.

Another important factor in the positive appraisal of UNCTAD by the CMEA was the fact that, in contrast to GATT or the IMF, UNCTAD is not an institution which imposes particular conditions and obligations on its members.[6] Ever since the GATT Agreement was signed in 1948, the Soviet Union in particular has urged that an international trade organisation be founded which would take greater account of the interests of developing countries — exploited according to the Soviet view by the industrial nations — and of the socialist countries.

From the outset it has, in fact, been the prime objective of UNCTAD to support the developing countries in expanding their world trade and accelerating their overall economic development. In this way it was hoped to eliminate the growing imbalance between the developing and Western industrialized countries. UNCTAD has also sought to promote trade between countries with different economic and social systems.

Not least because the USSR and in particular the smaller East European countries have experienced similar problems in expanding their international trade, they have always supported the demands of developing countries for a more extensive liberalisation of world trade and a new international economic order. The difficulties experienced by developing countries in gaining a foothold on the markets of Western industrialized countries are different from those of East European countries. The latter do not suffer so much from problems of poor diversification in their range of exports, but rather from their inadequate competitive strength on Western markets. But both groups of countries nevertheless have a number of problems in common. They have both been confronted by a drop in exports in the wake of sagging world demand since the mid 1970s, and both have had to cope with a substantial deterioration in their terms of trade. Both also suffer from a permanent shortage of foreign exchange. This is in large part due to the non-convertibility of their currencies which encourages the trend towards a bilateral settlement of trade balances. Finally both groups of countries have been integrated into world trade to a degree which can only be described as extremely unsatisfactory.[7]

As a consequence, both developing and CMEA countries are also greatly interested in creating larger markets for their exports in the Western industrialized countries which accounted for 66 per cent of world trade in 1982. They have therefore unceasingly demanded a further liberalization of world trade, and used UNCTAD as an important forum for the articulation of such demands. In UNCTAD the developing countries in particular could count on the unreserved support of the socialist countries as long as they continued to direct their demands exclusively at the capitalist nations. It is, however, paradoxical that the Third World's demands for more aid − based on the capitalist countries' special responsibility due to the "colonial exploitation" of the past − were supported by the socialist countries which, for their part, rejected financial development aid as inefficient.[8]

At the meeting of the Group 77 in Manila in February 1976 and continuing at the IVth UNCTAD in Nairobi that same year, the developing countries were no longer prepared to content themselves with only the verbal support of the CMEA countries and instead began to direct concrete demands at the socialist countries. The result was the Manila Declaration. This refered to the socialist countries' "modest" aid effort, which was around 0,01 % of GNP. It also noted the scant promotion of the sale and consumption of products from developing countries on socialist markets, the lack of tariff preferences, and the use of world market prices for exports from CMEA members to the developing countries.[9] In Nairobi, however, in contrast to this latter complaint about the world market prices expected for CMEA goods, there were demands for exchange prices conforming to world market levels in trade between the countries – irrespective of their economic system – with a view to achieving an "all-round, more profitable and hence fairer division of labour".[10]

Nairobi provided a forum for demands to lift or relax all tariff and non-tariff barriers to trade. With respect to the CMEA countries, the developing countries also demanded their special needs be considered when drawing up and coordinating CMEA national economic policies. The CMEA countries were also asked to depart from two-way bartering in trade with the developing countries but to allow favourable terms of payment and to expand cooperation with the developing countries. Furthermore, there were calls for the payments agreements on the transferable rouble to be extended to the developing countries, whereby "the surplus rouble holdings of individual developing countries" should be made "freely transferable in their dealings with CMEA countries" through the International Bank for Economic Cooperation (IBEC) in Moscow.[11]

The one demand in this whole array which seems particularly illusory is that on the transferable rouble which, contrary to its original intention, has not once been used for multilateral settlement even within the CMEA. In other words, rouble surpluses which a country earns in bilateral commodity trading are not cleared in trade with a third CMEA country. Any settlement of trade in transferable roubles with developing countries can therefore at best amount to bilateral clearing.

These demands made of the socialist countries by the Third World are in part contradictory and scarcely practicable. The fact that they are made, however, means the CMEA countries can no longer saddle the Western industrialized countries with all the responsibility of finding solutions to the fundamental economic problems of the developing countries. They must, on the contrary, offer "plausible alternative courses of action",[12] i.e. they must define in more specific terms their readiness to cooperate. In reply to the position adopted by the developing countries, the CMEA countries undertook among other things, to increase imports, to promote joint production with a view to developing export industries, to support the developing countries in developing their raw materials, and to recommend the stabilisation of raw material and agricultural prices. They further declared their readiness to arrange for the settlement of trade in transferable roubles, and to make credit facilities available to developing countries from a special fund via the International Investment Bank.[13] The CMEA countries believe that, in particular by intensifying economic cooperation, they have come up with an alternative to the development policy of Western nations. In line with their preference for institutionalized collaboration, this economic cooperation takes place essentially within the scope of bilateral agreements. There can be no doubt that the economic commitment in the Third World shown by the CMEA countries has been greatly strengthened in recent years.

The declared objective of East European foreign trade policy vis-à-vis the developing countries is to promote the reciprocal exchange of goods making full use of complementary economic structures. This is to be achieved with the help of a great many different agreements. In 1983, for example, over 100 long-term cooperation agreements were concluded between CMEA countries and Third World nations at government level.[14] However, according to UNCTAD reports, the trade surplus of the CMEA countries in trade with the Third World rose from 918 million roubles in 1980 through 4.8 billion roubles in 1981 to 8.3 billion roubles in 1982.[15] Also in their trade with Eastern Europe therefore, the developing countries are far removed from any balanced exchange of goods and services.

It nevertheless has to be said that the problems of the developing countries, whether in their relations with the industrialized West or with the CMEA, receive more attention in UNCTAD than, for example, in GATT. For this reason the Soviet Union views UNCTAD as important for the future creation of a new economic order which takes proper account of the interests of Third World countries.[16]

The Western industrialized countries have meanwhile joined the countries of the Third World in recognizing that a new world economic order cannot be decreed by North and South alone. New developments in trade including the growing importance of the Soviet Union as a trader in energy, raw materials and grain, call for greater efforts to include the socialist countries in the North-South dialogue. Moves were indeed made, particularly at the Vth UNCTAD in Manila in 1979, to urge the socialist countries to play a bigger part in negotiations.

The primarily Soviet demand of considerably widening UNCTAD into an international trade organisation which "might also assume responsibility for the complex of questions currently covered by GATT"[17] seems, however, unrealistic. In Manila for example, the demand for an extension of the UNCTAD mandate to deal with trade, foreign exchange and development problems, was rejected. It might be more realistic to think of closer cooperation between UNCTAD, GATT and the International Monetary Fund. Considering in particular the outcome of the 1983 UNCTAD in Belgrade, UNCTAD might then become more than it appears to be now: a forum for discussion with only few tangible results.

GATT

The General Agreement on Tariffs and Trade (GATT) was founded by 23 signatory countries on 1st January 1948 in order to begin trade-liberalization as soon as possible after the end of World War II. A multilateral agreement in which all members have mutual rights and duties, GATT's purpose is to shape trade relations so as to achieve a rising standard of living, full employment, real income growth, full utilization of the world's raw material resources, increased production, and a continual growth in the trade of goods.

To attain these goals, the agreement contains a number of fundamental provisions, most important of which is undoubtedly the rule of non-discrimination between trading partners, i.e. the most-favoured-nation (MFN) clause. Quantitative import restrictions (quotas) are prohibited under the agreement; the only exceptions granted are for serious balance of payments problems or for developing countries facing special difficulties (Art. XII). In practice, GATT adopts the IMF's criteria for establishing the existence and the extent of any balance of payments disequilibrium. With the exception of this special provision, tariffs alone should, in principle, be used to protect domestic industries. Obligatory pre-determined tariff levels are then intended to assure a stable basis for trade. However, allowance is made for regional trade agreements which provide for intra-regional free trade and a common external tariff, as in the case of the EEC. This necessarily involves the regionally agreed trade preferences being exempt from the most-favoured-nation principle.

By 1983, the number of GATT member countries had risen to 89. Four of these are CMEA countries, namely Czechoslovakia (a founding member), Poland (since 1967), Rumania (since 1971) and Hungary (since 1973). In addition, Bulgaria acquired observer status in 1967. Only the Soviet Union and East Germany have kept their distance from the GATT. It is really Poland's entry in 1967 which ought to be regarded as the first accession of a CMEA·country, because Czechoslovakia was initially no more than a sleeping partner and as such did not participate in GATT's tariff reduction rounds.[18]

When GATT was founded, it had been tacitly assumed that only market economy countries would become party to the agreement. There had been hardly any thought that intensive trade might be possible with state-trading economies.[19] Although this has now fundamentally changed, there are nevertheless still special provisions today for individual CMEA countries, not least because these were not involved in GATT at the outset. The special provisions are needed because problems arising out of their economic systems cannot be solved by the articles of GATT in their present form.

One special problem is that the majority of CMEA member countries do not actually have import tariffs as defined by GATT. They are therefore unable to offer any tariff reductions in return for trade preferences granted to them under the auspices of GATT. As a corollary, it is equally impossible for the benefits negotiated either bilaterally or in the context of general tariff reduction rounds to be applied to the countries of Eastern Europe. For this reason, special conditions were agreed on — with the exception of Hungary — for the accession of all the new member countries belonging to the CMEA. Poland, for example, committed itself in 1967 to a 7 per cent annual increase in imports from other GATT member countries as a means of achieving a similar effect to the reduction of tariffs. In 1971, Rumania declared itself willing to increase imports from GATT countries at at least the same rate as its total imports. Hungary was the only country regarded as having a functioning tariff system, so when it joined

GATT in 1973 it did so on the basis of mutual tariff reductions. The terms of accession for all three countries include clauses giving other GATT members the right to protect their economies from any damage that might result from trading with state-trading economies. This was to be facilitated by applying non-tariff controls — chiefly quantitative import restrictions. These clauses are closely linked with the problem of pricing in the individual CMEA countries. Prices are largely administratively determined and do not necessarily reflect the costs of production. Therefore GATT's intention — given the difficulties in making international price comparisons — was to allow effective defensive measures to be taken against exports at dumping prices. Czechoslovakia is also affected by these import restrictions even though, as a founder member, it was not strictly obliged to accept such special rules which clearly contradict Art. XIX of the GATT agreement.

Trade relations between the CMEA countries and the USA have always been subject to special restrictions within the context of GATT. On the basis of the 1962 Trade Expansion Act and of Art. XXXV of the GATT, the USA initially denied most-favoured-nation (MFN) treatment to all socialist countries except Poland and Yugoslavia. Even the 1974 Trade Act did not — as GATT's East European members had hoped — enable the U.S. administration to grant them unconditional MFN status. In fact, they were only able to obtain such status via bilateral trade agreements, and then it was only on a limited basis. Application of the MFN principle was further restricted by what is known as the Jackson-Vanik Amendment. This made the granting of trade preferences to communist countries conditional upon a more liberal attitude on the part of their governments towards emigration. Though Rumania and Hungary did obtain MFN status — albeit limited — in bilateral agreements, this form of discrimination has nevertheless been constantly and forcefully criticized.

The chief problem, however, has been that the provision on annual import increases agreed on by Poland and Rumania instead of tariff reductions has come to be a substantial burden for them. Both countries now face the dilemma that, under the pressure of their high debt burdens and limited ability to export to the West, they really need to drastically curtail their imports.

Indeed in 1981 the International Monetary Fund established that Rumania was suffering from a serious balance of payments disequilibrium and granted it a stand-by credit as balance of payments assistance within the framework of a three-year stabilization programme. The United States, however, made use of Rumania's inability to fulfil its GATT obligations to justify a — clearly politically motivated — threat of withdrawing its MFN treatment of Rumania. In a normal situation, i.e. if Rumania's membership of GATT had been based on mutual tariff reductions, it would undoubtedly have been able to resort to measures under Art. XII to curtail imports. The IMF had in any case demanded such a curtailment to consolidate Rumania's balance of payments. The only reason the withdrawal of MFN treatment did not go through was because Rumania declared its willingness to revoke emigration regulations of which the U.S.A. had disapproved.

The U.S.A.'s treatment of Poland in October 1982 was even tougher. Here MFN treatment was actually withdrawn, resulting in clearly discernible export losses for Poland in its U.S. trade. The explanation given was that Poland had not been fulfilling its GATT import obligations since 1978, and that bilateral consultations had failed to resolve the dispute. The Polish version of events is that such consultations never took place despite the fact that Poland had signalled its willingness to talk. The Poles say the withdrawal of MFN treatment was linked to the fact that martial law was in force in Poland at that time.[20] The effects of MFN withdrawal on the Polish economy − at present there are virtually no exports of lathes, bearings, sheet steel, dyes and pharmaceuticals to the U.S.A. because of high tariffs[21] − also clearly show the benefits normally accruing to CMEA countries from membership of GATT. There can be no doubt that multilateral GATT negotiations have offered them improved access to export markets in Western industrialized countries.

It was during the Tokyo Round (1973 to 1979) that the CMEA countries first actively participated in the multilateral trade talks in an attempt to articulate their interests more effectively. Their main concern was to secure the removal of the quantitative import restrictions which still persisted in some Western countries. Although the EC countries, first and foremost, agreed to liberalize their trade with the CMEA countries and, if possible, abolish import quotas altogether, the East European countries still find progress towards liberalization too slow. Even though in the Federal Republic of Germany, for example, 94 per cent of all types of goods are now free of import restrictions, those still subject to quotas are precisely the goods East European countries are strong potential suppliers of, namely agricultural produce, textiles and clothing, and indeed a range of iron and steel products.

Overall it must be said that the results of the Tokyo Round have remained of little comfort to Eastern Europe. This especially applies to Rumania and Poland. Having joined GATT, these later introduced, in 1974 and 1976 respectively, their own tariff systems with the hope that any tariff concessions they made during the Tokyo Round would be sufficient to fulfil the conditions of reciprocity. In other words, now that they were able to match tariff preferences granted to them with equivalent tariff reductions of their own, they hoped to be relieved of their quantitative import obligations. However, the EC and the U.S.A. took the view that a tariff reduction alone was not enough because their imports were much more controlled by administrative decisions of the state than by tariffs. Accordingly, they insisted on further commitments to import particular groups of goods, especially in the fields of agricultural produce and consumer goods. This, however, was met with a blank rejection by the East European countries.[22] The Western demands also applied to Hungary, which felt particularly hard done by because its tariff system had been accepted when it signed the

GATT. Ultimately, then, satisfactory solutions were not found during the Tokyo Round, either for the CMEA countries or for the Western industrialized countries.

Despite the failure to agree, the fact that CMEA countries took an active part in GATT negotiations for the first time must be seen as an important step towards their integration into the world economy. After some hesitation, even the U.S.A. welcomed their active participation, probably ultimately hoping that if Eastern Europe became more integrated into international trade flows its dependence upon the Soviet Union might be reduced. The U.S.A. might also have thought that the increased influence of world economic processes on the CMEA countries' domestic economic systems would increase pressure for economic reform in the shape of greater flexibility and more decentralization.

The International Monetary Fund

The International Monetary Fund (IMF) was founded in 1944. Despite the fact that the Soviet Union played an active part in the formative negotiations in Bretton Woods, and that Poland and Czechoslovakia were founder members, at the beginning of 1983 there were only two East European CMEA countries, namely Rumania and Hungary, among the IMF's 146 members. The Soviet Union never signed the agreement because it feared that the U.S.A. would exert too great an influence on Fund policy as a result of the projected distribution of quotas. In the early 1950s Poland withdrew because it also objected to the strong U.S. influence and was generally dissatisfied with Fund policy. In 1954, Czechoslovakia was excluded from the Fund for failing to comply with its duty to inform and consult.[23]

In principle, membership of the Fund is open to all countries, irrespective of their economic and political system. The only stipulation is that the country is prepared, and in a position, to meet the obligations associated with membership. These obligations are essentially defined under Art. VIII of the IMF Agreement (in the 1978 revised version).[24] At the time the IMF was founded, it was intended that centrally-planned economy countries such as the Soviet Union should also be entitled to become members. As early as in the Atlantic Charter of 1941, it was held that all countries should benefit from economic progress. Similarly, the draft of the White Plan for the formation of an international monetary union, submitted in April 1942, demanded that on no account should membership be dependent upon the type of economic system. In other words existence of a socialist economic system should not provide grounds for refusing any country admission to the Fund.[25]

In order to enable countries without free markets and with non-convertible currencies to also become members of the Monetary Fund, transitional arrangements were included in the IMF Agreement allowing economically weak countries to retain foreign exchange controls for an unlimited period. This facility is widely used. In late 1981, for example, 88 countries out of the then current total of 143 members applied the transitional arrangements of Art. XIV in order to maintain, either in full or in part, the exchange controls they operated when they joined the Fund.[26]

Rumania and Hungary, following their admission in 1982, also belong to this group of countries. It must, however, be said that, in the case of the socialist countries, the motives for maintaining exchange controls are conditioned primarily by the system, whereas developing countries retain restrictions essentially because of balance of payments problems. The centrally-planned economy countries' system of convertible currency management forms an integral part of their economic system and can hence scarcely be regarded as a temporary measure. It would appear therefore, that socialist countries are only entitled to become members of the Fund as long as the transitional arrangements can be applied for an unlimited period.

Although moves to integrate the Soviet Union into the Monetary Fund have not led to membership, they were nevertheless instrumental in incorporating principles into the IMF Agreement which subsequently enabled other socialist countries to join.

Rumania was first to make use of this opportunity. Not least in order to encourage other potential members from the CMEA, further amendments were made to the Fund Articles in 1978. The most important amendment for the East European countries was probably the revision of Art. IV, Section 3. This obliges the Monetary Fund to keep a watchful eye on the monetary and exchange rate policies of its members and to introduce special guidelines for such policies applicable to all members. At the same time, however, it commits the Fund to take reasonable account of the general political and socio-political conditions of a country in applying these guidelines. This also means that, when the Fund imposes economic policy conditions in connection with the borrowing of its resources, it must take account of characteristics peculiar to a specific country – e.g. the economic system – which may influence the ability of that country to alter its economic structure or economic policy or adapt to changes in the general trading environment.

Until the end of the 1970s, no Western observers thought it possible that the Soviet Union, or the other East European countries – with the exception of Rumania – would join the IMF. Despite the second amendment to the IMF Agreement which took effect in 1978, there were "scarcely any points of departure for the integration – irrespective of system – of the Soviet Union and the remaining CMEA countries into the international monetary system of the IMF".[27]

This still applies to the Soviet Union, which is not prepared to allow the West to, among other things, gain an insight into the strictly held secret Soviet gold production and gold reserve/gold export policy through obligations to inform the Fund. Another of the Soviet Union's main objections to the Monetary Fund relates to the break with gold – neutral in currency terms – as a principal international reserve asset. As noted above the other CMEA countries still shared this Soviet view at the IVth UNCTAD in Nairobi in 1976, but at least two CMEA members, apart from Rumania, have for various reasons since dissociated themselves from this stance.

In all probability, the main reason for Rumania's entry on 15th December 1972 was its desire to continue its policy, begun in the early 1960s, of achieving the greatest possible economic and political independence of the Soviet Union. At that time the country was under no pressure to join for reasons of its balance of payments policy. Rumania did not face acute balance of payments hardships at the beginning of the 1970s as, for example, Poland did or to some extent Hungary did in the early 1980s. In 1981, however, the advantages enjoyed by Rumania as a result of its membership in the Monetary Fund, could no longer be denied in view of the then bleak balance of payments situation.

When, in November 1981, Hungary surprised the world by applying for membership in the International Monetary Fund, its external position was substantially more stable than that of Rumania or Poland. In 1981 Hungary did at times face serious liquidity problems when, in the wake of the Poland crisis, short-term loans from Western banks were not extended as expected and access to new medium and long-term loans was largely blocked. Hungary nevertheless managed to service due debts. For their part, the Hungarians stress that application for membership was not made to bridge liquidity bottlenecks but rather reflected their resolute pursuance of the reform policy begun in 1968. In their view, membership of the Fund was designed to back Hungary's efforts to achieve even greater integration into the world economy and to secure the future provision of finance in order to expand the limited lending potential within the CMEA.[28] Moreover, the fact that membership of the World Bank is only possible via membership of the Fund was a decisive factor for Hungary – as indeed also for Rumania.

Poland has been trying to become a member of the Monetary Fund since November 1981. After the official lifting of martial law Poland's application has won increased support, particularly from the EC. Whether Poland can become a member as early as 1984 might, however, depend partly on the Fund's liquidity position and the development of East-West relations in general. The Fund's liquidity remains as tight as ever, despite the fact that a majority of Fund members have now approved the increase in overall quotas to 90 billion SDRs and the provision of the long-debated 6 billion SDR credit line to the Fund to finance its credit commitments to members in payments difficulties. This situation might ultimately prejudice the negotiations on Poland's entry, as Poland would undoubtedly desire substantial drawings.

Moreover, it should not be forgotten that the U.S.A. still has a great influence over Fund decisions through its voting share of about 20 per cent and that lending to socialist countries is a highly controversial subject in the U.S. Congress at present. Admittedly it is incompatible with the Articles of the Fund to discriminate against a country because of its economic or social system, but it cannot be ruled out that resistance on the part of the U.S.A. will at least delay Poland's entry.

Within the framework of a stand-by agreement, the Fund has made EAP (Enlarged Access Policy) resources available to both Rumania (June 1981) and Hungary (December 1982). In Rumania's case, for example, the total amount of stand-by credit which was originally to be paid in instalments by mid 1984 came to 1.1 billion SDRs. This amount would have corresponded to around 210 per cent of Rumania's new quota which, following the general increase in quotas in November 1983, rose from 367.5 million SDRs to 523.4 million SDRs.[29]

Rumania has not been able to draw the full amount, however. In the period 1981-83 the country made great efforts to implement the adjustment measures required of it, primarily in the field of demand management, by means of price, exchange rate and income policy measures to the detriment of the already low standard of living, but they were clearly more than it can manage. The Fund's hard line on conditionality has been strongly criticized of late by many of the countries affected. Rumania, which unquestionably was more than willing to adjust, began to resist the measures. For example, in October 1983 Nicolae Ceauşescu rejected the further increase in energy prices demanded by the IMF as inflationary.[30] In view of this non-fulfilment of one of the criteria laid down by the Fund, the IMF decided not to pay the final instalment of 285 million SDRs of the standby credit that had been planned for 1984. Rumania was compelled to accept the premature expiry of the standby credit agreement on 31st January 1984 and has therefore taken up only 817 million SDRs (156 per cent of the new quota), not 1.1 billion SDRs.

Rumania's inability to comply with the Fund's requirements in all respects has not only prevented the full payment of the current standby credit, but might also prejudice the Fund's future willingness to approve further loans that would be quite plausible in principle. The maximum cumulative access to conditional Fund resources is set at 408 per cent of quotas from 1984 onwards (3 x 102 per cent plus outstanding previous drawings). Rumania could theoretically draw a further 1.3 billion SDRs under a new standby credit in the next three years, if the Fund decided to grant further financial assistance on the grounds that a lasting stabilization of Rumania's balance of payments is unlikely to be achieved by 1984. If a further credit line were opened, and probably only then, Rumania might be in a position to repay maturing instalments of principal and interest to its Western creditors without further rescheduling.[31]

In the context of Fund conditionality, it is also debatable whether Poland would be in any position to cope with the adjustment measures which would undoubtedly turn out to be equally as severe. No matter how necessary these measures are to an economy which has lost its internal and external equilibrium as a result of years of excess domestic demand, they have always produced a very severe strain on the population. Any further drop in the standard of living in Poland could easily lead to a renewed wave of protests.

The inability of Rumania and other countries to fulfil the economic conditions imposed by the Fund might indicate that the time-scale of the IMF's attempts at consolidation is not sufficiently long. For example, the rigorous demandcurbing measures taken under the Rumanian three-year stabilization program have in any case caused a further contraction in the country's trade with the West in goods and services, thereby exacerbating the existing crisis. On the other hand, the IMF does not have adequate resources to undertake long-term financing. It is therefore all the more important for the IMF to be involved early-on rather than only when a country's balance of payments problems have become practically unmanageable. Within the framework of its regular consultations with all member countries the IMF should take steps in good time to prevent individual countries from contracting excessive debt. In the case of Rumania, however, the Fund was clearly unable to do this.

Whatever criticism one might make, greater East European cooperation in the IMF nevertheless appears desirable. At present the socialist members of the IMF (Hungary, Rumania, Yugoslavia, China and Vietnam) are confined to the position of debtors for economic and system-related reasons (their currencies are inconvertible) and they can exert little influence on Fund policy with their share of just under 5 per cent of the votes. The IMF is not an institution whose objectives are to promote trade directly between member countries, as are UNCTAD and GATT, but efforts to stabilize international monetary relations and to achieve balanced growth in world trade will undoubtedly have a beneficial effect on trade over the long term.

Given the present need for East European CMEA countries to adjust — mainly by reducing imports from the West and increasing CMEA integration — to foreign exchange bottlenecks and Western debts, it seems especially desirable that these countries should intensify their cooperation in the international economic and monetary organizations. This cannot but help achieve the goal of leading East-West economic relations out of their present period of stagnation.

The World Bank

Founded in 1945, the World Bank has 144 member countries which have subscribed to different size shares of the bank's capital depending on their economic strength. As a general rule participating countries only pay over 10 per cent of the sum subscribed to the bank, 1 per cent in freely convertible currency and the other 9 per cent in domestic currency. The remaining 90 per cent is not actually deposited, but can in principle be called upon by the World Bank in case of need, i.e. in the event that the Bank needs to fulfill obligations resulting from loans taken up or credits granted.

Before any country can be eligible to join the World Bank it must first be a member of the International Monetary Fund. Accordingly, the only CMEA countries which have so far been able to participate are Rumania and Hungary. Both countries are placed by both institutions in the category of European developing countries. This entitles them to apply for World Bank funds which are available either for long-term project-related financing or, since 1980, for structural adjustment loans granted on a conditional basis in close cooperation with the IMF. These World Bank loans, which are granted in addition to IMF balance of payments assistance, were a contributory factor in both Hungary's and Rumania's decision to join the International Monetary Fund. World Bank credit is especially attractive because facilities run for substantially longer periods, generally five years without any repayment of principal, with a maximum of 20 years to maturity. The average interest charges are also below market rates. In financial year 1982, the average interest rate on all of the World Bank's outstanding loans was 7.6 per cent, and in 1983 7.9 per cent.[32]

On joining the World Bank, Rumania subscribed to shares totalling 162.1 million SDRs. As a result of an agreement in 1980 on a global increase in the Bank's capital base, Rumania's share rose to 200 million SDRs in June 1983 (0.41 per cent of the total capital). Only 7.5 per cent of this contribution had to be paid over, of which only 10 per cent was in convertible currency.

Rumania benefitted from membership because it was able to draw upon substantial World Bank financial aid in return for a comparatively small contribution. Having actually paid over only 2 million SDRs, or $ 2.14 million, as its convertible currency capital contribution, Rumania had, by June 1983, drawn 33 loans with a total value of approximately $ 2.2 billion. Credit facilities still outstanding total roughly $ 1.5 billion.

In the 1981/82 financial year alone, the World Bank granted Rumania three loans with a total value of $ 321.5 million to support specific projects. These ensured partial financing for investment plans in the agricultural, energy and transport sectors. Like the IMF, the World Bank also supports Rumania's restrictive policies which are intended to consolidate its economic position. In 1981 World Bank representatives carried out a review of Rumanian investment plans for the period 1981-1985 and concurred with the proposed changes in the structure of capital investment. Priority was accorded to the energy sector, agriculture and exporting industries in the distribution of investment finance. In the World Bank's view this, combined with greater encouragement to production in less energy-intensive branches of industry, was an appropriate way of trying to eliminate the current bottlenecks in the Rumanian economy.

When Hungary joined the World Bank, it subscribed to shares totalling 204 million SDRs. Because it is categorized as a developing country, Hungary can both act as a supplier in Third World projects financed by the Bank, and also make use of direct financial assistance from the Bank. Hungary received its first two World Bank loans of $ 240 million in June 1983, the repayment period being

15 years. One loan, of $ 109 million, is intended to finance an energy conservation program and the other, of $ 130 million, to modernize cereal farming. The loans will cover the cost of the imports from the West needed to carry out these projects.

In the future, World Bank credit facilities may become more important for both countries. For some years the Bank has encouraged private sources of capital to return to the business of lending to developing countries. To this end it has promoted co-financing in which it finances projects in cooperation with commercial banks. These co-financings are intended to provide better security for the commercial banks, and longer repayment periods for the borrowing countries. To achieve these two aims, the World Bank does not recall its own outstanding credit until after all obligations to the participating banks have been met. Co-financings represent one possible way in which the flow of private capital to East European countries, which has almost completely dried up, might be brought on stream once more.

NOTES

1 OECD: *Foreign Trade Statistics.* Series A.
2 UN: *Economic Bulletin for Europe,* Vol. 35. 1983. p. 1.11.
3 Böhm, E./Bolz, K./Kebschull, D./Menck, W./Naini, A.: *Zur Rolle der sozialistischen Staaten im Nord-Süd Dialog.* Hamburg: 1978. p. 10.
4 Joint declaration of the socialist countries to the IVth United Nations Conference on Trade and Development. In: Supplement to: *Außenhandel der UdSSR.* No. 9. 1976. p. 2.
5 ibid. p. 14.
6 Baumer, M./Jacobsen, H.-D. 'CMEA and the World Economy: Institutional Concepts', in: *East European Economies Post-Helsinki,* Joint Economic Committee, Congress of the United States. Washington, D.C.: 1977. p. 1015.
7 For example, the non-oil-exporting developing countries' share of world exports (imports) in 1982 was just under 14 per cent (16 per cent); the equivalent shares for East European planned economy countries (including the USSR) came to only 9 per cent and 8 per cent respectively. Furthermore, approximately 50 per cent of the European CMEA countries' exports and imports were accounted for by intra-CMEA trade. UN: *Economic Bulletin for Europe.* Vol. 35. 1983. pp. 1.9, 3.12 and 3.14.
8 On this issue, see Markiewicz, W. 'The Main Directions of UNCTAD's Activity and the Stand of the Socialist Countries', *Studies on the Developing Countries.* No. 4. 1974. Warsaw. p. 34 ff.
9 Manila Declaration and Program of Action. UNCTAD Document TD/195. 1976; quoted in: Baumer, M./Jacobsen, H.-D.: *op.cit.* p. 1016.
10 Heise, H. 'Die neue Weltwirtschaftsordnung und ihre finanziellen Implikationen für sozialistische Industrieländer', *Osteuropa-Wirtschaft.* Vol. 23 (1978), No. 1, p. 55.
11 *ibid.*
12 Böhm, E. et al.: *op.cit.* p. 12.
13 'Die UdSSR und die Probleme der dritten Welt'. *Sowjetunion heute.* No. 12/13. 1st July 1976, and Misala, J. 'RGW und die Dritte Welt – fruchtbare Partnerschaft', *Der polnische Außenhandel (Warsaw):* No. 8. 1979.
14 *Handelsblatt.* No. 198. 13.10.83.
15 *ibid.*
16 Die UdSSR und die Probleme der Dritten Welt. *op.cit.*
17 Die UdSSR und die Probleme der Dritten Welt. *op.cit.*
18 Jacobsen, H.-D. 'Die osteuropäischen Länder im GATT: Abbau von wirtschaftlicher Diskriminierung und nationale Emanzipation', in: Gantzel, K.J. (Ed.): *Kapitalistische Penetration in Osteuropa.* Hamburg: 1976. p. 287.
19 Bratschi, P. *Allgemeines Zoll- und Handelsabkommen (GATT). Handbuch für Praktiker.* Zürich: 1973. p. 159.
20 *Die Wirtschaft des Ostblocks.* Vol. 29 (1983). No. 44. p. 2.
21 GATT, *GATT Activities in 1982.* Geneva: 1983. p. 73.
22 Orr, M.Z. 'Eastern European Participation in the Tokyo-Round of Multilateral Trade Negotiations', in *East European Economic Assessment,* Part 2

242

- Regional Assessments, Joint Economic Committee, Congress of the United States. Washington, D.C.: 1981, p. 807.

23 Gold, J. *Membership and Nonmembership in the International Monetary Fund.* Washington, D.C.: 1974. pp. 342 and 345 ff.

24 IMF *Articles of Agreement.* Washington, D.C.: 1978.

25 Gold, J. *Membership and Nonmembership in the International Monetary Fund: op.cit.* p. 129.

26 IMF Exchange Arrangements and Exchange Restrictions. *Annual Report,* 1982. p. 6.

27 Hamel, H. 'Zur Frage der Mitgliedschaft der RGW-Länder im Internationalen Währungsfonds (IWF)', in: Schüller, A. (Ed.): *Außenwirtschaftspolitik und Stabilisierung von Wirtschaftssystemen.* Stuttgart: 1980. p. 192.

28 Schröder, K. 'The IMF and the Countries of the Council for Mutual Economic Assistance', *Intereconomics.* No. 2 (March/April) 1982. p. 89.

29 Hooke, A.W. *The International Monetary Fund, Its Evolution, Organization and Activities.* Washington, D.C.: 1983. p. 71 ff.

30 *Der Spiegel.* No. 43. 24th October 1983.

31 Pissulla, P.: *Der Internationale Währungsfonds und seine Bedeutung für die osteuropäischen Länder – Rumänien, Ungarn, Polen.* Hamburg: 1983. p. 61 ff.

32 World Bank *Annual Report* 1983. p. 60.

Reinhard Rode

As the summary of economic relations has shown, these have not yet assumed such importance that they can be used to promote political détente or as an effective instrument of political leverage. Nor for that matter was the increase in East-West tensions at the beginning of 1980 prevented by the existence of economic relations, although they probably had a certain moderating influence.

The complex interrelationship between politics and economics is still generally unresolved, and also remains unresolved in the case of East-West relations. There is both a primacy of politics by virtue of the fact that security issues between antagonistic systems are involved, and a remarkable dynamism in economic relations. Politics, however, obviously provided the setting within which economic relations grew into an autonomous network of interactions.

There is therefore, validity in both of the Western assumptions concerning East-West trade. There is something in the functionalist assumption "change by trade" (Wandel durch Handel) which envisages positive pro-détente effects. But there is also some validity in the assumption from the tradition of power politics that economic relations can be used as an instrument of leverage. Both the functionalist and power politics approaches have been employed and found, with varying degrees of success, application in East-West economic relations.

Because both the détente and leverage approaches have a certain validity the comparative analysis of Western policies on East-West trade must ask what the specific conditions of success or failure were as well as indicating whether a given policy was or was not successful. Political analysis must, however, go beyond the question of cause and effect and include less "reasonable" policies even if these are not related to the level of economic relations and are therefore potentially unfounded. Decisions of political systems follow different rationales independent of the specific issue areas. Therefore an analysis based only on narrow economic relations is not enough. The preceeding studies of the East-West trade policies of the different Western countries have, for this reason, rightly considered foreign and security policy.

Western Interests

The picture which emerges from the analysis of economic and political relations of Western countries is one of differentiated Western interests. At first glance, interest in economic relations with the East appears to be dependent on the level of involvement. Because trade is the most important sector of interaction (see Peter Knirsch, in chapter 7 of this volume), the share of East-West trade in total foreign trade and the share of Eastern markets are useful measures for a ranking. As table 4 of Jochen Bethkenhagen's contribution demonstrates, East-West trade generally accounts for only a small share of total trade for Western countries, but given this limited significance of East-West trade the Federal Republic of Germany ranks top. This is especially the case in the 1970s for trade with CMEA (6) countries, but also to a lesser degree for trade with the Soviet Union. In terms of the shares of Western countries in CMEA markets the Federal Republic of Germany's leading position is even more obvious. According to an above source (table 4), West Germany accounted for 30 per cent of the CMEA (6) market and between 12 and 23 per cent of the Soviet market. This is a greater share than other members of the European Community such as France, Italy and Britain, and a much greater share than the United States. France and Italy hold approximately the same position with a stronger French accent on exports and an Italian on imports. Britain ranks behind the continent in East-West trade and also experienced the clearest decline during the 1970s. There is also a clear quantitative difference between Europe and the United States. The U.S.A.'s share of Eastern markets was generally below 18 per cent and the level of U.S. imports from the CMEA countries is below those of Western Europe.

Although the different rankings of particular Western countries indicate a differing degree of interest in East-West trade, this should not be overstated. First of all, the share of East-West trade in total trade is generally low. Furthermore, the overall figures do not show the position for particular branches. Specific branches or companies which are more involved in East-West trade may make specific demands and have a better chance of gaining political support than the diffuse mixed interests of large groups. While East-West traders have no guarantee of success, they cannot be written-off from the beginning. Their chances of success depend on the ability to form potential coalitions with other interest groups. Clearly, trade can best flourish if pro-trade lobbies dominate and anti-trade lobbies are absent or marginal.

Such an optimal combination did indeed occur in the Federal Republic of Germany during the 1970s and the first half of the 1980s. The business community, represented by its umbrella trade organizations and the "Ost-Ausschuß der deutschen Wirtschaft", vigorously and publicly supported East-West trade. They were supported by the Deutsche Gewerkschaftsbund (DGB) and its membership of large industry trade-unions. Criticism of low wage competition from Eastern imports remained exceptional and attracted little public support. One can therefore rightly speak of a pro-East-West trade consensus in the Federal Republic during the period considered which was not jeopardized by demands of the security establishment.

The situation in France was similar to that in the Federal Republic of Germany. In France interest in trade with the East was also reinforced by agricultural lobbies. The trade-unions supported this general line. However, the anti-traders, who were not heard in the Federal Republic, did articulate their position more forcefully in France, and criticism from intellectuals and representatives of the security establishment could not be overlooked, even if it did not prevail over the proponents of trade.

In Italy the pro-trader position adopted by business and trade-unions also prevailed. In Italy, as in the Federal Republic of Germany, there were no determined opponents of East-West trade, so that the pro-trade attitude became self-evident and there was often no debate on the issue.

In Britain there was also a consensus favouring trade with the East. Contrary to the continent, British trade-unions took a more neutral position, and as in Western Europe as a whole there was no effective anti-East-West trade lobby in Britain.

Within the framework of the European Community, the European level trade associations and interest groups found the lowest common denominator which was to preserve East-West trade. On the question of an agreement between the EC and CMEA as an organization, however, protectionist and anti-communist demands did play a certain role.

Such a relatively clear consensus in favour of East-West trade was not to be found in the United States. The pro-traders in the business community were faced by determined opponents on the political side. Industry and banks were reticent supporters of East-West trade during the second half of the 1970s and at the beginning of the 1980s, and only agriculture lobbied vigorously for its grain exports to the East. In contrast to Western Europe, the conservative security establishment made clear demands for strong export controls culminating in economic warfare. The trade-unions in the United States, in the form of the AFL-CIO, took a firm anti-East-West trade position and neglected the economic welfare and job arguments in favour of trade. The anti-traders were also supported by ethnic groups, particularly by American Jews and minorities from Eastern countries, although their interest was more in favour of linking trade to political concessions such as on emigration than restricting trade as such. But such minorities were used to further the political aim of trade restriction such as in the case of the Jackson/Vanik amendment.

Western Decisions

Vested interests are undoubtedly a major factor in decisions affecting East-West trade policy. But calls for continued or enhanced trade on the grounds of economic interest are not necessarily translated into decisions. Besides the economic welfare-oriented business interests there are also general foreign policy and security interests. The degree to which these influence East-West trade policy depends on the perceived importance of the East-West conflict and its role in specific countries. In this regard, there is a very complex picture within the West.

The Federal Republic of Germany has a special relationship with the German Democratic Republic (GDR) which, as long as overall German considerations play a role, has a great influence on political decisions. The objectives of guaranteeing a high degree of communication between the populations of both German states, and improving standards of human rights have often played an instrumental role in East-West trade policy. Economic concessions to the East were implicitly linked with reciprocal political concessions. This was typically implemented through diplomatic channels in order to satisfy the Eastern prestige, and often culminated in the denial of any connection. This positive linkage approach, offering positive economic inducements or carrots to Eastern countries, was an expression of the FRG's position of weakness in the political and military fields and its strength in the economic field. By pursuing such a strategy, West German governments were for example, able to have a certain amount of influence on the behavior of communist countries on the question of emigration.

Apart from these political considerations there were, of course, economic interests. From the beginning of the 1970s all West German federal governments permitted and promoted business with the East because of its positive economic welfare effects. In the case of the FRG political and economic interests also coincided. During the period analyzed here, no striking contradictions existed between the interests of both areas. Ever since the autumn of 1982, the liberal-conservative coalition has continued the policies of its social-liberal predecessors. Nor have West German governments found contradictions between their security and political, and economic goals in East-West economic relations. The West German perception of strategic defense saw increased economic relations with the East as an advantage rather than a dramatic danger of dependence.

French decisions in the field of East-West trade during the era of Giscard d'Estaing were the result of a mixture of France's desire for a special political relationship with the East and economic interests. A privileged political relationship with the East was seen as being in the French national interests for reasons of prestige; East-West trade was interpreted simply as a chance to promote export business. This approach under Giscard therefore, tended to neglect the interests of French security, which are normally given considerable weight. It was not until under François Mitterrand that the need to distance France from communist countries increased, which resulted in a greater emphasis on security. For domestic reasons the socialist President with communist members in his cabinet quite naturally wished to distance himself politically from communist states. Mitterrand therefore, wished to emphasize the fact that there had been a change of policy from that of his predecessor. There was, however, little change in the promotion of exports to the East. By separating politics and economics, therefore, he tried to deal with contradictions between ideology and economic necessity.

Of all the West European countries Italy's policy on East-West trade had the strongest emphasis on economic considerations. Despite multiple changes of government, the field of East-West trade policy was also characterized by continuity. Political special interests, which were present in the Federal Republic of Germany and in France, were absent in Italy. Italy represents a special case because of the separation of trade and foreign policy in order to preserve business interests and to avoid a debate on the security interests in East-West trade.

This position has some parallels in British policy. The preservation and, if possible, the expansion of East-West trade was self-evident for both Labour and Conservative governments. But for Britain there were no special political goals at stake. East-West trade was perceived as mutually beneficial, but this view stemmed more from a basic notion of foreign economic policy than from special East-West trade considerations. The fact that East-West trade is more marginal for Britain than for its continental European partners is, of course, of some importance. The fact that the Thatcher government and the Reagan administration shared some common conservative ideological positions on relations with the Soviet Union meant, however, that Britain was fairly receptive to American demands for control of East-West trade for security reasons, although opposition to American tutelage on export control, sanctions and restrictions of credit was as vigorous as in the case of France for reasons of national prestige.

Autonomous East-West trade policy decisions of the European Community, which would qualitatively go beyond the lowest common denominator of the member states, were impossible because of the Community's structure. The clear and relatively determined statements of the European Commission vis-à-vis the United States, therefore, represented the West European consensus against sanctions, intensified export control, credit restrictions, and extra-territoriality. Even this minimal consensus in Brussels permitted the use of a tougher language in opposing the position of the Reagan administration than individual national governments could have employed. Europe speaking with one voice did, therefore, have a greater effect on the leading power of the Western alliance. This West European consensus, however, conceals the spectrum of national policies discussed above despite all the short-term agreement. In particular the German position, which diverged most dramatically from the American policy, probably could not have been held in bilateral confrontation between the Federal Republic and the United States, but only with the support of the West European consensus and French and British "prestige" nationalism.

U.S. East-West economic policy differed from the West European policies because it showed far less continuity. From the mid-1970s it moved from a mainly positive linkage policy under Carter and then ended up with Reagan's attempts at economic warfare. Such shifts in policy would not occur in any West European country. The turning point in the U.S. approach did not, however, coincide with the change from Carter to Reagan. Carter himself pursued a range of policies from at first no linkage policy at all, followed by a policy of economic diplomacy which tried to reward and punish simultaneously, and finally ending up with the sanctions of 1980. The trend from the carrot to the stick was extended by President Reagan to include economic warfare. The economic warfare strategy of the hardliners within the Reagan administration suffered, from the beginning, from the contradiction between promoting agricultural exports and restricting industrial trade. The attempt to broaden the unilateral U.S. policy to a multilateral policy including Western Europe in order to make it more effective led inevitably to conflict with the West European countries. This was settled in 1982 when the United States retreated on its pipeline embargo, with some face-saving diplomatic phrases. In 1983 domestic pressure and West European resistance resulted in a further moderation of Reagan's East-West economic policy. The primacy of security interests favouring more effective export control, particularly for high technology, remained, but industrial exports were given more of the freedom agricultural exports already had. There were also more export licences granted, such as for Caterpillar pipe-layers.

1983 also showed that the main goal of Reagan's policy was world power competition and not general ideological anti-communism, because he liberalized technology exports to the People's Republic of China. This demonstrates the contradictions between security and welfare most clearly. Both administrations first of all pursued power politics towards the East. Carter first tried to allure with economic relations, but then used them to punish. Reagan aimed at pressuring the Soviet Union by economic denial in order to force them to transfer resources from the military to the civil sector in the long-term. Whilst pursuing different approaches they both overestimated their ability to use economic relations as an instrument to influence the Soviet Union.

The policies of international organizations (UNCTAD, GATT, IMF and World Bank) did not reflect different Western strategies very much. Only UNCTAD counts all the CMEA countries as members, and it is more a forum for discussion. The main cause of conflict, the Soviet Union, has not been a factor in the other international organizations mentioned, because it does not belong to them and has shown no signs, as yet, of any interest in participation. Western Europe and the United States have, however, supported countries such as Hungary and Rumania in their efforts to achieve greater autonomy by participating in multilateral organizations.

Western Convergence and Divergence

The summary of Western policies clearly indicates differences in transatlantic interests and strategies. The Federal Republic of Germany and the United States represent the two extreme positions of the Western spectrum of policies. They differed most clearly in the use of East-West economic relations as a policy instrument. Both had a stake in foreign policy objectives, but the United States has been shown to be committed to power politics towards the East, the Federal Republic of Germany to a policy of positive inducements. Because of political and military weakness, the Federal Republic has had to rely on economics as a means of attempting to influence developments in line with its interests in over-all German relations. General economic welfare and business interests played a major role in the FRG's self-image as an economic giant, but a political dwarf. Therefore the impact of trade on security was seen to be positive and East-West business seen as a stabilizing factor in general East-West relations. The assumption of "change by trade" (Wandel durch Handel) became a political credo because, given the specific West German situation, there was no alternative.

As a world power in competition with the Soviet Union, the United States saw things very differently. Given the political and especially military make-up of the USSR, economics remained the last sector of unchallenged American superiority. Given also the pressure to accept the Soviet Union as a superpower with equal rights and the U.S. rejection of such equality, it was inevitable that the U.S. administration would succumb to the temptation of using economic relations as an instrument in power politics. Failures were therefore, also inevitable because although the United States has the strongest economy, this strength is not such as to be able to force its allies and the neutral Western states into following U.S. policy. Consequently, the United States' ability to inflict major damage on the relatively autarchic Soviet economy was limited. This was even more the case when there was insufficient domestic support for power and security politics at the cost of economic welfare and profits. The limits and contradictions between the U.S. use of the economic instrument in power politics became evident in 1980 with the failure of Carter's grain embargo, and 1982 with Reagan's back-down in the natural gas pipeline dispute.

The other Western European countries lay between the West German and the U.S. positions. Because they had no fixation with the need to use economic relations as an instrument of policy they were able to put economic interests before security in East-West trade policy, or could strictly separate politics and trade like France under President Mitterrand. Without a strong commitment to either power politics or economic incentives they could easily compromise. There is therefore no need for the transatlantic conflict on East-West trade policy at the beginning of the 1980s to persist. West European opposition was provoked, not by fundamental differences in substance, but by the excessive demands of the United States in its pursuit of power politics and its lack of any respect for European interests. The Federal Republic of Germany benefitted from this, because it was able to pursue its relatively favorable approach to East-West trade under a European umbrella. A move away from U.S. unilateralism and towards transatlantic multilateralism may be possible if the United States desists from the pursuit of maximalist goals in the form of economic warfare and extraterritorial reach of U.S. controls, and emphasizes instead the real problems of export control and credits. All Western states share the problems of balancing political, economic and security interests. There is also no evidence of fundamental obstacles to a transatlantic compromise, provided neither the functionalist nor the power politics related simplifications prevail. As discussed above both these approaches may have some effect, but neither is guaranteed to succeed. Success or failure are, however, not arbitrary. It is, for example, no accident that the Federal Republic of Germany has, for the period in question, had a better record than the United States.

PART IV
EASTERN POLICIES

19
The Soviet Union

Heinrich Machowski

Introduction

When analysing Soviet economic relations with the West in the 1970s one cannot usefully use the economic warfare or détente approach, because the intensification of the economic relations with Western industrialized countries was in fact one of the basic motives for the Soviet (and East European) policy of détente. By the time this policy began in the spring of 1969 with the so-called Budapest appeal, Soviet leaders did not consider an economic war with the West as a political alternative. This chapter will therefore give (1) a short description of the Soviet economic policy toward the West; (2) a description of the factual development of the Soviet economic relations with the West since 1970, (3) a discussion of the special problems in economic relations with the West, which did not develop as Moscow had hoped or expected (particularly with the U.S.A. and Japan and between the CMEA and the EEC); and finally (4) a summing-up of the results from the Soviet point of view, with a special focus on the inter-relationship between the economic and political interests of the USSR.

One important fact must be mentioned at the very beginning. The relevant Soviet literature of the 1970s contains no views pointing out the dangers of an intensified cooperation with the imperialist West and thus opposed to the intended opening of the country to the West. Whilst the author, at least, has found no written opposition, we must, however, assume that there were and still are opponents to this foreign trade policy in the USSR. This assumption is based on numerous discussions with Soviet colleagues and specialists, and is confirmed, indirectly, by comments – more numerous after the U.S.A. imposed sanctions against the USSR – emphasizing that the Soviet economy has not fallen into a dangerous dependence on imports from the West. Bogomolov for example, states that "the imports of the USSR from capitalist countries never had a decisive influence on the perspectives of the socio-economic development of the Soviet Union".[1] Given the present political situation, however, scholarly discussion with these domestic opponents to the Soviet policy of détente is not possible.

An Outline of the Soviet Economic Policy in the 1970s

During the phase of industrialization before, and in the first few years after the Second World War, the USSR attached only minor importance to foreign trade. Soviet foreign trade policy of that time was characterized by three factors.

- Imports were no larger than necessary to fulfil economic plans ("minimization of trade");
- Only investment goods were imported and then only those serving the production of investment goods. Imports were financed by the export of raw materials and food ("industrialization by trade");
- The conflict between "minimization of trade" and "industrialization by trade" was solved by developing industries in order to minimize imports ("import substitution").

The USSR is indeed one of the very few countries of the world in which the economic conditions for industrialization based on the domestic market exist, i.e. a domestic market and a rich supply of endogenous natural resources. But the Soviets realized that in the course of time this kind of policy would, necessarily, be accompanied by a decrease in wealth. This realization, combined with the new foreign policy goals of the post-Stalin era, brought a change in approach to foreign trade under Khrushchov. Cooperation among the CMEA countries was to be intensified. This was also in reaction to the first successes of the EEC. The chemical industry and − later on − the automobile industry were to be developed faster with the help of Western technology, and for the first time greater amounts of grain were imported from the West. Trade and development aid were also used as a tool to gain political influence in the Third World.

Then the conditions of growth for the Soviet economy changed so that "by the beginning of the 1970s, the exploitation of the advantages of international trade" was the last major source of potential Soviet economic growth not yet opened up.[2] The political leadership under Brezhnev reacted to this situation with a new foreign trade policy concept in which the development of cooperation with the West played an important role. This concept was presented to and passed by the XXVth Congress of the CPSU in the spring of 1976. In his report to the Party Congress[3] Brezhnev rejected self-sufficiency and saw that "a peculiarity of our time is the increasing utilization of the international division of labour for the development of any country, irrespective of its wealth and its actual economic standard". The inevitable consequence from this statement was an export oriented growth strategy and a renunciation of the "Stalinist industrialization" with its domestic market orientation. This strategy was also stressed in several Party Congress documents, especially in the speech of Kosygin[4] in which he found that "as foreign trade had become an important branch of the economy", special export enterprises suited to the "specific requirements of the foreign market", were needed in order to increase the profitability of exports and thus make a maximum contribution to economic growth. At the same time imports were supposed to be used as a means of realizing "the economic strategy underlying the state plan". They were in particular supposed to promote the acceleration of technical progress and to diversify the supply of goods for the people. Thus imports – as well as exports – were to become constituent parts of the economic plans and no longer primarily a "stopgap" when a plan was disrupted.

The "primacy of foreign policy" was, however, reaffirmed by Brezhnev, who regarded "foreign trade as an effective means of achieving political as well as economic tasks", and saw "foreign trade relations as a complex of policy and economy, diplomacy and business, industrial production and trade". As before, the USSR gave priority to foreign policy in any clash between the interests of foreign policy and foreign trade.

According to Brezhnev, the further development of "economic, scientific and technical relations with capitalist countries" should serve as the strengthening and extension of the "material basis of the policy of peaceful coexistence". The USSR also wanted to develop trade and economic relations faster with those countries in the West, "which showed a sincere willingness to cooperate and which took care to ensure normal and equal conditions for the development of cooperation" (Kosygin). Only in such cases were "solid economic relations, which find their expression in our economic plans, possible" (Kosygin).

In the speeches at the Party Congress the Soviet Union also expressed the wish "to add new qualitative aspects to economic relations with the developed capitalist countries" (Kosygin), such as to develop "new forms of foreign trade relations which exceed the framework of traditional trade" (Brezhnev). What they had in mind were compensation agreements, "according to which new enterprises, totally owned by our state, were to be established in cooperation with foreign enterprises. The Soviet Union was to receive credits, equipment and licenses, and pay for them with a part of the goods produced in these or other enterprises" (Brezhnev). This form of cooperation with the industrialized West, which had so far been used predominantly in the field of raw materials – though there are no statistical data indicating its scale – was, according to Brezhnev, to be extended in the five-year plan period from 1976 to 1980 to the manufacturing industry as well. It remains to be seen, whether Brezhnev's statement on the need to consider other new forms of cooperation will be acted upon. New forms of cooperation would include for example the highest form of industrial cooperation, namely "joint ventures" which have significant consequences concerning the share of risk and profits. It was no surprise that the Soviet side wanted to promote those compensation transactions which were "of greatest use" and always guaranteed a "balance in trade accounts between the partners". The desire to do so, however, was an indication of Soviet problems with their balance of payments with the West.

Soviet Economic Relations With the West Since 1970

From 1970 to 1981 there was a real increase in Soviet exports to the West[5] of 40.5 per cent (see table 1).[6] This was lower than the growth rate of the country's total exports (+ 61 per cent). The share of exports to the Western industrialized countries in total Soviet exports therefore fell by 3 percentage points to 16 per cent. Measured in current prices, however, (see table 2) the market share of the industrialized West increased from 19 per cent (1970) to 30 per cent (1981 and 1982). In the same period Soviet imports from the West increased by 215 per cent in real terms, much faster than total imports, which grew by + 136 per cent. As a result the West's share in total Soviet foreign purchases reached about a third compared to only about a quarter in 1970. Unlike exports, the West's share in total Soviet imports differed little between real and nominal current figures.

A major factor in the expansion of the Soviet trade with the West during the 1970s was the favourable development in the relative prices of Soviet exports and imports. During this period the Soviet terms of trade improved by more than 150 per cent. Therefore as noted above, the USSR was able to increase its imports from the West, in real terms, to a much greater extent than its exports to the West, without reaching a critical limit of indebtedness. In this respect the development since 1978 in the wake of the "second oil price shock" is very interesting. Exports to the West have been decreasing since 1978 and have fallen by 10 per cent in real terms, while imports from the West rose by 35 per cent in real terms.

Compared to overall economic performance with real growth in national income of 68.5 per cent, the income elasticity of exports to the West was 0.83 per cent for the period from 1970 to 1981. In other words the Soviet propensity to export to the West declined during this period. The estimated share of exports to the West in the total Soviet economy is at present about 0.9 per cent (1970: 1.1 per cent), so its dependence on these exports is accordingly very small.

The overall distribution of goods, the distributed national income, grew at 60 per cent in real terms in the same period, much slower than the volume of imports from the West. The income elasticity of imports therefore came to almost 2 per cent, showing an increase in the import dependency of the Soviet economy on trade with the West during the 1970s. In macroeconomic terms, the share of Western imports in national income increased by 1.5 percentage points, to 2.9 per cent at the end of this period. But this is still a relatively low level. It is therefore possible to draw two general conclusions. With regard to trade in goods the Soviet economy is much more trade dependent on the import side than on the export side, but of all the modern industrialized countries, the Soviet Union is the one with the lowest degree of economic interdependence. Consequently, the Soviet economy is less dependent on events occurring in the world economy, and the country's economic security is accordingly higher. The increased trade dependence with the West on the import side must be seen against this background.

Despite improvements in its terms of trade, the USSR has accumulated a deficit in its trade with the Western industrialized countries of -13.5 billion transfer rubles (t.r.). Payments between the USSR and this group of countries − except Finland − are performed in hard currency, predominantly U.S.-Dollars. Consequently the prices on Western markets strongly influence prices in Soviet trade with the West. Thomas A. Wolf has proved that even in those markets "in which the Soviet market share and hence potential market power is greatest", the Soviet foreign trade organizations "may 'follow' rather than lead price developments".[7] In order to finance its trade deficit in hard currency the USSR has raised loans on Western capital markets, and Western estimates put its net debt (liabilities minus claims) at between 8 and 10 billion U.S.-Dollars at the end of 1982. This figure includes more than 4 billion U.S.-Dollars of net liabilities with commercial banks reporting to the Bank of International Settlements (BIS). The figures of the BIS are certainly the most reliable Western source on Eastern debt. This debt is, however, unlikely to be a great problem for the Soviet economy, which will probably manage its debt problems easier than the other CMEA countries. The debt service ratio (interest payments as a percentage of the revenues from exports to OECD markets) was estimated at 4 per cent in 1982, against 31.5 per cent for the smaller East European countries as a whole.

This low debt service ratio is due to the fact that almost half the Soviet liabilities to the West are the result of long-term compensation agreements. By the end of 1970 the USSR had concluded compensation agreements for a total of 60 projects in the oil and gas, chemical, petrochemical, timber, paper and cellulose and other branches of the industry.[8] Whilst the repayment of loans raised to finance such projects is therefore secured by the Soviet delivery and the Western purchase obligations, the present ill-balanced and asymmetric composition of Soviet trade with the West is also unlikely to change in the future.

Fuels, mineral raw materials and metals accounted for more than 85 per cent of Soviet exports to Western industrialized countries in 1982 (see table 3). The USSR was able to increase revenue from its energy exports from 1.3 billion t.r. in 1973 to 15 billion t.r. in 1982, even though the export volume only increased from 76 million to 127 million tonnes coal equivalent. Thus price increases on the energy market were the decisive factor in growth in the Soviet trade with Western countries ("windfall profits"). In addition, according to an American estimate [9] the USSR sold 2320 tons of gold valued at $ 14.5 bn between 1971 and 1981. Sales of gold are not included in the official trade statistics of the USSR. Finished products, however, are all but insignificant in Soviet exports to the West which is evidence of the export weakness of Soviet industry.

The composition of Soviet imports shows a different picture. In 1982 32 per cent of Soviet imports from Western industrialized countries were machines including equipment and means of transport (see table 3). There is no easy

answer to the question of what share of these Soviet purchases of machines en-
corporate the highest technology items. According to one American estimate 12
per cent of all Soviet imports of finished products from Western industrialized
countries in 1981 were products encorporating "highest technology"; in 1970 it
was 18 per cent.[10] In any case goods that serve the maintenance of current production (pos. 2, 3 and 4) accounted for a larger share of Soviet imports from the
West. This corresponds to the anticipated behaviour of bureaucrats in centrally
planned economies, who attach more importance to the fulfilment of the
current plan than to future economic growth.

There has been a dramatic increase in the amount of hard currency absorbed
by imports of agricultural goods. Between 1971 and 1981 the USSR spent about
$ 49 billion on agricultural imports, $ 25.5 billion of which was on grain alone.
This covers imports in hard currency trade with the Western industrialized countries, excluding Finland, and all those developing countries, with which the USSR
has concluded payment agreements on hard currency basis, and is higher than the
sum spent on investment goods ($ 43.5 billion). In the period between 1971 and
1982 the USSR imported about 175 million tons of grain (the figures are partly
based on estimates), of which more than 90 per cent came from Western countries. For these grain imports the USSR spent more than 15 billion t.r. The imported grain accounted for an increasing share of the total domestic grain consumption. Between 1971 and 1975 imports accounted for an annual average of 4
per cent of consumption, between 1976 and 1980 an annual average of 9 per
cent, but 19 per cent in 1981 and 18 per cent in 1982.

Western Europe was the predominant market for Soviet exports. In 1982
95 per cent of all Soviet exports to the West went to Western Europe, compared
to 81.5 per cent in 1970, the exports consisting mainly of energy. Japan played
a relatively minor role taking only 4 per cent of total Soviet exports in 1982
compared to 1.5 per cent in 1970, and even the U.S.A. held only a marginal
position (with 0.8 per cent and 2.7 per cent respectively).

On the import side only two thirds of the Soviet imports from the West
came from Western Europe compared to 76 per cent in 1970. More than 15 per
cent came from Japan, compared to 12 per cent in 1970, where the USSR mainly purchased machines and equipment for its energy industry. The share of the
U.S.A. in Soviet imports was, depending on Soviet purchases of grain, between
4 per cent (1970) and 11 per cent (1982). The Soviet balance of trade deficit
with the U.S.A. of nearly $ 20 bn for the period 1971-1981, which was to a
large extent a consequence of grain purchases, was more than balanced by a $ 21
bn export surplus in the trade with the EC countries. The deficit with Japan
which was just short of $ 11 bn, had to be financed by other means, such as
loans on Western capital markets.

Special Problems of the Soviet Economic Policy Toward the West

The normalization of the trade relations, especially with the U.S.A., was an important goal of the Soviet policy of détente at the beginning of the 1970s. In the spring of 1969 American businessmen were presented in Moscow with a "shopping list" of what the Soviet Union wished to import, that amounted to a total of $ 5 bn in 1969 prices. In that year the Soviet Union actually imported goods from the United States worth almost $ 120 m. In June 1971 the U.S.A. signalled its willingness to extend trade with the USSR.[11] It began by taking unilateral measures to stimulate the economic exchange such as granting credits, a less restrictive interpretation of export controls and the establishment of a Bureau of East-West trade in the Department of Commerce. In May 1972 the first summit meeting between President Nixon and General Secretary Brezhnev took place in Moscow, despite the fact that the American President had only a few weeks before given the order to bomb North Vietnam and to impose a blockade on the port of Haiphong.[12] During the meeting an official joint trade commission was established, the task of which was to negotiate the conclusion of a trade agreement (including most favoured nation treatment), the conditions for the granting of credits, long-term joint projects, and a mechanism for the solution of trade conflicts.

Finally, in the second half of 1972, and after a series of intensive negotiations the U.S.A. and the USSR concluded several agreements dealing with economic problems, among which the most important were the following:

(1) "Lend-lease" agreement. This agreement settled the terms of repayment of the Soviet liabilities from the Second World War. The U.S.A. insisted on a settlement of this set of problems, and linked it to their readiness to grant most favoured nation treatment and credits.
(2) Trade agreement. This provided for a tripling of the bilateral trade within a period of three years. It granted the USSR most favoured nation (MFN) treatment, and promised Exim Bank credits and guarantees for purchases in the U.S.A.

The Soviet government regarded the granting of MFN treatment, which settled the question of what trade barriers the U.S.A. would impose on imports from the USSR, as the litmus test for U.S. behaviour, as well as a symbol of goodwill and relations in the spirit of détente.[13] The Soviet position was influenced by its main foreign policy goal of the last 25 years, namely to gain U.S. recognition of the USSR as a world power equal in every respect to the U.S.A.

It was no surprise therefore that the Soviet Union reacted in no uncertain terms when the U.S. Congress imposed conditions on the granting MFN treatment. These linked the granting of credits and/or MFN treatment to Soviet emigration policy (Jackson/Vanik Amendment), limited credits granted to the USSR by the Exim Bank to 300 million U.S.-Dollars (Stevenson Amendment) and prohibited official credit for certain Soviet energy projects (Church Amendment).

Only one week after the U.S. Congress passed the "Trade Act", containing these three amendments in January 1975 the USSR, referring to interference with its internal affairs, gave notice of its intention to terminate the trade agreement of 1972. Since this time the economic relations between the two superpowers have existed in the vacuum of no formed agreement, as indeed they did before.

The political dialogue between the Soviet Union and Japan, which established diplomatic relations in 1956, has remained acrimonious. The territorial problem of the northern islands and the problem of the fishing rights in this area are still unsolved. While Japanese Prime Ministers Tanaka (1973) and Suzuki (1982) paid visits to Moscow, these visits have not been returned by Soviet politicians. There is a strong and almost insurmountable antagonism between the two countries on the question of the concept of defence for the Far East. Japanese-Soviet relations deteriorated further in 1980 after the Japanese government – following its closest ally the U.S.A. – imposed economic sanctions against the USSR following the invasion of Afghanistan. The Japanese Export-Import-Bank was prohibited from granting new credits to the Soviet Union, and the export of modern technology, mainly in the field of energy equipment, was forbidden. As a consequence the Soviet side broke-off negotiations on Japanese involvement in several projects in Siberia. The Soviet Union has nevertheless made efforts to improve the political climate for its trade with Japan. "The Soviet Union worked very hard on an economic rapprochement policy vis-à-vis Japan. ... in which their principal policy objective was to extract the greatest possible economic cooperation from Japan".[14] What the Soviet Union wants first of all is a long-term economic cooperation agreement similar to those it concluded with most of the West European countries and Canada in the 1970s and Japanese involvement in some copper, asbestos and timber projects, as well as in the mining of coal and iron ore in Siberia. The Soviet-Japanese negotiations on these and other large-scale projects, such as gas deliveries from Sakhalin to Japan, were continued in 1983, but there has recently been a worsening rather than an improvement in the political climate between the two countries.

There is a third set of so far unsolved problems in East-West economic relations concerning relations between the CMEA and the EC.[15] During the CSCE negotiations the USSR could not but realize that the EC countries acted politically "in unison". This happened and happens in the framework of the so-called European Political Cooperation (EPC), which has evolved in the form of direct cooperation between the foreign ministers of the EC member states outside the EC itself. As a result the USSR also makes the CMEA act as a homogeneous community, and has introduced it on the European political stage as a counterpart to the EC. Although the economic integration of Eastern Europe has always been a political objective of the Soviet Union it was only demonstrated in the form of a joint CMEA foreign trade policy after the EC countries acted jointly in the CSCE.

Since 1973 therefore, the CMEA had been making efforts to establish official contacts with the EC. In February 1976 these efforts resulted in the presentation by the CMEA of a draft treaty on the "foundations of mutual relations" between the two communities, in which cooperation in many fields, including trade and credit policy, as well as the establishment of a Joint Commission ("maximum offer") were proposed. In November 1976 the EC advanced a counter-proposal which only provided for "working relations" between the two communities and in which trade policy was to be arranged bilaterally by agreements between the EC on one side and individual CMEA countries on the other ("minimum offer"). From 1978 until the beginning of 1980 there were several rounds of negotiations between the two sides on the basis of these two contrasting proposals, but no progress was made.

The lack of any success in these negotiations means that there have been no trade agreements between the two sides since 1975. Since then the CMEA countries have had no influence on EC trade policy toward the East ("autonomous trade policy"), which is a major disadvantage for them. Obviously, this disadvantage is not too serious for the Soviet economy. Soviet exports, mainly consisting of energy and raw materials, find almost free access to West European markets. But the supply of finished products from the smaller CMEA economies – three quarters of which are consumer goods, mainly clothing – is hit by the high customs barriers and quantitative limitations of imports in Western Europe. It is the smaller CMEA countries who have to bear the economic costs of the Soviet policy toward the EC.

Conclusions

The balance of the Soviet economic relations with the West in the 1970s shows positive as well as negative aspects. One of the major items on the positive side is without doubt the improved provision of the Soviet domestic market by the increase in imports of intermediate goods, technological hardware and grain. This has not resulted in a Soviet dependence on Western supplies at either the sectoral level or – especially – the macro level. The most important item on the negative side must be the fact that the USSR has not managed to create a powerful export industry or raise its trade with the West on the desired "higher quality level". Its projected compensation transactions with the West are limited exclusively to raw materials and energy supplies, and energy still accounts for most of its exports to the West. There can be no question of a deeper involvement of the Soviet economy in the international division of labour.

At the beginning of the 1970s the USSR's political and economic interests in its relations with the West were nearly identical. From the Soviet point of view this far-reaching identity of interests was to be consolidated by a process in which flourishing East-West trade would provide the "material basis" for the policy of détente, which would in turn intensify economic relations and help make such a policy irreversible. The Soviet Union declared its willingness to maintain close economic relations, especially with those capitalist countries which played an active role in the policy of détente and cooperation ("positive linkage policy").

In the case of conflicts between its political and economic interests, for whatever reasons, during the 1970s the Soviet Union reacted according to the concrete situation. It did not ratify the Soviet-American trade agreement negotiated in the middle of 1972 because it was unwilling to surrender to the public pressure applied by the U.S.A. on Soviet emigration policy. But economic relations with the U.S.A. were not broken-off. On the contrary the Soviet Union continued, and even increased, its grain imports from the U.S.A. and concluded two medium-term agreements with the U.S. government in 1975, and even 1983, concerning the volume and the conditions of grain imports. On both occasions the economic interests – and this is true for both sides – took priority over foreign policy. The "loss of face" involved, however, was more severe for the U.S.A., because the Reagan Administration has explicitly made the grain agreement "embargo-proof". In other words it contracted to renounce the only significant economic weapon it has in relations with the USSR.

With regards to its relations with Japan the Soviet Union showed another pattern of behaviour. In this case the USSR tried, in vain, to intensify its economic relations with Japan and to encourage greater Japanese involvement in the opening up of Siberia despite a continuous worsening of the political climate since 1979 if not before. It is interesting that the USSR never considered making political concessions to Japan in order to promote economic relations, but made a sharp division between politics and economics, giving politics a clear priority.

In the Soviet relations with the West in the 1970s there was no evidence of the application of economic instruments in pursuit of anything other than economic goals. In particular it is not true that the USSR tried once again "to gain influence over Western Europe and to separate Europe from the United States".[16] The Soviet Union does not even have an economic instrument it could use for this purpose. The Soviet dilemma is one of economic weakness accompanied by military equality with the U.S.A. The positive linkage policy of the Soviet Union mentioned above has in fact turned out to be nothing but passivity.

In its relations with the West the USSR is in a special position to make clear distinctions between politics and economics, ideology and economic necessities, and economic welfare and security. Given the Soviet social system, particular economic interests obviously do not have an influence on the major political goals of the CPSU leadership of security on the international level and maintenance of the system on the domestic level. This is even true in the case of the opening up of Siberia, where there is certainly more than a particular regional or sectoral interest involved (Siberia is not Soviet Alaska).

It is argued in the West that the intensification of the Soviet economic relations with the West may cause a fundamental change of the Soviet economic system, or that these relations are regarded by the Soviet leadership as a substitute for deeper economic reforms.[17] Both arguments are clearly opposed to each other. On the one hand it is argued that the realization of some major investment projects such as the Fiat works in Togliatti, the Kama works, the Baikal-Amur Railway, the West Siberian oil and gas complex, "require considerable Western economic involvement and seem to be moving from traditional lines of control".[18] On the other hand it is stressed that close cooperation with the West "is seen as an alternative to the politically more dangerous economic reforms and as a promise or bait of a better standard of living for the elite".[19]

In both cases the overall economic importance of the Soviet trade with the West is grossly overestimated.[20] Moreover, a false evaluation of the recent factual development of the Soviet economic reform – or better of the "improvement of the economic mechanism" – has become evident. The mechanism of planning and management has neither adapted itself to Western management methods under the influence of Western technology, nor have changes been abandoned. The goal of the changes was in any case the better adaptation of the trade with the West to the Soviet economic system.

It is indeed remarkable that none of the measures to improve the organization of planning affected foreign trade. The Soviet economic planners continue to try to retain full control of the influence which foreign trade exerts on the domestic economy. This control is exercised by means of both a strict handling of the foreign trade and foreign exchange monopoly of the state, and the maintenance of the domestic character of the ruble. Inconvertibility is in the last instance a precondition for quantitative planning and the management of bilaterally balanced foreign trade relations and thus an instrument of central control over these relations. The conclusion therefore is that the Soviet leadership will continue to try "to maximize Western technology imports while not changing their economic system".[21]

NOTES

1 O.T. Bogomolov: Economic Relations Between Socialist and Capitalist Countries. In: *MEMO*, No. 3/1980, p. 50.
2 *Strukturentwicklung der sowjetischen Wirtschaft und deren Rückwirkungen auf den Außenhandel.* Arbeiten aus dem Osteuropa-Institut München. Editors: Wolfram Schrettl, Volkhart Vinzentz. Vol. 1, 1981, p. 175.
3 *Neues Deutschland* of 25.2.1976.
4 *Neues Deutschland* of 2.3.1976.
5 "West" applies here to the 24 member states of the OECD.
6 The indices of volumes and prices for 1982 cannot (yet?) be calculated.
7 Thomas A. Wolf: Soviet Market Power and Pricing Behaviour In Western Import Markets. In: *Soviet Studies*, No. 4/1982, p. 529.
8 See V. Malkevich: East-West: Economic Cooperation. Technological Exchange. Moscow 1982, p. 89.
9 Joan Parpart Zoeter: USSR: Hard Currency Trade and Payments. In: *Soviet Economy In The 1980s: Problems And Prospects.* Part 2. Washington 1983, p. 479.
10 John A. Martens: *Quantification of Western Exports of High-Technology-Products to Communist Countries.* Washington 1983, p. 13.
11 Hanns-Dieter Jacobsen: *Die Ostwirtschaftspolitik der USA. Möglichkeiten und Grenzen einer "linkage"-Politik.* Ebenhausen 1980, p. 25.
12 Marshall I. Goldman: Interaction of Politics and Trade: Soviet-Western Interaction. In: *Soviet Economy in the 1980s: Problems and Prospects.* Part 1. Washington 1982, p. 121.
13 See Hanns-Dieter Jacobsen, *op.cit.* p. 27.
14 Kazuo Ogawa: *Japan-Soviet Economic Relation: Present Status and Future Prospects.* Manuscript. Tokyo 1982, p. 2.
15 See Heinrich Machowski: Zur Politischen Ökonomie der Beziehungen zwischen dem RGW und der EWG. In: *Beilage zur Wochenzeitung Das Parlament*, Nr. B12/1982, p. 33.
16 Angela Stent: Economic Strategy. In: *Soviet Strategy Toward Western Europe.* Edited by Edwina Moreton and Gerald Segal. London, Boston, Sydney 1984, p. 204.
17 A good summary of the pros and cons of these two arguments can be found in: Eugene Zaleski and Helgard Wienert: *Technology Transfer Between East and West.* OECD. Paris 1980, p. 186.
18 *Ibid.*, p. 188.
19 *Ibid.*, p. 195.
20 See Jochen Bethkenhagen und Heinrich Machowski: *Entwicklung und Struktur des deutsch-sowjetischen Handels – Seine Bedeutung für die Volkswirtschaften der Bundesrepublik Deutschland und der Sowjetunion.* Sonderheft des DIW. Berlin 1982, p. 186.
21 Eugene Zaleski and Helgard Wienert, *op.cit.* p. 196.

Table 1: *The Development of Soviet Foreign Trade 1970 – 1982*

Groups of countries	1975/70	1980/75	1980	1981	1982
Exports (real annual growth in per cent)					
all countries	4,9 [5]	4,8 [5]	1,6	0,4	6,3
Socialist countries[1] among these:	5,3 [5]	4,9 [5]	4,0	-1,1	-2,4
CMEA countries[2]	5,3 [5]	4,7 [5]	3,6	0,2	-4,0
Western industrialized countries[3]	4,8 [5]	2,8 [5]	-2,0	-3,3	
Developing countries[4]	3,8 [5]	7,8 [5]	-0,4	14,7	18,5 [6]
Imports (real annual growth in per cent)					
all countries	10,4 [5]	5,8 [5]	7,3	8,2	9,1
Socialist countries[1] among these:	7,6 [5]	6,0 [5]	3,4	4,9	12,9
CMEA countries[2]	7,0 [5]	5,7 [5]	0,7	2,7	14,1
Western industrialized countries[3]	17,1 [5]	6,4 [5]	7,3	4,8	
Developing countries[4]	9,8 [5]	2,9 [5]	33,4	33,8	6,2 [6]
Terms of Trade[7] (annual growth in per cent)					
all countries	1,2 [5]	5,4 [5]	5,4	4,9	5,8
Socialist countries[1] among these:	1,2 [5]	2,8 [5]	2,6	8,7	9,9
CMEA countries[2]	1,6 [5]	4,3 [5]	1,4	9,2	10,9
Western industrialized countries3)	5,1 [5]	14,0 [5]	17,1	2,4	
Developing countries[4]	-1,8 [5]	-0,7 [5]	-8,4	-3,6	1,5 [6]
Balance of Trade[8] (in billion t.r.[9])					
all countries	1,11	-	14,38	18,86	25,62
Socialist countries[1] among these:	2,50	-	11,71	16,16	19,48
CMEA countries[2]	0,56	-	8,42	13,37	16,97
Western industrialized countries[3]	-5,79	-	-12,77	-13,63	-13,67
Developing countries[4]	4,41	-	15,45	16,34	19,82

Note: Exports and imports: fob prices. Countries of destination and origin. Figures for 1982 are provisional.

1) CMEA countries plus People's Republic of China, Yugoslavia, People's Republic of Korea, Laos.-2) Albania, Bulgaria, Czechoslovakia, GDR, Cuba, Mongolia, Poland, Rumania, Hungary, Vietnam.-3) OECD countries except Turkey.-4) All other non-European developing countries; specification by groups.-5) Annual average.-6) Industrialized plus developing (non-socialist) countries.-7) Index of export prices in relation to index of import prices.-8) Quantities cumulated from 1970 up to the current reported year 1975, 1980, 1981 and 1982; surplus: +, deficit:-.-9)Current prices.

Sources: Foreign Trade of the USSR 1922-1981, Jubilee issue;
Foreign Trade of the USSR 1982 (both in Russian).

264

Table 2: *Regional Structure of Soviet Foreign Trade 1970–1982 – per cent*

Groups of countries	1970 a	1975 a	1975 b	1980 a	1980 b	1981 a	1981 b	1982 a	1982 b
Exports									
All countries					100				
Socialist countries[1]	65,4	66,6	60,7	66,0	54,2	65,1	54,6	59,7	54,0
among these: CMEA countries[2]	59,4	62,0	56,3	60,9	49,0	60,8	50,0	55,0	49,3
Western industrialized countries[3]	18,7	18,6	25,5	16,6	32,0	16,0	30,2	40,3[5]	29,8
Developing countries[4]	15,9	14,8	13,8	17,1	13,8	18,9	15,2		16,2
Imports					100				
All countries									
Socialist countries[1]	65,1	57,3	52,4	57,8	53,2	56,0	50,8	58,0	54,6
among these: CMEA countries[2]	61,4	52,5	48,5	52,3	48,2	49,6	44,9	51,9	48,8
Western industrialized countries[3]	24,0	32,3	36,3	32,9	35,3	31,8	34,4	42,0[5]	33,5
Developing countries[4]	10,9	10,4	11,3	9,3	11,5	12,2	14,8		11,9

a: Prices of 1970; b: Current prices.

Note: Exports and imports: fob prices. Countries of destination and origin. Figures for 1982 are provisional.

1) CMEA countries plus Peoples Republic of China, Yugoslavia, Peoples Republic of Korea, Laos. - 2) Albania, Bulgaria, Czechoslovakia, GDR, Cuba, Mongolia, Poland, Rumania, Hungary, Vietnam. - 3) OECD countries except Turkey. - 4) All other non-European developing countries; specification by groups. - 5) Industrialized plus developing (non-socialist) countries.

Sources: Foreign Trade of the USSR 1922 - 1981, Jubilee issue; Foreign Trade of the USSR 1982 (both in Russian)

Table 3: *Structure of Goods in Soviet Foreign Trade 1982 in per cent*
(all goods = 100)

Groups of goods	Exports					Imports				
	a	b	c	d	e	a	b	c	d	e
1. Machines, equipment means of transport	12,9	17,5	18,1	1,7	18,0	34,4	43,4	45,2	31,1	2,3
2. Fuels, mineral raw materials, metals	60,8	60,1	59,9	85,6	16,9	14,9	8,2	7,7	20,8	28,6
3. Other commercial raw materials, building materials	5,3	5,9	5,6	5,6	2,6	6,3	2,7	2,1	9,9	12,9
4. Chemical products, fertilizers, caoutchouc	3,1	3,7	3,5	2,7	2,1	4,4	3,2	3,1	6,9	2,9
5. Agricultural raw materials, animals, food and beverages	1,6	2,1	2,1	0,9	1,3	23,7	18,8	19,7	25,1	42,3
6. Industrial consumer goods	1,9	2,3	2,4	1,9	0,5	12,7	17,9	16,3	4,9	10,9
7. Goods not specified	14,5	8,4	8,4	1,6	58,6	3,6	5,8	6,1	1,3	0,2

Deviations in sums result from rounding of the figures.
a: All countries; b: Socialist countries[1]; c: CMEA countries[2]; d: Western industrialized countries[3]; e: Developing countries[4].
1) CMEA countries plus People's Republic of China, Yugoslavia, People's Republic of Korea, Laos.-2) Albania, Bulgaria, Czechoslovakia, GDR, Cuba, Mongolia, Poland, Rumania, Hungary, Vietnam.-3) OECD countries except Turkey.-4) All other non-European developing countries; specification by groups.
Sources: Foreign Trade of the USSR 1922-1981, Jubilee issue; Foreign Trade of the USSR 1982 (both in Russian).

20

EASTERN EUROPE (CMEA 6)*

Franz-Lothar Altmann

The present stagnation or even recession in East-West trade and the general
uncertainty concerning future trends affects the smaller CMEA-countries much
more severely than the Soviet Union. This study looks at the differences between the interests of the individual CMEA (6)-countries and the performance
of the respective national policies in the field of foreign trade.

Trends in the West trade Relations of the CMEA(6)-Countries in the 1970s

As early as the 1960s there was a significant growth in the CMEA(6)-coun-
tries' foreign trade. Between 1960 and 1970 the average annual export growth
lay between 7,0 per cent in the case of Czechoslovakia (CSSR) and 13,3 per
cent for Bulgaria, while imports grew at an average annual rate of between 7,6
per cent in the case of the USSR and 11,7 per cent for Rumania.[1] The period of
extensive industrialization, characterized in particular by an emphasis on heavy
industries, was more or less terminated at the end of the 1950s in all the CMEA-
countries, and replaced by the so-called intensive phase of economic development. In 1962 the first attempts to create an enforced international division of
labour in the CMEA were made in the form of the "Fundamental Principles of
International Socialist Division of Labour". These should have brought about a
flourishing of Intra-CMEA-trade, but there were already distinct signs of moves
towards nationally oriented foreign trade policies seeking more independence
from Moscow.

Table 1 and graph 1 show that, with the exception of Poland and Bulgaria in
the second half of the 1960s, all European CMEA-countries including the Soviet
Union, experienced faster growth in their trade with the West than within the
CMEA even during the 1960s. This is still the case even when one takes account
of the fact that the data in table 1 and graph 1 only give nominal figures, because of the very distinct differences between growth in Intra-CMEA trade and
trade with the West. Price developments in industrial commodities and raw
materials can give a distorted view of real trade flows. For example, East-West
trade can appear nominally more important than it really is when prices of
manufactured goods, which predominate in East-West trade, grow faster than
raw materials, which characterize Intra-CMEA trade. Given the distinct differences between the respective rates of growth in trade, these price effects only
justify a partial qualification of the finding that East-West trade has increased
more rapidly than Intra-CMEA trade. Furthermore it only applies to imports,

Table 1: *Foreign Trade of the CMEA Countries, 1960–1980*

| | Average Annual Rates of Growth (percentages) | | | | | | Trade balances in Mill. TRbl (Surplus: +; Deficit: –) in Trade with | | |
| | Exports to | | | Imports from | | | | | |
	CMEA[2]	Western Ind. Count.	Developing Countries	CMEA[2]	Western Ind. Count.	Developing Countries	CMEA[2]	Western Ind. Count.	Developing Countries
Bulg. 1961–70	12.8	14.9	20.8	10.4	14.9	19.1	– 79	– 544	+ 147
1971–75	14.2	4.7	26.3	18.2	24.8	16.4	– 111	– 1.112	+ 432
1976–80	11.7	27.3	19.5	11.5	2.9	8.5	– 787	– 969	+ 1.978
ČSSR 1961–70	7.2	9.1	4.8	7.3	10.2	2.5	+ 316	– 411	+ 611
1971–75	11.9	10.7	10.3	14.4	13.9	11.6	+ 59	– 1.097	+ 500
1976–80	11.0	13.5	11.5	10.1	9.7	9.6	– 1.242	– 2.456	+ 888
GDR[1] 1961–70	7.6	8.5	7.5	8.2	10.4	7.1	+ 2.113	– 832	+ 365
1971–75	13.0	13.3	13.9	13.1	15.9	16.8	+ 1.055	– 2.755	– 40
1976–80	9.0	11.9	21.6	8.7	11.0	17.7	– 821	– 5.397	– 171
Pol. 1961–70	11.4	9.8	5.5	10.6	7.7	7.2	– 1.123	– 176	+ 148
1971–75	17.7	21.7	21.6	14.0	40.7	19.9	– 218	– 5.103	+ 530
1976–80	7.3	10.7	11.5	11.2	– 0.1	21.9	– 820	– 7.494	+ 497
Rum. 1961–70	7.0	14.5	16.3	8.0	17.7	19.0	– 99	– 1.072	+ 186
1971–75	13.0	21.1	35.8	11.7	19.9	34.8	+ 414	– 1.042	+ 483
1976–80	14.1	15.7	17.3	13.3	9.7	39.8	– 148	– 1.501	+ 713
Hung. 1961–70	10.4	12.6	9.0	9.7	11.1	11.9	– 998	– 1.363	+ 641
1971–75	16.1	9.0	14.1	16.3	16.2	15.4	+ 253	– 1.023	– 112
1976–80	4.7	11.2	11.9	3.4	7.0	5.1	– 373	– 4.093	– 147
USSR 1961–70	8.3	9.0	19.7	9.0	9.7	9.1	+ 1.872	– 1.445	+ 3.722
1971–75	16.4	23.3	12.5	16.4	30.7	21.2	+ 320	– 5.638	+ 4.317
1976–80	12.7	20.9	15.7	10.7	10.1	11.2	+ 7.851	– 6.977	+ 11.238

1 Includes trade with the Federal Rep. of Germany;
2 CMEA (9), i.e. the 7 European countries and Cuba and Mongolia, plus Albania. For Czechoslovakia also Vietnam.

Sources: V.I.E.C.: Comecon Foreign Trade Data 1982, London: McMillan Press Ltd, 1983.
Medzheryanı, F.: Vneshnaya torgovlya evropeyskikh stran-chlenov SEV, *Revue Roumaine des Sciences Sociales*, Vol. 27, No. 1/1983, p. 61.
Calculations of the author.

268

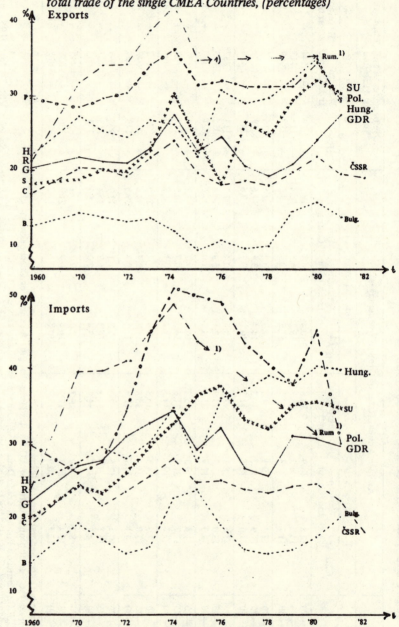

Graph 1: *Share of foreign trade with western industrialized countries in the total trade of the single CMEA Countries, (percentages)*

1) Since 1976 the Rumanian trade with the West includes also the trade with the developing countries. Data for 1980, however, indicate only export resp. import with the industrialized West.

Sources: Own calculations after CMEA-Yearbook, and Kleer, J., op. cit.

where the simplified distinction between plant and equipment in imports from the West and raw materials and semi-finished products from the CMEA, mainly from the USSR, is valid. In exports the regional commodity structure shows a totally different picture. Here the Intra-CMEA deliveries of all CMEA-countries, with the exception of the Soviet Union, are characterized by plant and equipment, whereas commodities of the CTN groups 2-5 (fuels, raw-materials, fertilizers, construction material etc.) account for major shares of exports to the West. Even though these patterns of trade have recently changed for countries such as Hungary, Poland and Bulgaria, there seems little doubt that there was a marked preference for trade with the West in the 1960s. Several factors which facilitated or influenced this development were still important in the 1970s. Towards the end of the 1950s a change occurred in the European socialist countries' evaluation of the impact and importance of foreign trade relations. During the period of extensive economic growth and Cold War, economic policy was characterized by a desire for national autarky, and imports, in particular those from the non-socialist countries, only served to fill gaps in domestic requirements, mainly production. Exports to the non-socialist countries were therefore only seen as a necessary means of paying for the imports. As J. Bognár put it: "No import policy could develop which saw imports as a component of a rational economic structure and exports as a component of growth policy."[2]

The 1960s saw a fundamental change in approach in Eastern Europe. On the one hand this was certainly facilitated by an easing of international tensions, but on the other hand it also reflected the requirements of the "intensive" growth policy. This new approach recognizes the stimulative effect of foreign trade relations on domestic economic development. The resultant interest of the CMEA-countries in increased trade with the West takes a number of forms:[3]

– Only increased imports of Western means of production were seen to be able to create the necessary climate for – and make a direct contribution to – a more rapid industrialization. This view could be found in countries whose economies were still in the transition from an agro-industrial to an industrial society, as well as in Czechoslovakia and East-Germany which already had developed economies.

– A more intensive engagement of the national economies in an international, world-wide division of labour, not only meant larger markets, which could promote growth, but also provided the planners with additional arguments, such as the need to improve quality to compete, which could be used to increase pressure on domestic producers to improve quality and increase productivity.

– In terms of domestic policy, imports of Western consumer products also offered the possibility, initially to a very limited degree, of raising the level of consumer satisfaction. Such an effect was, however, only perceptible in Hungary and Poland in the 1970s.

It was obvious that these advantages of foreign trade could not be achieved by trading with socialist partners because they suffered from the same basic structural deficiencies. It is noteworthy however, that the differences between the rates of growth of imports from and exports to the West were not as great in this initial phase of intensified relations with the West as in the later phase in the first half of the 1970s. Nevertheless, all CMEA-countries had persistent trade deficits through the period 1961-1970. The scale of deficits varied from Hungary and Rumania at top of the deficit list in 1970, to Poland (which 10 years later became the problem-country number one) which was way down the list and practically free of debt!

There was an enormous increase in imports from the West by all European CMEA-countries in the first half of the 1970s and up until 1974, in which imports from the West were again more dynamic than imports from the East. The only exception was Czechoslovakia, which for political reasons following the violent end to the Prague Spring, was oriented towards the CMEA. With the exception of Rumania, which kept about the same growth rates for exports and imports, all the CMEA-countries allowed substantially higher rates of growth for imports from the West than for exports to the West. The result can be seen in the accumulated trade deficits (see table 1).

The impact of the first oil-price shock, in the form of higher import prices, higher interest rates and a decline in exports due to economic recession in the West, is clearly shown in the development of CMEA trade with the West in the second half of the 1970s. Imports were already curtailed in this period, and not only as is often claimed after 1980. This is most clearly demonstrated in the cases of Bulgaria and Poland, where the respective average annual increases of imports from the West were reduced from 24,8 per cent and 40,7 per cent during the period 1971-75, to 2,9 per cent and -0,1 per cent in the period 1976-80!

Higher rates of growth in imports from the East and a concomitant preference for exports to the West show an attempt to shift deficits into Intra-CMEA trade, in particular trade with the Soviet Union (see the accumulated trade balance between the USSR and the CMEA for the years 1976-80 in table 1) and to slow the growth in Western debt. The fact that only Bulgaria succeeded in slowing the growth in debt was due to the enormous imbalances in CMEA-countries' trade with the West in the middle of the 1970s. These imbalances took the form of large annual trade deficits which meant that a return to more balanced trade and thus repayment of debt could only be achieved in the longer term. For example, Poland could only cover 53 per cent of its imports from the West with exports to the same destination.[4] Consequently although Poland ceased to import from the West and increased its exports to the West by an annual average rate of 10,7 per cent from 1976, it took until 1981 to achieve a trade balance. Not until 1982 after drastic import curtailments could Poland achieve its first marginal trade surplus with the West.

All CMEA-countries therefore recognized the need for a fundamental change in their policies on trade with the West in the middle of the 1970s. But the inherent dynamic of the existing structures militated against more radical policy changes. By 1974 all CMEA(6)-countries except Hungary had reached their maximum degree of economic interdependence with the West, even though the levels of course differed (see graph no. 1). Despite the reduction of the West's share of total trade in all CMEA-countries since 1975, trade dependence is still higher than in 1970 not to mention 1960. The only exception to this is Rumania due to its extreme curtailment of Western imports.

Different Interests in the CMEA(6)-Countries

Despite the existence of several fundamental common features there are nevertheless distinct differences between the CMEA-(6) with regard to their specific national interests, the policies they pursue as well as trends in the actual development of their trade with the West.

Fundamental differences existed from the very outset in terms of the level of development and general economic conditions pertaining in the individual countries. If one compares, for example, the GDR and Rumania at the end of the 1950s, trade with the West accounted for roughly the same share of total trade in each, but the GDR was an industrialized country whereas Rumania was still on the threshold of industrialization, in which the absolute value of per capita foreign trade was $ 73, compared to $ 225 in the GDR.[5] It goes without saying that given such different levels of development the commodity structures of foreign trade differed between the countries. Deliveries of the commodity group CTN 1 (plant and equipment in the CMEA nomenclature) accounted for 48.2 per cent of all GDR exports in 1960, compared to only 16.7 per cent in Rumania. Even 20 years later plant and equipment still accounts for only 26.2 per cent of Rumanian exports. There can be no doubt that the GDR has bene-fitted from the special trade relations with the Federal Republic of Germany. But one should also not neglect the very intensive political and economic links with the Soviet Union which have in the past brought some advantages in terms of purchases of raw materials, although this provided little in the way of further development impulses for the already industrialized GDR. Such impulses could only come from Czechoslovakia, but here only temporarily, and the trade with the West, which offered prospects for trade that could stimulate and promote technological advance.

East Germany and Czechoslovakia have therefore been interested in an ex-pansion of their trade with the West in order to maintain some contact with developments in new growth industries. For the other smaller CMEA-countries the problem was completely different. The technologies offered by GDR and Czechoslovakia displayed, to an increasing extent, development lags vis-à-vis comparable Western standards. They could also only be delivered in a limited volume because the Soviet Union was given preference. For East Germany and Czechoslovakia it was necessary to export to the USSR because they have become widely dependent on the Soviet Union for raw materials and energy. For the smaller CMEA-countries it also made sense to look for the most up to date technology on offer, especially if they had ambitious industrialization plans and when Western equipment promised higher competitiveness on international markets and thus increased sales in both East and West. Last but by no means least, offers of credit tied to the purchase of Western equipment did not play an unimportant part in purchasing decisions. CMEA trade, which is based on the principle of bilaterally balanced trade, did not offer comparable opportunities. In particular, East Germany and Czechoslovakia were not able to provide equipment of comparable levels of technology on long term credit.

This deliberate policy of creating an import surplus with the aid of Western supplier, bank, and government credits, in order to bring about a rapid modernization of industrial structure, has often been called the "Polish approach", because it was above all Poland and Hungary who chose to follow it. Both countries, however, also displayed relatively liberal import policies with regard to consumer goods in the 1970s, so that many imports merely served to improve the standard of living in these countries, rather than being channelled into investment in future modern production.

From the time of the "universal socialization" in the 1960s, *Poland* was encumbered by large structural imbalances. Industrial development went hand in hand with neglect of the – mainly private – agricultural and the consumer products sectors. Hence, Gierek's policy for the 1970s now aimed at using consumption, or a substantial increase of the standard of living, as a lever for economic expansion. A content consumer as a more compliant worker could sustain the rescue operation for the Polish economy. In the early years double digit growth rates in national income were achieved thanks to a Soviet stand-by credit in Western currency supplemented by long-term consolidation credits from the West, a liberalization of the political life in the form of more independence for the political parties, improved travel possibilities, better relations between government and church, and less discrimination against private agriculture. By the middle of the 1970s, however, the government became too self-confident, and there was a return to the fundamental principles of the Soviet model. For example, the political option of sacrificing standard and quality of living for economic growth was reemphasized, political promises such as on trade unions were not realized but conveniently forgotten and the superiority of socialist agriculture was once again stressed. All this resulted in a change of the socio-political context of the Polish approach so that it no longer corresponded with Gierek's original intentions. Popular political support, purchased by credit-financed imports, dissolved as gaps in supply opened up and the purchasing power of the Zloty decreased. Moreover, the expected benefits of modernization were not realized. The Polish economy was, by itself, not sufficiently innovative. The innovations grafted from outside in the form of imports, also showed up deficiencies in skilled manpower, qualifications and structure. Difficulties in the application of new technologies were reported from everywhere. In the middle of the 1970s the Polish National Bank reported that there was no prospect of exports repaying credit in more than 60 per cent of the credit financed investment projects completed between 1971 and 1973. At that time there was not yet talk of "investment ruins", which are today a major relic of the import policy of the 1970s.

Although at first glance *Hungary's* approach during the 1970s appears similar to Poland's it exhibits clear differences in two of its essential component parts.

Through the whole period Hungary has consistently pursued a deliberate policy of promoting agriculture including the private sector. In contrast Poland, and also Rumania, have been characterized by a constant shifting from one fundamental political resolution to another in agricultural policy, which has eroded the confidence of agricultural producers, especially in the private sector. From the point of view of foreign trade policy this meant that Hungary, with a strong agricultural sector, could concentrate on technology imports for the industrialization of the country. Whereas the share of food and agricultural products in Poland's imports from the West increased from 9.9 per cent to 20.2 per cent between 1974 and 1980, reaching even 27.8 per cent in 1981, there was a decrease in the share of such products in Hungary's imports over the period from 6.9 per cent to 3.7 per cent. Hard currency saved on food imports could therefore be put to better use in the purchase of machinery and equipment, as well as industrial consumer goods to improve the standard of living.

The second and perhaps even more important difference between the Polish and the Hungarian approach was that whilst the policy of trading with the West was accompanied by economic reform in Hungary, it led to a postponement of reform in Poland.

The Polish economic leaders relied upon the expected effects of the imports of machinery: in the case of Poland therefore it was imports of technology *instead* of economic reform. Hungary, however, has pursued a consistent policy of economic reform since 1968 and also carefully conceded a gradual liberalization in social life. In Hungary's case it was imports from the West *and* economic reform.

Czechoslovakian economic policy in the 1970s was characterized by an absence of both a relative increase in the importance of trade with the West and economic reform. After the traumatic experience of 1968, and the subsequent political re-orientation towards Moscow, Czechoslovakia displayed an accentuated reserve in its trade with the West and an increased economic and political dependence on the Soviet Union. The option of using Western credits to facilitate the already overdue modernization of some hopelessly obsolete plant and

274

equipment was not even considered. In this decision, based more on political and ideological than economic considerations, the régime argued that the country should not surrender financially to the class enemy. But this reserve has prevented Czechoslovakia reaching a level of development that it otherwise would have and has increased dependence on the Soviet Union.

In Czechoslovakia Intra-CMEA trade accounts for a higher share than any other country. Czechoslovak planners can, however, now proudly claim that, among the smaller CMEA-countries, Czechoslovakia has by far the smallest hard-currency debt, regardless of whether it is measured in terms of absolute debt to the economic potential of the country, to Western exports or to the number of inhabitants. Distrust and suspicion of any kind of economic reform rounded off the picture of the politicians in Prague and Bratislava after 1968. For Husák, Bilák and Štrougal the experience of the speed with which demands for liberalization in the relatively narrow economic sphere could spill-over into other, and in particular socio-political domains, was still too fresh in their memory.

The general hostility towards any reform in the *Rumanian* leadership was probably based on similar considerations. But it was not a hindrance to Rumania increasing its trade with the West in the 1960s; with the result that by 1970 Rumania had a clear lead over the other CMEA-countries when Eastern Europe in general began to expand its trade with the West. The driving force behind Rumanian endeavours to increase trade with the West, however, is the desire to strengthen the country's independence from Moscow by greater freedom in the choice of the trading partners. Ambitious industrialization targets clearly also played an important role, and a developed industry can serve in strengthening the ability of a country to maintain a more autarkic position despite the demands for specialization in the CMEA.

Bulgaria is in a completely different position. For decades Bulgaria has, of all the smaller CMEA countries, maintained the most intensive political and economic allegiance to the Moscow line. Only Prague sometimes now outdoes Sofia in this respect. Nor has Bulgaria ever made economic relations with the West a topic of primary significance, but has on the contrary, tried, from the very beginning of the CMEA, to take advantage of the intra-bloc specialization and cooperation. The scope for a more marked increase in economic relations with the West is also limited by the fact that more than 50 per cent of Bulgaria's trade is with the Soviet Union. The extreme dependence of the country on deliveries of raw materials from the USSR locks large parts of the economy into the existing foreign trade relations.

Interest groups in the CMEA(6)-Countries

The previous section sought to sketch out differences in the fundamental interests of the six smaller European CMEA-countries with regard to their trade with the West. This clearly showed that each of these countries is characterized by completely different fundamental requirements. Each has therefore also pursued a different strategy. The following will seek to identify the various interest groups and their preferences with regard to various strategy options.

Reformists and Conservatives. A simple differentation between those seeking reform and those wishing to retain dogma and central control, makes it quite easy to distinguish supporters and opponents of trade with the West. Hungary and Czechoslovakia are useful examples here. Increased economic relations with the West require changes in the domestic decision making structures, such as broader fields of responsibility and decentralization in order to achieve the flexibility needed to respond to the rapidly changing conditions and requirements of the Western markets. More imports inevitably lead to an increase in exports, and therefore render the domestic economy more exposed to the influence of Western market forces. The necessary incentives to improve efficiency and modernize, however, will only come from competition which cannot be found within the CMEA. A decision for the modernization of an economy therefore, also constitutes a decision for trade with the West and subsequently also for economic reforms including the main issues of decentralization and some market forces.

This can, however, be seen another way. If one desires economic and sociopolitical reforms, and one inevitably leads to the other — as Czechoslovakia in 1968 and Hungary showed — then the promotion of trade with the West presents a useful means of bringing pressure to bear in pursuit of the desired reform. Conversely, conservative dogmatists also recognize the danger in any intensification of trade with the West. Conservatives such as Vasil Biľák in Czechoslovakia are therefore understandably firm in their clear reserve or even extensive disapproval of such an intensification of trade with the West. Every economic reform sooner or later results in a relaxation of political structures and imperils the absolute claim to power of the ruling elite. The alternative is to protect oneself from the West and extend socialist integration within the CMEA.

Planners and Managers in Industry. The distinction between supporters and opponents of trade with the West becomes more difficult if one considers the narrower group of economic planning staff and the highest level of the directors of industrial enterprises. The position of the economic planners is probably largely determined by classifying them as reformists or conservatives. Their duties are, however, limited to the specific domain of economic development, where their interest is concentrated on economic growth and increased efficiency. This means that they are not primarily concerned with the socio-political implications of decisions. One can therefore assume that the expectations of improved productivity with Western technology as well as of general economic stimuli from trade with the West will result in planners being positively disposed towards trade with the West.

Directors of industrial enterprises are, however, likely to be far more ambivalent. Certainly one can assume that most of them − in so far as they are not "Party Directors" as many Czechoslovak directors were in the first years after 1968 − would like to see increased productivity, improved quality and range etc. Any improvement in the performance of the enterprise also means an increase in their personal, professional and social standing as well as of their income. They are aware that more engagement in the world wide division of labour can help bring about such advances, but are also very well aware that the cold wind of competition bites harder than most of them can endure on Western markets.

Even the first step of importing Western machinery and equipment can cause more problems than it solves for the industrial managers concerned. Inevitably such a modernization process creates greater demands on their own qualifications as well as on those of their employees, and the central plan will expect the new equipment to produce big improvements in the performance of the whole enterprise. This would not be so bad if central planning staff did not quasi automatically also expect increased exports to the West to materialize from such investment. In other words substantial incentives are necessary if managers are to be enticed into supporting a policy of increased trade with the West.

The Military. The military must also be considered. Although partly covered by the discussion of orthodox dogmatists, this interest and power group is important enough to deserve more specific consideration. As the military's basic task is to set up and maintain a highly developed powerful army for the defense of the country, it can be assumed that this group is interested in continuous technological advance in arms production, but also in the entire economy as a whole. Technology imports from the West as well as a general extension of economic relations with the West would therefore, in the first instance, be supported by the military if it results in economic growth and modernization. For the military economic ties with the West become questionable or even undesirable if they result in sensitive sectors of the domestic economy becoming dependent on Western imports, which could weaken economic capability and thus the fundamentals of national defense in the event of conflict.

In addition, one can assume that the military in the East, similar to its counterparts in the West, is predominantly conservative with respect to the existing socio-political system. Consequently it will not be at all happy with the fact − discussed above − that increased economic relations with the West can generate increased pressure for reforms in socialist society which would not correspond to its conservative views.

The military, being deeply rooted in a strong tradition of hierarchy, must in principle be inclined to favour centrally administered systems with regard to both the pursuit of political power and the entire sphere of economic decisions. It must therefore, distrust any decentralization which "softens" the existing decision structures, even if these are at present limited to economic controls.

The 1980s

The decline in economic activity in the Western industrialized countries at the end of the 1970s, followed by distinct symptoms of a recession at the beginning of the 1980s, hit the CMEA(6)-countries' trade with the West just when they were beginning to make progress in balancing their trade. The weaker demand in the West affected, in particular, those, such as Hungary, who had followed the recommendations of their Western partners and tried to enhance and diversify their exports by supplying more manufactured goods. This included products manufactured in factories which were modernized or even fully equipped by Western imports of machinery and equipment. But it was precisely these manufactured goods which not only faced strong international competition on the Western markets but also turned out to be especially sensitive to the economic climate. Efforts to withstand the pressures caused by this largely unforeseeable situation by means of additional credits failed due to the *de facto* credit refusal of Western banks and governments, who put all the CMEA-countries in the same pot after the Polish shock. To stop or even reduce imports remained the only way out. From the Western side these were accompanied by sanctions against Poland and the USSR, and a general increase in protectionism, not only against the CMEA-countries.

In this very difficult world economy climate the smaller CMEA-countries are now faced with two main problems. First their main supplier of raw materials, the Soviet Union, has made it clear that in future the volume of supplies will fall but prices must rise due to the general Intra-CMEA price formula. This means that the CMEA purchasers must either buy elsewhere, but then for hard-currency which they do not have, or they must make substantial savings on energy and raw materials. Such savings are, however, scarcely possible given the present technological capabilities of the domestic economies. This means that the purchase of raw materials and energy saving technologies in the West must be considered, which is again constrained by limited hard currency and access to credit.

The second urgent problem is the satisfaction of consumers' demands. With the exception of Hungary all CMEA-countries report shortages in supplies from time to time. These difficulties are of course partly due to the drastic import reductions, which not only reduced the supply of finished consumer goods, but also affected supplies of semi-finished products and spare parts in such a fashion that domestic production in countries such as Poland, Rumania, and Yugoslavia was disrupted. The examples of Poland and Rumania demonstrate that extensive shortages can endanger the stability of the existing political systems. In comparison Hungary's relative political stability can be attributed to the permanent improvement in the standard of living. Czechoslovakia also used this instrument in order to elicit at least a passive toleration of its citizens for the unpopular system imposed after 1968. The danger with such a policy of consumption socialism is, however, that unfulfilled expectations and demands can have the reverse destabilizing effect as was clearly shown by Gierek's economic and subsequent political failure.

The interest structure of the smaller European CMEA-countries therefore seems to be fairly clear. In addition to the increased dependence on Soviet raw materials and energy, the restructuring and partial modernization in the 1970s has also created a dependence on Western technology and supplies of plant and semifinished products. Given the current dilemma in financing deliveries of such imports which are needed if production of manufactured goods is to grow, there are some major problems for the planners. Any longer term curtailment of Western imports would have to be accompanied by a basic re-orientation towards more Intra-CMEA trade. In the short as well as in the long-term, however, this must result in lost economic growth. Integrationalists have again and again pointed to the danger of any excessive dependence on the West of which Poland is seen as an example. As a result of these warnings one certainly saw a strengthening of the CMEA integration arguments for coordinated planning of the next five year plan period (1986-90) at the 36th meeting of the CMEA Council in Budapest in 1982. Nevertheless in most CMEA-countries those favouring a maintenance of the economic relations with the West prevail.[6]

It is easier for the smaller CMEA-countries to adopt such a trade policy because in recent years they have seen their share of East-West trade decline whilst the Soviet Union has benefitted from a larger share of trade with the West.[7] In 1970 the USSR accounted for 40 per cent of CMEA-OECD-trade, but by 1982 the USSR already accounted for 64 per cent of OECD-imports from the CMEA and 63 per cent of OECD-exports to the CMEA. Arguments from Moscow favouring more restraint and caution in trade with the West can therefore be more easily refuted. This then raises the question of Moscow's interest in the current situation. There are certainly attempts to utilize the predicament of the smaller CMEA partners for a revitalization of the idea of CMEA integration. It is indeed ironic that it was precisely during the years following the adoption of the Bucharest program in 1971 that there was an explosive growth in trade with the West. During the 1970s there was no practical way for the Soviet Union to counter this trend because it too was actively engaged in trade promotion with the West. It is therefore undoubtedly a great temptation to make a new effort to get East-West trade firmly under Soviet control.

Moscow is very aware that the CMEA-partners already represent an economic burden which can only increase with further CMEA integration. The USSR's accumulated surplus in trade with the smaller CMEA-countries during the years 1976-80, 7,85 billions TRbl, see table 1, was based largely on credit. Moscow can therefore expect a relief from this burden to come from a revitalization of the CMEA(6)-countries' trade with the West. In addition, there is also something in the Hungarian argument that the individual CMEA countries cannot do without the stimulus of trade with the West even as they seek more intensive integration in the CMEA with its increased cooperation and specialization.[8]

Outlook

In summary therefore the CMEA (6)-countries are still basically interested in an intensification of their trade relations with the West. This objective was included in the basic political position adopted in the Prague declaration of the Warsaw Treaty states in early 1983.[9] The chances of achieving this objective, however, depend more on factors outside rather than within the competence of the countries themselves. At present the general world economic climate dominates and it is difficult to see any increase in demand for Eastern products or any relaxation of tensions in the overall financial situation. One must wait and see whether the CMEA-countries can, for their part, do anything to stimulate trade. Hungary's move to achieve a new basic trade agreement with the European Community suggests that even Moscow is looking to the CMEA for new initiatives in the revitalization of East-West trade, because such a softening of the long standing principle of no trade agreements between the European Community and the single CMEA-countries is inconceivable without Moscow's approval.

Whilst these final remarks are generally valid for all the CMEA(6)-countries it is necessary to reemphasize the fact that all exhibit differences in the economic, foreign policy and socio-political premises on which policy decisions are based.

The further development of East-West trade will also be characterized by differences between the targets in and degree of involvement of the respective countries. The CMEA-community has not and will not present a homogeneous picture.

280

NOTES

*   Bulgaria, CSSR, GDR, Hungary, Poland and Rumania. In this article the term CMEA-Countries includes only the seven European member countries of the CMEA, i.e. the above mentioned CMEA(6) and the Soviet Union.

1   Kleer, J. *Strategia gospodarcza krajów RWPG.* Warsaw 1975, p. 226.

2   Bognár, J.: 'Ost-West-Handel und Entspannungsprozeß', in. Levčik, F. (Ed.): *International Economics – Comparisons and Interdependences.* (= Studien über Wirtschafts- und Systemvergleiche, Vol. 9). Wien-New York. 1978, p. 127.

3   See also Bognár, J., *op.cit.,* p. 127 f.

4   See inter alia: Machowski, H.: 'Die Verschuldung der VR Polen gegenüber dem Westen: Gegenwärtiger Stand und Ausblick.' Expertise of DIW, Berlin 1981, Tab. A. 2.

5   Kleer, J.: *Strategia gospodarcza krajów RWPG.* Warsaw 1975, p. 225.

6   See for example Köves, A.: 'Turning Inward or Turning Outward: Reflections on the Foreign Economic Strategy of CMEA Countries,' *Acta Oeconomica,* Vol. 26, No. 1-2/1981. Zabza, J.: 'Wirtschaftsbeziehungen Ost-West. Ihre Probleme und Perspektiven,' *Außenhandel der Tschechoslowakei,* No. 6/1982. Kroc, V.: 'Reserven in der Ausnutzung der Kooperation', *Außenhandel der Tschechoslowakei,* No. 6/1982. Freiberg, P./Nitz, J.: "Tendenzen im Ost-West-Handel am Beginn der achtziger Jahre", *IPW-Berichte,* Vol. 12, No. 5/1983.

7   Kádár, B.: 'East-West Trade in a New Epoch', *Acta Oeconomica,* Vol. 29, No. 3-4/1982.

8   Köves, A.: *op.cit.,* p. 61.

9   See: *Neues Deutschland,* 7. January 1983.

PART V

POLITICAL AND ECONOMIC CONSEQUENCES

21
The Efficiency of Embargoes and Sanctions

Gunnar Adler-Karlsson

An old story

"Déjà vu" is the concept that most easily comes to mind for somebody who has followed the embargo policy close to 25 years.[1]

CoCom, the Co-ordinating Committee, was created in the late 1940s. At that time it was absolutely secret. Nobody wanted to admit that the intention was to carry out offensive economic warfare against the communist bloc in general and the Soviet Union in particular. The present secrecy is but a pale reflection of that time.

The U.S. desire to include many more goods and services in the lists of forbidden items, than the West European nations, was a problem from the very beginning. It surfaced as a small conflict right after Stalin's death in March thirty years ago. The U.S. pressure upon the West European nations is also more than thirty years old, even if the forms have changed and the issue of extraterritorial application of U.S. legislation has grown in importance. The factual inefficacy of the embargo and the ease of circumvention were also facts of life from the beginning. In short all the embargo issues that today create trouble between the United States and Western Europe are old, déjà vus.

In this chapter, however, it will be argued that the mix of components has changed, and changed in a way that is dangerous for the Western alliance, and positive for the long-run Soviet policy of splitting the West and "finlandizing" Western Europe. This has to do with more general considerations, with which we will begin.

---

1   In 1968 I published my book on "Western Economic Warfare 1947-1967. A Case Study in Foreign Economic Policy." (Almqvist & Wiksell, Stockholm). I had started to follow the embargo policy already in 1959. After 1968 I had written half a dozen articles on it. This paper should be understood as a general reflection upon the subject.

282

Three eternal problems of power

Our cultural development began some 10.000 years ago. The world was then made up by several tens of thousands, let us say one hundred thousand small, independent family kingdoms. Today the United Nations has 158 sovereign members. The remaining ninety-nine thousand eight hundred and forty-two sovereign social units have been wiped out from the map by that long-run trend of violent social integration which has dominated our "culture".

The East-West conflict is, to my mind, the latest variation of this long trend, and it continues. Of the 158 UN members, a handful are formally independent East European nations, lacking any serious real independence. In the West our close economic relations have created a real integration that is far stronger than formal sovereignty. Factual integration continues, even if the formal does not, at least not yet.

This long term trend is the outcome of ever fewer and bigger social units — nations or alliances of nations — standing against each other, conducting warfare, losing and disappearing, or winning and moving up the ladder to new and greater conflicts. The Soviet-American conflict is the present form of this development, according to this philosophy of history.

Throughout this long struggle, one can observe three types of interdependent conflicts.

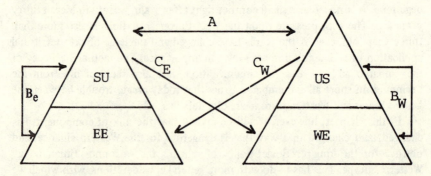

The major conflict is always between the leaders of the strongest groupings, A., in which "the other side" is normally seen as the incarnation of Evil. God has usually been fighting on one's own side. Bronfenbrenner has termed it "the mirror image", in the East-West conflict. A secondary form of conflict always exists within nations or alliances, that is between the strong at the top and the weak at the bottom of the social pyramid. Historically the weak have often been defeated, former enemies. In modern ideological language this conflict is called "class struggle", in polished social science, "tension between different social strata". Today it can be seen as an obscured conflict between the Soviet Union and its East European "satellites", B_e, as well as in the more openly discussed conflicts between the United States and its West European allies, B_W. We could add the North-South and the Sino-Soviet conflicts, but these are of less importance to the embargo problem. The third form of conflict is created — or intensified — by the natural tendency of the leaders on one side to create trouble within the ranks of the enemy by wiping up the hostility between the strong and the weak on the other side. By supporting the weak on the enemy side, C, so as to exacerbate the natural internal conflicts, B, both leaders can hope to gain advantages in the major struggle, A. The Western support for 'Solidarnosc' in Poland, and the Soviet financing of Western communist newspapers, and of "freedom movements" in southern Africa are normal examples.

It can, with some justification, be said that this C-type of conflict is more of a conflict strategy than a group of conflicts in itself. But one can easily maintain, however, that a conflict like the recent one in Grenada, would never have involved a single U.S. soldier, had it not been for the Cuban-Soviet attempts to exploit the situation. Thus this group of intensified conflicts can be understood as sui generis. The intensified embargo conflict is another example.

All these three types of conflict have been important in the embargo policy. Let us call them the "type A"-, "type B"- and "type C"-conflicts. The embargo has been intended as an instrument to weaken the Soviet Union in its struggle for world hegemony with the United States, a Type A conflict. It has created conflicts both within the United States itself and especially between the United States on the one hand and Western Europe and Japan on the other, type B-conflicts. The Soviet Union has also consciously and patiently used this intra-western conflict to widen the natural gap between the major Western nations, a type C conflict. What is dangerous for the Western alliance is that the relative importance of these various elements has changed over time.

The objective of the Western statesman must be to try to optimize the sum of the embargo effects, considering all the three major aspects. Today this seldom seems to be the case. On the contrary embargoes seem to be slapped on in a rather haphazard fashion whenever there is nothing else that can be done in response to any given Soviet action.

Let us now consider the embargo policy during three major periods, as a means of illustrating the relevance of these more general considerations.

1947–1953: Against Stalin

In the United States an anti-Soviet embargo policy was discussed soon after the end of the Second World War. In 1946 Bernard Baruch suggested such a policy. In early 1948 it had advanced so far that a special section dealing with embargo policy was included in the legislation granting the Marshall Aid to Europe. This stipulated that U.S. aid could not go to a country that exported a commodity to the Soviet Union which the United States had forbidden their companies to export. A year later CoCom was created, and by 1950 the whole embargo machinery was in place. Since then it has functioned in more or less the same manner for 35 years.

Until Stalin's death on March 5, 1953, the embargo policy was clearly conceived as an instrument for restraining the Soviet economy. Two issues were of particular importance. First, there was the atomic bomb. Here the United States had a monopoly which it wanted to keep as long as possible. All commodities that could in the slightest contribute to the production of the Soviet A-bomb were therefore denied Stalin's economy, in order to retain the monopoly for a longer period.

Second, the embargo was intended to contribute to the policy of restraint, containment or roll-back, intended to check Stalin's expansionary lust. This was part of the same package as the Marshall Aid and related economic policies. It took some time for Western Europe to come out of the economic disaster that the war had brought. The communist parties in the West, notably in Italy and France, were strong and there were fears that what happened in Prague in February 1948 could also come to take place in Rome and Paris. Western Europe had therefore to be strengthened economically and the Soviet Union weakened, so that it could not afford to give help to its supporters in the West. An embargo on the export of all important commodities to the Soviet Union and its "satellites" was thus believed to contribute to such a relative strengthening of the Western position.

In the United States there were some with even higher hopes for the effects of the embargo. This was the time of Dulles' "roll-back strategy", and several participants in the U.S. debate, in a rather typical American way, exaggerated the importance of the economic factors. They believed, expressly, that when the United States started to deny its wealth to the war-stricken Soviet economy, the communist leaders would come on their knees begging for necessities and offering to "liberate" the East European nations as a small price in return. In short there can be no doubt that the embargo policy of the period was conceived of as a purely foreign policy instrument in the great power struggle, a clear example of a type-A policy in the introductory scheme.

This being the case, the United States wanted to make the embargo into an open and declared policy. From the very outset, however, a conflict came to the fore, type B in the above scheme, between the United States and Western Europe.

There were several reasons for this conflict. To start with there were different political situations. In the United States anti-communism was as sacred a duty of every American as fighting the "Red" Indians had been in an earlier period. No communist parties of importance existed. McCarthyism was already strong, and the whole political life was religiously anti-communist.

In Europe it was different. Communist parties were strong in several nations. Memories of the wartime alliance with the Soviet Union lingered on, as did the wish not to return to the capitalist system that had created the crisis of the 1930s with all its unemployment and misery. In such a situation it was difficult to openly accept a U.S.-led, overtly aggressive, anti-communist trade policy. If it had to be accepted it should at least be secret and hidden, not from the Soviet Union, nor from the businessmen forbidden to sell, but from the electorates in the West, who should not be told what was actually happening. This was especially true in France, Italy, Denmark, and Norway. CoCom was therefore created as a top secret committee, a "gentlemen's agreement", without any formally binding rules that had to be ratified by the West European parliaments in the normal way. This is an early fact that still has a considerable importance for the way the embargo policy is conducted.

On top of the political situation, at least two other differences existed between U.S. and West European politicians, at this time led by the British, and not least by the later prime minister, Harold Wilson. One was the interest in trade with the Soviet Union that existed in Western Europe. Several important raw materials, wood and oil among them, could be obtained from the Soviet Union without use of the scarce hard currency such as the dollar. The other was West European doubts about the wisdom of the embargo policy, already now appearing, which were possibly a rationalization of an interest in trade. It was pointed out that trade is a two-way affair and that Western Europe would forego just as great a benefit as would the Soviet Union. Furthermore the embargo was not in conformity with the free trade policy, proclaimed in all other contexts.

The practical expression for these differences within West was found in the length of the lists of items which could not be exported to the Soviet Union and other communist nations, including China after 1949. On the strength of arguments that "even plastic combs could contribute to the intensity of female work in the Chinese armament factories", exports of almost everything was forbidden to the communist area in this early period. The embargo lists were very long, very comprehensive, and in reality blocked almost all East-West trade.

The West European objections to this were efficiently silenced in the 1951 U.S. Battle Act, named after its creater, a Representative Battle. This law made explicit and fortified what had been implicit in section 117d in the Marshall Aid Law of 1948. According to this act, no aid could go to any nation that did not effectively cooperate with the United States in its embargo policy against the communist nations. As American aid at this time was infinitely more profitable for Western Europe than any potential trade with the East could be, good opportunism required an obedient submission to the U.S. embargo demands in all official − but secret − contexts. The B-conflict, in the scheme already existed, but it was not very strong at this early stage. The A-part of the embargo policy, combined with the realistic West European attitudes to U.S. political demands and economic aid, was of overriding importance.

The C-part of the embargo policy also played some role during Stalin's lifetime. One element in the American policy considerations which has already been alluded to, was that the economic difficulties created by the embargo in the Soviet bloc would result in a splitting away of the satellites from the Soviet Union. More realistic observers quickly pointed out that the East European nations might instead become even more dependent upon the Soviet Union. The creation of the "Council for Mutual Economic Assistance" and later policy confirmed that such realism was more in place.

More important from our point of view, however, was Stalin's attempts to utilize the splits inside the West for his own purpose. This was not easy at that time, but on one plane it succeeded in that through paying high prices for cherished goods, Stalin was able to get many Western businessmen to engage in smuggling of the forbidden commodities. There are good reasons to believe that the West European governments consciously closed their eyes to this circumvention of the embargo rules, thereby opportunistically keeping both the American aid and the benefits of trade with the East. A student of this period, in which everybody tried to fool everybody else, can easily become a Machiavellian cynic.

1953–1968: The failure

In 1949 the Soviet Union exploded its own atom bomb. Four years later both the United States and the Soviet Union exploded their first H-bombs, at about the same time. The embargo had evidently not had much of the hoped for effect of slowing Soviet possession of nuclear technology. Both the Soviet Union and the East European communist nations made a surprisingly fast recovery to their prewar levels of economic strength, about as fast indeed as the Marshall aid receiving West European countries. In other words neither the U.S. aid to the West, nor the negative embargo employed against the East European countries, seemed to have much effect, at least not relatively speaking, and it was the relative development that counted. The Soviet bombs, as well as the fast Soviet economic growth came during the period of the most intensive embargo policy, when almost everything was included in the CoCom embargo lists. The Soviet successes were in spite of the embargo. In the late 1950s the Soviet economic growth had been so impressive that Nikita Khrushchov was brash enough to predict that the Soviet Union would have caught up with, and overtaken, the United States in per capita production by 1970. In 1983 the Soviet Union was only half way towards that goal, but 25 years ago the prophecy was taken seriously by many, as the Soviet growth performance in the 1950s was considerably better than that of the United States. In spite of the almost complete embargo therefore, the Soviet economy continued to strengthen. As a result it could no longer be claimed that U.S. policies favouring embargoes were an effective instrument in the A-type struggle for world hegemony. From that point of view it was widely recognized by, say, about 1968, that the embargo was a failure.

This realization led to an increase in the intensity of the B-type conflict over embargo policy between the United States and its own allies. This conflict was argued out in the CoCom meetings. The resulting balance of forces turned out to be against the United States, as is revealed by the continuous shortening of the embargo lists of forbidden goods. This trend can be seen as the beginning of a development that later continued into the conflict about West German Ostpolitik. The basic question was can Soviet communism be rolled back, as Dulles had wanted, by harsh and unfriendly policies of isolation, such as the embargo, or must it be seen as a fact of life that we must live with and, if possible, mollify from within by increasing confidence-building relations of various sorts, including trade?

Stalin's death in 1953 led to some optimism in the West, which was reflected in a long drawn-out review of the CoCom lists, and resulted in a considerable shortening of them in late 1954. The increasing realization in Western Europe that the embargo did not prevent Soviet economic growth, combined with an increased interest in West European industrial circles in finding new markets in the East, led to a similar review and shortening of the remaining lists in 1957-58.

During the next ten years there were continuous reviews in CoCom of the lists. The United States refused to recognize the failure of the policy and generally wanted longer lists of controlled goods. The West Europeans became increasingly bitter and pressed for ever shorter lists. The issue became more and more heated. In the 1960s France, under de Gaulle, withdrew from the CoCom cooperation. This step fortified the other governments, as they could now all claim that if they were not permitted to export a particular good to a communist nation, France would do so in any case.

All these CoCom reviews were, however, cloaked in as much secrecy as was possible at the time. Until 1954 the very existence of CoCom was considered to be top secret. To repeat, not secret for the Soviet Union, nor for the Western businessmen, but secret for the general Western public. The West had broken its own principles of openness and democracy, had started and now carried on an aggressive economic warfare that it dared not tell its own electorates about.

One personal piece of evidence on the success of this secrecy may be permitted. When my book on "Western Economic Warfare" was published in 1968 it was formally an academic "Habilitationsschrift". The conservative professors of Stockholm University, who were to judge it, considered it an unfounded Soviet-inspired anti-American slander. In their ignorance they had never heard about the embargo before.

This secrecy surrounding the embargo policy had — and still has — one important effect. The West European governments cannot use public opinion as a means of strengthening their resistance to American pressure. Thus the negotiations of the 1950s and 1960s were never backed by a serious public discussion in Western Europe. For somebody who followed the few editorials written at that time, and spoke to the people involved, there can, however, be no doubt that the West European frustrations surrounding the embargo policy sometimes became very bitter.

It was not only the West European frustration at lost export opportunities that grew, but also American bitterness about "weak, bad, appeasement-minded and ungrateful" allies. The U.S. policy makers could not demonstrate the efficiency of the embargo but they had staked their pride on it and wanted it to continue. Consequently they demanded submission of the West European allies, whom they had saved from Hitler and Stalin and whose economies they had rebuilt with generous Marshall aid.

This American bitterness had to be given an outlet. The opening accepted by the West European governments was that they acquiesced in the U.S. extraterritorial extension of the embargo regulations in a manner that formally infringed upon West European sovereignty. This was accepted, but disliked! Today this is one of the most contentious issues in the embargo policy, and creates a high level of tension between the United States and Western Europe. The lessons of the extraterritorial application are as follows.

The conflict between the United States and Western Europe about the content of the embargo lists was not resolved. CoCom agreed upon a shorter list, reflecting the West European willingness to trade with the East. The United States maintained much longer lists, including many more goods which could not be sold to communist nations under U.S. legal jurisdiction. The difference between the two lists is called "the embargo differential". It is of course natural that American companies in the United States had to follow the U.S. legislation. But it was resented that subsidiaries of U.S. multinationals, registered in other Western nations and thus formally non-American legal subjects, were forced to follow the American legislation. The United States thus created a serious conflict by enforcing an economic police system, combined with threats of economic reprisals via its embassies and their "economic defense officers", in an effort to get all foreign companies with close contacts to the United States to follow the U.S. and not the CoCom-West European laws. It was – and remains – a clear violation of the sovereignty of allied nations, a clear case of extraterritorial legislation, a clear case of intimidation.

As the CoCom list shortened and the embargo differential grew, the United States relied more and more upon this type of extraterritorial control of exports. The conflict over the embargo policy therefore also increased in intensity within the Western alliance after 1968 and has continued to do so.

As the Bw-type of conflict grows the scope for C-type stimulation of the B-conflict also increases. This has indeed probably been the case, even if the author has never seen a good study of this aspect of embargo policy. The Soviet Union made constant propaganda references to the American embargo policies. It stimulated private traders to circumvent the policy and European governments to close their eyes to such circumvention. Considering the way the Soviet Union itself behaved, with continued internal repression of anything akin to human rights and external violent suppression in Hungary in 1956 and in Czechoslovakia in 1968, few people in the West are likely to have taken the Soviet actions in the field very seriously. When opportunistic profit opportunities were available connivance was likely, but not because of any belief in the Soviet system.

1968–1983: Déjà vu

By 1968 at the latest the present economic-political configurations of the embargo policy had been well established.

With reference to the analytical scheme again, very few people in the field still believed that the embargo policy was an efficient instrument of Western policy in the continuing – and probably secular – East-West conflict, that is, in the major A-conflict. Only a few die-hards still supported or at least professed to support such a policy. In the period that followed, it was also possible to see a change in the emphasis of the discussion within the United States with regard to the expected results of the policy. In the early years, Dulles had hoped that the embargo would help to "roll back" the Soviet Union from Eastern Europe. Earlier it was hoped that the embargo would strengthen the Western side in the continuing competition between the systems for the minds of men. In later years, however, such effects are rarely claimed. Various embargo actions were referred to as "sanctions", that is, as revenge and punishment for various Soviet brutalities, such as those in Afghanistan and Poland. This conforms well with the conclusion of one scholar who studied a number of different embargoes in the 20th century. An embargo, he concludes, is an expression of deep disgust for the actions of a foreign government but, at the same time, also of an inability to do anything about it.

Trade is a two-way affair. Sanctions cut off trade, and thus the benefits accruing to *both* sides. If one is prepared to forego some profit in order to demonstrate one's deep disgust for some political action, knowing full well that it will not change anything, then, and only then, can embargoes be looked upon as rational policies.

For several good reasons, not least the sheer size of East-West trade in Europe compared to the United States, the West European nations have been disinclined to lose money in order to demonstrate moral indignation. The Europeans, like the Russians, are much more Machiavellian, much more cynical, and much less moral in their political judgements than are the Americans.

This can be seen as good hardheaded realism. But it can also be seen as selling-out those ideals that may in the long term be the only thing that preserves belief in a political system. Moral demonstrations may be a good thing, but if so they should be presented as such, not as efficient policy instruments. Nobody believes in the morality of embargoes on pipelines from Europe, when American grain is flowing freely! The best course may be to engage in some moral sanctions combined with a total realism about their inefficiency, leading to a serious search for other and better policy instruments. This is, essentially, how one can look upon the Ostpolitik of Willy Brandt. But such alternatives fall outside the scope of the present essay.

However the embargo sanctions after 1968 are to be judged, it is a political fact of life that they have increased tensions between the United States and Western Europe. The West European decision-makers involved express the same dismay and contempt for the U.S. stupidities in the field, as have the numerous editorials and other comments in the public opinion.

The outlook for the Western alliance is therefore decidedly worse as a result of the continuing embargo actions. Any Western statesman should ask himself whether a policy that contributes to the break-up of an alliance is a wise policy!

The Soviet propaganda machinery is, of course, whipping up the animosity surrounding the embargo within the West. They play on the purely egoistic West European interests. When the Western markets are unstable or even decline, as they did after the oil crisis of 1973/74 and 1979/80, the Russians will stress the stability of state-trading, the increasing importance of stable energy flows through direct pipelines from Siberia to Western Europe, and the positive employment effects of exports to the East. The worse the Western economic crises get, the greater the opportunities for Soviet propaganda. From the very beginning of the embargo policy the Soviet Union has also constantly told all potential exporters that "if YOU refuse to sell, somebody else will get the order." This may or may not be true. Most likely it often is. Regardless of whether these statements are based on factual circumventions of the rules, or not, they have succeeded in intensifying commercial rivalry between the United States and Western Europe. One of the items most discussed in CoCom over the last 15 years has been computers. The United States has wanted to prohibit sales of almost all computer technology to the East and has largely succeeded. At the same time, however, IBM has had two large affiliates, one in France and one in Vienna, specializing in the needs of the Soviet and East European market. West European companies and diplomats were convinced that should IBM succeed in gaining an order before its European competitors, the CoCom lists would have been changed in favor of IBM and the Soviet Union, just as the United States makes the distinction between European pipes and American grain. This is superb Russian propaganda material – and it has been fully exploited.

Summary

This chapter has first presented a generalized model of international conflict containing three types of conflict:
the A-type conflict between the two most powerful competing nations;

the B-type between the top and the bottom within each competing nation or alliance; and the

C-type conflict by which one of the A-leaders tries to stimulate B-conflict within the potential enemy nation or alliance.

An effort has also been made to show the development of these three types of conflict in the specific field of Western economic warfare in the entire post-war years. The results can be summarized in the following diagram which shows the intensity of the three conflicts in embargo policy over time.

Diagram: Intensity of the three types of conflict in embargo policy.

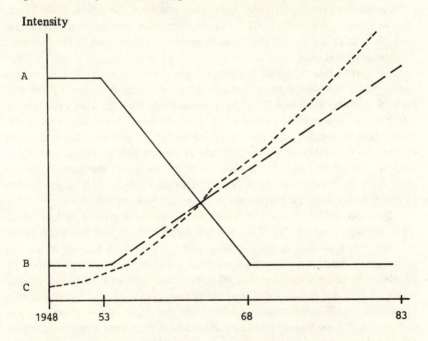

No firm values can of course be attached to these curves. But most serious observers of the embargo policy would surely agree that policy has developed as outlined below.

The type-A conflict fully justified the embargo policy from its inception until Stalin's death in 1953. Later there was a decline in both the efficacy and the sensible use of the embargo policy as a serious instrument in the East-West or Soviet-American struggle for world hegemony.

By 1968 all serious observers agreed that some type of weapons and weapon technology should, of course, be on the CoCom embargo lists, but that an embargo on important goods in the civil economy would be a failure. There has been a consolidation of this position in Western Europe. Its correctness is also revealed by the fact that the United States talks about "sanctions" rather than embargo policy. Embargoes are no longer seen as efficient longterm instruments of economic policy. They are short-term emotional reactions to hostile behaviour.

Conflicts over embargo policy between the United States and Western Europe had virtually no importance at the time of the Prague coup of 1948, the Berlin blockade, the Korean war, and Mao's assumption of power in China. From 1953 the lack of belief in the efficacy of the embargo as an instrument in the great power contest went hand in hand with a growing conflict on this issue within the Western alliance.

As diagram one suggests, with the curves crossing in the middle of the 1960s, one must conclude that the costs for the Western alliance of continuous embargo quarrels have exceeded any contribution embargoes have made in the East-West struggle since that time.

After 1968 this imbalance between costs and benefits to the West of the embargo policy has surely risen. Doubts about the general wisdom of the U.S. leadership in the Western alliance have arisen every time this issue has come up. Combined with a number of other U.S. mistakes and failures, the embargo has surely undermined the general support for the NATO alliance. This is reflected in the serious doubts about the wisdom of placing new American missiles in Western Europe in 1983. If the losses from the B-conflict are greater than the gains from the embargo in the A-type of struggle, a policy of embargo ceases to be a wise policy from the perspective of long term Western interests.

The bottom-line is that the Soviet Union has been given a perfect instrument for whipping up the intra-Western B-conflicts. In the beginning Soviet behavior was such that it could hardly affect the Western alliance at all. But with Stalin's death, the objective tendencies towards "détente", combined with a widespread desire to believe that what was considered as Soviet misbehaviour was a result of one person and not of the system, gave the Soviet Union a chance to exploit intra-Western divisions. After 1968 the efforts of the Soviet policy in this direction have intensified. These efforts have even been more intense than the intra-Western embargo conflict as such, which is why the C-curve has been drawn above the B-curve.

The future

If the main elements of this analysis are correct, a continuation of the American embargo efforts are positively harmful for the future of the U.S.-West European side of the East-West ideological conflict. The latter East-West conflict is, so far as one can judge, of a secular type. It is possible that the communist leadership in the Soviet Union — also in this respect, much like the Catholic church — has a longer time-perspective than Western leaders, who come up for re-election at short intervals.

The long-term strategic goal of the Soviet Union must surely be first to split the Western alliance. If the United States, Western Europe and Japan could be efficiently split up, they would pose much less of a threat and less of an obstacle to Soviet policy. Second, having achieved this the next goal would be to split up Western Europe, so that a real "Finlandization" could take place in stages and thus remove any possible threat to established Soviet rule. Only when this has been achieved in Western Europe, could we realistically expect the Soviet leaders to permit the trends towards diversification in Eastern Europe to be translated into a mild form of sovereignty in foreign policy matters.

A central instrument in this long-term strategy must be the German situation. From an historical point of view it is completely natural that the German people should desire re-unification. This goal is totally disregarded today but it is of importance in long-term planning, and the Soviet Union has that card completely to itself. For the United States the importance of this fact has still to be fully realized.

Today the only, or at least the main way, the two Germanies can express their desire for unity is in trade and economic relations, so that the United States' attempts to prevent such trade plays into the hands of the Soviet policy. If the embargo policy continues to be handled as unwisely as it has been over the last two decades, it may in the long run lead to the loss of what must be judged as the most important Western ally, the Federal Republic of Germany.

In short, more than twenty years of closely following and studying embargoes have led to the following two conclusions: In the short term the losses from the embargo policy to the West in form of conflict and ill-feeling within NATO, are much greater than the gains in the East-West or Soviet-American power struggle. In the long term a continuation of the current trends in the U.S. embargo policy, which is now 35 years old, is bound to be more advantageous to the Soviet Union because it favours the long term Soviet strategy of decoupling Western Europe from the United States.

22
Economic Relations as a Prop for Détente?
Hanns-D. Jacobsen/Reinhard Rode

This chapter will pick up some of the main themes emerging from the different contributions in order to address the questions posed in the introductory chapter. From this it is evident that in a field such as economic relations between East and West, in which politics and economics are so inextricably linked it is very likely that research will not be able to come up with more than tentative results, on the basis of presumptive evidence, for a long time to come. Given the lack of adequate theory precise statements concerning the relationship between cause and effect are simply not feasible. Parallel developments and correlations between trade with the East and détente are not the same as stable or even compelling connections. Indeed, the ambivalence of all the possible effects studied remains a central result of all the contributions, which leads one to consider working from the premise of less far reaching questions.

Even an updated, detailed analysis of the different economic and political issue areas on the basis of the new developments at the beginning of 1980, gives us no clear answer to questions concerning the interrelationship between trade with the East and détente. It is possible to draw this conclusion by simply considering the interests of both sides.

The interest of the Eastern countries in improving trade ties with the West has been primarily of an economic nature. Each Eastern country has accepted a certain — though varying — degree of dependence on the trade with the West with the associated destabilizing effects on their societies, in order to obtain Western technology and credits and thus further their economic development. These countries' trade dependence on the West is, at nearly one third of total trade, remarkably high, and it has led to an increased sensitivity to political, and particularly economic disturbances originated in the West. Even for the East European countries who have a higher dependence than the USSR, however, the dependence has remained too small to have had any significant influence on their domestic or foreign policy behavior.

Within the whole spectrum of East-West relations, economic interactions have a rather secondary relevance. In only certain fields such as technology transfer, energy, and credit does some degree of mutual dependence exist. This interdependence is, however, of asymmetrical nature, meaning that any politically or economically motivated reduction or even interruption of economic relations would result in more economic disturbance or relatively higher adjustment costs in the East than in the West.

The interests of the Western countries, in particular of the Federal Republic of Germany, in East-West trade have been of both an economic and political nature. First of all trade with the East has been — and still is — welcomed as a means of developing new markets and tapping secure sources of supply of scarce raw materials and energy. Developments in East-West trade since the mid-1970s have, however, proved that the euphoric expectations of the early détente period were much too high. The OECD's trade with the East, as a share of its total trade, has never been higher than 5 per cent. Given the stagnation and even decline in the relative importance of East-West trade since the mid-1970s, it is also very unlikely that there will be a change in this trend in the foreseeable future.

This relatively limited importance of East-West economic relations has also led to a dampening of related political expectations. As it turned out economic relations alone have not been sufficient to propell the process of détente. Although new forms of economic interaction between East and West such as industrial cooperation in the form of licensing, coproduction and joint ventures were created, their relevance remained limited. This was partly because of the reluctance with which the Eastern partners created new economic and legislative foundations, and partly because Western companies would not accept the high bureaucratic and organizational burdens. The simple functionalist approach, in which increased economic links would automatically lead to economic reforms in the USSR and Eastern Europe and thus in turn to political, social or even systematic change proved to be of little relevance.

All in all the economic relations have proven to be a necessary but by no means a sufficient element in stabilizing the overall relationship between East and West. The relative importance of economic relations grew, however, as East-West relations in other fields, such as arms control, deteriorated. East-West trade has become an important part of the détente process, and even though it alone is not capable of furthering détente, a reduction or even interruption of East-West trade is very likely to fuel the tensions between the antagonistic systems.

Thus, if the concept of "change through trade" goes too far in its optimism about improved relations, the use of economic relations as an instrument for the realization of political goals is also of limited impact. The experience of the United States in its economic relations with the USSR and Eastern Europe has shown that economic incentives can be more effective than negative sanctions in the form of embargoes or boycotts but their efficiency is in no way guaranteed. In particular the FRG, in its relations with the GDR and other Eastern countries, has shown that Western actors can derive certain political concessions of the East by using economic incentives, especially as far as humanitarian issues are concerned. Western governments also stand more chance of achieving their objectives in dealings with the Eastern countries, if they employ economic leverage, when at all, in a favorable political-psychological climate. Above all the use of such an instrument should not be overdone, nor should one raise undue expectations, or simply ask for too much in return for any given economic concession. Such linkages proved to be particularly successful when they were not publicized and were handled in such a manner as not to damage the prestige of the target country. Too much publicity can provoke counterproductive results by provoking reactions from the target country which are detrimental to the goals of the country imposing the positive sanctions or incentives.

Even though the economic relations with the Eastern countries have in general a relatively limited relevance in the foreign economic relations of the West European countries, their importance for certain sectors should not be underestimated. Imports of oil and natural gas from the USSR, for instance, contribute to the regional diversification of West European energy supplies, and exports of machinery and large-diameter pipe have — compared to the overall exports of these products — reached above-average levels. The interest groups affected, such as certain branches of industry, firms, and even trade unions, have therefore always tried to prevent a deterioration of East-West relations. In so doing they find a mutual interest with those in the East who seek reform and increased flexibility and efficiency. In neither East nor West, however, have such groups been able to prevent developments in the political and military fields from undermining the basis for improved economic relations and more intense forms of cooperation. The relevance of economic relations has remained limited or even declined. Nevertheless it remains the most stable element in the web of East-West relations but one with more of a tension dampening than a détente promoting effect during this period. Those who benefit from East-West trade certainly have an interest in easing conflict but their impact has been limited so far. The conflict of military security interests in East-West relations constrains the room for manoeuver of such interest groups.

In general terms East-West economic relations have shown ambivalent results as far as détente is concerned. Although both sides have complained, they have also benefited economically from trade. On the Western side there were certain reservations concerning unfair competition and dumping. This was to be expected given the general increase in global import competition from all sources, the strong protectionist tendencies, and especially given the systemic differences in the way prices are determined in which Eastern prices are seldom or indeed almost never based on real production costs. These reservations, however, had only a minor impact on the development of East-West trade. The same was true of Eastern fears that an intensification of relations with the West could lead to political and economic penetration of their systems and thus result in an erosion of socialist goals. For East European countries the economic benefits derived from the trade with the West turned out to be so important, particularly for smaller countries such as Hungary and the GDR, that whilst such fears certainly still exist they have remained subdued in the past few years. It is evident that economic relations, particularly when linked to non-economic issue areas such as in the case of the CSCE Final Act, contributed to a relative opening of East European societies and to a much lesser extent of Soviet society. The intensification of relations with Eastern countries, mainly in the economic sphere has, however, also had some destabilizing effects, as in the case of Poland, which have negatively influenced the general development of East-West relations.

As far as the effects of embargo and sanction policies are concerned the following differentiated conclusions can be drawn. The East never tried seriously to impose economic sanctions on the West for the simple reason that it lacks an effective economic leverage. The West as a whole pursued embargo policy after World War II and the United States has subsequently made some unilateral efforts. The reason for the failure of such policies has been the fact that the main target country, the USSR, was not a suitable target for economic pressure because of its remarkable capacity for autarky and independence. The East-European countries are more vulnerable to Western economic pressure. Whilst the West can bring its economic power to bear on East European countries it would be of little use because such a step would not correspond to the West's political goals. Just as the East tries to exploit differences in interest between Western countries, the Western side is eager to further the autonomy tendencies of East European countries vis-à-vis their hegemonial power, the USSR. This cannot be done by forcing such autonomy by threatening to use economic leverage. This is clearly illustrated by the case of sanctions against Poland after the declaration of martial law. The U.S. sanctions had certain disadvantages for Poland, but their main result was to bring about even deeper ties with the USSR. This is another example of how carrots are more effective than sticks. Sanctions might be effective when a powerful nation faces a weak one. Similarly strong powers may impose economic burdens on each other, but as this means both incur costs it cannot be considered as an effective sanction unless the country imposing sanctions has some sort of symbolic gesture in mind.

The overall picture of East-West economic relations and détente, therefore, shows a gap between the interests and policies of the leading powers of the respective blocs and their smaller allies. Traditionally, the United States has been least engaged in East-West trade. As trade with the East is not important for the United States it has been able to employ embargo and sanction policies at relatively little economic cost to itself. West European countries have benefited much more from trade and are, therefore, inclined to preserve economic ties. Without doubt the FRG is the Western country with the biggest stake in détente and trade with the East. The FRG not only benefits most from trade with the East, it also stands to lose most in political-humanitarian terms from any disruption of East-West relations because of its special relationship with the GDR.

There is a similar gap in the East in which the GDR is without doubt the country which benefits most from its trade with the West. The GDR has always let the FRG pay for concessions that have been made for better communication between both Germanies, and also benefits substantially from the fact that the FRG does not wish to treat it as a foreign country in economic terms. A consequence of this is the implicit participation of the GDR, a member country of the Council for Mutual Economic Assistance (CMEA), in the European Economic Community.

All the other East European countries have basically the same interest in good relations with the West. Any deterioration in détente policy and in East-West economic relations increases their already substantial dependence on the USSR which dominates them militarily, politically, and economically. The position of the USSR is due to its role as a world power and can, therefore, be compared with that of the U.S. Certainly, the USSR is economically weaker than the U.S. and cannot, for this reason, exert any sanction power of its own. The Soviet Union is able, however, to reduce or even neutralize the impact of Western sanctions. The USSR can also derive benefits from block-transcending economic relations and from détente policy, but is at the same time also able to bear the burden of an interruption of such relations. The USSR is, therefore, free to evaluate whether the benefits of trade with the West are sufficient to compensate for the associated potential political costs such as the emigration of Soviet Jews after the Jackson/Vanik amendment of 1974. The exercise of American economic power against the USSR thus has very narrow limits and is at best mainly symbolic.

For most West European countries, and this is particularly true for the Federal Republic of Germany, the alternative of economic warfare or détente makes no sense. At least since the end of the sixties the West European countries have been following an approach aimed at a long-term reduction of tensions between East and West. Western Europe did not just act according to its own economic interests by creating favorable political conditions for the improvement of East-West economic relations through, for example, the conclusion of long-term Cooperation agreements with the Eastern countries. It also views trade as a stabilizing factor in the détente process. For both political and economic reasons East-West trade never attained such an importance that – in a functionalist sense – it could fulfill this role. Therefore, the use of trade as an instrument of economic power policy or even economic warfare against the Eastern countries is simply not feasible. East-West economic relations are not important enough to be employed as a lever in order to realize essential political objectives. They could however, be used to a limited extent, to extend the web of interrelations with the East in order to further and even to improve détente.

The divergencies within the West on how to pursue the right foreign economic policies toward the East, therefore, reflect the difference between the global power policies of the U.S. and West European regional détente policies. Economic interests fit more easily into the latter so that for the West European countries a conflict between security and economic interests did not occur. Such a conflict did, however, exist in the United States and it has resulted in considerable disadvantages for U.S. business since 1980. European policies have recently helped to dampen this trend. Despite basic differences in interest, therefore, compromises within the West seem to be at least within reach.

ABOUT THE AUTHORS

Gunnar Adler-Karlsson is Professor at the Roskilde University Center in Denmark and Director of the Capri Institute for International Social Philosophy, Italy. Among other works, he is author of *Western Economic Warfare 1947–1967* (Stockholm 1968) and "Instruments of Economic Coercion and Their Use", in Frans A.M. Alting von Geusau/Jacques Pelkmans, eds., *National Economic Security – Perceptions, Threats, and Policies* (Tilburg, The Netherlands 1982).

Franz-Lothar Altmann is Research Fellow at the Osteuropa-Institut München and Editor of *Osteuropa Wirtschaft* and *Jahrbuch der Wirtschaft Osteuropas*. His publications include "Die Koordinierung der Volkswirtschaftspläne der RGW-Mitgliedsländer (Plan Coordination of CMEA Member Countries)", in *Südost-Europa* No. 11-12, 1983; *Die Kompensation als Instrument im Ost-West-Handel* (Compensation as an Instrument in East-West Trade) (München 1979).

Jochen Bethkenhagen is Research Fellow at the Deutsches Institut für Wirtschaftsforschung (DIW), Berlin (West). His recent writings include "Erdöl und Erdgas im Ost-West-Handel" (Natural Oil and Gas in East-West Trade), *Vierteljahreshefte des DIW*, No. 4, 1983; *Entwicklung und Struktur des deutsch-sowjetischen Handels* (Development and Structure of Trade between the FRG and the USSR), Sonderheft des DIW No. 136 (Berlin 1982) (with H. Machowski).

Klaus Bolz is Head of Department "Sozialistische Länder und Ost-West-Wirtschaftsbeziehungen" at the HWWA-Institut für Wirtschaftsforschung, Hamburg. He is editor of *Die wirtschaftliche Entwicklung in den sozialistischen Ländern Osteuropas zur Jahreswende 1983/84* (Economic Development in the Socialist Countries of Eastern Europe) (Hamburg 1984) and co-author (with H. Clement and P. Pissulla) of *Die Wirtschaftsbeziehungen zwischen der Bundesrepublik Deutschland und der Sowjetunion* (The Economic Relations between the FRG and the USSR) (Hamburg 1976).

Renata Fritsch-Bournazel is Scientific Advisor at the Fondation Nationale des Sciences Politiques and Lecturer at the Institut d'Etudes Politiques of Paris University. Her publications include *Les Allemands au coeur de l'Europe* (The Germans at the Heart of Europe) (Paris 1983); *Rapallo: naissance d'un mythe* (Rapallo: The Birth of a Myth) (Paris 1974).

Hanns-D. Jacobsen is Research Fellow at the Stiftung Wissenschaft und Politik, Ebenhausen near München. His recent writings include "Foreign Trade Relations of the GDR" in K.v.Beyme/H. Zimmermann, eds., *Policymaking in the German Democratic Republic* (New York 1984) and *Ost-West-Wirtschaftsbeziehungen als deutsch-amerikanisches Problem* (East-West Economic Relations as a German-American Problem) (Baden-Baden, forthcoming).

Mathias Jopp is Research Fellow at the Peace Research Institute Frankfurt. He is author of *Militär und Gesellschaft in der Bundesrepublik Deutschland* (The Military and Society in the FRG) (Frankfurt 1983) and "Embargo oder Business?", in PRIF, ed., *Europa zwischen Konfrontation und Kooperation* (Frankfurt 1982).

Peter Knirsch is Professor at the Osteuropa Institut of the Free University of Berlin. His publications include "Interdependence in East-West Economic Relations", in OECD, *From Marshall Plan to Interdependence* (Paris 1978); *Strukturen und Formen zentraler Wirtschaftsplanung* (Structures and Forms of Central Planning) (Berlin 1969).

Heinrich A. Machowski is Research Fellow at the Deutsches Institut für Wirtschaftsforschung (DIW), Berlin (West). Among other works, he is author of *Sowjetunion – Wachstumsfaktor Außenhandel* (USSR – Foreign Trade as a Factor of Growth) (Berlin 1979); *Außenwirtschaftliche Reformen in den RGW-Staaten* (Foreign Trade Reforms of CMEA Countries) (Berlin 1970).

Friedemann Müller is Research Fellow at the Stiftung Wissenschaft und Politik, Ebenhausen near München. He is editor of *Wirtschaftssanktionen im Ost-West-Verhältnis* (Economic Sanctions in the Relationship between East and West) (Baden-Baden 1983) and author of *Außenwirtschaftstheorie in der Planwirtschaft* (Foreign Economic Theory in the Planned Economy) (Berlin 1975).

Harald Müller is Research Fellow at the Peace Research Institute Frankfurt. He is co-author (with R. Rode) of *Osthandel oder Wirtschaftskrieg?* (East-West trade or Economic Warfare?) (Frankfurt 1982) and author of *Energiepolitik, Nuklearexport und die Weiterverbreitung von Kernwaffen* (Energy Policy, Nuclear Exports, and the Proliferation of Nuclear Arms) (Frankfurt 1978).

Jürgen Nötzold is Head of the Group "Eastern Countries" at the Stiftung Wissenschaft und Politik, Ebenhausen near München. He has published extensively in the area of East-West trade and technology transfer. He is also co-author (with W. Beitel) of *Deutsch-Sowjetische Wirtschaftsbeziehungen in der Zeit der Weimarer Republik* (German-Soviet Economic Relations during the Weimar Republic) (Baden-Baden 1979).

Petra Pissulla is Head of the Group East European Countries at the HWWA-Institut für Wirtschaftsforschung, Hamburg. She is author of *Der Internationale Währungsfonds und seine Bedeutung für die osteuropäischen Länder* (The IMF and Its Relevance for East European Countries) (Hamburg 1983) and co-author (with K. Bolz) of *Die Erfahrungen deutscher Unternehmen aus der Kooperation mit polnischen Wirtschaftsorganisationen* (The Experiences of German Companies from the Cooperation with Polish Economic Organisations) (Hamburg 1981).

Reinhard Rode is Research Fellow at the Peace Research Institute Frankfurt. His publications include *Amerikanische Handelspolitik gegenüber Westeuropa* (American Trade Policy Toward Western Europe) (Frankfurt 1980) and *Die Südafrikapolitik der Bundesrepublik Deutschland* (The FRG's Policy vis-à-vis South Africa) (München 1975).

Giuseppe Schiavone is Professor of International Organization at the Faculty of Political Science at the University of Catania, Italy. He is author of *The Institutions of COMECON* (London 1981) and editor of *East-West Relations: Prospects for the 1980s* (London 1982).

Klaus Schröder is Research Fellow at the Stiftung Wissenschaft und Politik, Ebenhausen near München. His publications include *Die polnische Wirtschafts- und Verschuldungspolitik in den vergangenen zehn Jahren* (Polish Economic and Indebtedness Policy during the last Decade) (Ebenhausen 1981) and *Die Kooperationspolitik der Bundesrepublik Deutschland gegenüber den Ländern des RGW* (Cooperation Policies between the FRG and the CMEA Countries) (Berlin 1979).

Angela E. Stent is Associate Professor of Government and Director of the Russian Area Studies Program at Georgetown University, Washington, D.C. Among other writings, she is author of *From Embargo to Ostpolitik – The Political Economy of West German-Soviet Relations, 1955-1980* (Cambridge 1981) and *East-West Technology Transfer – European Perspectives*, The Washington Papers No. 75 (1980).

Stephen Woolcock is Spaak Fellow at the Center for International Affairs of Harvard University, Cambridge, Mass. His publications include "Atlantic Trade Relations", in L. Freedman, ed., *The Troubled Alliance*. Joint Studies in Public Policy, No. 8 (London 1983) and *Western Policies on East-West Trade*, Chatham House Paper No. 15 (London/Boston 1982).